California
TRIPS

68 THEMED ITINERARIES **1147** LOCAL PLACES TO SEE

Ryan Ver Berkmoes,
Alexis Averbuck, Amy C Balfour, Andrew Bender, Sara Benson,
Alison Bing, Nate Cavalieri, Dominique Channell, Beth Kohn

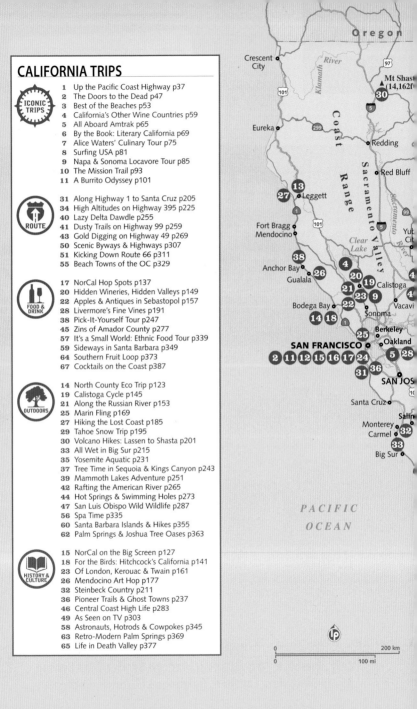

CALIFORNIA TRIPS

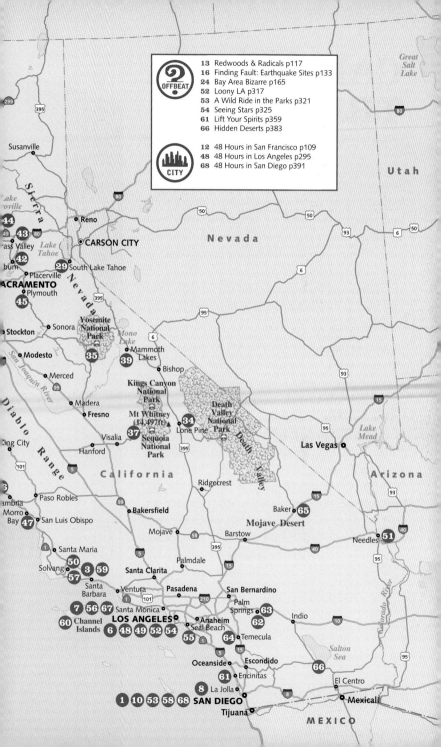

CALIFORNIA TRIPS

At home, in the office, stuck in the commute, we all fantasize about doing more; of getting to truly see world-famous coastlines, iconic cities, hidden parks and wilderness roads…or just sitting back with an astonishingly great glass of wine. But where to start? Trying to make sense of the myriad sources, opinions and references can leave one, well, driving in circles. And that's before you've even left. What you want is inspiration and a plan so you have but one thing to do. Go.

Thanks to our authors you can do just that. They've driven California's roads hither and yonder and scoured every corner of the state to bring you 68 of the best trips for spa seekers, beach bummers, wilderness hikers, celebrity spotters, family road-trippers, city hipsters and heritage lovers. Our trips range from San Francisco alleys to lost deserts, from Hollywood glitz to Hwy 1 bliss. You can find a burrito, hang ten, run a river, ride Amtrak and maybe even discover gold. Day-trippers can trip and weekenders can find an ideal weekend. More time means more joy and a chance to link one trip to another. Your biggest challenge: stopping.

UP THE PACIFIC COAST HIGHWAY p37
Coastline from Rocky Point, Big Sur

"Day-trippers can trip and weekenders can find an ideal weekend. More time means more joy…"

AUTO LOVE

California is the global home of car culture. Most of the world's automakers have design studios in the state where car trends begin and driving is a religion.

Iconic Trips

Seeing the surf from the beach (p53) and the beach from the surf (p81), stoic adobe missions (p93) and a mission-style burrito (p101), "LA Woman" (p47) and Raymond Chandler's LA (p69), a bottle of Napa wine (p85) and meals that put the art in artisan (p75)…they all mean California. Each is an icon of a place with far more than its fair share. Everyone has their image of the state; this book has 11 iconic trips to help you find your own vision of California.

"...this book has 11 iconic trips to help you find your own vision of California."

CALIFORNIA'S CLASSIC ROAD

Part of the Pacific Coast Hwy, that most Californian of roads, Hwy 101 runs for 807 miles, from downtown Los Angeles through Santa Barbara, Monterey, San Francisco, Marin and Redwood Country.

THE MISSION TRAIL p93
Mission Santa Barbara

SURFING USA p81
Surfing Big Sur

ALICE WATERS' CULINARY TOUR p75
Hog Island Oyster Bar, Ferry Building Marketplace, San Francisco

"...its significance echoes for those who recall a time when a mere drive could change your destiny."

Routes

California has more than 15,000 miles of highways, some whose numbers alone are filled with meaning. Look for 10 classic routes in this book. **Hwy 1** (p37 and p205), the route of the coast, of rocky shores, cool beaches and hot beach towns, says "get a convertible and drive me." **Route 66** (p311), the highway to the California dream, was always the road from tragedy to hope. Today its significance echoes for those who recall a time when a mere drive could change your destiny. **Hwy 99** (p259; fitting that it's 66 upended) runs like a ribbon through the heart of the state, avoiding the glossy extremes; it was where people did – and do – get down to work. **Hwy 395** (p225) traverses the high Sierra and the peaks separating the state from the deserts beyond.

Ⓐ **KICKING DOWN ROUTE 66** p311
America's "Mother Road" leads to the promised land – California

Ⓑ **BEACH TOWNS OF THE OC** p329
Refueling at a classic 1950s-style diner in Laguna Beach

Ⓒ **HIGH ALTITUDES ON HIGHWAY 395** p225
Sierra Nevada's Lone Pine Peak and Mt Whitney, Alabama Hills

AWARD-WINNING HIGHWAY 1

The US Dept of Transportation has designated Hwy 1 an "All-American Road," one of 27 recognized in the US for scenery that makes them tourist destinations.

Food & Drink

If there's an even more popular refrain from the back seat (and front seat) than "Are we there yet?" it's "Let's get something to eat!" Whether you're wandering the world simply by roaming the byways of LA in search of amazing **ethnic food** (p339) or focusing on the search for the perfect **burrito** (p101), you'll find 14 ways to enjoy California's best food and drink in this book. Take a food tour with the legendary **Alice Waters** (p75), find the best **wineries** in Napa (p85) and across the state (p59, p149, p191 and p277), get sideways in **Santa Barbara** (p349), slurp sunset **cocktails** over the Pacific (p387) or hop on out to the best **microbreweries** (p137). And for something healthy, explore the **farms** that put the golden in Golden State and **pick your own** (p247).

"Take a food tour with the legendary Alice Waters, find the best wineries in Napa..."

FAST-FOOD FAST LANE

The modern day fast-food joint was invented by the McDonald brothers in San Bernardino in 1948. Ray Kroc saw their success and took the concept worldwide.

IT'S A SMALL WORLD: ETHNIC FOOD TOUR p339
California is a melting pot and a smorgasbord, from seviche to *injera* to Korean barbecue

PICK-IT-YOURSELF TOUR p247
Pick your own lunch

COCKTAILS ON THE COAST p387
The Abbey in West Hollywood offers 24 varieties of martini

"One moment you're trapped in traffic, the next you've found your own perfect waterfall."

OUTDOOR HIGH

Hwy 120 crosses the Sierra Nevada, connecting the Eastern Sierras to Yosemite National Park. At 9945ft, the pass is the highest in the state.

Outdoors

It doesn't take long. One moment you're trapped in traffic, the next you've found your own perfect waterfall. California's beauty is all around and you can forsake civilization for naturalization quicker than you think. There are 19 ways to get out and into the state's great outdoors in this book. Cycling the vine-lined byways of **Calistoga** (p145), **hiking forgotten trails** (p185), tracking a **butterfly** (p287), searching for **desert oases** (p363), flying like a bird in **Lake Tahoe** (p195) or just lazing on the **Russian River** (p153), you won't be inside for a minute. And there's no shortage of big names (and big trees), in places like **Yosemite** (p231) and **Sequoia and Kings Canyon** (p243), to make you feel small but happy.

TAHOE SNOW TRIP p195
Divine views of Heavenly Valley, Lake Tahoe

PALM SPRINGS & JOSHUA TREE OASES p363
A date farm in the Coachella Valley

MAMMOTH LAKES ADVENTURE p251
Exploring the wilderness at Mammoth Lakes

History & Culture

California's population exploded after somebody yelled **"Gold!"** The discoveries in the Sierra foothills started the rush to the state, which hasn't stopped yet. Touring the surprisingly evocative towns (p237) where dreams came true and hopes were dashed over 150 years ago is one of 14 trips in this book that explore the state's long history and rich culture. Witness the inspirations for the words of **Eugene O'Neill** (p69), **Jack Kerouac** (p161) and **John Steinbeck** (p211). Or look for the California of the silver screen; movies and the state go together like butter and popcorn. Follow **Hitchcock** from *The Birds* to *Vertigo* (p141), see the town that inspired **American Graffiti** (p127) and find the most famous **locations** in LA (p303). Or, for a different kind of art, plumb the galleries of **Mendocino** (p177).

TWAIN, MISQUOTED

San Francisco may feel like Antarctica in July, but Mark Twain never said, "The coldest winter I ever spent was summer in San Francisco."

"*Witness the inspirations for the words of Eugene O'Neill, Jack Kerouac and John Steinbeck.*"

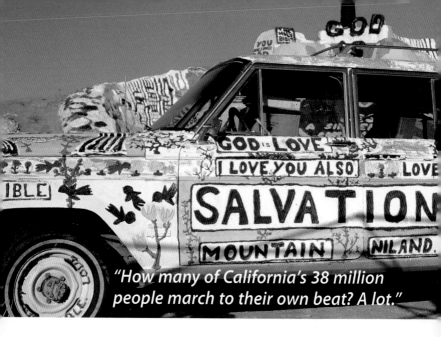

"How many of California's 38 million people march to their own beat? A lot."

 # Offbeat

How many of California's 38 million people march to their own beat? A lot. In fact, many would say the state thrives on the offbeat. In this book you'll find eight trips that go places and meet people not hyped in the tourist brochures. The radicals of the **far north forests** (p117) owe their roots to the beatniks, the deserts attract their share of **characters** (p383), LA's celebrity stomping grounds overflow with **oddball attractions** (p317 and p325) and the Golden State marches to its own beat during **earthquakes** (p133). If you're feeling beat, recharge at some of the most sensational **spas** and **New Agey hangouts** (p359). Or scream your head off at Disneyland or another SoCal **theme park** (p321). Need we say? These trips are hard to beat.

WEIRD NAMES

Avocado, Bivalve, Clapper Gap, Fort Dick, Hooker, Mad River, Plaster City, Scarface, Shrub and Weed are some of California's odder town names…and then there's Zzyzx.

"California's great cities are trips in themselves and you might have a hard time leaving."

Cities

California's great cities are trips in themselves and you might have a hard time leaving. In this book there are trips covering the very best that San Francisco, Los Angeles and San Diego have to offer. Weird, wild and wonderful **San Francisco** (p109) has always taken pride in a personality that trumps even its gorgeous location on the bay. **Los Angeles** (p295) is flash and brash: every local has a story of seeing a star at the 7-Eleven, an experience every visitor fervently hopes to replicate. Down in **San Diego** (p391) is the place weather announcers retire to at age 30. Permanently balmy days and mild nights are just right for plunging into the Pacific by day and chilling outdoors with a margarita by night.

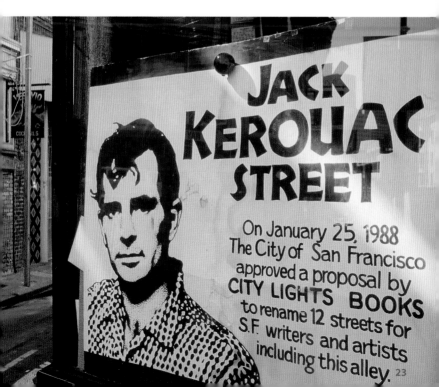

CALIFORNIA'S BEST TRIPS

48 HOURS IN SAN FRANCISCO p109
Mist over the Golden Gate Bridge

CALISTOGA CYCLE p145
Cycling through wine country in Napa

Contents

CENTRAL CALIFORNIA TRIPS 223

TRIP

SOUTHERN CALIFORNIA TRIPS 293

TRIP

Trips by Theme

ROUTES

TRIP

FOOD & DRINK

TRIP

OUTDOORS

HISTORY & CULTURE

OFFBEAT

CITIES

 **DAY TRIPS**

Trips by Season

Expert-Recommended Trips

The Authors

RYAN VER BERKMOES
Ryan Ver Berkmoes grew up close to Hwy 1 near Santa Cruz. As a young fair-haired moppet, he and his friends took delight in giving lost tourists wrong directions. (His angelic face was so believable…) He hopes to make up for this now with his trips in this book. When not toiling away as an author, he'd just as soon track *every* movie location in California. His website is www.ryanverberk moes.com

ALEXIS AVERBUCK
Alexis Averbuck lives in Greece and returned to her home state to further explore the back roads of northern California. An Oakland native and a travel writer for two decades, she has lived in Antarctica, crossed the Pacific by sailboat and still adores the Mendocino coast. She's a painter – see her work at www.alexisaverbuck.com.

AMY C BALFOUR
In the last six years Amy Balfour has hiked, biked and four-wheeled her way across SoCal. She wrote Lonely Planet's *Los Angeles Encounter* and contributed to *Coastal California, LA & Southern California* and the upcoming *California*. Her favorite trips are Sideways in Santa Barbara p349 and 48 Hours in San Diego p391.

SARA BENSON
Sara lives in San Luis Obispo County and has contributed to dozens of Lonely Planet titles, including *California* and *Road Trip: Route 66*. Her travel writing has featured in print and online for the *Los Angeles Times* and *San Francisco Chronicle*. Her favorite trip was The Mission Trail (p93).

NATE CAVALIERI
Nate Cavalieri writes about music, food and travel and lives in Sacramento. His titles for Lonely Planet include *Puerto Rico*, *Chicago* and *Volunteer: A Traveler's Guide to Making a Difference Around the World*. The double-big beers and cowboy dancing at Buck Owen's Crystal Palace were highlights of researching this book.

ALISON BING
In San Francisco for over 15 years, Alison has done everything you're supposed to do in the city and many things you're not, including falling in love on the 7 Haight bus and gorging on Mission burritos before Berlioz symphonies. Alison holds degrees in art history and international diplomacy — respectable credentials she regularly undermines with opinionated culture commentary for radio, newspapers, magazines and books, including Lonely Planet's *San Francisco* and *San Francisco Encounter* guides.

ANDREW BENDER
Andy loves showing people around Southern California, his home since the early 1990s. Since he transitioned out of film production, his travel and food writing has appeared in the *Los Angeles Times*, *Forbes*, *Hemispheres* and *SilverKris* (in-flight magazines of United and Singapore Airlines respectively). His website is www.andrewbender.com.

DOMINIQUE CHANNELL

Dominique Channell lives in the Bay Area. She is coauthor of Lonely Planet's *San Francisco* and *USA* guides and writes about far too much eating and drinking in California and Argentina. After researching Calistoga Cycle (p145) she was inspired to buy a real road bike to pedal it all off. You can usually find her in a favorite internet café or rowing with the Lake Merritt women's crew team in Oakland in the verrrry early morning.

LONELY PLANET AUTHORS

Why is our travel information the best in the world? It's simple: our authors are independent, dedicated travelers. They don't research using just the internet or phone, and they don't take freebies, so you can rely on their advice being well researched and impartial. They travel widely, to all the popular spots and off the beaten track. They personally visit thousands of hotels, restaurants, cafés, bars, galleries, palaces, museums and more – and they take pride in getting all the details right, and telling it how it is. Think you can do it? Find out how at lonelyplanet.com.

BETH KOHN

From her home base in San Francisco, Beth Kohn has authored four titles for Lonely Planet, including *Yosemite, Sequoia & Kings Canyon National Parks*. For this guide, she tested High Sierra hot springs and read Raymond Chandler in the bathtub. Her favorite trip was High Altitudes on Highway 395 (p225).

CONTRIBUTING EXPERTS

Scott Armstrong is a white-water guide, whose family business, All-Outdoors Whitewater Rafting, was the first operator on the American River's Middle Fork. He leads us down the American on p265.

George Baker, a member of the Modesto Film Commission, and his wife, Louise, helm The Fireside Foundation (www.firesidefoundation.com), which sponsors NorCal film festivals. His combined passions for moviemaking and the northern counties contributed to our NorCal film sites trip (p127).

Mike Connolly, Jr is a California State Park Interpreter at the Coastal Discovery Center on San Simeon Bay. He reveals local natural history highlights on the San Luis Obispo wildlife trip (p287).

Douglas Fir (www.douglasfirphotography.com) is a photographer and environmental professional whose other vocational pursuits include builder, mediator and bon vivant. Fir brought his 40 years' experience in southern Humboldt to bear on a Lost Coast hiking trip (p185).

Jennifer Godwin is an associate editor, reporter, and Watch with Kristin blogger at E! Online. To increase your odds of spotting a star, check out Godwin's inside scoop on p325.

Charles Hodgkins is the founder and editor-in-chief of Burritoeater.com, San Francisco's top resource for *taquerias* and mustaches. Try his recommendations on p101.

Bryan Hope, founder of Santa Barbara's Sustainable Vine Wine Tours, whisks guests to ecoconscious wineries in a sleek, biodiesel van. On p349, Bryan gives us the goods on the area's sustainable wineries and ecominded businesses.

David Keene, visionary publican and beer lover, has been the owner of San Francisco's renowned Toronado beer pub (Northern California's first beer bar; www.toronado.com) for over 20 years. He recommends some of his favorite breweries in NorCal (p137).

Kerry Kellogg, Wilderness and Trails Manager in the Los Padres National Forest's Santa Barbara Ranger District, has hiked, biked, kayaked and camped all over Santa Barbara County. Kellogg, who grew up in the area, shares outdoor adventure hotpots on p355.

Tony Merchell is a well-known architectural historian of southern California's desert regions.

He talks about his love of midcentury modern design in Palm Springs (p369).

Andy O'Neill lives in Los Angeles where he reports on the LA taco scene at his blog The Great Taco Hunt (http://tacohunt.blogspot.com). He advises us on which taco truck to target on p101.

Joel Patterson, SoCal native and lifelong surfer, is the current editor-in-chief of *Surfer* magazine and the former editor-in-chief of *Transworld Surf* magazine. He recommends California's best surf spots on p81.

Kent Rosenblum is the President, CEO and Director of Winemaking at esteemed Rosenblum Cellars (www.rosenblumcellars.com). He shared his joy in winemaking and expertise in wine-growing regions when he helped craft a stellar hidden wineries trip (p149).

Brad Suhr has cycled solo cross-country for cancer research and raced in sprint triathlons and 24-hour adventure races. After moving to Calistoga from Martha's Vineyard, he opened a pro shop offering wine tours and extended rides. He shows us around Calistoga on p145.

Alice Waters, chef and author, revolutionized modern eating by championing local, organic, sustainable foods, which she does for us on p75. Her groundbreaking restaurant, Chez Panisse, is in Berkeley.

CALIFORNIA ICONIC TRIPS

Driving the Pacific Coast Hwy from Mexico to Oregon…can there be anything more iconically Californian than this 1050-mile beauty? Sure there can (although the scores of happy holidaymakers navigating their rented convertibles down Big Sur as you read this might beg to differ). In fact, there are so many icons, you might need to narrow your focus: look at the oodles of often-deserted beaches along the coast, the ceaseless tubular waves that inspired an entire lifestyle called surfing, or ditch the car and let Amtrak navigate the turns while you marvel at the views. On most parts of the coast, you're never far from the trail used by the Spanish padres when they colonized California in the 18th century. That heritage lingers in California's favorite road food: the burrito. But if folks in the Golden State know how to eat humble, they also know how to eat well.

PLAYLIST ♫

Each note of these songs can't help but conjure a vision of California. The Beach Boys, Joni Mitchell, Art Pepper, Los Lobos; man, the hits go on and on…

- "Sally Let Your Bangs Hang Down," Rose Maddox
- "Sin City," The Byrds
- "Ball & Chain," Big Brother and the Holding Company
- "The Valley," Los Lobos
- "Surfer Girl," Beach Boys
- "California Love," Tupac
- "Big Yellow Taxi," Joni Mitchell
- "Straight Life," Art Pepper

Food legend Alice Waters has favorite places to dine across the state. And what goes with good food but good wine? And what goes with good wine but good tunes and maybe a good book…

BEST ICONIC TRIPS

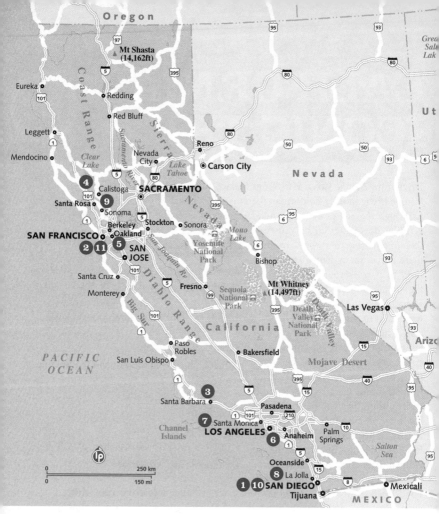

ICONIC TRIPS

Up the Pacific Coast Highway

WHY GO Our top pick for classic California dreamin' hugs the coast from the border with Mexico all the way north to Oregon. Summer is the busiest, but still the best time to drive the PCH. Gawk at elephant seals, uncover secret beaches and touch the tallest trees on earth.

TIME
5 – 7 days

DISTANCE
1050 miles

BEST TIME TO GO
Apr – Oct

START
San Diego

END
Crescent City

ALSO GOOD FOR

Even if you've lived in California all your life, you know there's no such thing as too much time by the beach. Once you get rolling on the Pacific Coast Hwy (PCH), it'll be almost painful to leave the sea behind for too long. This trip never strays far from the coast, except to be tempted by some easy detours inland, including through coastal California's three big cities – San Diego, LA and San Francisco.

Start at the bottom of the state map, just outside San Diego, where the pretty peninsular beach town of Coronado is connected to the mainland by a long, narrow spit of sand called the Silver Strand. If you've seen Marilyn Monroe cavort in *Some Like It Hot,* you may recognize the ❶ **Hotel Del Coronado**. Dating from 1888, this National Historic Landmark has hosted US presidents, celebs from Babe Ruth to Brad Pitt, and the Prince of Wales, later King Edward VIII, who gave up his throne for the love of a Coronado divorcée, Wallis Spencer Simpson. Wander the labyrinthine corridors of this turreted timber palace, then sup at a table overlooking the sea or throw back margaritas at the founders' Babcock & Story Bar.

You can't help but feel a thrill while speeding over the 2-mile-long Coronado Bridge as it snakes its way across San Diego Bay. Turning north, you'll pass by San Diego's beach towns, each with its own quirky personality. After Ocean Beach ("OB" for short), SoCal's answer to boho Santa Cruz, comes Mission Beach, where an old-fashioned amusement park is dwarfed by SeaWorld, and then funky, surfer-friendly Pacific Beach ("PB"). Suddenly, you'll find yourself in hoity-toity La Jolla, like a Beverly Hills by the beach. Recently revamped, chic ❷ **Georges at the Cove** has ocean vistas to match the artistry of the contemporary Euro-Cal cuisine on your plate inside the California Modern restaurant, or upstairs at the parasol-shaded Ocean Terrace café.

Leaving the luxe life of La Jolla behind, roll downhill toward the sea and ❸ **Torrey Pines State Natural Reserve**, harboring the rarest pines in North America and a lagoon frequented by migrating seabirds. This stretch of coast is astonishingly wild, looking much as it must have done when Kumeyaay tribespeople made their seasonal camps here.

It's a fast trip along I-5 into Orange County (aka the "OC"), about 75 miles from San Diego and less than 50 miles from LA. Life behind the conservative "Orange Curtain" is a lot different than in most other California beach towns, where the motto usually is "the more freaks, the merrier." Here desperate housewives drive gas-guzzling SUVs over to Starbucks, and there are easily more shopping malls than museums. But here you can also ferret out the California beach resort culture of yesteryear. Just slingshot around Dana Point, then speed by the wealthy artists' colony of Laguna Beach to Crystal Cove State Park. Hidden inside the park are the beautifully restored 1920s and '30s beachfront ❹ **Crystal Cove Cottages** and the famous Shake Shack (try a date shake!). Time seems to stop and move backward here – it's really that relaxing. Another tribute to California beach traditions is the ❺ **International Surfing Museum** in Huntington Beach, now legally trademarked "Surf City USA." Oahu-born surfer George Freeth introduced the royal Hawaiian sport of wave riding on the beach here in 1908. Further north, Seal Beach pier has mild surf that's perfect for riding your first wave, while ❻ **Walt's Wharf** is everybody's favorite place for fresh fish – some drive down from LA for it.

Hwy 1 heads inland before Long Beach, but the more scenic route sticks to the coast. In Long Beach, the biggest stars are the touristy RMS *Queen Mary* ocean liner and the Aquarium of the Pacific. An often overlooked coastal pleasure is the ❼ **Long Beach Museum of Art**, sitting pretty on an ocean bluff. Exhibits focus on California modernism, with surprisingly cool contemporary art in mixed media. In an early-20th-century mansion, the museum's gourmand café has killer weekend brunches and postcard-perfect views.

Wind your way slowly around the Palos Verdes peninsula, with its rocky precipices and rugged coastline. You may spy Catalina Island out there, if LA's everyday haze doesn't pitifully obscure the views. Hwy 1 rolls north from missable Redondo Beach into turbo-charged Hermosa Beach, where you can stay right on the paradisiacal SoCal sands at the blissful ❽ **Beach House**. Further north along the coast, Manhattan Beach has a swanky singles' scene,

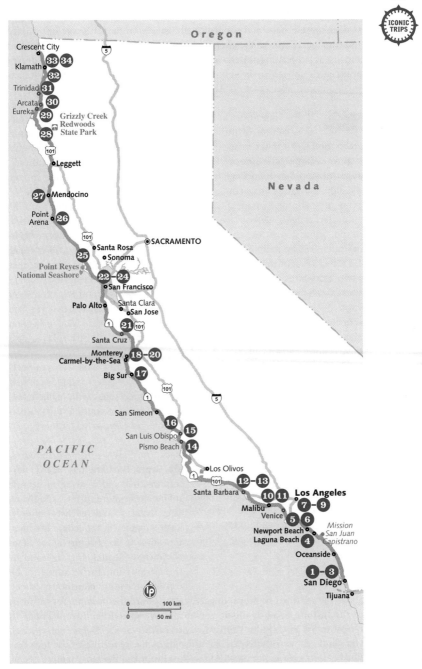

as does more urbane and sophisticated Santa Monica. If it's way-out, wacky and wild local flavor you're after, there's no place like ❾ **Venice**. Idiosyncratic and just as left-leaning as Berkeley, this beatnik haven was originally the dream of eccentric tobacco heir Abbot Kinney, who envisaged building an Italian seaside resort. Well, sort of. Although you'll find canals here, the main attraction is Venice's Ocean Front Walk, where a tragicomic carnival of humanity comes together in a cauldron of creativity. Amuse yourself with this surreal slice of life on the boardwalk, being sure to look up at the murals painted on the beachfront buildings.

DETOUR

If the plasticky, unholy pop culture of the "OC" gets you down, detour 10 miles inland from Laguna Beach for a high-culture dose of history and art at **Mission San Juan Capistrano** (☎ 949-234-1300; www.missionsjc.com), the best-preserved of California's many historic missions. It's located at 26801 Ortega Hwy, San Juan Capistrano; admission is $9/5 per adult /child, and it's open 8:30am to 5pm. Every year on March 19, the Festival of the Swallows celebrates the migratory birds' return from South America to nest in the mission walls.

Leaving LA, PCH really hits its stride on the breezy 20-mile drive north to Malibu. You'll feel like a movie star walking around here – except that real Hollywood celebrities live in gated compounds and are rarely seen in public. One mansion that you can actually get a look inside is the ❿ **Adamson House**, next to Malibu Lagoon State Beach. Just west of Malibu Pier, this 1930s Spanish Moorish villa is awash in Arts and Crafts details such as colorful hand-painted tiles. Make time for frolicking on one of Malibu's famous beaches, like Point Dume, Zuma or Surfrider, too. At the Ventura County line, surfers, Harley riders and kids covered in sand chow down at ⓫ **Neptune's Net**, a seafood shack with picnic tables and fresh (sometimes live!) seafood cooked just the way you want it.

ASK A LOCAL

"For a fun way to cool off, bring the family out to **Santa Monica Pier** (www.santamonicapier .org). Not only do you get a great view of the ocean, you can get up close and personal with sea urchins, sharks and rays at the aquarium run by the nonprofit organization Heal the Bay. When you're done learning, head up top for a spin on the carousel used in *The Sting,* or the solar-powered Ferris wheel."

Amy S, Los Angeles

Back on Hwy 101 northbound, ⓬ **Santa Barbara** has nearly perfect weather and a string of beautiful beaches, where surfers, kite flyers, dog walkers and cyclists mingle. Take a gander at the iconic Mediterranean-style architecture along State St downtown, including an innovative art museum, then clamber to the top of the county courthouse, rising above the red-tiled rooftops, to gaze south toward the busy harbor or north to the historic Spanish mission. Skip the overpriced beachfront hotels to retreat to ⓭ **El Capitan Canyon** resort, further north. Deluxe safari tents, yurts and cabins with fireplaces and Jacuzzi tubs are for those who love getting back to nature, but hate waking up with dirt under their nails.

Keep following high-speed Hwy 101 or take scenic Hwy 1, which squiggles along the coastline; both highways meet up again at ⑭ **Pismo Beach**, about 100 miles north of Santa Barbara. A classic California beach town, Pismo once laid claim to being the "Clam Capital of the World." Turn up for the family-friendly clam festival every October, also when monarch butterflies return to their seaside grove. After walking out onto Pismo's pier at sunset, revert to childhood with all of the retro attractions on nearby side streets, from bowling alleys, billiards halls and video arcades to fast-food stands.

Further north, the CalPoly student town of ⑮ **San Luis Obispo** (aka "SLO") comes alive every Thursday night for a downtown farmers market. Join throngs of locals as they demolish piping-hot dishes from fresh-food vendors, listen to live indie bands, and enjoy the street carnival.

DETOUR The Mediterranean climate around Santa Barbara is perfect for growing grapes. About a 40-minute drive northwest of Santa Barbara along Hwy 154 lies the Santa Ynez Valley wine country, made infamous by the 2004 indie flick *Sideways*. Jump-start your grape-loving tasté-buds at the **Los Olivos Tasting Room & Wine Shop** (☎805-688-7406). It's located at 2905 Grand Ave, Los Olivos, and is open from 11am to 5:30pm. Then, strike out on your own along the Foxen Canyon wine trail, which eventually rejoins Hwy 101 north at Santa Maria.

Hwy 1 keeps cruising north through SLO County, passing landmark Morro Rock. Pull off the highway for the little surf town of Cayucos. ⑯ **Ruddell's Smokehouse** is a tasty place for fresh-off-the-boat seafood transformed into succulent smoked slabs; the fish tacos come slathered in an apple-and-celery relish. Make sure your gas tank is full before you blow by the hilltop mansion of Hearst Castle and plunge into the big-trees scenery of the Big Sur coast, where rocky headlands and precipitous cliffs with leaping waterfalls dominate the seascape. Known for its counter-cultural tendencies, Big Sur feels like a rural mountain community with an arty, hippie bent. Nature preserves and beaches beckon along Hwy 1, as do high-end resorts and hidden retreats where San Franciscans come to escape the noise. Only open to the public after midnight, the natural hot-springs baths of the ⑰ **Esalen Institute** are worth the crazy effort of making reservations for, with au-naturel pools perched on an ocean ledge and stormy moonlit surf crashing below.

As Big Sur loosens its talons on the coastal highway, Hwy 1 rolls gently downhill toward Monterey Bay, about a 100-mile drive from Hearst Castle. This fishing community is the heart of Steinbeck country, and although Cannery Row today is a touristy claptrap, it's worth strolling down solely to step inside the mesmerizing ⑱ **Monterey Bay Aquarium**, inhabiting a converted sardine cannery. All kinds of aquatic denizens are on display here, from sea stars and sea dragons to pot-bellied seahorses and comical sea otters. Drive alongside the waterfront over to Pacific Beach for dinner at ⑲ **Passionfish**, a down-to-earth, sustainable seafood restaurant with a phenomenal wine list.

Then dart north into the sand dunes outside Marina to the ⑳ **Sanctuary Beach Resort**. Spoil yourself with a sleek, modern suite with an ocean-view balcony, so you can sleep soundly next to the surf.

Before making the 115-mile run up to San Francisco past Half Moon Bay and Pacifica, where Hwy 1 conquers the tricky, washout-prone Devil's Slide,

"…with au-naturel pools perched on an ocean ledge with stormy moonlit surf crashing below."

stop briefly by ㉑ **Santa Cruz**. Here the flower power of the 1960s lives on, and bumper stickers on surfboard-laden woodies loudly protest "Keep Santa Cruz weird." Built in 1907, the Santa Cruz Beach Boardwalk has a glorious old-school Americana vibe, with the smell of cotton candy mixing with salty sea breezes. The fun-for-all atmosphere is punctuated by squeals from nervous nellies on the stomach-turning Giant Dipper, a 1920s wooden rollercoaster that's a National Historic Landmark, as seen in the vampire cult classic movie *The Lost Boys*.

The gridlock of San Francisco may shock your system after hundreds of miles of wide-open, rolling coast. But don't despair. Hwy 1 runs straight through the city's biggest and most breathable green space, ㉒ **Golden Gate Park**, which dates from the Victorian era. You could easily lose yourself all day in the conservatory of flowers, arboretum and botanic gardens, perusing the galleries of the de Young Museum of fine arts, then taking tea underneath pagodas in the Japanese Tea Garden, or romantically renting a rowboat at petite Stow Lake.

To get out of the city, drive over the ㉓ **Golden Gate Bridge**. Guarding entry to San Francisco Bay, this iconic 2-mile-long bridge is named after the straits it spans and not for its color, which is "international orange." Thanks to the saltiness of the air and the whipping winds, repainting the bridge is a never-ending job. Dash into the parking lot before the toll plaza on the south side of the bridge, then out onto the brick-laden pedestrian walkway for a photo.

On the other side of the bridge lies Marin County, an enclave of rich folks who passionately love the outdoors – and all the cosmopolitan perks of the good life, like exceptional food and wine and, yes, hot tubs. At ㉔ **Cavallo Point**, an eco-conscious lodge built on the grounds of old military Fort Baker inside Golden Gate National Recreation Area, guests can enjoy all kinds of freebie activities, from fireside chats with park rangers to yoga in the healing-arts spa and guided walking tours with green-living, art and architectural themes.

Past Sausalito, abandon Hwy 101 for torturously twisted Hwy 1, which sets a slow pace for the next 200 miles along a gloriously uninterrupted stretch of PCH. Along the coasts of Sonoma and Mendocino Counties you will uncover wild NorCal beaches and lagoons where rare birds flock, laid against emerald pasturelands where dairy cows and goats graze. Fishing communities still eke out a living, with Tomales Bay prized for its oysters. At the historic Valley Ford Hotel, **25** **Rocker Oysterfeller's** kitchen and saloon has a sense of humor, but is dead serious about satisfying even picky eaters with its artisan cheeses, raw seafood plates and organic beef and seasonal veggies sourced from local farms.

The fishing fleets of Bodega Bay and Jenner's harbor-seal colony are the last things you'll see before PCH dives into California's great rural northlands. Hwy 1 twists past a lineup of state parks packed with hiking trails, sand dunes and beaches, rhododendron groves and a 19th-century Russian fur-trading fort. At Sea Ranch, don't let the exclusive-looking vacation homes prevent you from following public-access trailhead signs down to more remote beaches and across windy ocean blufftops. Don't linger so long that you miss seeing **26** **Point Arena Lighthouse**, the only lighthouse in California that you can actually climb to the top of. Check in at the museum, then ascend the 115ft tower to inspect the Fresnel lens and view the jagged San Andreas Fault below.

More like Cape Cod than California, the too-quaint town of Mendocino blooms with rose gardens, while white picket fences surround New England–style cottages with redwood water towers. Since this yesteryear timber town and shipping port was "discovered" by artists and bohemians in the 1950s, the not-so-humble community, with its dramatic headlands jutting into the Pacific, has served as a backdrop in over 50 movies. After you've browsed the treacly sentimental streets lined with souvenir shops selling everything from driftwood carvings to housemade fruit jams and preserves, relish the **27** **Joshua Grindle Inn**, Mendo's very first B&B and a must for aficionados of historic homes. Or dash north to workaday Fort Bragg, with its simple fishing harbor, roadside motels and brewpub.

DETOUR A rough-hewn beauty, **Point Reyes National Seashore** (www.nps.gov/pore) lures marine mammals and birds, as well as scores of shipwrecks. It was here that Sir Francis Drake repaired his ship the *Golden Hind* in 1579 and, while he was at it, claimed the land for England. North of Olema, follow Sir Francis Drake Blvd out to the edge-of-the-world lighthouse, whipped by ferocious winds, where you can observe migrating gray whales in winter, near the Chimney Rock elephant seal colony.

Amid roaring surf and endless sightlines, Westport is the last hamlet along this rugged stretch of Hwy 1. The coastal route rejoins Hwy 101 northbound for 200 miles through the Redwood Empire up to the Oregon border. Don't miss the exit for the "Avenue of the Giants," a 32-mile-long parkway with two narrow lanes passing among incredible stands of redwoods, the tallest trees on earth. In the early morning, the heavenly light filtering through the dense greenery of the forest is transcendent; many visitors walk out into the Founders Grove with a respectful silence usually not seen outside of a cathedral. Much of the land belongs to **28** **Humboldt Redwoods State Park**, which maintains a worthwhile natural- and human-history museum at the visitor center in Weott.

Hwy 101 trundles past the company logging town of Scotia and the turnoff for Humboldt Bay National Wildlife Refuge, a major stopover for migratory birds. Next comes the sleepy railroad town of ㉙ **Eureka**. Check out the ornate Carson Mansion (corner of M and 2nd Sts), built in the 1880s by a timber baron and adorned with dizzying turrets, towers and gables. Opposite is an almost equally impressive Queen Anne Victorian, painted in cake-frosting pink.

While prim-and-proper Eureka rolls up the sidewalks at 9pm sharp, its trippy-dippy northern neighbor ㉚ **Arcata** may just be getting started. It's a bastion of student-led radicalism and, let's be honest, a helluva lot of pot smoking. The more scenic route north travels across the lonely, windswept Samoa Peninsula before reaching Arcata's town square, ringed with bohemian coffee shops, global fusion eateries, student bars and outdoor outfitters. If you want to converse about politics or metaphysics, just about anyone on the street will oblige you.

Before the scent of patchouli knocks you out, keep motoring up Hwy 101 into ㉛ **Trinidad**, where a trim lighthouse keeps watch over the bluffs that tumble down into a deep harbor. After touching the tide-pool critters at the university-run marine laboratory and traipsing on the beach at Trinidad Cove or white-sand Moonstone Beach, continue north. Hwy 101 drops out of the trees by the Humboldt Lagoons, where kayakers wend their way across the marshy waters. At long last the highway reaches ㉜ **Redwood National & State Parks**. Commune with the coastal giants on their own mossy turf inside the Lady Bird Johnson Grove or the majestic but less-accessible Tall Trees Grove (free permits required). For more untouched virgin redwood forests, drive along the 8-mile Newton B Drury Scenic Parkway, passing tempting trailheads and meadows where Roosevelt elk roam.

> **ASK A LOCAL**
>
> "To find the best hidden redwood groves, **Grizzly Creek Redwoods State Park** (www.parks.ca.gov) is the place. It's smaller than other parks, but so out of the way that it's pristine. The Cheatham Grove in particular has the most lush sorrel carpets under the trees. And it's along the Van Duzen River, which has great summer swimming holes. Bonus factoid: scenes in *Return of the Jedi* were shot here."
>
> *Richard S, Eureka*

Giant cast-metal golden bears stand sentry over the bridge leading into tiny Klamath. Watch out for Paul Bunyan and his blue ox Babe outside the ㉝ **Trees of Mystery**, a shameless tourist trap with a gondola ride through the redwood canopy. The free End of the Trail Museum displays Native American art and artifacts; enter through the gift shop. If you can't bear to leave the big trees behind, ㉞ **HI Redwood Hostel** awaits inside an early-20th-century farmhouse, tucked into a craggy section of truly wild coast overlooking blustery Klamath Cove. Further north, Crescent City is a utilitarian stopover just before you reach the beach-resort towns of the Oregon coast.

Sara Benson

TRIP INFORMATION

GETTING THERE
From Los Angeles, take I-5 south to San Diego.

DO

Adamson House
Informative guided tours of the beach-front mansion are first-come, first-served. ☎ 310-456-8432; www.adamsonhouse .org; 23200 Pacific Coast Hwy, Malibu; adult/child $5/2, cash only; ⏱ 11am-3pm Wed-Sat, last tour 2pm

Esalen Institute
Reservations are required for the clothing-optional hot-springs baths. ☎ 831-667-3047; www.esalen.org; 55000 Hwy 1, Big Sur; admission $20; ⏱ public bath entry 1am-3am

Hotel Del Coronado
Pretend to live like royalty at this historic seaside resort. ☎ 619-435-6611; www .hoteldel.com; 1500 Orange Ave, Coronado; ⏱ 24hr

Humboldt Redwoods State Park
Be amazed by a canopy of the tallest trees you may have ever seen. ☎ 707-946-2263, camping reservations 800-444-7275; www .parks.ca.gov, www.reserveamerica.com; Avenue of the Giants; ⏱ visitor center 9am-5pm Apr-Oct, 10am-4pm Nov-Mar; &

International Surfing Museum
Chronicles the iconic sport's history through photos, film, music and memorabilia. ☎ 714-960-3483; www.surfingmuseum.org; 411 Olive Ave, Huntington Beach; admission free; ⏱ noon-5pm Mon-Fri, 11am-6pm Sat & Sun

Long Beach Museum of Art
Ever-changing exhibitions of California art range from pinhole photos to giant sculptures. ☎ 562-439-2119; www.lbma.org; 2300 E Ocean Blvd, Long Beach; adult/child $7/free; ⏱ 11am-5pm Tue-Sun

Monterey Bay Aquarium
Avoid long lines by going early or purchasing tickets online in advance. ☎ 831-648-4800; www.mabyaq.org; 886 Cannery Row, Monterey; adult/child $25/16; ⏱ 10am-6pm; &

Point Arena Lighthouse
Still standing on an unbelievably windy point since 1908. ☎ 707-882-2777; www.point arenalighthouse.com; 45500 Lighthouse Rd, Point Arena; adult/child $5/1; ⏱ 10am-3:30pm; &

Redwood National & State Parks
Get oriented to the big trees at the visitors center south of Orick, or along the scenic Newton B Drury Parkway. ☎ 707-464-6101; www.nps.gov/redw; state park day-use fee $6; ⏱ visitors centers 9am-5pm; &

Trees of Mystery
Leave your cynicism at home; it's retro family-vacation fun. ☎ 707-482-2251, 800-638-3389; www.treesofmystery.net; 15500 Hwy 101, Klamath; adult/child $13.50/6.50; ⏱ 8am-6:30pm Jun-Aug, 9am-4:30pm Sep-May; & &

Torrey Pines State Natural Reserve
Breathe in the fresh marine air, perched high above the beach. ☎ 858-755-2063; www .parks.ca.gov; Hwy 1, btwn La Jolla & Del Mar; day-use fee $6; ⏱ 8am-sunset, visitors center from 9am; &

EAT

Georges at the Cove
Reservations are essential at La Jolla's top-tier epicurean destination. ☎ 858-454-4244; www.georgesatthecove.com; 1250 Prospect St, La Jolla; mains $10-40; ⏱ café 11am-10pm, restaurant 5:30-10pm

Neptune's Net
Order up lobster, crab and jumbo shrimp at this 1950s roadhouse. ☎ 310-457-3095; www.neptunesnet.com; 42505 Pacific Coast Hwy, Malibu; mains $4-17; ⏱ 10:30am-8pm Mon-Thu, 10:30am-9pm Fri, 10am-8:30pm Sat & Sun, closes 1hr earlier Nov-Mar; & &

Passionfish
Fresh, inventive seafood dishes and organic, slow-food produce earn a devoted following. ☎ 831-655-3311; www.passionfish.net; 701 Lighthouse Ave, Pacific Grove; mains $17-24; ⏱ 5-8:45pm Sun-Thu, 5-9:45pm Fri & Sat

Rocker Oysterfeller's
Cozy up to the Old West bar for oyster shooters and some spicy Sonoma-grown zinfandel. ☎ 707-876-1983; www.rockeroysterfellers.com; 14415 Hwy 1, Valley Ford; mains $9-34; ⏱ 10am-2pm Sun, 5-9pm Wed-Sun

Ruddell's Smokehouse
Grab-and-go, made-to-order tacos and seafood jerky made by "Smoker Jim." ☎ 805-995-5028; www.smokerjim.com; 101 D St, Cayucos; mains $4-10; ⏱ 11am-6pm; ⏱ ⏱

Walt's Wharf
Oak-grilled surf-and-turf platters pack the house, especially on weekends. No reservations. ☎ 562-598-4433; http://waltswharf.com; 201 Main St, Seal Beach; mains $9-41; ⏱ 11am-3:30pm & 4pm-close; ⏱

SLEEP

Beach House
Fall asleep to the sounds of the surf in lofty condo-like suites with high-tech modern amenities. ☎ 310-374-3001, 888-895-4559; www.beach-house.com; 1300 The Strand, Hermosa Beach; r $305-485; ⏱

Cavallo Point
Sleep inside a former military officer's house or more contemporary rooms on the hillside, which have Golden Gate views. ☎ 415-339-4700, 888-651-2003; www.cavallopoint.com; 601 Murray Circle, Fort Baker, Sausalito; r $250-750; ⏱

Crystal Cove Cottages
Reservations sell out immediately by phone and online, starting at 8am on the first day of the month, six months prior to your stay.

☎ reservations 800-444-7275; www.crystal covebeachcottages.org, reservations www.reserveamerica.com; 8471 North Coast Hwy, Laguna Beach; r $52-345; ⏱

El Capitan Canyon
Go "glamping" in Santa Barbara; a two-night minimum stay applies on weekends. ☎ 805-685-3887, 866-352-2729; www.elcapitan canyon.com; 11560 Calle Real, Santa Barbara; r $145-350; ⏱

HI Redwood Hostel
Basic shared and private rooms in an unbeatable locale. ☎ 707-482-8265; www.norcal hostels.org/redwoods; 14480 Hwy 101, Klamath; dorms/r $21/52; ⏱ check-in 4-10pm Mar-Oct, some weekends Nov-Feb; ⏱

Humboldt Redwoods State Park
Roadside campgrounds come with hot showers, potable water and hike-in "envirosites." ☎ 707-946-1811, reservations 800-444-7275; www.reserveamerica.com; Avenue of the Giants; campsites $12-20; ⏱ most campgrounds mid-May–mid-Oct, some year-round; ⏱ ⏱

Joshua Grindle Inn
Bright, airy and uncluttered rooms in a Victorian house, weathered saltbox cottage and water tower are perennially full. ☎ 707-937-4143, 800-474-6353; www.joshgrin.com; 44800 Little Lake Rd, Mendocino; r $189-425; ⏱

Sanctuary Beach Resort
Deluxe rooms and suites next to the beach, without any maddening crowds or traffic. ☎ 831-883-9478, 877-944-3863; www.thesanctuarybeachresort.com; 3295 Dunes Dr, Marina; r $169-279; ⏱

USEFUL WEBSITES
www.parks.ca.gov
www.visitcalifornia.com

LINK YOUR TRIP

www.lonelyplanet.com/trip-planner

The Doors to the Dead

WHY GO Chase the trail of iconic California rockers between San Francisco's hippie crossroads and the deafening din of West Hollywood. Eat the Beach Boys' burgers, party all night at the Riot House and catch shows at landmark West Coast venues.

Right there in the first few seconds of the Mamas and the Papas' oldies warhorse "California Dreamin'" – amongst the tinny ring of guitars and ghostly cluster of harmonies – there's a certain thread that the astute listener can hear in most iconic songs about this place. You hear it in the rumbling rave-up of the Doors' "LA Woman" and the sparkling acoustics that introduce the Eagles' "Hotel California." You hear it in Joni Mitchell's acrobatic soprano in "California" and Otis Redding's view from the dock of the bay. Like the other great musical muses – love and drugs – it's about a kind of yearning, the essential, mysterious promise that's hardwired in the idea of California.

California musicians have long bucked convention and changed history, from the plucky country revolution that was created by Bakersfield artists like Buck Owens, the punk takeover that snarled out of the Bay Area with Green Day, or the young emcees whose takeover of suburban America began with swapping mix tapes in Compton parking lots. The culture-shaping influence of California's rock 'n' roll can't be overstated, and this dedicated trip, which follows the sound from the crowded streets of the Bay Area to the desolate skies of Joshua Tree, barely scratches the surface.

Day and night, weekdays and weekends, in rain and fog and sunshine, people line up to have their picture snapped under the street sign of the often mythologized corner of ❶ **Haight-Ashbury**. This was the corner where the tie-dyed love revolution in the mid '60s took hold,

TIME
4 – 5 days

DISTANCE
632 miles

BEST TIME TO GO
Year-round

START
San Francisco

END
Joshua Tree

ALSO GOOD FOR

HISTORY &
CULTURE

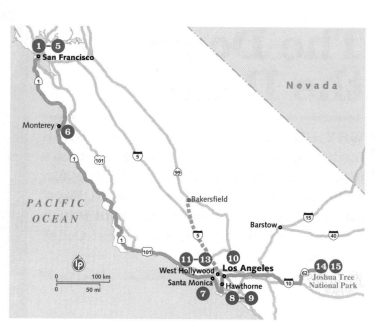

and fragmentary reminders (read: burnouts) of the trippy days remain, despite the fact that chain stores have encroached on the spot. Just up the hill at 710 Ashbury is the house that the Grateful Dead called home and a few blocks northwest, at 2400 Fulton St, is where Jefferson Airplane laid their head. At the end of Haight St, in a converted bowling alley at the edge of Golden Gate Park, lies the enormous Amoeba Music. You can stock up on the requisite tunes to accompany your journey and wander through the park, where plenty of other enhancements for the trip are also readily available.

"...the Dead named it for a hotel down the street, with rooms by the hour..."

Get the car and head downtown. Park at the lot at **2** **827 Folsom St**, the site of the Automatt Studio, where the Grateful Dead cut their mid-'70s watermark *From the Mars Hotel* (the Dead named it for a hotel down the street, which rents rooms by the hour). Other tunes recorded in this studio-turned-parking lot include Steve Miller's faux-psych blockbuster "Fly Like an Eagle."

One of San Francisco's iconic recording houses still stands just on the other side of Market, at **3** **Hyde Street Studios**. This is the studio where Creedence Clearwater Revival cut "Bad Moon Rising" and four of their LPs between 1969 and 1970. It's a functioning studio and isn't open for tours, but if you want to join your heroes, book their overnight sessions, available at discounted rates.

Before leaving San Francisco, see a show – any show – at ❹ **The Fillmore**. Once booked by legendary concert promoter Bill Graham, the spacious ballroom is still a favorite of touring acts. The interior is a museum of San Francisco's rock heyday: walls are lined with posters and photos of recent acts and alumni that include psych and jam godfathers like the Dead and Country Joe and The Fish. On the way out, grab an apple from the big bin by the door, an homage to Graham's legendary hospitality. After the show, bunk down at the ❺ **Phoenix Hotel**, a hip, nearby 1950s motor lodge. Even though they're no longer incognito at the hotel known as the city's rocker crash pad, the rock stars continue to check in – along with the obligatory groupies. Unlike most hotels in the city, this one actually has a swimming pool.

Leave San Francisco via Hwy 1 south and travel three hours into Monterey. Take the Casa Verde Exit to reach the ❻ **Monterey Country Fairgrounds**, home to the 1967 Monterey Pop Festival, held during the peak of the summer of love. Today, the sleepy grounds host tamer annual events, like the Monterey Jazz Festival each September, where some of the 60,000-plus Bay Area kids who once dropped acid and took in sets from Hendrix, The Who, Jefferson Airplane and Otis Redding now sit enjoying smooth jazz and chardonnay.

The complete box set of the Monterey Pop Festival performances were put to disc in the late '90s and later reissued, which makes good road music for the long six-hour drive south on Hwy 101 toward Los Angeles. It was probably Hendrix that stole the show when he ended the set by setting his guitar on fire, a move that helped introduce him to American audiences.

To buy an ax you too can torch, hit the West Coast's best guitar shop, ❼ **Truetone Music**, in Santa Monica. The shop is lined with brightly polished vintage guitars that will bring out the gearhead in anyone. The staff has hocked merchandise to both Tom Petty and his right-hand man, Mike Campbell, as well as Don Henley and Prince.

Getting back out to I-10, continue on I-405 south to the Imperial Hwy exit and cue up *Pet Sounds* while cruising the same streets the Beach Boys did. Take a right off the broad Hawthorne Blvd, to pass ❽ **Foster's Freeze**. There's some debate as to whether or not this is the actual hamburger stand that the young lass was cruising to in "Fun, Fun, Fun," but today you can get your grease on with onion rings, burgers and double thick shakes. Take the Wilsons' favorite cruising route by going left on 120th Ave for a mile and left on Kornblum Ave, to arrive at the ❾ **Beach Boys Historic Landmark**, a brick-and-bronze wall that stands at the location of Brian and co's former front lawn. The large white stone carving in the center of the monument depicts the boys carrying a long board, a nod to the Beach Boys' seminal *Surfer Girl* album.

Get back on I-105 and head east for three minutes, connecting with I-110 north, to the heart of the city. After 8 miles, go west on I-10 and exit at Arlington. Go a block north and two blocks east on 21st St and stop at ⑩ **2101 S Grammercy**. Leave some flowers for Marvin Gaye, who was shot and killed here by his father, a day before his 45th birthday.

Between the driving and the memorial, it's time for a drink, so get back on I-10 and go west. Exit after 3 miles at the signs for S La Cienega Blvd, which leads to the heart of the Sunset Strip.

First, grab some sun at the rooftop pool at the ⑪ **"Riot House,"** a notorious rock and roll hotel on Sunset that has been partially destroyed at different times by members of Led Zeppelin (who rode motorcycles in the hallway), the Stones (who mooned the public from their rooms) and Guns n' Roses (who threw steaks from a balcony grill to a crowd below). If it's not under renovation or occupied, choose room 319, which Little Richard lived in for the better part of two decades.

The walk west on Sunset Strip offers a disorienting mess of high-volume bars, over-the-top clubs and dog-eared rock venues, but head east, past the Chateau Marmont, where John Belushi famously died of an overdose in 1982.

Take a left at N Doheny Dr and walk to the corner of Santa Monica to the ⑫ **Troubadour**, the most noble of Los Angeles' remaining venues. The place has some bragging rights – first performances by solo Neil Young, Buffalo Springfield and Guns n' Roses, and the discovery of Tom Waits – but the casual, cozy room wears its history without pretension. The best seats are behind the bar, facing the stage where the rock-star spotting happens on a nightly basis.

> **DETOUR**
>
> Enough of this rock and roll racket! Hit the sun-washed streets of Bakersfield, the home of a twangy high-volume brand of country called the "Bakersfield Sound." Buck Owens and Merle Haggard put Bakersfield on the map in the 1950s by rebelling against the soggy, sentimental ballads of Nashville.
>
> Today, sharp-dressed cowboys and girls crowd the dance floor at **Buck Owens' Crystal Palace**, but a more intimate roadhouse is **Ethel's Old Corral Café** where homespun pickers keep the rebellious dream alive. Bakersfield is two hours north of LA via I-5 and Hwy 99.

Walk up Santa Monica a mile to grab some pizzas at ⑬ **Benvenuto Caffé**. This building housed The Doors' office between October 1970 and February 1971. The food? Nothing to write home about. The bathroom? It served as the vocal booth to the title track of their classic "LA Woman."

The only way to clear your head of the frantic carnival of Hollywood is to get back on the road and head into the desert. Go east two hours on I-10 and take CA 62 north into Joshua Tree, a nearby refuge where rock stars from Keith Richards to U2 (who holed up here to write part of their famous record of the same name) have ventured to get away. After half an hour on CA 62, you'll see the humble facade of the ⑭ **Joshua Tree Inn**. Do it right by staying in the peach-colored room 8, where Gram Parsons, former member of The Byrds and The Flying Burrito Brothers, died of an overdose in September 1973. Parsons' pilgrims scrawl adoring notes on a notebook by the bed. If you want to stay in Gram's room, book in advance.

Half a mile east, go right on Park Blvd, entering the 50,000 acres of harsh, high desert of the Joshua Tree National Park. Twenty minutes south, the road turns sharply near a disorderly pile of boulders called ⑮ **Cap Rock**, a site that marks the

STRAIGHT OUTTA COMPTON

Eazy-E, a Compton dope dealer with a high-pitched voice, turned the musical world on its head when he founded NWA (Niggaz With Attitude). Joined by Dr Dre and Ice Cube, the group terrorized suburban mothers with lyrics that glamourized the tough-as-nails street life of South Central Los Angeles and minted Gangsta Rap. NWA became the most polarizing group of the '90s, breaking racial barriers, becoming unlikely crusaders for the First Amendment and forever changing the landscape of pop music.

end of Parsons' strange journey, and ours. In accordance with Parsons' wishes, his road manager and confidant, Phil Kaufman, brought him here to perform an impromptu cremation with appropriate mystical form. Look for messages that people paint or carve into the rock to honor the singer and songwriter's memory. It's a surreally desolate way to end the aptly expansive journey, and a place to hear the sound of California on the wind.

Nate Cavalieri

TRIP INFORMATION

GETTING THERE
Cue up some tunes and start in San Francisco, at the site of California's first revolutionary rock scene, Haight-Ashbury.

DO
Beach Boys Historic Landmark
This historic marker is parked on the site of the Wilson brothers' childhood lawn. 3701 W 119th St, Hawthorne; admission free; ⛹ ⛹

Hyde Street Studios
Creedence Clearwater Revival and Jerry Garcia have haunted the studios of this landmark facility. ☎ 415-441-8934; www.hydestreet.com; 245 Hyde St, San Francisco; from 8 hours $325; ✷ by appointment

The Fillmore
Legendary promoter Bill Graham booked this definitive West-Coast rock venue, littered with mind-blowing memorabilia. ☎ 415-346-6000; www.thefillmore.com; 1805 Geary Blvd, San Francisco; admission $10-50; ✷ 8pm-2am

Monterey Country Fairgrounds
This is the site of the concert that paved the way for Woodstock; it's now home to annual festivals and breezy picnic grounds. ☎ 831-372-5863; www.montereycountryfair.com; 2004 Fairgrounds Rd, Monterey; ⛹ ⛹

Riot House (ANdAZ West Hollywood)
Many a TV has learned to fly from the windows of this Sunset Strip hotel, which is nearly always under renovation. ☎ 323-656-1234; 8401 Sunset Blvd, West Hollywood

Troubadour
There are plenty bigger and badder, but this is SoCal's best small venue. ☎ 310-276-6168; www.troubadour.com; 9081 Santa Monica Blvd, West Hollywood; admission varies; ✷ most shows 8pm

Truetone Music
Don't take our word for it – Tom Petty gets his gear here. ☎ 310-393-8232; www.truetonemusic.com; 714 Santa Monica Blvd, Santa Monica; ✷ 11am-9pm Mon-Thu, 11am-7pm Fri-Sat

EAT & SLEEP
Benvenuto Caffé
Even if you skip the passable Italian food, use the restroom – once Jim Morrison's vocal booth. ☎ 310-659-8635; www.benvenuto-caffe.com; 8512 Santa Monica Blvd, West Hollywood; mains $9-15; ✷ lunch & dinner

Foster's Freeze
Just before daddy took the T-Bird away, this is where she might have been cruisin'. ☎ 310-644-9654; 11969 Hawthorne Blvd, Hawthorne; mains $2-10; ✷ 10am-9:45pm Mon-Sun; ⛹

Joshua Tree Inn
On the edge of the national park, this humble motel draws Gram Parsons' faithful followers. ☎ 760-366-1188; www.joshuatreeinn.com; 61259 29 Palms Hwy, Joshua Tree; r $85-175; ✷ office 3-8pm

Phoenix Hotel
Rooms are midcentury modern vamped up with tropical decor. Down a cocktail at the Bambuddha Lounge on-site. ☎ 415-776-1380; www.jdvhospitality.com; 601 Eddy St, San Francisco; r $150-190 with seasonal variations

USEFUL WEBSITES
www.rockandrollroadmap.com

LINK YOUR TRIP

www.lonelyplanet.com/trip-planner

Best of the Beaches

WHY GO More than 300 miles of sun-splashed coast stretches between Santa Barbara and San Diego. These are the shores of America's daydreams, an embarrassment of riches that can prove bedeviling when deciding where to unfurl your beach towel. Surf-centered? Family-friendly? Romantic? Off the beaten path? Reduce the competition with these seven "Bests."

TIME
4 – 5 days

DISTANCE
215 miles

BEST TIME TO GO
Apr – Oct

START
Santa Barbara

END
La Jolla

ALSO GOOD FOR

OUTDOORS

For a "Best of the Beaches" trip, there's no more appropriate launch pad than ❶ East Beach in ❷ Santa Barbara at the southern end of State St. For sheer supremacy in all the key categories – looks, accessibility, family friendliness and adventure appeal – this breezy, palm-lined golden girl wins "Best All-Round."

For natural beauty, just look north. The Santa Ynez Mountains flank a Mediterranean-style downtown where red tile roofs glow in the evening sun. To the south, Stearns Wharf frames a deep blue, yacht-dotted sea. Did we mention it's sunny nearly 300 days of the year? No wonder Santa Barbara's been dubbed America's Riviera. East Beach is a cultural charmer as well, with nearly 250 local artists displaying their work every Sunday during the Santa Barbara Arts & Crafts Show. Within a few blocks are Mission-era buildings, historic theaters, the Santa Barbara Museum of Art, and a Spanish-Moorish courthouse that's a work of art in itself.

But it's not all about looks and art. Just ask the helmet-clad cyclist pedaling past on the beachfront bike path, or the barefoot girl diving for a spike on the beach volleyball court. East Beach is family friendly too (but watch the traffic on Cabrillo Blvd). Kids can sing along with

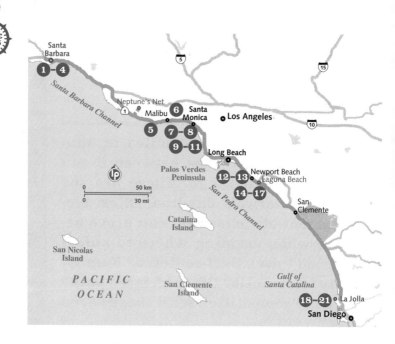

whale karaoke at ❸ **Ty Warner Sea Center,** or the whole clan can pedal the bike path in a four-person surrey from ❹ **Wheel Fun Rentals.**

Leaving urban comforts behind, follow Hwy 101 south, breaking off after Ventura to continue on Hwy 1, also called Pacific Coast Hwy (PCH). After zigzagging through tiny Oxnard, the road unfurls between mountain foothills and crashing surf. Approaching Malibu, the scenery kicks up a notch as Harleys swoop up behind you and sleek titanium road bikes flash into view ahead. Keep your eyes peeled for a line of cars parked bumper-to-bumper on PCH, an alert that ❺ **Zuma Beach** is just ahead. If you see a spot, nab it. Otherwise, pay a small fee (usually $6) to park in the sprawling, 2025-space lot.

With its gentle swells and wide beaches, Zuma wins "Best for a Lazy Beach Day." The only requirement is selecting your plot of sand and plunking into your chair. Though it can be amusing to ponder your options. Join the boogie boarders ripping toward shore? Dive for a volleyball on the pearly sand? Or maybe cast a line in the surf. Let's nap on it, shall we?

To flash that hard-earned tan, follow Hwy 1 south to ❻ **Geoffrey's Malibu,** where parking on PCH simply won't do. They have valet, darling, please use it. Inside, an open flow between the inside bar and flower-dappled patio draws eyes toward bluff-top views. Here, the air-kisses brigade nibbles shrimp salad and ahi tartar as light ocean breezes tease their highlighted tresses.

Swapping fashionistas for freaks, continue south on PCH (called Lincoln Ave in parts of LA) to **7** **Venice Beach**, where the most difficult part of a beach visit is actually getting to the sand. As the "Best Beach for People Watching," there are simply too many distractions. Like that shaggy-haired skaterat weaving past like Tony Hawk. Or the hustling hip-hop kid pressing his CD into your palm. Grimacing bodybuilders hoisting weights in The Pit. Where's the beach again?

For a less frenetic experience, grab a patio perch at **8** **Sidewalk Café**, where the views are as interesting as the literary-minded dishes, from the hearty Larry McMurty burger to the spare Emily Dickinson omelet. Perhaps a subtle reminder to visit the adjacent bookstore, Small Word Books, for a beach read in case you make it to the sand.

For sweeping views of Santa Monica Bay, on a road typically off-radar to visitors, follow PCH south, turning right onto Culver Blvd and following it past the bird-filled rushes of Ballona Wetlands – LA County's largest remaining wetlands – to Vista Del Mar. This four-lane road runs parallel to the beach on a small bluff behind LAX. Below, cyclists whoosh over a bike path, known locally as The Strand, that's part of the 22-mile South Bay Bicycle Trail.

FRIED SHRIMP & BEER BY THE SEA

It would be easy to dismiss the Harley-lined shack slumped near the Malibu line as just another biker joint. But that would be a mistake. **Neptune's Net** (www.neptunesnet.com) may not look like anything special but the fried-shrimp-and-beer hospitality inside this weathered Rte 1 outpost is can't-miss. Yeah, the food is mostly fried and the bathroom sitch sketchy, but the porch is breezy and the beach is just across the street. Best of all, those people slurping chowder beside you? They're freaks for the open road, just like you.

Next up is **9** **Manhattan Beach**, looking like it stepped from the pages of *Coastal Living*. This "Most Stylish" of SoCal beaches is a place where bright bougainvillea bursts from picket fences, perfectly tousled children scamper over soft sand, and brightly shuttered cottages terrace up gentle hillsides, all with an ocean view. Residents here – who include Mia Hamm and Luke Walton – are a healthy, outdoorsy bunch always looking effortlessly put together and breezy cool, whether playing volleyball, pushing a baby stroller or riding a bike with a chihuahua tucked in a basket.

Once here, don your best Lululemon sweats then join a beach volleyball game, rent a surf board or power walk on The Strand. Inside the compact, red-roofed **10** **Roundhouse Marine Studies Lab & Aquarium**, perched at the end of the 928ft Manhattan Beach Pier, kids can touch a slimy sea cucumber, ogle a clicking garibaldi, or stare at fins flickering inside the 3500-gallon shark tank. Three blocks from the beach, **11** **Shade Hotel** provides the trendiest digs in town – and possibly the whole South Bay. Sleek rooms sparkle with iPod docking stations, margarita blenders and other handy amenities.

Driving into ⑫ **Huntington Beach** – "Best for Surf Culture" – it's not the sight of actual surfers that tips you off to the city's obsession with the sport. It's the two megaliths, Jack's Surfboards and Huntington Surf & Sport, towering over the Main & PCH intersection that set the tone. Even the city's gone commercial, licensing products under its trademarked moniker, Surf City USA, inspired by Jan & Dean's classic song. To be fair, there's a statue of the city's patron saint, Hawaiian surfer Duke Kahanamoku, at the same intersection and if you look down you'll see names of legendary surfers engraved in granite at the Surfing Walk of Fame. A few blocks east, the International Surfing Museum also honors these legends.

"The only requirement is selecting your plot of sand and plunking into your chair."

To watch surfers in action, pull into the Huntington City Beach parking lot and join the crowds on the 1853ft Huntington Beach Pier. From here, catch up-close views of daredevils barreling through tubes, often looking to catch the eye of sponsors. The surf here may not be the ideal place to test your skills, however. Locals can be territorial. In late July, come here for the US Open of Surfing, a six-star competition drawing more than 600 world-class surfers, 400,000 spectators, and a mini-village of concerts, motocross demos and skater jams. As for the actual beach, it's wide and flat in these parts – a perfect place to snooze on a giant beach towel. Make a day of it by snagging a fire pit just south of the pier and building an evening bonfire.

For surfer haute cuisine, drive a few blocks north to ⑬ **Chronic Tacos**. Any trepidation you feel approaching this sticker-covered shack with a locals-only vibe dissipates once you step inside. With Casey Jones rolling from the speakers, surf dudes chilling beside the pool table, and friendly staff prepping your meal right at the taco counter, you might be tempted to ditch your everyday life.

Cruising south, take a moment to admire the tricked-out yachts, the gleaming BMWs and fancy mansions…then keep going. We won't be stopping in Newport Beach today, not with the natural charms of ⑭ **Laguna Beach** waiting just ahead. In fact picking a "best" for Laguna's beaches is problematic. With its palms trees, bougainvillea-dotted walkways and sweeping oceanside bluffs, Laguna's famous ⑮ **Heisler Park** is easily the most romantic spot on the coast. But wait…what are all those people doing on the beaches below the park? They're not holding hands. They're diving, snorkeling, tidepooling – and putting Laguna's northern beaches in the running for "Best for Underwater Exploration."

The compromise? "Best for Honeymooning Scuba Divers." For the best one-two punch of romance-and-regulators, descend the staircase just north of Heisler Park to Diver's Cove. From this bluff-protected swath of sand, the Laguna Beach Marine Life Refuge – one of the county's best underwater parks – is just a few kicks away.

Postdive, watch the sunset and swap fish tales with your sweetheart from the outdoor Jacuzzi at ⑯ **By The Sea Inn**, a 36-room inn winning repeat guests with its hardwood floors, flat screens, big pillows and helpful service. It's also close to the northern beaches and an easy stroll from romance and margaritas at ⑰ **Las Brisas**. Though locals roll their eyes at any mention of this bluff-top stalwart, the cove-and-ocean views from the patio are spectacular. Bring your camera.

Continuing south, PCH hooks up with I-5 heading into San Diego County. For views of surf and sand, rejoin Hwy 101 at Carlsbad, following the train tracks through San Diego County's northern beach towns – Carlsbad, Encinitas, Solana and Del Mar – before rolling into ⑱ **La Jolla**. With its boutiques, jewelry stores and mansions, La Jolla earns its rep as a glitzy enclave for San Diego's upper crust, but the sea caves, tide pools, gentle surf and diverse wildlife bordering its cliff-topping downtown make it great for families and worthy of the title "Best for Active Families." Former resident Theodor Geisel, more famously known as Dr Seuss, would surely agree.

At La Jolla Shores, moms and daughters can learn to surf from the ever-patient gals at ⑲ **Surf Diva** or the whole family can snorkel off La Jolla

> **ASK A LOCAL**
>
> Local dad Paul Anderson recommends taking kids to the **children's pool**, south of Ellen Browning Scripps Park (just east of La Jolla Cove). But not for swimming. Seals and their pups have taken to lolling on the protected beach in recent years, and children now come to watch the pinnipeds. The pool has garnered headlines recently, as swimmers want the seals removed and the pool returned to its intended status as a swimming beach for children. Stay tuned.

Cove in downtown. Prefer staying on top of the water? Take a guided kayak tour to explore the sea caves just east of the cove or descend 145 steps inside the dark, dripping-wet sandstone tunnel leading from the bluff-top Cave Store to Sunny Jim Cave. Shake off the gloom inside bright, spare ⑳ **Burger Lounge** at the corner of Wall St and Herschel Ave. It may look new-millennium mod, but the burgers are old-school messy. Made from organic grass-fed beef, these juicy numbers are best cut in half to avoid a soggy mess. The fresh-cut fries are made for sibling snatching. After dinner, return to the bluffs for a palm-framed sunset from the well-manicured lawns of ㉑ **Ellen Browning Scripps Park**.

Amy C Balfour

TRIP INFORMATION

GETTING THERE
From Los Angeles, drive 95 miles northwest via Hwy 101.

DO

Roundhouse Marine Studies Lab & Aquarium
Touch tanks, shark tanks and aquariums are packed tight at pier's end. ☎ 310-379-8117; www.roundhouseaquarium.org; Manhattan Beach Pier; suggested donation $2; ☽ 3pm-sunset Mon-Fri, 10am-sunset Sat & Sun; ♿

Surf Diva
Women, learn to catch a wave with encouraging surfer chicks as your guide. ☎ 858-454-8273; www.surfdiva.com; 2160 Avenida de la Playa, La Jolla; lessons or "guys on the side" per hr $75, 2-day clinics $150; ♿

Ty Warner Sea Center
Kids can touch a shark, who's probably not thrilled about the whole thing. ☎ 805-962-2526; www.sbnature.org; 211 Stearns Wharf, Santa Barbara; adult/2-12yr/student/13-17yr & senior $8/5/6/7; ☽ 10am-5pm; ♿

Wheel Fun Rentals
Rent slingshots, deuce coupes or four-seater surreys. ☎ 805-966-2282; www.wheelfun rentals.com; 23 E Cabrillo Blvd, Santa Barbara; bike 2hr/half-day $16/18, four-seater surrey 2hr/half-day $35/65; ☽ 8am-8pm; ♿

EAT & DRINK

Burger Lounge
It may be gourmet, but piles of messy napkins are a sign they're keeping it real. ☎ 858-456-0196; www.burgerlounge.com; 1101 Wall St, La Jolla; mains $6-8; ☽ 11am-9pm Mon-Thu, 11am-10pm Fri & Sat, 11am-8pm Sun; ♿

Chronic Tacos
Don't judge a taco shack by its cover. This hole-in-the-wall serves awesome "fatty tacos."

☎ 714-960-0339; www.eatchronictacos.com; 328 11th St, Huntington Beach; mains $2-7; ☽ 9am-10pm Sun-Fri, 8am-10pm Sat; ♿

Geoffrey's Malibu
Baked brie and Caesar salad are popular with nibblers scoping the view. ☎ 310-457-1519; www.geoffreysmalibu.com; 27400 Pacific Coast Hwy, Malibu; mains brunch & lunch $16-36, dinner $22-77; ☽ lunch and dinner daily, brunch Sat & Sun

Las Brisas
Swoon for the view – then sip margaritas – on a bluff overlooking Laguna's Main Beach. ☎ 949-497-5434; www.lasbrisaslaguna beach.com; 361 Cliff Dr, Laguna Beach; mains $14-20; ☽ patio and bar open until 11pm weekdays, 1am weekends

Sidewalk Café
It's hard not to gape from this center-of-the-action patio. ☎ 310-399-5547; www.theside walkcafe.com; 1401 Ocean Front Walk, Venice; mains $8-22; ☽ 8am-11pm; ♿

SLEEP

By the Sea Inn
Romantics return year after year for comfy beds, proximity to Heisler Park and reasonable-for-Laguna prices. ☎ 949-497-6645; www.bytheseainn.com; 475 N Coast Hwy, Laguna Beach; r $250-379

Shade
Average-sized rooms sport sleek decor befitting the South Bay's hippest hotel. ☎ 310-546-4995; www.shadehotel.com; 1221 N Valley Dr, Manhattan Beach; r $395, ste $535-795

USEFUL WEBSITES
www.surfrider.org
www.watchthewater.org
www.lonelyplanet.com/trip-planner

LINK YOUR TRIP
TRIP

California's Other Wine Countries

WHY GO Everybody knows the Napa and Sonoma Valleys. So, now it's time to venture into California's less-famous wine regions, where family-owned wineries welcome novices and experts alike, and tasting fees are low. Most of these well-hidden wine countries are near the San Francisco Bay area, perfect for weekend escapes.

TIME
4 days

DISTANCE
650 miles

BEST TIME TO GO
Apr – Oct

START
Hopland

END
San Luis Obispo

ALSO GOOD FOR

Beyond Napa and Sonoma, and past the Russian River Valley, lie the wineries of Mendocino County. No more than 100 miles north of San Francisco, this unsung winemaking region is hospitable to rich Mediterranean reds and brawny, fruit-forward zinfandels. Family farms line Hwy 101 just south and north of Hopland, a tiny farm town. The downtown wine shop ❶ Sip! Mendocino should be your first stop. There the expert proprietor pours handpicked flights of wines ranging from across the county, including rare vintages you might not even get to taste at the wineries themselves. Down the street next to a bakery, sunlight-filled ❷ Graziano Family of Wines brings together four different labels, distilled from the fruits of labor of the owner's grandparents, Italian immigrants who planted the first grapes in Mendocino County before the Prohibition era. For earthy, flavor-packed wine-country cooking, dash north to ❸ Patrona in Ukiah. Locally grown ingredients glow in garden salads, flatbread pizzas and seasonal game dishes, exhibiting equal helpings of French and Italian tastes.

The biggest appellation in Mendo is the Anderson Valley, known for its delicate Alsatian whites and sparkling wines as much as for its specialty pinot noirs, all thanks to sun-drenched days and coastal fog drifting over the vineyards at night. Follow winding Hwy 153 west to the podunk town of Boonville. Rest up for more tastings at the

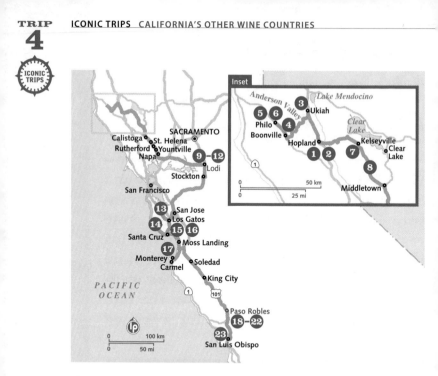

4 **Boonville Hotel**, with its chicly rehabbed, yet still rustic rooms over-hanging the highway. A short drive past Philo, Hwy 128 is lined with family run wineries. With a redwood-built tasting room and picnic deck, **5** **Navarro Vineyards** is the most popular stop. Starring on a lengthy tasting menu are Navarro's dry, estate-bottled gewürtztraminer and a smoky pinot noir. The sparkling wines of **6** **Roederer Estate** are handcrafted by the same French family that makes Cristal champagne. At this humble countryside winery, delicate pressings of chardonnay and pinot noir grapes use only 70% of the cuvée (ie the first 120 gallons of juice) – the winemakers are picky, and it pays.

In the northern San Joaquin Valley of central California, where breezes from the Sacramento River delta soothe the hot vineyards of Lodi, more zinfandel grapes are grown than anywhere else in the world. Particularly old vines have often been tended by the same family for over a century. Lodi's diverse soil is sometimes rocky, sometimes a fine sandy loam, giving its zins distinctive character. To get here from Hopland, the scenic route takes you east into Lake County around Clear Lake, which boasts its own noteworthy winemakers like deeply rooted **7** **Steele Wines**, where an adventurous lineup of whites and reds includes Writer's Block pinot noir, bottled with a portrait of the Bard; and high-society **8** **Langtry Estate & Vineyards**, a Napa-style winery that makes a bright, soft petite sirah from vineyards planted in the late 19th century by actress Lillie Langtry.

Hwy 29 flows slowly south through Calistoga, St Helena, Yountville and finally Napa, after which Hwy 12 slingshots east across the delta toward Lodi. Get your first taste of Lodi's powerful, sun-soaked zins at the **9** **Lodi Wine & Visitor Center**, where 100 local vintages are sold by the solid-wood tasting bar. Then drive out into the vineyards to sample straight from the source. **10** **Michael-David Winery** is shockingly touristy, with its farm stand, café and tasting-room complex, but its flagship 7 Deadly Zins, a jammy blend of seven different old-vine grapes, merits a stop. Boutique wineries and experimental labels by more famous names are poured at the Italian-style **11** **Vino Piazza**, where you can park your car, order a bistro lunch and afterward amble between tasting rooms. For zin lovers, it's heaven to sample dozens of different vineyards to detect the subtle differences of *terroir* (a French word describing the unique flavor of a geographical place, based on climate, soil and topography). With historical atmosphere and ultramodern amenities, the bed-and-breakfast inn **12** **Wine & Roses** distinguishes itself with a sophisticated Cal-Ital restaurant, where apple-spinach pizzas and braised pot roast with parsnips are served on a leafy patio.

> **ASK A LOCAL**
>
> "My favorite hidden California winery? **Husch Vineyards** (http://huschvineyards.com). Mmmmm, their pinot noir (insert a Homer Simpson–sound of satisfaction here). Their chardonnay is likewise very complex. Both have an excellent finish, but are not too fruit-forward – just the right amount. The tasting room and the winery owners are mellow, too."
>
> *Evan B, San Francisco Bay Area*

Backtracking to the Bay area, you'll pass the emerging Livermore wine country, then coast down the peninsula into the Santa Cruz Mountains. Vines were first planted among these coastal redwood forests in the mid-19th century. One of the first US regions to be awarded its own appellation, it was a cabernet sauvignon from these rugged, little-known mountains that bested mighty French Bordeaux in the Judgment of Paris in 1976. Taste the championship winemakers' most recent harvests at legendary **13** **Ridge Vineyards**. Heading over the mountains on twisted Hwy 9 or Skyline Dr to Santa Cruz, you'll pass dozens more wineries, most open for tastings only on Saturday afternoons or during the quarterly "Passport Weekend" festivals. In case you're wondering, estate-bottled pinot noirs are the specialty around here.

Along the coast north of Santa Cruz, **14** **Bonny Doon Vineyard** has a cult following for its unusual varietals and original Rhône blends like Le Cigare Volant ("The Flying Cigar" – ask about the actual French law that prohibits UFOs from landing in vineyards). In downtown Santa Cruz, **15** **Vinocruz** is an airy wine shop with a modern stainless-steel tasting bar, where an ever-changing lineup of wines by famous Santa Cruz Mountain winemakers like Kathryn Kennedy, Thomas Fogarty and David Bruce, to name just a few, are poured. Also downtown, **16** **Soif** (French for "thirst," get it?) is where bon vivant foodies flock for a heady selection of 50 international wines by the glass and tempting Old and New World tastes.

Further south, Monterey County is a much younger wine region. Although most of its vineyards are found far away from the coast, you can taste vintages from as far away as the Santa Lucia Highlands right on Cannery Row at **17 A Taste of Monterey**. This wine shop and tasting room has panoramic sea views and thoughtful exhibits on barrel-making and cork production. East of Carmel-by-the-Sea, Carmel Valley Rd takes you past organic farms, vineyards and equestrian ranches and into the tiny village of Carmel Valley, where many established Monterey County wineries have tasting rooms, and country bistros have invitingly shady garden patios.

GREENING THE VINEYARDS

Some of California's smallest wineries and wine regions are among the "greenest," environmentally speaking. A buzz word you'll hear as you travel about is "biodynamic," referring to vineyards that create self-sustaining farm ecosystems and aim to keep crop quality high. Organic, pesticide-free vineyards at wineries using solar-energy panels and biodiesel-fueled vehicles abound, especially in Mendocino County, where you can tour the educational **Solar Living Institute** (☎ 707-744-2017; www.solarliving .org). It's located at 13771 S Hwy 101, Hopland, and is open from 10am to 7pm in summer, until 6pm the rest of the year.

Further south is **18 Paso Robles**, a hot spot for San Luis Obispo County wines. With an unprepossessing tasting room, **19 Martin & Weyrich** is a stand-out producer of Italian varietals, including noteworthy Tuscan blends. Travel west along Hwy 46 to discover scores of small family-run wineries, including many zinfandel specialists, like **20 Dark Star Cellars**, which also crafts outrageously rich reds and Bordeaux-style blends. Closer to Hwy 101, **21 Zenaida Cellars** is a Zen master of zin, along with lush estate-bottled red blends like Fire Sign and Zephyr. Rent its Winemaker's Loft and watch the sunset over the vineyards from your own private porch.

> *"…ask about the actual French law that prohibits UFOs from landing in vineyards."*

Paso Robles' downtown square is bordered by even more boutique tasting rooms and outstanding California and European-style wine-country restaurants. **22 Vinoteca** wine bar will send you soaring with its wine flights, artisan cheese plates and tapas. Further south in downtown San Luis Obispo, **23 Taste** is a friendly co-op tasting room for the off-the-beaten-path Edna Valley wineries, best known for crisp chardonnays and subtle syrahs. Take Taste's enomatic wine-dispensing system for a spin with a Riedel tasting glass in hand, then pick up an Edna Valley winery map for more lip-smacking explorations tomorrow.

Sara Benson

TRIP INFORMATION

GETTING THERE
From San Francisco, take Hwy 101 across the Golden Gate Bridge and north to Hopland.

DO & DRINK
Bonny Doon Vineyard
Out-of-this-world wines from the original "Rhône Deranger" Randall Grahm. ☎ 831-425-4518; www.bonnydoonvineyard.com; 10 Pine Flat Rd, Santa Cruz; tasting fee $5; 🕙 11am-5pm

Dark Star Cellars
For stellar, intense reds – zinfandel, cabernet sauvignon and yes, even merlot. ☎ 805-237-2389; www.darkstarcellars.com; 2985 Anderson Rd, Paso Robles; tasting fee $3; 🕙 10:30am-5pm Fri-Sun

Graziano Family of Wines
Makes classic French and Italian varietals, and bolder, Mendo-style zinfandels and petite sirahs. ☎ 707-744-8466; www.grazianofamilyofwines.com; 13251 S Hwy 101, Hopland; tasting fee $5; 🕙 10am-5pm

Langtry Estate & Vineyards
With a unique *terroir,* this elegant winery owns the Guenoc Valley appellation. ☎ 707-987-9127; www.langtryestate.com; 21000 Butts Canyon Rd, Middletown; tasting fee $5; 🕙 11am-5pm

Lodi Wine & Visitor Center
Pick up wine-tasting maps here and ask about the ZinFest in May. ☎ 209-365-0621; www.lodiwine.com; 2545 W Turner Rd, Lodi; tasting fee $5; 🕙 10am-5pm

Martin & Weyrich
Italianate winery with a westside York Mountain vineyard producing pinot noirs and European whites. ☎ 805-238-2520; www.martinweyrich.com; 2610 Buena Vista Dr, Paso Robles; tasting fee $4-10; 🕙 10am-6pm daily summer, 10am-5pm Sun-Thu, 10am-6pm Fri & Sat winter

Michael-David Winery
Famous for its zinfandels, all fruit-forward, fully loaded bombs. ☎ 209-368-7384; www.lodivineyards.com; 4580 W Hwy 12, Lodi; tasting fee $5; 🕙 10am-5pm

Navarro Vineyards
By far the busiest, but also the least fussy tasting room in the Anderson Valley. ☎ 707-895-3686; www.navarrowine.com; 5601 Hwy 128, Philo; tasting free; 🕙 10am-5pm

Ridge Vineyards
Top-tier producer astride Monte Bello Ridge is known for its utterly complex, age-worthy European reds. ☎ 408-867-3233; www.ridgewine.com; 17100 Monte Bello Rd, Cupertino; tasting free-$5; 🕙 11am-5pm Sat & Sun Apr-Oct

Roederer Estate
French sparkling-wine specialists conduct winery tours and weekend "wine camps" for aspiring oenophiles. ☎ 707-895-2288; www.roedererestate.com; 4501 Hwy 128, Philo; tasting fee $3; 🕙 11am-5pm

Sip! Mendocino
Expertly selected wines of all types, often served with chef-made appetizer plates on Thursday and Saturday nights. ☎ 707-744-8375; www.sipmendocino.com; 13420 S Hwy 101, Hopland; tasting fee $5; 🕙 11am-6pm

Steele Wines
No varietal goes unfermented here! Dare to sip its cabernet franc rosé or Black Bubbles, an Aussie-inspired sparkling syrah. ☎ 707-279-9475; www.steelewines.com; 4350 Thomas Dr at Hwy 29, Kelseyville; tasting fee $4; 🕙 11am-5pm

Taste
Meet real-life San Luis Obispo County winemakers on Wednesday nights, taste flights on Fridays, or double your money on Two-Oz Tuesdays. ☎ 805-269-8279; www.taste-slo.com; 1003 Osos St, San Luis Obispo; tasting fee varies; 🕙 11am-9pm Mon-Sat, to 5pm Sun

A Taste of Monterey
This winery also has a cheaper, less picturesque, tasting room in Salinas, off Hwy 101.

☎ 831-646-5446; www.tastemonterey.com; 700 Cannery Row, Monterey; tasting fee $10-15; ⏱ 11am-6pm

Vino Piazza

Almost a dozen independent wineries offer tastings here; the dinosaur-fossil displays are an odd but interesting bonus. ☎ 209-727-9770; www.vinopiazza.com; 12470 Locke Rd, Lockeford; tasting fee varies; ⏱ most tasting rooms noon-5pm Fri-Sun

Vinocruz

Unlock the secrets of the Santa Cruz Mountains at this chilled-out wine shop. It's off Cooper St, between Front St and Pacific Ave. ☎ 831-426-8466; www.vinocruz .com; Abbott Sq, Santa Cruz; tasting fee $9; ⏱ 11am-7pm Mon-Thu, 11am-8pm Fri & Sat, noon-6pm Sun

EAT

Patrona

A "simply seasonal" bistro and wine bar adheres to a sustainable-food mission. ☎ 707-462-9181; www.patronarestaurant.com; 130 W Standley St, Ukiah; mains $15-33; ⏱ 5-9pm Tue-Sat

Soif

Extensive wine bar and mostly organic California cuisine make for a swanky local hangout. ☎ 831-423-2020; www.soifwine .com; 105 Walnut Ave, Santa Cruz; mains $14-40; ⏱ noon-2pm Wed-Sat, 4-10pm Sun, 5-10pm Mon-Thu, 5-11pm Fri & Sat

Vinoteca

Romantic wine bar with cushy sofas and satisfying bowls of olives and cheese fondue.

☎ 805-227-7154; www.vinotecawinebar .com; 835 12th St, Paso Robles; mains $10-23; ⏱ 4-9pm Sun & Mon, to 10pm Tue-Thu, to 11pm Fri & Sat

Wine & Roses

Seasonally classic California wine-country cuisine with a European twist. ☎ 209-334-6988; www.winerose.com; 2505 W Turner Rd, Lodi; mains $10-16; ⏱ 11:30am-1:30pm Mon-Fri, 10:30am-1:30pm Sat & Sun, 5-9pm Sun-Thu, 5-10pm Fri & Sat

SLEEP

Boonville Hotel

For urbanites who refuse to abandon style in the country. Just don't expect good service. ☎ 707-895-2210; www.boonvillehotel.com; 14050 Hwy 128, Boonville; r $125-275; ▣

Zenaida Cellars

Bring friends to the apartment-style loft in this winery (tastings $3), or get romantic in an ecofriendly suite with bamboo furnishings, organic cotton sheets and an outdoor hammock. ☎ 866-936-5638; www.zenaida cellars.com; 1550 W Hwy 46, Paso Robles; r $250-375

USEFUL WEBSITES

www.gomendo.com
www.lakecountywinegrape.org
www.montereywines.org
www.pasowine.com
www.scmwa.com

LINK YOUR TRIP

www.lonelyplanet.com/trip-planner

All Aboard Amtrak

WHY GO Beaches, beaches, beaches. That's the theme for this trip down California's coast. Leave the driving to Amtrak while you enjoy sandy vistas and chances to pause at numerous stops for everything from wine tasting to iconic meals to a baseball game.

Amtrak's *Coast Starlight* begins its 1377-mile run far north in Seattle but to start this trip you'll hop aboard in ❶ Oakland for a 464-mile daylight run through the heart of California to San Diego. The train skirts the San Francisco Bay and runs through the middle of sprawling Silicon Valley. You can extend this trip over many days by getting on and off the train at various stops, the most interesting of which are detailed below.

As you near ❷ Salinas, the tracks enter the Salinas Valley, which fully lives up to its hackneyed moniker "America's Salad Bowl." Lettuce, broccoli, celery, strawberries and much more grow here in profusion. Try not to feel too guilty as you recline in your seat watching squads of people laboring amidst the orderly rows of produce.

After 100 miles of agricultural splendor, the terrain gets brown and hilly as you reach ❸ Paso Robles. You'll notice striations across the landscape, which are the twisted vines of the region's vast vineyards. More than 100 wineries produce some excellent zinfandels and syrahs. If you exit the *Coast Starlight* here you can spend the night at the century-old ❹ Paso Robles Inn, and the next morning tour wineries with the ❺ Wine Wrangler before boarding the next train.

The line then makes a dramatic looping descent to ❻ San Luis Obispo. The next 120 miles or so are among the most spectacular of any railroad in the world. Trains hug the Pacific Ocean, passing countless isolated

TIME
2 – 4 days

DISTANCE
600 miles

BEST TIME TO GO
Mar – Oct

START
Oakland

END
San Diego

ALSO GOOD FOR

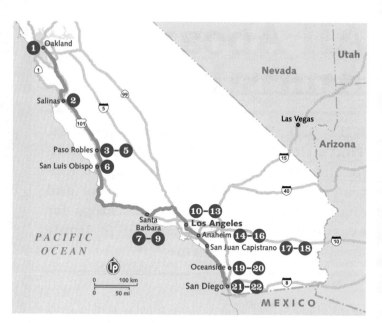

beaches, some deserted except for the odd puffin and seal, others dotted with
frolicking naked sunbathers (sit on the right side for views of the wildlife, fur-
clad and otherwise). A good portion of this segment lies within the off-limits
expanse of Vandenberg Air Force Base. Look for the gantries used for launching spy satellites poking up amidst the rugged terrain.

A perfect place to break your journey, **7** **Santa Barbara** combines beautiful
buildings, a top-notch beach and orange blossom–scented air in one beguil-
ing package. Only three blocks from the train station and near the beach, the
8 **Villa Rosa Inn** has the city's signature old Spanish architecture. Nearby

State St is one of the most beautiful main streets in the US;
perfect for walking, it is lined with shops, cafés and fine restaurants such as locally beloved **9** **Tupelo Junction**.

"…sit on the right side for views of the wildlife, fur-clad and otherwise."

There are frequent trains south from Santa Barbara all the
way to San Diego. The next important stop is 100 miles
south in **10** **Los Angeles** and it's a big one: **11** **Los Angeles
Union Station**. This 1939 Mission-style gem has commodi-
ous leather chairs in its waiting area and is a popular location for films.
Nearby **12** **Olvera St** is a Mexican marketplace in the middle of LA's oldest neighborhood. Amidst plenty of tourist tat are stalls selling quality arts
and crafts and numerous restaurants as authentic as any in Mexico City. Or
head just north to **13** **Philippe the Original**, where the French dipped sand-

wich debuted a century ago. Photos show trains at Union Station through the decades.

The tracks to San Diego first head east through an endless sprawl of factories and warehouses. After about 30 minutes the route turns south through thickets of suburbs. Views open up at ⑭ **Anaheim**, where the station sits right across the parking lot from ⑮ **Angel Stadium of Anaheim**, home of the equally ponderously named Los Angeles Angels at Anaheim. Fortunately the team is more deft on the field and frequently sparks flamboyant displays of fountains and fireworks with their home runs and victories. Less than 3 miles from Anaheim (and linked to the station by shuttle bus), ⑯ **Disneyland** is *the* stop on many a SoCal itinerary.

About the time you may be reaching subdivision fatigue, the train pulls into ⑰ **San Juan Capistrano**, some 27 miles south of Anaheim. This cute-as-a-button village exudes old California for several blocks in all directions from the station. Amidst the quaint shops, cafés and attractions is the local star: ⑱ **Mission San Juan Capistrano**, which dates from 1776. As you wander the flower-bedecked grounds and breezeway-surrounded old buildings, you'll see why it's not just swallows that flock here.

As it did up north, the rail line now heads straight for the coast and follows the beaches most of the way to San Diego. Unlike the stretch north of Santa Barbara, these beaches are lined with people sunning themselves between bouts of volleyball and surfing. At the classic beach town of ⑲ **Oceanside** you can revel in surf culture at the ⑳ **California Surf Museum**, just two blocks from the station.

DETOUR

One block from the station, Salinas's **National Steinbeck Center** (www.steinbeck.org) gives context to both the Salinas Valley and the John Steinbeck works set here, such as *East of Eden*. Spend the night in Salinas or nearby Monterey before continuing on the train the next day.

RIDING AMTRAK

North of San Luis Obispo, Amtrak's **Coast Starlight** service runs only once a day. It has comfy coaches and a diner, and you can splurge and enjoy wine tastings in the private Pacific Parlor Car. South of SLO, most services are on frequent **Pacific Surfliner** trains featuring double-deck coaches, big windows and snack bars.

Full fare from Oakland to San Diego is $65. Reserve in advance for the *Coast Starlight,* which is often full (www.amtrakcalifornia.com).

Your Amtrak adventure hits the end of the line 130 miles south of LA, in downtown ㉑ **San Diego**. The best way to start your explorations of this town, which mixes sunshine, beaches, loads of attractions and the navy, is on a tour of the vast bay. ㉒ **Hornblower Cruises** depart the waterfront from the historic old train station. Bon Voyage!

Ryan Ver Berkmoes

TRIP INFORMATION

GETTING THERE
Oakland is just across the Bay Bridge from San Francisco. Amtrak buses link the train station with stops across the city.

DO

Angel Stadium of Anaheim
The fun-filled home of Major League Baseball's Los Angeles Angels at Anaheim. ☎ 888-796-4256; www.losangeles.angels .mlb.com; 2000 Gene Autry Way, Anaheim; tickets $12-200; ☯ Apr-Sep; ♿

California Surf Museum
Boards galore and tributes to surf culture dating back almost 100 years. Look for the motorized surfboard. ☎ 760-721-6876; www.surfmuseum.org; 233 N Coast Hwy, Oceanside; admission free; ☯ 10am-4pm; ♿

Disneyland
Adults are often as entranced as the kids at the Magic Kingdom. ☎ 714-781-4565; www.disneyland.com; Anaheim; adult/child from $66/56; ☯ various; ♿

Hornblower Cruises
One- and two-hour tours of the famous San Diego harbor include Coronado Island and the Pacific Ocean. ☎ 619-725-8888; www.horn blower.com; The Embarcadero, San Diego; adult/child from $20/10; ☯ various; ♿

Mission San Juan Capistrano
This vast old Spanish Mission is famous for both the annual migration of swallows (mid-March) and its evocative buildings and ruins. ☎ 949-234-1300; www.missionsjc.com; 26801 Ortega Hwy, San Juan Capistrano; adult/child $9/5; ☯ 8:30am-5pm; ♿

Olvera St
Unearth some Mexican treasures at this chaotic market in the midst of buildings that are ancient by LA standards (the 1870s!). www .olvera-street.com; Los Angeles; ☯ 10am-7pm; ♿

EAT & DRINK

Philippe the Original
Everyone loves Philippe's. Order a crusty roll filled with meat and hunker down at communal tables on the sawdust-covered floor. ☎ 213-628-3781; www.philippes.com; 1001 N Alameda St, Los Angeles; sandwiches $5-6; ☯ 6am-10pm; ♿

Tupelo Junction
Local organic ingredients star in dishes with a Southern flair; enjoy 'em at the sidewalk tables. ☎ 805-899-3100; www.tupelojunction .com; 1218 State St, Santa Barbara; mains $8-25; ☯ breakfast, lunch & dinner

Wine Wrangler
Let this enterprising tour company haul your besotted butt between some of the area's best wineries. ☎ 805-238-5700; www.the winewrangler.com; Paso Robles; tours from $92; ☯ call for details

SLEEP

Paso Robles Inn
Many of the 108 rooms here have spas; all have views of the beautiful gardens. ☎ 805-238-2660, 800-676-1713; www.pasorobles inn.com; 1103 Spring St, Paso Robles; r $115-330

Villa Rosa Inn
An 18-room inn wrapped around a flower-festooned courtyard with swimming pool and whirlpool. ☎ 805-966-0851; www.villarosa innsb.com; 15 Chapala St, Santa Barbara; r $150-300

USEFUL WEBSITES
www.amtrakcalifornia.com
www.visitcalifornia.com

LINK YOUR TRIP

www.lonelyplanet.com/trip-planner

TRIP
32 Steinbeck Country p211
59 Sideways in Santa Barbara p349
68 48 Hours in San Diego p391

By the Book: Literary California

WHY GO Stalk the haunts of your literary heroes as you book shop and bar-hop up the coastline. From LA's gumshoe detectives to the Bay Area Beats, sniff out the places where authors gathered, the solitary houses they lived in and the eccentric artifacts they left behind.

Freeway-carved ❶ **Los Angeles** may be better known for the glaring spotlights and paparazzi flashbulbs of the movie industry, but its literary tradition goes deep and ever so dark. The breeding ground for '40s noir and mystery crime novels, it's where Raymond Chandler fans can channel the exploits of detective Philip Marlowe and other fictional personas…if they know where to look.

William Faulkner mixed his own mint juleps behind the bar and some of the smartly red-jacketed wait staff have been on the books for more than 40 years. The oldest restaurant in Hollywood, the ❷ **Musso & Frank Grill**, was already on the scene when the studios opened in the 1930s, becoming the favored spot for writers like TS Eliot, Dashiell Hammett and Ernest Hemingway when they worked stints in the film industry. With the Stanley Rose Bookshop next door (selling bootleg booze during Prohibition) and the Writers Guild office catty-corner across the street, this was where writers migrated to blow out their livers. When the bookstore closed, the restaurant expanded in, and a dedicated "Writers' Room" was born. With clubby red booths and the original sports player–themed wallpaper stained by nicotine and time, the restaurant still exudes old-school Hollywood glamour. In contemporary times, it's become a mainstay of Michael Connelly's Harry Bosch novels.

Take Hwy 101 south to sample some fruit and grab a snack at the covered open-air ❸ **Grand Central Market**. A bustling warren of

TIME
3 – 4 days

DISTANCE
520 miles

BEST TIME TO GO
Year-round

START
Los Angeles

END
Martinez

ALSO GOOD FOR

HISTORY &
CULTURE

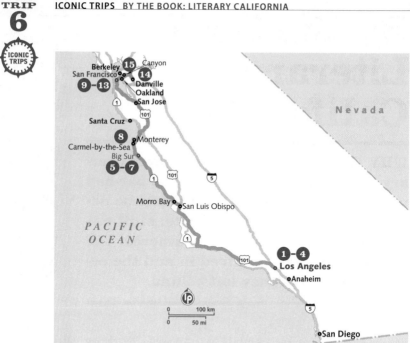

produce stalls and food counters dating back to 1917, it sits at the foot of a Downtown neighborhood once dotted with magnificent Victorians. The market featured in John Fante's *Dreams from Bunker Hill* and Charles Bukowski's poem "Crucifix in a Death Hand," – both authors wrote of being down-and-out and getting free fruit from market merchants.

For a site-specific voyage into Raymond Chandler's world, head 2 miles west to read a copy of "I'll Be Waiting" in the historic 14-story ❹ **Mayfair Hotel**. Besides being the setting for this gritty short story, Chandler stayed and boozed here during a separation from his wife, calling his friends and threatening to jump out the window. Not quite the art-deco head-turner it was in its youth, it's still a comfortable lodging and a five-star stop for Chandler fans. Head 200 miles north on Hwy 101 to San Luis Obispo and join the coastal route on Hwy 1. Fifteen miles later, pause at the ocean at Morro Bay to gasp at the 578ft peak of Morro Rock jutting offshore. Then continue north another 90 or so miles along one of the most breathtaking seaside roads in the world. Many writers have found solitude and inspiration in the cliffside region of ❺ **Big Sur**. The newly (and awkwardly) successful Jack Kerouac recounted battling his demons here in a book by the same name.

In the summer of 2008, Big Sur survived weeks of frightening wildfires, and firefighters staved off flames closing in on the doorstep of the ❻ **Henry Miller Library**. The iconoclastic author of *Tropic of Cancer* lived in Big Sur for 18 years. This former friend's home celebrates his life and work and contains a great collection of books by Beat and Big Sur writers, as well as a Ping Pong table. Check the website calendar for listings of its eclectic cultural events.

When the fog rolls across, settle in a half mile south at rustic redwood-shaded ⑦ **Deetjen's Big Sur Inn** and try to snag a room with a fireplace. Nestled along Castro Creek, the homey 1930s rooms and wooden cabins were built by Norwegian immigrant Helmuth Deetjen as one of the first accommodations in the area. Nosh on homemade granola for breakfast or sit by the fireplace for a candlelit dinner of organic filet mignon or a hearty cassoulet in the converted-barn restaurant.

Forty miles north on Hwy 1, the swish town of Carmel-by-the-Sea also has a history as a retreat for artists and writers. Perched on a pastoral rise along the Pacific, ⑧ **Tor House** looks a trifle anachronistic amid the more modern residences next door. Inspired by ancient Irish stone towers, the poet Robinson Jeffers helped build a low cottage with granite from the cove below and then, without any assistance, pieced together a castlelike turret called Hawk Tower. Writing from his home, he and his wife also played host to the literary luminaries of the day, including Langston Hughes, Sinclair Lewis and Edna St Vincent Millay. Visitors can climb Hawk Tower, tour the house and stroll the beautiful gardens.

ON THE BUS

Can't find the scrawling grounds of your favorite writer? Though LA's literary legends etched many of the city's landmarks into the backdrops of their works, many of the buildings no longer exist or are unmarked. Helpfully finding these secret spots, **Esotouric** (www.esotouric .com) runs eclectic literary coach tours visiting the haunts of some of LA's legendary writers, including James M Cain and John Fante. Don't miss the two separate Raymond Chandler tours and a Bukowski outing titled "Haunts of a Dirty Old Man."

Head northeast on Hwy 68 to Salinas and jump on north Hwy 101 for the two-hour drive to ⑨ **San Francisco**. In a city renowned as a breeding ground for writers, the North Beach neighborhood has howled and boozed with the best of the Beat Generation. Poet Lawrence Ferlinghetti's ⑩ **City Lights** bookstore, opened in 1953, remains a bohemian and literary magnet, with frequent readings. The store earned notoriety in 1957, when it published Ginsberg's poem "Howl" (banned for obscenity), which led to a well-publicized trial. Browse the fiction and magazine sections while eyeballing picture-window views of the frenetic neon-accessorized neighborhood, or venture down the creaky wooden stairs to peruse shelves on People's History, Stolen Continents and Class War. Finally, duck behind the pie slice–shaped building to admire the brilliant Zapatista solidarity mural on Jack Kerouac Alley.

Walking south through Chinatown, hushed alleys reverberate with the clack of mah-jongg tiles. A few blocks away is the neighborhood's central gathering place, Portsmouth Sq (Kearny St between Washington and Clay Sts), where elderly residents move hypnotically through their morning tai chi. Site of the first public school in California, a number of markers and statues dot this well-utilized patch of urban open space. Look for a masted galleon crowning a **11 memorial to Robert Louis Stevenson**, which commemorates the time he spent here while visiting San Francisco in the late 1870s. The marker quotes from his essay "A Christmas Sermon."

Further south in the sunny Mission District, eyepatches, spyglasses and message-ready bottles stock a pirate-supply shop that's a swashbuckling front for the writers of the future. A non-profit writing and tutoring center for youth started by author Dave Eggers, the **12 826 Valencia store** helps fund the free programs out back. Kids can keep any treasure they unearth in the store's overflowing cauldron of sand, but only if they barter it for a riddle. The store also sells literary magazines – and lard – though the many excellent restaurants on Valencia St are recommended for a tastier meal.

Stay the night at the literary-themed **13 Hotel Rex** and imagine yourself back at the Algonquin Round Table. Put pen to paper at your room's writing desk, power up your laptop for free wi-fi, or come browse the books in the library lobby bar and quaff a drink under the glow of a reading lamp. Author events occur sporadically, though the hotel boasts of frequent literary guests. Comfortable modern rooms with thick mattresses flaunt some color

MAXINE HONG KINGSTON & EARLL KINGSTON'S BAY AREA

We asked award-winning author Maxine Hong Kingston and her husband, actor Earll Kingston, about some of their favorite literary Bay Area spots.

"We met on (**UC Berkeley**) campus. It was amazing in those years at Cal. It was before bookstores like Cody's had readings, and there were always authors coming to read at Wheeler Auditorium.

Our friends Jeanne Wakatsuki and Jim Houston have a house a block from the ocean in **Santa Cruz**. It has a widow's walk on top that can be viewed from the top of the roller-coaster at the Santa Cruz Boardwalk, and a redwood interior with no nails that dates back to the 1880s. Jim writes about the area and wrote a book called *Snow Mountain Passage* about the Donner Party, because Patty Reed, who was a girl during the winter of the Donner Party, died at the house.

Canyon is a gorgeous spot. When we have friends that haven't been to the area we like to take them there. It's a community east of Oakland in Contra Costa County, just over Skyline Blvd, an old beatnik hippie town down in an arroyo and shielded from the city. There used to be a train line there to St Mary's College. The redwood stands and eucalyptus grow to monster heights, competing to get sunlight. It's worth a drive just to see the trees, and people run around barefoot."

and guests are encouraged to earmark a donation for the 826 Valencia youth writing program.

The following day, drive east over the Bay Bridge and navigate I-580 to Hwy 24 and on to I-680 south for the city of Danville. Advance reservations are required to visit the **⑭ Eugene O'Neill National Historic Site**, also known as the Tao House, where the Nobel Prize–winning but reclusive playwright lived and wrote classics including *The Iceman Cometh*. From downtown, the park shuttles in visitors to tour his former home, a greenbelted oasis that draws influences from Spanish colonial and Chinese architecture. Learn about his legacy in American theater, and about some of the bleaker aspects of his personal life. After docents wrap up the indoor presentation, visitors can wander the grounds of fruit and nut orchards.

"His 'scribble den' has been left as it was during his life, with crumbled papers overflowing..."

Lastly, go north on I-680 to Hwy 4 west for the **⑮ John Muir National Historic Site**, a pastoral patch of farmland in bustling modern Martinez. Acres of his fruit orchard still stand, and visitors can enjoy seasonal samples. Though Muir wrote of sauntering the High Sierra with a sack of tea and bread, his house may be a shock for those familiar with the iconic Sierra Club founder's ascetic weather-beaten appearance – it's a model of Victorian Italianate refinement, with a tower cupola, a daintily upholstered parlor and splashes of fussy white lace. His "scribble den" has been left as it was during his life, with crumbled papers overflowing from wire wastebaskets and dried bread balls – his preferred snack – resting on the mantelpiece.

Beth Kohn

TRIP INFORMATION

GETTING THERE
From Los Angeles, take Hwy 1 to Big Sur and then Hwy 68 to Hwy 101 and on to San Francisco.

DO
826 Valencia store
A goofy pirate store fronts Dave Egger's writing workshop for local youth. ☎ 415-642-5905; www.826valencia.org; 826 Valencia St, San Francisco; ⊙ noon-6pm; ♿

City Lights
A North Beach literary fixture since the Beat Generation, it's still one of the best bookstores in the Bay Area. ☎ 415-362-8193; www.citylights.com; 261 Columbus Ave, San Francisco; ⊙ 10am-midnight

Eugene O'Neill National Historic Site
Book reservations to visit the house the famed playwright built with his 1936 Nobel Prize money. ☎ 925-838-0249; www.nps .gov/euon; Danville; admission free; ⊙ tours 10am & 12:30pm Wed-Sun

Henry Miller Library
An offbeat arts space celebrating the life, work and values of former Big Sur resident Henry Miller. ☎ 831-667-2574; www .henrymiller.org; Big Sur; ⊙ 11am-6pm Wed-Mon

John Muir National Historic Site
See the home where the Sierra Club founder penned many of his environmental essays. ☎ 925-228-8860; www.nps.gov/jomu; 4202 Alhambra Ave, Martinez; adult/child $3/free; ⊙ 10am-5pm Wed-Sun

Tor House
Reserve in advance to tour the rugged home of poet Robinson Jeffers. ☎ 831-624-1813; www.torhouse.org; 26304 Ocean View Ave, Carmel; adult/student $7/2; ⊙ hourly tours 10am-3pm Fri & Sat

EAT & DRINK
Grand Central Market
The oldest and largest open-air market in Los Angeles, it has produce stands and restaurants. ☎ 213-624-2378; www.grandcentral square.com; 317 S Broadway, Los Angeles; ⊙ 9am-6pm

Musso & Frank Grill
Literary and movie history hangs thickly in the air at Hollywood's oldest eatery, which is going on 90 years old. ☎ 323-467-7788; 6667 Hollywood Blvd, Hollywood; mains $14-38; ⊙ 11am-11pm Tue-Sat

SLEEP
Deetjen's Big Sur Inn
An enchanting conglomeration of rustic rooms, redwoods and wisteria along Castro Creek, built in the early 1930s. ☎ 831-667-2377; www.deetjens.com; Big Sur; r $80-200

Hotel Rex
With a nod to the local 1920s arts salon scene, the Rex exudes an old-guard men's club atmosphere. ☎ 415-433-4434, 800-433-4434; www.jdvhotels.com/rex; 562 Sutter St, San Francisco; r $189-299; ▨

Mayfair Hotel
A former hole-up spot for Raymond Chandler's many benders and a setting for his hard-boiled writings. ☎ 213-484-9789, 800-821-8682; www.mayfairla.com; 1256 W 7th St, Los Angeles; r $99

USEFUL WEBSITES
www.californiaauthors.com
www.litquake.org

SUGGESTED READS
- *Slouching Towards Bethlehem*, Joan Didion
- *Tales of the City*, Armistead Maupin
- *Chicano*, Richard Vasquez
- *Devil in a Blue Dress*, Walter Mosley

www.lonelyplanet.com/trip-planner

LINK YOUR TRIP

Alice Waters' Culinary Tour

WHY GO Alice Waters' vision for local, organic food continues to change and challenge the way we think about what we put in our bodies. True to this vision, her tour of California eating focuses on foods that stay close to the source, ending with dinner at her own Chez Panisse.

If you were to close your eyes and go by your nose on any given Wednesday in Santa Monica, you might thank California food pioneer and restaurateur Alice Waters for your ability to identify the season – from the broad-shouldered sweetness of stone fruit and strawberries in the summer to the weighty earthiness of root vegetables in the fall. Standing on the sun-soft pavement of the ❶ **Santa Monica Wednesday Farmers Market**, the smell that's most distinct is that of a food revolution in full swing.

Waters herself has little to do with that particular public market in Santa Monica (there are four weekly), but it's hardly too bold to credit her with this particular food revolution. By championing fresh, organic, local, seasonal produce, she forever changed the face of American food. When you ask Waters how she eats while traveling, her response is simple: "Find the nearest farmers market. That's what I do. That's always my first stop."

The 9000 shoppers at the market are shoulder to shoulder with some of the country's best chefs, whom Waters also helped liberate from the sauce-drowned old-world standards of "fine cuisine" when she plunked down a bit of goat cheese on a bed of airy greens and invented the fusions of California cuisine. It's a little more expensive, and getting to her favorite spots takes some hunting, but to Waters it's unquestionably worth it. "We have to start looking at food as a right and not a privilege," she says flatly. "That is important."

TIME
4 days

DISTANCE
536 miles

BEST TIME TO GO
Late summer

START
Santa Monica

END
Berkeley

ALSO GOOD FOR

FOOD & DRINK

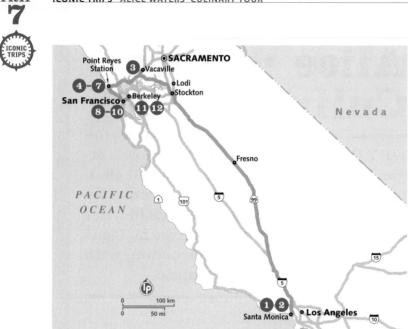

Asked about menus she admires, her response is uncomplicated: "It's about seasonality, no question," she says. "And obviously locality. I'm looking for people who are using organic produce and meat. So I want grass-fed beef. I want organic vegetables. I want organic breads. I want people who care about farmers and ranchers. I'm looking," and she pauses just a beat, "for the *purists*."

West on Wilshire about a mile takes you to the doorstep of one of those purists, Josiah Citrin, the chef of ❷ Mélisse. Citrin's restaurant is more formal and more Frenchie than Waters' Chez Panisse (the waiters wear suits, and so do many of the diners), and the atmosphere might bring to mind a date scene in a mid-'90s sitcom, but Citrin's focus is on food – an immaculate French presentation that changes seasonally and is mostly pulled from the market down the street.

"...ask Waters how she eats while traveling: 'Find the nearest farmers market. That's what I do.'"

To tour California based on Waters' principals, head north on I-5 and take Hwy 99 through the big sky and broad horizons of California's 400-mile-long Central Valley, which grows about one-quarter of the food America eats. Many of the fields you'll pass on that long, hot six-hour drive are huge swaths of industrially farmed land that don't jive with Waters' palate, but hidden among them is a thriving network of small producers. And it doesn't get fresher than the stuff sold at the many fruit stands marked by hand-painted signs along the route.

Two hours north on Hwy 99, exit at Lodi and take CA 12 an hour across the Sacramento River Delta. Go north on I-80 and exit at Pena Adobe Rd. The winding Cherry Glen Rd crosses under the highway to come to Pleasant Valley Rd, home of ❸ **Soul Food Farm**. Run by Alexis Koefoed, it earns Waters' raves and supplies chickens and eggs to a select handful of other restaurateurs throughout the Bay Area.

Waters reminisces about Soul Food's humanely raised "Freedom Rangers" breed, which peck around the 45 acres. "I had one of those the other week. I made it at home, this simple chicken, and you know what, I'm pretty used to good chicken. It tasted like no other chicken I've had in the United States. The dark meat was richer, more flavorful, and it was a revelation. It reminded me of the chicken I had 35 years ago in France." Pick up some of the eggs from the cooler at the end of the drive and leave your money in the jar. "Her eggs are fantastic," Waters says. "I just feel like I'm making a donation to the cause."

From Vacaville, go south on I-80 for 20 minutes and follow the exit for CA 37, which skirts the marshes of the San Pablo Bay and leads into Novato.

THE ENDANGERED ELBERT PEACH

At **Masumoto Family Farm**, near Fresno, you can sink your teeth into the endangered Elbert peach, a variety deemed "too fragile" for the modern supermarket. Waters calls the farm "one of the most gratifying places on earth," but the public can only visit if they adopt a tree through www.masumoto.com. The adoptive parents harvest the buttery peaches themselves – all 400lbs to 500lbs of them. "Its no vacation," Masumoto says. "But it's the kind of thing that really helps people understand the rhythms of nature."

Take Point Reyes-Petaluma Rd 20 miles west of town to Point Reyes Station, home to a pair of Waters' favorite destinations in the north bay and an ideal stop for picnic supplies. Begin at ❹ **Bovine Bakery**, for a crusty loaf of their fire-baked Brickmaiden Bread and organic, fresh-brewed coffee.

With loaf under arm, step down the block to the restored barn that houses ❺ **Cowgirl Creamery**, one of the nation's most sought-after cheese makers. In springtime the must-buy is their St Pat's, a smooth, mellow round that comes wrapped in nettle leaves; the Mt Tam (available year-round) is pretty damn good too. There is also a gourmet deli and tour available on Friday mornings.

For the perfect picnic spot, Waters says to look on the surrounding coast. "Go up there in the headlands and find a little spot on the way out by Bolinas and Inverness and along the ❻ **Point Reyes National Seashore**," she says. "I think that is one of the greatest park areas I've ever been in." Another idyllic picnic spot awaits 10 minutes north of Point Reyes Station at the salty turnout for the ❼ **Hog Island Oyster Company**. It has a handful of silky oysters available to go (by the pound) but, to Waters, "there's nothing better than eating them right there on the beach." For a fee you can arrange for a table and borrow some shucking tools. The company even offers lessons on how to crack open and grill the oysters for those who like them barbecued.

PANISSE PROTÉGÉS

"When you operate a restaurant for 37 years, a whole lot of people come through the kitchen," Waters says. Of her alumni in San Francisco, try Michael Tusk, who offers shrewd Italian-French fusions at Quince, or Gayle Pirie, who operates Foreign Cinema, a gourmet movie house in the Mission District. More casual eats are across the bay, where Charlie Hallowell offers immaculate wood-fired pizzas at Pizzaiolo, and Alison Barakat marries brilliant comfort food with '50s kitsch at Bakesale Betty.

After lunch, explore the misty coastal forests before winding down Hwy 1 back into San Francisco. From the center of the Golden Gate Bridge, it's possible to view the clock tower of the city's **⑧ Ferry Building Marketplace**, which hosts not only a broad selection of gourmet organic produce, but is also a one-stop destination for many of Waters' recommendations.

"The day to go, of course, is Saturday," she says. "Inside there are really quite exceptional vendors. It's one of the only places where you can get real food all in one place – real meat, real chicken, raised at Soul Food Farm and Prather Meat. There's obviously Cowgirl Creamery and Acme Bread and McAvoy Olive Oil."

When it comes to McAvoy, she showers the local producer with high praise. "I just think they've put a lot of energy figuring out what varietals of tree can grow up there, south of Petaluma. They've set the standard. There are loads of little boutique producers of olive oil that are happening now, but they've set the standard."

To stay within skipping distance, check into the bay-front luxury **⑨ Hotel Vitale**. Those worn out from all the organic veggie hunting can blow off some steam in the rooftop soaking tubs surrounded by a bamboo forest.

For dinner, a San Francisco institution is just up Market St at **⑩ Zuni Café**, a place Waters merrily refers to as her "home away from home." She'll quickly admit that it's a distinctively different atmosphere than the one at Chez Panisse, but adds, "Zuni is run in the right spirit. It's real food." By the way she offers these straightforward compliments – her voice going from a kind of gregarious, playful lilt to dead-serious in a second – it's clear that a declaration of "real food" is her highest praise. It's not doled out all that often and is saved for a select handful of students who have passed through the kitchen of her restaurant and other like-minded chefs in what she calls "the cause."

Certainly one of the most celebrated of these is Steve Sullivan, the master baker behind ⑪ **Acme Bread Company**. Cross the Bay Bridge to Acme's original location in Berkeley, the only place that carries their entire line of artisan breads, other than the Ferry Plaza, and another place that Waters refers to as "setting the standard." Sullivan started bussing tables at Chez Panisse while a student at UC Berkeley and began what local foodies refer to as the "San Francisco bread revolution." On the western end of the so-called "Gourmet Ghetto" – a neighborhood that married the revolutionary ideals of Berkley in the late '60s with a haute dining sensibility – you can smell the cinnamon bread floating across Shattuck St, intoxicating passersby every morning.

To cap Waters' tour of California, end with her legendary restaurant, ⑫ **Chez Panisse**, just up the street. It's casual and unpretentious, and every mind-altering, soul-sanctifying bite of the food served in the dining room downstairs and the slightly less formal café upstairs is emblematic of her principles. The service is impeccable, the atmosphere is comfortably elegant and the kitchen is open for a peek behind the scenes. The harmonious menu changes every day, so if you close your eyes and take a nibble you might even be able to tell what season it is.
Nate Cavalieri

SEASON'S EATINGS

California is the most agriculturally diverse region in the United States and its farmers markets stay open year-round. Look for these seasonal delights during your romp through the state: spring's artichokes, mushrooms, snow peas, lettuce greens and onions; summer's berries, watermelon, peppers, zucchini, corn and stone fruit; fall's squash, tomatoes, apples, pumpkins and cucumbers; and winter's Swiss chard, cabbage, fennel and kale.

TRIP INFORMATION

GETTING THERE
From Santa Monica, travel on Hwy 99 north for 350 miles to the Bay Area, ending in the East Bay.

DO

Ferry Building Marketplace
This landmark is a one-stop shop of Waters' favorites. ☎ 415-693-0996; www.ferrybuildingmarketplace.com; One Ferry Building, San Francisco; admission free; 10am-6pm Mon-Fri, 9am-6pm Sat, 11am-5pm Sun; ⛦

Santa Monica Wednesday Farmers Market
Santa Monica hosts four markets a week, but the best is on Wednesday. ☎ 310-458-8411; www.santamonica.com; Arizona Ave at 2nd St, Santa Monica; admission free; ⏱ Tues market 10am-2pm; ⛦

Soul Food Farm
It raises chickens that Waters claims are the best in America; also available at Bay Area farmers markets. ☎ 707-469-0499; www.soulfoodfarm.com; 6046 Pleasant Valley Rd, Vacaville; ⛦

EAT

Acme Bread Company
Waters' student Steve Sullivan ignited the "San Francisco bread revolution." ☎ 510-524-1327; 1601 San Pablo, Berkeley; ⏱ 8am-6pm Mon-Sat, 8:30am-3pm Sun

Bovine Bakery
It gets loaded on the weekends with spandex-clad cyclists drawn to the divine baked goods. ☎ 415-663-9420; 11315 Shoreline Hwy, Pt Reyes Station; pastries $1-8; ⏱ 6:30am-5pm; ⛦

Chez Panisse
Waters' defining restaurant is nothing short of soul affirming. ☎ 415-663-9218; www.chezpanisse.com; 1517 Shattuck Ave, Berkeley; café $20-30, restaurant prix fixe $60-95; ⏱ café 11:30am-3pm, restaurant 5-11:30pm

Cowgirl Creamery
Their triple-cream soft cheese has a nation-wide rep; helpful staff guide you through tastings. There's also a branch in San Francisco's Ferry Building. ☎ 415-663-9335; www.cowgirlcreamery.com; 80 Fourth St, Pt Reyes Station; artisan cheese per lb from $26; ⏱ 10am-6pm Wed-Sun; ⛦

Hog Island Oyster Company
Their sustainably farmed oysters can be grilled on the beach. ☎ 415-663-9218; www.hogislandoysters.com; 20215 Hwy 1, Marshall; 12 oysters $13-$16, picnic area fee $8; ⏱ 9am-5pm Mon-Sun

Mélisse
The farmers market goes French. Request a booth to savor the people-watching too. ☎ 310-395-0881; www.melisse.com; 1104 Wilshire Blvd, Santa Monica; mains $40-55; ⏱ 6-9:30pm Mon-Thu, 6-10pm Fri, 5:45-10pm Sat

Zuni Café
This hip spot is great for mesquite-grilled meats, brick-oven pizzas and people-watching. ☎ 415-552-2522; www.zunicafe.com; 1658 Market St, San Francisco; mains $15-30; ⏱ 11:30am-midnight Tue-Sat, 11am-11pm Sun

SLEEP

Hotel Vitale
Deep soaking tubs and huge views of the Bay Bridge are an easy stroll from the Ferry Building Marketplace. ☎ 415-278-3700; www.hotelvitale.com; 8 Mission St, San Francisco; r from $319

USEFUL WEBSITES
www.chezpanisse.com
www.ccfm.org
www.lonelyplanet.com/trip-planner

LINK YOUR TRIP

Surfing USA

WHY GO With so many waves, where to start? We got recommendations from So-Cal native and lifelong surfer Joel Patterson, current editor-in-chief of Surfer magazine and former editor-in-chief of Transworld Surf magazine. Check out these beaches on any given day and you're almost guaranteed to find a good break.

TIME
3 – 4 days

DISTANCE
580 miles

BEST TIME TO GO
Year-round

START
La Jolla

END
San Francisco

ALSO GOOD FOR

Head north of downtown La Jolla to a spot called ❶ Black's Beach, near the Scripps Pier. Pick your way down a steep canyon to reach the undeveloped beach. "With the right combination swell, it's the perfect wave. It's mostly a left-hand wave but a right too, though it can be scary on a big day." It's also a nudist beach. Patterson jokes that surfers quickly learn that "nudity and surfing don't necessarily go that well together."

A 1920s jewel, La Jolla's ❷ La Valencia Hotel has beautiful rooms facing the ocean, and a built-in bonus for surfers: on a clear day, you can check the surf from some of the rooms. The hotel bar feels "like you've walked into San Diego in 1948."

Located at the river mouth of a nature preserve, the surf spots known as ❸ Trestles are at the southernmost tip of Orange County, north of Camp Pendleton off I-5. Leaving your car near the freeway, the traffic noise fades away, the path turns lush and you can hear "birds chirping and animals moving in the bushes next to you." The sandy beach is wild in each direction, with no development anywhere nearby except for the *Surfliner* train track.

San Clemente is the nearest town, a sleepy little beach community that's managed to hold onto an element of surf culture. Patterson has a hint for visitors: "If you know who the pro surfers are, ❹ Sonny's

Pizza is the place they all go after they get out of the water." A little Italian restaurant, it's a local hot spot slinging great pizza.

> *"See boards ridden by greats, from Duke Kahanamoku through to Kelly Slater..."*

Also in San Clemente, the ❺ **Surfing Heritage Foundation** museum tells the history of surfing through surfboards. See boards ridden by greats, from Duke Kahanamoku through to Kelly Slater, and the huge planks of redwood and balsa wood that people used 100 years ago.

In Orange County, an audience forms to watch surfers ride breaks on both sides of the ❻ **Huntington Beach Pier**. Home of the surf industry, ❼ **Huntington Beach** hosts the huge annual US Open of Surfing competition in July. The city takes its surfing credentials so seriously that the visitors bureau tussled with Santa Cruz for years over the exclusive right to be called "Surf City, USA" (and won).

In addition, two of the biggest surf shops in the world, ❽ **Jack's Surfboards** and ❾ **Huntington Surf & Sport**, sit right at the base of the pier. Patterson says "it's where every buyer from every surf retail outlet in the world goes to see what the trends are."

Owned by the family of one of surfing's "modern explorers," the ❿ **Sugar Shack Café** sits on the busiest street in town. Anyone who has anything to do with surfing eats breakfast here (the Main Street breakfast burrito or omelettes with hash browns). It's hard not to notice that "everyone's tan or sunburnt."

Continuing up the coast, Patterson notes one no-brainer. "If you're surfing in California, you *have* to do ⑪ **Surfrider Beach** in Malibu. It's the original surf break where Miki Dora pioneered technical surfing, and LA's real surf beach." He adds, "it's like a little village, but you can see all the stars." Spot more celebrities over at ⑫ **Nobu Malibu**, a five-minute walk from Surfrider Beach. "The food's really good, and if you want to see Matthew McConaughey eating sushi, this is where you go."

Right on exclusive Carbon Beach, less than a mile south of Surfrider, the ⑬ **Casa Malibu Inn** sports a ho-hum motel facade but an amazing location overlooking a small private beach. Lana Turner even lived here for a while.

> **DETOUR**
>
> "Golf's a big thing in the surf community – most of the surfers I know are golfers too. In La Jolla, the **Torrey Pines Golf Course** (www.torreypines golfcourse.com) is insanely stunning. The whole west side of the course is the Pacific Ocean and you're right above the break. It's probably one of the most challenging courses in the world."
>
> *Joel Patterson*

While it lost the battle to be Surf City, Santa Cruz remains a high-caliber surf town. Because the water's cold, it's home to many wetsuit companies and their research. Patterson recommends ⑭ **Steamers Lane,** off West Cliff Drive: "a right-hand point break that builds along a big cliff with a rocky shore-line." After your session, check out the ⑮ **Santa Cruz Surfing Museum,** located in a lighthouse building overlooking the beach. A regional history gem, it exhibits early equipment and photos of surf history going back a century.

WOMEN IN THE WATER

Want to learn the basics or just fine-tune your goofy technique? Spend a weekend in La Jolla's warm water with **Surf Diva** (www.surfdiva.com). It runs two-day women's surf workshops every weekend, with female instructors coaching you on how to paddle out there, stand up and ride that wave.

Most people don't think of San Francisco as a surf town but Patterson admires the ⑯ **Ocean Beach** break. "You see a lot of older equipment, and not everyone's tan," he says. "You're out there with everyone from accountants to truck drivers." Ocean Beach abuts the Sunset and Richmond districts.

The nearby ⑰ **Mollusk Surf Shop** rides the recent retro surfing craze, selling beavertail wetsuits and trunks from the 1950s and '60s. At the northern end of the beach, the ⑱ **Cliff House** is a handy place to stop by when you're chilled to the bone. You can get a meal or "have a beer at sunset and look south and see all the peaks breaking."

Beth Kohn

TRIP INFORMATION

GETTING THERE
From Los Angeles, take I-5 south to San Diego or Hwy 152 north towards San Francisco.

DO

Jack's Surfboards
Experience the joy of surf-equipment overload while visiting this massive shop at the base of the Huntington Beach Pier. ☎ 714-536-4516; www.jackssurfboards.com; 101 Main St, Huntington Beach; ⊙ 8am-10pm

Huntington Surf & Sport
One of California's (and the world's) largest surfing emporiums. ☎ 714-841-4000; www.hsssurf.com; 300 Pacific Coast Hwy, Huntington Beach; ⊙ 8am-9pm Sun-Thu, 8am-10pm Fri & Sat, extended summer hours

Mollusk Surf Shop
Check out the cool art and artisan boards at this friendly shop near the beach and Golden Gate Park. ☎ 415-564-6300; www.mollusk surfshop.com; 4500 Irving St, San Francisco; ⊙ 10am-6:30pm

Santa Cruz Surfing Museum
Housed in a tiny lighthouse building, it archives the region's surfing history. ☎ 831-420-6289; www.santacruzsurfingmuseum .org; 701 West Cliff Dr, Santa Cruz; admission free; ⊙ noon-4pm Thu-Mon, extended summer hours

Surfing Heritage Foundation
Trace the history of surfing, as shown in this museum through the evolution of the surfboard. ☎ 949-388-0313; www.surfing heritage.com; 101 Calle Iglesia, San Clemente; admission free; ⊙ 9am-5pm Mon-Fri year-round, 11am-3pm Sat Jul–mid-Sep

EAT

Nobu Malibu
A restaurant empire with a famous clientele, it serves creative Japanese fare and tasty sushi. ☎ 310-317-9140; 3835 Cross Creek Rd, Malibu; sushi $7-12, mains $20-40; ⊙ 5:45-10pm Sun-Thu, 5:45-11pm Fri & Sat

Sonny's Pizza
Yummy pizza; popular with locals and surfers. ☎ 949-498-2540; 429 N El Camino Real, San Clemente; mains $8-16; ⊙ 11am-10pm Sun-Thu, 11am-11pm Fri & Sat ⑤

Sugar Shack Café
Where the local surf industry and freshly out-of-the-water folks come to eat breakfast. ☎ 714-536-0355; 213½ Main St, Huntington Beach; mains $5-7; ⊙ 5am-4pm Thu-Tue, 5am-8pm Wed ⑤

DRINK

Cliff House
Two casual but snazzy restaurants at this shoreside institution. Or just sidle up to the bar for drinks. ☎ 415-386-3330; 1090 Point Lobos, San Francisco; mains $13-36; ⊙ 9am-9:30pm

SLEEP

Casa Malibu Inn
Let the crashing surf lull you to sleep at this "California Dreamin'" beachfront getaway on Carbon Beach. ☎ 310-456-2219, 800-831-0858; casamalibu@earthlink.net; 22752 Pacific Coast Hwy, Malibu; r $199-500

La Valencia Hotel
"The Pink Lady of La Jolla," this salmon-colored Mediterranean palace spills down the hillside toward the ocean. ☎ 858-454-0771, 800-451-0772; www.lavalencia.com; 1132 Prospect St, La Jolla; r from $275 ⑧

USEFUL WEBSITES
www.surfline.com
www.surfrider.org

www.lonelyplanet.com/trip-planner

LINK YOUR TRIP
TRIP

Napa & Sonoma Locavore Tour

WHY GO Sun-honeyed fields, toast-colored hills and rows of vines carpeting the valleys – wine country is a feast for the eyes. But it's also full of organic fresh-from-the-farm eats and environmentally minded wineries, so renting a hybrid and sampling the buffet of offerings can be a hedonistic and planet-saving experience all at once.

The "locavore" movement is in full swing in Napa and Sonoma, where the eco-conscious try to eat only locally grown, sustainable food from within a 100-mile radius. Hand in hand with this is the trend of wineries, hotels and restaurants adopting green practices, like using solar energy and recycled and reclaimed materials. Departing from Santa Rosa and winding your way down through Sonoma Valley and up Napa Valley makes for a pleasant weekend trip chock-full of feel-good stops.

Simplicity is key at ❶ **Beltane Ranch**, a lemon-yellow-painted 1890s B&B with a wraparound porch, 13 miles east of Santa Rosa. Spending your first night here means no phone, TV or air-conditioning, but you'll have breakfasted upon the likes of sweet-potato latkes or oatmeal pancakes with homemade fig-merlot syrup in an idyllic setting. Once on the road, dipping just west of Glen Ellen on Arnold Dr/London Ranch Rd sets you up with the best crash course in winemaking and biodynamic vineyard practices at ❷ **Benziger Winery**. A red tractor takes you through the vineyard; afterward, you can check out the caves – and the cabernets. The tour's the thing, though. You'll learn about the difference between organic and biodynamic farming – biodynamic systems work to achieve a balance with the entire ecosystem, going beyond organic practices. With your newfound expert knowledge of what goes on behind the scenes, you can drive with confidence back on Sonoma Hwy to ❸ **Imagery Estate**, Benziger's

TIME
2 – 3 days

DISTANCE
70 miles

BEST TIME TO GO
Sep – Nov

START
Glen Ellen

END
Calistoga

ALSO GOOD FOR

FOOD &
DRINK

sister winery with bottle labels designed by local artists; the art changes with each vintage and varietal. A gallery currently houses the entire collection of artwork – 190 pieces that all have the winery's signature Parthenon symbol interpreted in them. The heavy-sweet viognier and moscato are popular, and all wines are certified biodynamic.

A little ways further down the road you'll come upon ❹ **Oak Hill Farm**, with acres upon acres of organic flowers and produce, hemmed in by lovely steep oak and Manzanita woodland. The farm's Red Barn Store is a historic dairy barn filled with handmade wreaths, herbs and organic goods reaped from the surrounding fields. Try the heirloom tomatoes, pumpkins and blue plums.

As you enter Sonoma, keep a lookout for the mobile *taquerías* on Hwy 12's east side, between Boyes Blvd and Agua Caliente. The best local "taco truck" has a picture of a giant, beckoning Jesus on the side, aka the "come to Jesus truck": if it's there, you can't miss it.

DETOUR

On the Sonoma Coast an hour's drive from Glen Ellen, **Bodega Artisan Cheese** (www.bodega artisancheese.com) comprises a 60-goat farm and dairy, where Patty Karlin, a veteran goat rancher who lives "off the grid," shows ecotourists how she eliminates her power and water bills. Under the solar panels and pond-fed irrigation system, you can marvel at her fresh goat manchego and creamy ricotta.

If you can resist the Lord's temptation and stay on the organic eating path, your next stop is ❺ **El Dorado Kitchen**, an earthy but sleek and minimalist restaurant right off Sonoma Plaza, which incorporates all kinds of green practices; it converts its fryer oil to biodiesel fuel and uses ecofriendly takeout containers. Mouthwatering faves are the pizza topped with local forest mushrooms or the Niman Ranch steak with broccolini and truffle fries. The upstairs ❻ **El Dorado Hotel**, equally chic, is floored and furnished with reclaimed materials and cleaned with all-natural products. The staff reduce their ecological "footprint" by walking, biking or carpooling to work.

If you're inclined toward somewhere less fancy, take a rain check for locally grown and raised fare at the dinner-only ❼ **Harvest Moon Cafe**. The married co-owners bring culinary skills from their previous lives at Alice Waters' Chez Panisse in Berkeley and La Toque in Napa. The menu changes daily but could include handmade lamb ravioli, chilled fennel soup and local halibut, all served up bistro-style on a casual patio with cheerful red chairs.

Just steps away are the ❽ **Bungalows 313**, where you might choose to stay the night; the apartment-like suites include breakfast delivered to your room. The outdoor courtyard is lovely with citrus trees and bougainvillea, and a block away there's a half-mile walking trail that winds prettily through vineyards and farmhouses to Ravenswood Winery.

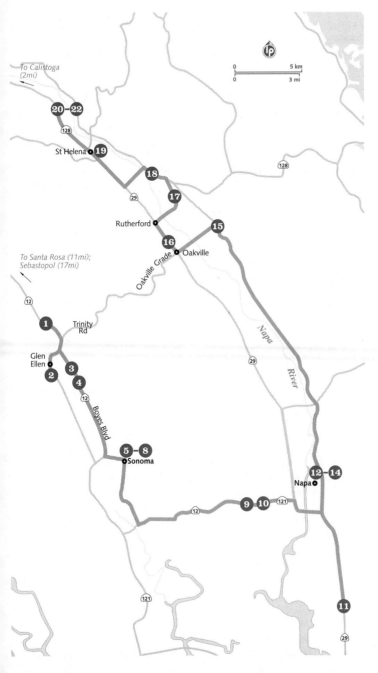

To Calistoga
(2mi)

20—22

128

St Helena 19

18

17

128

Rutherford

29

16

Oakville Grade • Oakville

15

To Santa Rosa (11mi);
Sebastopol (17mi)

12

1

Trinity
Rd

Napa

Glen
Ellen

2 3

4

River

12

Boyes Blvd

29

5—8

Sonoma

12—14

Napa

9 10 121

12

11

121

29

Perhaps you have time for a late-afternoon wine tasting first at **9** **Madonna Estate**, a few miles east on Napa Rd (and a slight left on Old Sonoma Rd as you enter Napa Valley). The grapes are 100% organically grown and the Bartolucci family uses only biodynamic and dry farming techniques, meaning that in areas of limited precipitation, growing methods are selected that make the most efficient use of the soil's moisture. The tasting room isn't fancy, but the wine (at $5 for tasting, and possibly the valley's cheapest shipping) can be quite decent. Try the sweet whites, which can only be found at the winery.

If the Sonoma sleeping options aren't your style, you'll crash elegantly at the serene, private **10** **Carneros Inn**, about half a mile on Sonoma Hwy toward Napa. The 86 semidetached, corrugated-metal units look like itinerant housing – in fact, they were styled on barns, silos and ranchers' cottages. Inside they're contemporary and luxurious, with cherry-wood floors, poured concrete fireplaces, Frette linens, heated bathroom floors and rocking-chair patios. The indoor and outdoor showers speak to the place's romantic privacy, surrounded by acres of vineyards, apple orchards and farmland. And there are no fewer than *three* swimming pools: an infinity pool overlooking the vineyards, a lap pool lined with cabanas and a kiddie pool. If you can manage dinner, there's in-house organic dining that's sourced from a 150-mile radius.

> **DETOUR**
>
> A 25-mile drive from Glen Ellen, Sebastopol boasts one of the few true farm stays in Sonoma County. At **Full House Farm** (www.fhfarm.com) you get your very own kitchen garden, with everything from blackberries to green beans, and freshly laid organic eggs from hens that roam on the 23-acre grounds. The rest of Sebastopol is worth seeing, too: ask around for the organic creamery and the mushroom hut.

In the morning, continue down the Sonoma–Napa Hwy, then turn south on Route 29. After about 8 miles you'll cross the railroad tracks at Napa Junction. At Napa Junction Rd, turn right and right again on Lombard Rd until you come to **11** **Marshall's Farm Honey**. Fascinating beekeeper tours allow you to get up close with a netted helmet and taste thick, sticky honey straight from the hive; the farm produces 35 varieties of organic honey, including ones made with Napa Valley wildflowers, blackberries and eucalyptus. Call ahead to reserve an individual tour, given on one or two Sundays a month in the dry season, or a group tour during the week.

After such a sweet amuse-bouche you'll be craving a more substantial meal, so the next stop on your route is 9 miles north in downtown Napa, at the new Oxbow Market. Inside, stands offer everything from fresh-roasted organic coffee to cranberry baguette sandwiches with pea shoots and fontina. Sample a beef frank at the counter of **12** **Five Dot Ranch**, an all-natural beef purveyor with a holistic, sustainable, open-pasture program combined with low-stress handling. The family's been raising California livestock for seven generations.

A couple of stands over, top it off with the funky-creative flavors of ⓭ **Three Twins Organic Ice Cream** – try the Strawberry Je Ne Sais Quoi, where the creaminess is cut with an unexpected dash of balsamic vinegar. For those of you just dying to chomp into a good deli sandwich, you'll find it outside and around the corner at ⓭ **Fatted Calf Charcuterie.** For those who live nearby, it's the place to find a pasture-raised Berkshire roasting pig or a chicken that's lived a happy life in a lush green field (check out the cute photo from Soul Food Farms). But until you're lucky enough to live down the street, you'll have to settle for some of the house-smoked jerky or a baguette with meat that's been cured on site.

Once fully sated, set out on the scenic Silverado Trail, a mellower alternative to traffic-heavy Hwy 29, for a stint of Napa Valley or-

WINE TASTING 101

Even if you know nothing about wine, you can enjoy it with gusto. Inhale the wine's aroma by burying your nose deep in the glass. Swirl it and look at its color before letting it hit every part of your tongue. It's OK not to drain every glass (in fact, it'll dull your taste buds if you do). Use the containers on the counter to empty your glass and prepare for your next taste. You won't be offending anyone!

ganic wine tasting. Napa is known for its full-bodied, rich cabernets, but some more unusual Alsatian varietals (vin gris, dry rosé and cab franc) are deliciously refreshing at ⓯ **Robert Sinskey Vineyards**. The winery, with its dramatic high-ceilinged tasting room, is two-thirds solar powered and biodiesel-fueled, and the vineyards have hawk perches to keep the biodynamically grown grapes safe.

Continue north on the Silverado Trail and cut across Oakville Cross Rd to Hwy 29, turning right at the Oakville Grocery. On your left, you'll see the behemoth ⓰ **Robert Mondavi Winery**. While it's somewhat of a corporate-winery experience, the grounds are gorgeous and the winery does use careful environmental practices in its farming, managing 1000 acres of naturally farmed vineyards. For a far different experience, you must call ahead to get in (if you're lucky, the day of) at the irreverent ⓱ **Frog's Leap** in Rutherford, found by cutting back across Conn Creek Rd toward the Silverado Trail. "Time's fun when you're having flies," especially when meandering through the magical gardens and fruit-bearing orchards surrounding an 1884 barn and farmstead. All grapes are organically grown.

When you've come back to earth, journey north back to the Silverado Trail, feeling the cooler air from Lake Hennessey to the east, well hidden past Sage Canyon Rd. You'll come to the entrance to ⓲ **Quintessa**, high atop a hill; look for the insectory (made to attract insects away from the vineyards) before you begin the drive up. If you can fork over the $65 tasting fee, you'll be treated to a personal sit-down session with gourmet food pairings, including local cheeses.

Also, you can find out anything you'd like to know about the winery's environmental practices. At Quintessa, unused grape skins are composted back into fertilizer. The vineyards are guarded by two white owls and, apparently, a wild pack of coyotes (one is believed to have eaten the owner's Chihuahua).

Further up the Silverado Trail, head over to St Helena via Pope St. A little ways southeast on Main St is ⓳ **Go Fish**, with its watery blue-green decor and cool marble-topped raw bar, where you can order creative sushi rolls made with sustainably harvested fish. The brandade (salt cod) cakes, with fava shoots and Meyer lemon aioli, are to die for. Make a note to come back at the end of the day for dinner. For now, there's one more winery on the route: ⓴ **Ehlers Estate**, on the little spur road Ehlers Lane off St Helena's Main St heading north. Dating from the 1880s, Ehlers is a local favorite, with its Aussie shepherd, Ripley, and its well-meaning nonprofit status: all proceeds benefit cardiovascular research (look for the sideways heart in the "E"). It's also completely biodynamic and organic-farmed, solar-powered from 2009, and its shipping materials are pulp, not Styrofoam. Check out the blind sensory table in the center of the tasting room, and test what you've learned!

> **DETOUR** If you have an extra hour to spare, a little-used and beautiful route between Napa and Sonoma also begins at Glen Ellen. From Hwy 12, take Trinity Rd east to Dry Creek Rd and on to Oakville Grade. It takes you through the Mayacamas Mountains in 30 minutes (each way) of gorgeous scenery and empty road.

Half a mile further up St Helena Hwy, cruise by the all-organic locale of ㉑ **Goat's Leap Cheese**. The farm doesn't have the capacity for visitors, but you can spot the tiny-eared LaMancha dairy goats, amid the chaparral in the farmhouse fields, from the road before sampling the creamy rounds found in local stores.

THE GOURMET POET

Sonoma Valley is well known for arts and gastronomy, but it isn't widely known that these things go together, especially in one person: Armando Garcia-Davila (☎ 707-591-0595; www.armandogd.com), known as the Gourmet Poet. If you are in a friend's home, or a time-share, call him. He will come to your abode and, while you dine, regale you with the poetry that has made him a local living treasure.

At the outskirts of Calistoga, turn left into ㉒ **Bothe-Napa Valley State Park**. It's kind of a locals' secret (most tourists head to Calistoga's spas), with year-round campsites, a seasonal swimming pool and miles of trails through redwoods and to the historic Bale Grist Mill, with its recently restored 36ft water wheel, built in 1846. You can even buy sacks of ground flour and cornmeal at the mill shop. Afterward, pitch that tent that you stowed in the back of the hybrid. What more appropriate place to rest your head than in all natural surroundings, under towering trees and the stars?

Dominique Channell

ICONIC
TRIPS

TRIP INFORMATION

GETTING THERE

Santa Rosa is 55 miles from San Francisco on Hwy 101 and 429 miles from Los Angeles on Hwy I-5 N and Hwy 580 W.

DO

Five Dot Ranch

Ground chuck and steaks from open-range, sustainably ranched Napa Valley Angus cattle. ☎ 530-254-6987; www.fivedotranch.com; 610 First St, Napa; ☺ 9am-7pm

Goat's Leap Cheese

Drive by tiny-eared LaMancha dairy goats; sample the goat cheese at local stores. ☎ 707-963-2337; www.goatsleap.com; 3321 St Helena Hwy, St Helena

Marshall's Farm Honey

Taste up to 25 varieties of pure organic honey right out of a beehive. ☎ 800-624-4637; www.marshallshoney.com; 159 Lombard Rd, American Canyon; weekend tours adult/4-18yr $20/10, tasting & visiting free; ☺ 9am-6pm Mon-Fri, call to reserve tours; ♿

Oak Hill Farm

Forty-five acres of organic flowers and produce, bordered by oak and Manzanita woodland. ☎ 707-996-6643; www.oakhill farm.net; 15101 Sonoma Hwy, Glen Ellen; ☺ 11am-6pm Wed-Sun Apr-Dec; ♿

Three Twins Organic Ice Cream

Creative twists on traditional flavors, like Strawberry Je Ne Sais Quoi (with a splash of balsamic vinegar). ☎ 707-257-8946; www .threetwinsicecream.com; 610 First St, Napa; ☺ 9am-7pm; ♿

EAT

El Dorado Kitchen

Sleek and atmospheric with an open kitchen and a "farm-driven" menu. ☎ 707-996-3030; www.eldoradosonoma.com; 405 First St W, Sonoma; mains $11-38; ☺ 11:30am-2:30pm Mon-Sat & 5:30-9pm daily

Fatted Calf Charcuterie

House-cured meats and smoked jerky, all natural and from free-range animals. ☎ 707-256-3684; www.fattedcalf.com; 644C First Street, Napa; sandwiches $7.50; ☺ 9am-7pm

Go Fish

This sushi restaurant takes care to select sustainable fish. ☎ 707-963-0700; www.go fishrestaurant.net; 641 Main St, St Helena; mains $9-35; ☺ 11:30am-9:30pm Mon-Fri, 11:30am-10pm Sat & Sun

Harvest Moon Cafe

Locally grown and raised meats and fish in a casual patio setting. ☎ 707-933-8160; www .harvestmoonsonoma.com; 487 First St W, Sonoma; mains $20-25; ☺ 5:30-9pm Sun-Thu, 5:30-9:30pm Fri & Sat; ♿

DRINK

Benziger Winery

Biodynamic, educational winery with red tractor–led tours. ☎ 707-935-3000, 888-490-2739; www.benziger.com; 1883 London Ranch Rd, Glen Ellen; tasting fee $5-10, tour $10; ☺ 11am-3:30pm

Ehlers Estate

"Ghost" winery from the 1880s; biodynamic and organic with all proceeds going to cardiovascular research. ☎ 707-963-5972; www.ehlersestate.com; 3222 Ehlers Lane, St Helena; tasting fee $20; ☺ 10am-4pm

Frog's Leap

Wine snobs aren't allowed at this fun, 100% organic winery. ☎ 800-959-4704, 707-963-4704; www.frogsleap.com; 8815 Conn Creek Rd, Rutherford; admission free; ☺ 10am-4pm Mon-Sat (reservations required by phone or email: ribbit@frogsleap.com)

Imagery Estate

An art-gallery winery with fascinating bottle-label artwork. ☎ 707-935-4515, 877-550-4278; www.imagerywinery.com; 14335 Sonoma Hwy, Glen Ellen; tasting fee $10; ☺ 10am-4:30pm Sun-Thu, 10am-5pm Fri & Sat

Madonna Estate
One hundred percent organically grown grapes. ☎ 707-255-8864, 866-724-2993; www.madonnaestate.com; 5400 Old Sonoma Rd, Napa; tasting fee $5; ⊗ 10am-5pm

Quintessa
Stellar high-end wines from vineyards protected by white owls and an insectory. ☎ 707-967-1601; www.quintessa.com; 1601 Silverado Trail, Rutherford; tasting fee $65; ⊗ 10am-4pm by appointment only

Robert Mondavi Winery
The giant of winemakers uses natural farming and conservation practices and recycles water and materials. ☎ 888-766-6328; www.robertmondaviwinery.com; 7801 St Helena Hwy, Oakville; tasting fee $15; ⊗ 10am-5pm

Robert Sinskey Vineyards
Two-thirds solar-powered and biodiesel-fueled, with hawk perches to keep the grapes safe. ☎ 707-944-9090; www.robertsinskey .com; 6320 Silverado Trail, Napa; tasting fee $10; ⊗ 10am-4:30pm

SLEEP

Beltane Ranch
Pretty yellow B&B sans TV and phone, with delectable gourmet breakfasts. ☎ 707-996-6501; www.beltaneranch.com; 11775 Sonoma Hwy, Glen Ellen; r $150-220

Bothe-Napa Valley State Park
Year-round campsites, a summer-only swimming pool and miles of trails through redwoods and to the historic Bale Grist Mill. ☎ 707-942-4575; www.parks.ca.gov; 3801 St Helena Hwy, Calistoga; campsites $20-25; ♿

Bungalows 313
Uniquely homey suites with little luxuries and their own secret vineyard walking path. ☎ 707-996-8091; www.bungalows313.com; 313 First St E, Sonoma; r Dec-Mar $160-250, Mar-Aug $219-319, Sep-Oct $239-339

Carneros Inn
Chic, luxe standalone cottages, truly away from it all. ☎ 707-299-4900, 888-400-9000; www.thecarnerosinn.com; 4048 Sonoma Hwy, Napa; r $480-655

El Dorado Hotel
Hip, stylish, minimalist hotel on the plaza built with recycled and reclaimed materials. ☎ 707-996-3220, 800-289-3031; www.eldo radohotel.com; 405 First St W, Sonoma; r Jan-Mar $155-175, Apr-Nov $175-195

USEFUL WEBSITES
www.71miles.com
www.farmtrails.org
www.sustainablesonoma.org

LINK YOUR TRIP

www.lonelyplanet.com/trip-planner

The Mission Trail

WHY GO Unravel strands of California's multicultural tapestry along the historic path of Spanish colonization, from San Diego north to Sonoma. This pilgrimage ties together the most fascinating of California's 21 historic missions, with atmospheric inns and eateries along the way. Travel in spring, when mission gardens are in bloom.

TIME
4 days

DISTANCE
650 miles

BEST TIME TO GO
Mar – May

START
San Diego

END
Sonoma

ALSO GOOD FOR

HISTORY & CULTURE

Traveling north, California's beautiful missions follow El Camino Real (The Royal Road), forged by Spanish conquistador Gaspar de Portolá in the late 18th century during his failed search for Monterey Bay. As the Spanish crown made inroads into the New World, more soldiers, missionaries and colonists followed. It took over 50 years for the chain of 21 missions to be established. Each was just a day's ride on horseback from the next, meant to strengthen Spanish, and later Mexican, command over the fruitful land – and its indigenous peoples.

The early mission system was envisioned as a way to convert Native Americans to the Christian faith, to teach them agricultural and trade skills, and eventually to establish thriving Spanish-style pueblos. But the plan failed: more Native Americans died than were converted, mostly from introduced European diseases, forced labor and ill treatment at the hands of the Spaniards. Many of the missions fell into disrepair after they were secularized by a newly independent Mexico starting in 1821. Restoration efforts beginning with the Civilian Conservation Corps (CCC) in the 1930s have brought new life to the missions, some of which are still active Catholic parishes. Try to attend a mass inside one of the historic chapels to get the full dramatic effect.

Let's start at the beginning. On July 1, 1769, a forlorn lot of about 100 missionaries and soldiers, led by military commander Gaspar de

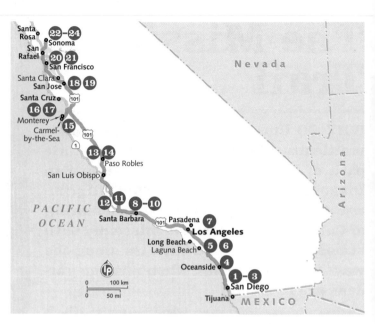

Portolá and Franciscan priest Junípero Serra, struggled ashore at San Diego Bay. After sailing for weeks up the coast from Baja California, a journey during which over half of the party died, many of the aspiring Spanish colonizers were sick and near death. It was a very inauspicious beginning for ❶ **Mission San Diego de Alcalá**, the oldest link in California's chain of missions. "The Mother of the Missions" was originally established at the Spanish presidio on a hill near the harbor, but was later moved inland in 1774. In an act of resistance to colonization, the indigenous Kumeyaay tribespeople burned the Catholic church to the ground and killed Luis Jayme, California's first Catholic martyr, still buried in the cemetery here. The attack did not deter Padre Serra, who rebuilt the mission using adobe walls and tiled roofs to make them fireproof. The mission's gardens today are filled with olive and avocado trees and boldly flowering bougainvillea.

Head west toward the ocean and summit of Presidio Hill to visit the ❷ **Serra Museum**. On the site of the colonists' original military fort, this modern Spanish-revival building is actually a 20th-century invention modeled after the early missions. Exhibits explore the Native American, mission and Mexican periods of San Diego history. Be sure to climb the tower for ocean views. A short drive downhill into the streets around Old Town takes you to ❸ **El Agave** restaurant. With nods to Spanish, Mexican and Hispanic cooking traditions, El Agave's proud mestizo menu is best known for its soulful mole sauces made with chilies and chocolate. Alongside this is a collection of 1200 types of tequila that will make cactus-juice connoisseurs swoon.

The first part of El Camino Real, which is marked throughout the state by free-standing bronze mission bells placed in the 1920s, follows I-5 north from San Diego. ❹ **Mission San Luis Rey de Francia** was one of the last missions established. It proclaims itself "The King of the Missions," not only because it was named after Louis IX of France, a fervent Catholic crusader, but also for its great size and wealth, which made it a much sought-after spoil following the Mexican revolution. Architecturally, this mission is one of the most beautiful you'll see, with its skillful execution of Spanish, Moorish and Mexican influences. Like many churches along the Mission Trail, San Luis Rey has been shaken by several earthquakes in the past, and has been rebuilt and restored many times over the centuries. The cruciform shape of its chapel is a unique feature among California's missions, shared only with Mission San Juan Capistrano.

If you have time for just one stop along the mission trail, pick ❺ **Mission San Juan Capistrano**. Rightfully calling itself "The Jewel of the California Missions," here archaeologists, engineers and restoration artists have done an exquisite job of keeping the mission alive. The Serra Chapel, where the padre celebrated mass in 1783, is considered California's oldest building; even the mighty San Andreas fault hasn't been able to topple it yet. Built around a series of arcades, the mission complex encloses bubbling fountains and gardens awash with monarch butterflies in winter. Every year on March 19, the city of San Juan Capistrano celebrates the Festival of the Swallows, when the birds return from their Argentine sojourn to make their nests in the walls of the mission, normally lingering until October 23. Touristy restaurants abound near the mission, but old ❻ **Señor Pedro's** *taquería* is the best for burritos, *sopes* (filled corn-dough bowls) and fried-chicken and veggie tacos.

ASK A LOCAL

"Stop by **Old Town State Historic Park** (www.parks .ca.gov) to see well-preserved buildings from the Spanish and early American periods of California history, and to get a true taste of Hispanic-American culture. One of the best things about Old Town is its resident ghost! There's an atmospheric, almost private cemetery behind the Whaley House Museum too."
Pam C, San Diego

Or hold off on eating altogether until you reach downtown LA and colorful ❼ **El Pueblo de Los Angeles Historical Monument**, where you can jostle with crowds down block-long Olvera St, stuffed with souvenir shops and Mexican-food vendors. Near the site of the City of Angels' founding in 1781, this historical monument delves into the multicultural heritage – Native American, European and African – of LA's early settlers. Peek inside historical buildings like the 1818 Avila Adobe, then unwind on the plaza in front of the wrought-iron bandstand, where mariachis often play on sunny weekend afternoons.

Take Hwy 101 up the coast to Santa Barbara. After a magnitude 6.3 earthquake hit this city in 1925, urban planners rebuilt downtown in a faux-Mediterranean style, with whitewashed adobe walls, red-tile roofs and strings of waving palm trees. State St, with its boutique shops, gourmet restaurants and student-driven bars, has remarkable architectural integrity, including the masterpiece of the **8 Santa Barbara County Courthouse**. Step inside its 2nd-floor Mural Room for an artistic take on California's Spanish colonial history, and climb the bell tower for arched panoramas of the Pacific and the Santa Ynez Mountains. A victim of the 1925 quake, **9 Mission Santa Barbara** calls itself "The Queen of the Missions." Standing in front of its imposing Doric facade, an homage to a chapel in ancient Rome, look at the twin bell towers atop the chapel, a unique feature that sets this mission apart. Founded in 1786 on the feast day of St Barbara, the mission has been continuously occupied by Franciscan priests, and so escaped Mexico's enforced policy of secularization. Back downtown, the Spanish-revival style **10 Inn of the Spanish Garden** harbors two dozen romantic rooms and suites, each with a balcony or patio overlooking a gracious fountain courtyard.

HOLY HARVEST

It wasn't until the late 18th century, when Spanish missionaries imported vines from the Old World, that the art of making wine took off in California. At the missions, wine was used for holy communion during mass and as an everyday table beverage. The first vintages emerged from Mission San Juan Capistrano in the 1780s. Although none of the missions still produce wine today, Napa Valley's Robert Mondavi Winery continues to harvest Mission, or Criolla, grapes.

In the Santa Ynez Valley, reached most scenically by rural Hwy 154 from Santa Barbara, **11 Mission Santa Inés** was established among the indigenous Chumash, who, although tolerant of the missionaries, carried out a revolt in 1824 against Spanish soldiers who had flogged one of their own. Today the historic Catholic mission is incongruously situated in the town of Solvang, founded by Danish protestant immigrants in 1911. Inside you'll find a typical collection of vestments, religious paintings and statuary, and artifacts from the early mission era. Out back a manicured garden in the shape of a Celtic cross is worth a wander. West of Hwy 101, drive through the hills past brilliantly colored commercial flower fields over to **12 La Purisma Mission State Historic Park**, an impressively restored complex that was resurrected by the CCC during the Depression. Here almost a dozen buildings have been restored to their original 1820s appearance, including soldiers' living quarters, a weaving room and a blacksmith's shop. Soak up the sunshine as you amble past grassy fields where cows, horses and goats graze.

The mission town of San Luis Obispo is a natural break in the journey. Although its mission is very modest, the bells are still rung in traditional patterns, pealing loudly around downtown. Chain motels line the highway north to Paso Robles. Next to Paso's town square, epicurean ⑬ **Villa Creek** is a wine-country restaurant that marries early Spanish-mission cooking traditions with sustainable and organic ingredients; envision shepherd's plates of artisan cheese, sausages and olives, and rancho-style cassoulet with duck. Afterward, steal yourself away among the vineyards at ⑭ **Wild Coyote Winery Bed & Breakfast**, where adobe-walled casitas echo the pueblos of the Southwest and a complimentary bottle of wine waits by the kiva (beehive-style) fireplace.

Once the domain of salt-of-the-earth artists and writers like Jack London, today Carmel-by-the-Sea is a wealthy enclave. Its gloriously restored ⑮ **Mission San Carlos Borromèo de Carmelo** is the final resting place of Padre Serra, who moved the mission here from Monterey in 1771. Long after Serra's death, the original adobe chapel was replaced with a beautiful basilica made of stone quarried in the Santa Lucia Mountains. It's a short hop north to the fishing bay of Monterey, once the capital of Alta California. Today its downtown district and wharf area protect the best-preserved collection of Spanish colonial and Mexican adobe buildings in California, all connected by the walkable "Path of History" through ⑯ **Monterey State Historic Park**. Pick up a self-guided tour brochure at the Pacific House Museum, which has fascinating historical exhibits worth an hour's browsing, including Native American cultural displays upstairs. When hunger strikes, seek out ⑰ **Wild Plum Cafe & Bakery**, with its bountiful egg breakfasts and deli-style lunches made even tastier with organic, local and sustainable produce; the ginormous apple pull-aparts and fresh-baked muffins sell out fast.

> "…unknowingly built directly atop the San Andreas Fault, the mission has been rocked by earthquakes."

Named for St John the Baptist, ⑱ **Mission San Juan Bautista** has the largest church of all of California's missions. Because it was unknowingly built directly atop the San Andreas Fault, the mission has been rocked by earthquakes. Here the padres taught Ohlone tribespeople to play European musical instruments using a color-coded system of musical notation. Bells hanging in the tower today include chimes that were salvaged after the 1906 San Francisco earthquake toppled the original mission. Parts of Alfred Hitchcock's thriller *Vertigo* were shot here, although the bell tower in the final scene was just a special-effects prop, sorry. Around the mission, the dusty, frontier town of San Juan Bautista is crowded with Mexican restaurants and antique shops. At ⑲ **San Juan Bakery**, pick up fresh loaves of cinnamon and banana-nut bread to sustain you during the drive north to San Francisco.

Named for St Francis of Assisi, **20 Mission San Francisco de Asís** is known locally as Mission Dolores, after the nearby Arroyo de los Dolores ("Creek of Sorrows"). The adobe-walled chapel with its shimmering gold altar and redwood beams decorated with Native American artwork is the only intact original mission chapel in California, having stood firm in the 1906 earthquake. The graveyard out back, where Kim Novak wandered around looking hypnotized in *Vertigo,* might seem small, but 5000 Ohlone and Miwok who died in measles epidemics are said to be buried there, along with early Mexican and European settlers. Today Mission Dolores anchors the Mission district, a bohemian SF neighborhood of colorful murals, where traditional Mexican *taquerías* mix with cutting-edge hipster hangouts. Ask locals which place makes the best burrito, then as their impassioned debate heats up, slip away to **21 El Toro**, a corner shop with a fast-and-furious assembly line churning out custom-made Mission-style burritos, each big enough to feed two. Look for the iconic black bull sign outside.

Cross over the Golden Gate Bridge and into the vineyards of Sonoma County. The gentrified town of Sonoma is not only the site of the last Spanish mission established in California. It also happens to be the place where European settlers declared independence from Mexico in 1846 when they raised the famous Bear Flag over the plaza. Presiding over the northwest corner of the square, the 1880s **22 Sonoma Hotel** has demure elegance that evokes past centuries without being chintzy. The hotel's quietest aeries face away from the street. Downstairs, **23 the girl & the fig** is a little Provençal-inspired bistro held in high esteem for its seasonal soups and salads, country-style game and seafood dishes, and aromatic "salon de fromage" (cheese-tasting cart). Tomorrow morning, walk down the block to Mission San Francisco Solano, part of **24 Sonoma State Historic Park**, which includes military barracks and an old Mexican general's home. The petite mission itself contains five original rooms, and incidentally was formerly owned by newspaper magnate William Randolph Hearst. It's also the finish line for El Camino Real.

Sara Benson

> **DETOUR** If you don't mind snarled freeway traffic, there are two hidden missions in the Bay Area worth finding. On the Santa Clara University campus, decorous **Mission Santa Clara de Asís** (500 El Camino Real, Santa Clara), open from sunrise to sunset, has an original 18th-century wooden cross standing outside. East of the bay, **Mission San José** (www.missionsanjose.org), in Fremont, is an awesome reproduction of the 1809 original, with a fascinating and eerie graveyard out back.

TRIP INFORMATION

GETTING THERE
From Los Angeles, take I-5 south to San Diego.

DO

El Pueblo de Los Angeles Historical Monument
Touch living history in Downtown LA, then plunge into the open-air marketplace of Olvera St. ☎ 213-628-1274; www.lacity.org /elp; Olvera St, off Hwy 101, exit Alameda St, Los Angeles; admission free; ☼ visitor center 9am-4pm Mon-Fri, Olvera St restaurants & shops 10am-8pm daily; ♿ ⊛

La Purisma Mission State Historic Park
Guided interpretive walks are given at 1pm daily. ☎ 805-733-3713; www.parks.ca.gov; 2295 Purisma Rd, Lompoc; admission $4; ☼ 9am-5pm

Mission San Carlos Borromèo de Carmelo
A jewel-like mission worth going out of your way for; it's also Junípero Serra's burial site. ☎ 831-624-3600; www.carmelmission.org; 3080 Rio Rd, Carmel; adult/child $5/1, guided tour $7; ☼ 9:30am-5pm Mon-Sat, 10:30am-5pm Sun

Mission San Diego de Alcalá
Start walking in Serra's footsteps at California's first mission, overlooking San Diego's Mission Valley. ☎ 619-281-8449; www .missionsandiego.com; 10818 San Diego Mission Rd, San Diego; adult/child $3/2; ☼ 9am-4:45pm

Mission San Francisco de Asís
Time seems to stand still here, in the frenetic heart of San Francisco. ☎ 415-621-8203; www.missiondolores.org; 3321 16th St, San Francisco; adult/child $5/free; ☼ 9am-4:30pm May-Oct, 9am-4pm Nov-Apr

Mission San Juan Bautista
Just across the plaza from the old stables, hotel and houses of San Juan Bautista State Historic Park. ☎ 831-623-4528; www.old missionsjb.org; 406 2nd St, San Juan Bautista; adult/child $4/2; ☼ 9:30am-4:30pm; ♿

Mission San Juan Capistrano
Snippets of oral history on the audio tour vividly bring the old mission to life. ☎ 949-234-1300; www.missionsjc.com; 26801 Ortega Hwy, San Juan Capistrano; adult/child $9/5; ☼ 8:30am-5pm; ♿

Mission San Luis Rey de Francia
Avoid visiting on Saturday, when weddings often close the church. ☎ 760-757-3651; www.sanluisrey.org; 4050 Mission Ave, Oceanside; adult/child $6/4; ☼ 10am-4pm

Mission Santa Barbara
See beautiful cloisters, artwork done by Chumash tribespeople, and a centuries-old cemetery. ☎ 805-682-4713; www.sbmission .org; 2201 Laguna St, Santa Barbara; adult/ child $5/1; ☼ 9am-5pm

Mission Santa Inés
Escape the madness of kitschy Danish-themed Solvang at this quiet mission. ☎ 805-688-4815; www.missionsantaines.org; 1760 Mission Dr, Solvang; adult/child $4/free; ☼ 9am-4:30pm

Monterey State Historic Park
Call ahead for schedules of free walking tours of the historic houses and gardens. ☎ 831-649-7118; www.parks.ca.gov; visitor center, 20 Custom House Plaza, Monterey; admission free; ☼ visitor center 10am-4pm Sat-Thu, 10:30am-4pm Fri; ♿

Santa Barbara County Courthouse
Join a docent-led tour at 2pm Monday to Saturday or 10:30am Monday, Tuesday and Friday. ☎ 805-962-6464; www.santabarbara courthouse.org; 1100 Anacapa St, Santa Barbara; admission free; ☼ 8am-5pm Mon-Fri, 10am-5pm Sat & Sun, tower closes 15min earlier

Serra Museum
Peaceful hilltop museum narrates Native Americans' struggles with mission life. ☎ 619-297-3258; www.sandiegohistory .org; 2727 Presidio Dr, San Diego; adult/ child $5/2; ☼ 10am-4:30pm Jun-Aug,

11am-3pm Mon-Fri & 10am-4:30pm Sat &
Sun Sep-May; ♿

Sonoma State Historic Park
Guided mission tours are available four
times daily on Friday, Saturday and Sunday.
☎ 707-938-9560; www.parks.ca.gov;
mission 20 E Spain St, Sonoma; adult/child
$2/free; ⏱ 10am-5pm; ♿

EAT
El Agave
An upmarket, downtown Mexican restaurant
for the culinary cognoscenti. ☎ 619-220-
0692; www.elagave.signonsandiego.com;
2304 San Diego Ave, San Diego; mains $12-
30; ⏱ 11am-10pm

El Toro
A smattering of Spanish will help you concoct
the perfect burrito, with dozens of filling
choices. ☎ 415-431-3351; 598 Valencia St,
San Francisco; mains $2-10; ⏱ 10am-10pm

San Juan Bakery
Treats at this beloved bakery often sell out
early in the day. ☎ 831-623-4570; 319
3rd St, San Juan Bautista; mains $2-4;
⏱ 7:30am-5pm; ♿

Señor Pedro's
Devour generously portioned Mexican takeout outdoors at picnic tables with mission
views. ☎ 949-489-7752; 31721 Camino
Capistrano, San Juan Capistrano; mains $3-6;
⏱ 10am-8pm; ♿ ⚄

the girl & the fig
A five-star wine list is not the only prize at
this Cal-French bistro; reservations advised
for dinner. ☎ 707-938-3634; www.thegirl
andthefig.com; 110 W Spain St, Sonoma;

mains $12-25; ⏱ 11:30am-10pm Mon-Thu,
11:30am-11pm Fri & Sat, 10am-10pm Sun

Villa Creek
Spanish-influenced sustainable California
cuisine soars alongside rich red wine flights;
reservations recommended. ☎ 805-238-
3000; www.villacreek.com; 1144 Pine St,
Paso Robles; mains $20-40; ⏱ 5:30-10pm

Wild Plum Cafe & Bakery
Simple sidewalk café with an eco-conscious
kitchen churning out seasonal goodness.
☎ 831-646-3109; 731 Munras Ave, Monterey;
mains $6-11; ⏱ 7am-6:30pm Tue-Fri, 7am-
5pm Mon & Sat; ♿

SLEEP
Inn of the Spanish Garden
A luxury boutique hotel heralding the deca-
dence of the Spanish colonial era. ☎ 805-
564-4700, 866-564-4700; www.spanish
gardeninn.com; 915 Garden St, Santa
Barbara; r $259-519

Sonoma Hotel
Sixteen tasteful rooms and petite suites,
some with iron bed frames and claw-foot
bathtubs, complete this historic inn. ☎ 707-
996-2996, 800-468-6016; www.sonomaho
tel.com; 110 W Spain St, Sonoma; r $100-250

Wild Coyote Winery Bed & Breakfast
A romantic retreat among the rolling hills of
the Paso Robles wine country. ☎ 805-610-
1311; www.wildcoyote.biz; 3775 Adelaida
Rd, Paso Robles; r $225-275

USEFUL WEBSITES
http://missionsofcalifornia.org
www.parks.ca.gov

LINK YOUR TRIP
www.lonelyplanet.com/trip-planner

ICONIC
TRIPS

A Burrito Odyssey

WHY GO No food in the Golden State commands as much devotion and stirs as much controversy as the humble, unofficial food of the region: the burrito. Two expert bloggers, Charles Hodgkins and Andy O'Neill, guide us through variations of California's hand-held Mexican delights from north to south.

TIME
3 – 4 days

DISTANCE
515 miles

BEST TIME TO GO
Year-round

START
San Francisco

END
San Diego

ALSO GOOD FOR

FOOD & DRINK

The sensation is instantaneous: the perfect texture, temperature and flavor, an ideal blend of spices and ingredients. When it's just right, this is no mere burrito, no mere tubular construction of tortilla-encased bean, of meat and salsa, of vegetables raw or grilled, of rice or no rice, or even of french-fried potato. No, no. This is heaven.

Juan Mendez, an enterprising burro-riding bit player in the Mexican Revolution, first served the burrito – a tortilla-encased meal, whose name literally translates to "little donkey" – in the early 20th century. But Californians took the hand-held delicacy and ran with it. Intricately distinct regional styles spread north, with varieties that developed cultish admirers, each following a variation on Mendez' theme. Burritos in San Francisco's Mission district had meat and rice added; in San Diego the specialty included seafood or french fries. Other parts of the country may have their signature dishes – Chicago with its loaded hot dogs and New York City with its bagels – but California's favorite dish is something as complex and diverse as the folks that have made it the state's unofficial lunch.

Hefting a breakfast burrito at San Francisco's ❶ **Taqueria Castillito** starts the trip with a display of the burrito's evolved variety – the savory mess of cheese, chorizo and egg makes Taco Bell seem unfit for the dog. Lunch and dinner staples, like the sweetly caramelized el pastor pork and *pollo en salsa roja* earn equal raves. Castillito ain't the

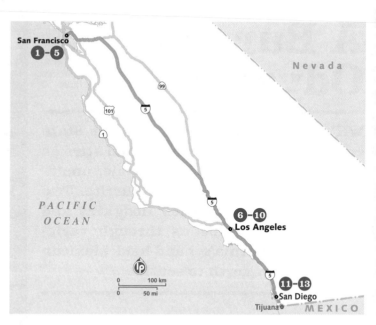

Ritz; it's brightly lit and clean enough (though probably not if you look too close) but the burritos here are some of San Francisco's best. It's just a few blocks south of what Charles Hodgkins, burrito expert and author of Burritoeater.com, calls "the miracle mile of San Francisco burritos" – a stretch of 24th St between Potrero Ave and Valencia St that is jammed with *taquerias* on almost every corner. "The belt-busting burritos here are often among San Francisco's finest," Hodgkins says. "No *taqueria* works more magic with grilled tortillas and melted cheese."

It's difficult to pin Hodgkins down on his favorite San Francisco burrito shop. He speaks as rhapsodically about the grilled steak at a taco stand behind a car wash as he does about the smoky mole sauce in the outer reaches of the city. A well-studied fan of music, his most fervent analogy comes when he tries to equate San Francisco *taquerias* to bands of the British invasion. His advice is to walk one block south from Castillito to the corner of Mission and 24th, and arrive at the crossroads of San Francisco's great *taquerias*.

For lunch, hit up ❷ **Taqueria San Francisco** for the perfect construction of the "San Francisco style" burrito which, in addition to the traditional blend of meat and beans, includes rice. Burrito purists from other parts of the state may well decry the extra starch, but the stylistic twist of the San Francisco burrito went global thanks to the comparatively bland Chipotle chain. Hodgkins calls Taqueria San Francisco "as quintessential as its name implies." It does the city's namesake burrito right: the carne asada super burrito is a perfect mix of ingredients, tightly wrapped in a slightly flaky, grilled tortilla.

If Taqueria San Francisco is too crowded, take a few strides south on Mission to ❸ **Taqueria El Farolito**. It's a narrow little storefront where a vegetarian burrito might include a misplaced chunk of pork, but many claim the humble joint is the best of the best (granted, judging by the late-night patrons, it might be liquor talking). Hodgkins lauds the decor – helped by a faux-cubist depiction of a pork rotisserie, and deafening Latino power ballads on the jukebox – and the consistently fine burritos. Wash them down with the neighborhood's best *agua fresca,* being sure to try the cantaloupe-flavored variety.

"It does the city's namesake burrito right: the carne asada super burrito is a perfect mix of ingredients..."

San Francisco's organic culinary bent is infused with the burrito tradition just a short walk up 24th St (at Valencia) at ❹ **Papalote**. Small and immaculate, this neighborhood favorite is more upscale, with organic meats and local art on display. "The Cal-Mex menu is built to make everyone happy," Hodgkins says. "Top-shelf grilled meats, exceptional vegetarian and vegan options, Mexican beverages galore and San Francisco's most delicious salsa." Papalote's salsa is so addictive that a national food magazine had it sent to a laboratory to deconstruct its ingredients. Here, vegetarian diners are more than an afterthought.

Any burrito-based exploration of the neighborhood will take time, so if you need another day, crash at ❺ **Elements Hotel** (part hostel, part budget hotel), with stylish, clean, minimalist rooms and efficient service.

Had enough of San Francisco's ricey burritos and foggy skies? Head east on I-80 for an hour and a half until you hit I-5 south. Drive five hours through the central valley before coming upon the bright lights of Los Angeles. Head east on Hwy 101 and check in Downtown at the ❻ **Figueroa Hotel**, with its bougainvillea- and cactus-laden poolside garden, Moroccan-themed rooms and Veranda Bar. Spend some time tootling around ❼ **El Pueblo de Los Angeles**, a car-free historic district with buildings dating back to the city's days as a dusty, lawless outpost. Walk along Olvera St and shop for Chicano art, slurp thick Mexican-style hot chocolate or pick up handmade candles and candy. At lunchtime, construction workers and cubicle slaves swarm the little eateries for tacos, tortas (sandwiches) and burritos.

Though more regarded as a "taco town," LA keeps a mobile homage to Mendez by serving burritos from trucks that either park in regular spots or rove East LA after dark.

Andy O'Neill, a blogger who obsesses about Los Angeles taco trucks at www .tacohunt.blogspot.com, says all you have to do to find a good taco truck is look for the one with the biggest crowds. "The locals know which truck has the best tacos," he says. "Look for people standing around eating their tacos. If the tacos are really good you won't see a lot of people taking them to go. They'll eat them right there on the street so they can go back for more."

O'Neil says that the best tacos are in East LA because there's more competition and the trucks have to be on their game to compete. "A bad taco truck can't survive on the eastside; it's the major leagues," he says. "There's a stretch of **8** **Olympic Blvd** in East LA that's referred to as LA's taco mecca among the taco faithful. The boulevard is lined with taco trucks that are at the top of their game."

CALIFORNIA BURRITO DECODER

Decoding the origin of California's handheld favorite can be done in a single bite. The San Francisco burrito originated in the Mission district in the '60s; they're stuffed with rice, meat, salsa and optional black beans. Though Los Angeles is more of a taco town, you can tell an Angeleno's favorite burrito by its weight; this is where the "burritos as big as your head" thing started. The California burrito is a drunkard's delight: the classic variation has grilled steak, sour cream and french fries.

The *carnitas* burritos from El Diablo, a stand in the back of the **9** **Alameda Swap Meet**, are killer. They come filled with moist, smoky slow-cooked pork and are sided with fresh salsa verde. Dessert comes by wandering the surrounding market – a sure bet for cinnamon-coated, kettle-fresh churros, which soak through their brown paper bags. Housed in a brightly painted building, and cluttered with candy, fresh produce and piñatas, it demands a few hours of attention. On some weekends the market even hosts Mexican wrestling matches.

Five minutes north on Alameda you'll cross I-101. Take a left on Cesar Chavez and another on N Evergreen St. After a few blocks, look for the line snaking out the door of **10** **El Tepeyac Café**, Los Angeles' most revered burrito shop. At El Tepeyac, bigger equals better – those with restrictive medical conditions shouldn't even attempt hefting one of the gargantuan stuffed beasts. The steak is the crowd favorite, and stays true to Mendez' original intent for the burrito – feeding an army.

It's getting late; time to head south on I-5 to San Diego, the final destination of the odyssey. Just past Del Mar, take I-805 into the heart of the city. Drive 12 miles and take the exit for El Cajon Blvd, turning right on Park to arrive at the city's unmatched **11** **El Zarape**, where the burritos come stuffed with fresh seafood. The calamari, salmon and scallop varieties are delicious, but nothing tops the lobster burrito, which comes dressed in a rich white sauce. They also offer soy burritos and beer, catering to the nearby population of college

ICONIC
TRIPS

students. Of San Diego's more innovative burrito ingredients, it's the french fries that are a key ingredient in the boldly, contentiously named "California Burrito," for which the city is famous. Naturally, this tastes best with a belly full of beer, so negotiate the designated driver before you head back to I-5. Take exit 21 to Sea World Dr, which turns into Sunset Cliffs Blvd.

Turn right on Newport and head to the beach, where you can belly up to the ⑫ **South Beach Bar & Grill**. It's not the burritos that are the draw, it's the happy hour, which starts with $1 pints at 11am and gets incrementally more expensive (and rowdy) throughout the day. The view of the surf and laid-back vibe introduce San Diego's oceanside community. If you get hungry, go for the crispy, cabbage-dressed Baja Fish or grilled Mahi tacos, or wander through the neighborhood for some fresh seafood.

DETOUR For *muy authentica* Mexican food, head south of the border to Tijuana, Mexico. From San Diego, just hop on I-5 for 45 minutes, park your car and walk across the border into the Zona Norte, where taco stands hock stuff that's fresher and fattier than most north-of-the-border proxies. Jump on a bus to Zona Rio where **Carnitas Uruapán** offers the house namesake (spit-roasted pork), which is so tender, smoky and perfectly spiced, that you may never return stateside.

The perfect thing to right the ship after an afternoon of drinking comes from ⑬ **Lolita's Taco Shop**. Don't stray from the house special – a legendary California Burrito, which will quickly straighten up the overly indulgent bar hounds with its stuffing of broiled steak, salsa, sour cream and french fries. It's a greasy, gargantuan mess, the evolution of which is nearly impossible to imagine from the little donkey stand that Mendez began a century ago. At Lolita's the fries are crispy and the blend of ingredients is just perfect. As you sink your teeth into it, it might seem like the trip ends in heaven.

Nate Cavalieri

TRIP INFORMATION

GETTING THERE
Begin in the Mission District of San Francisco, and follow I-5 to California's two other burrito capitals: Los Angeles and San Diego.

DO
Alameda Swap Meet
Filled with fresh produce, cheapie toys and fresh-fried churros, this is in the heart of taco-truck central. ☎ 323-233-2764; 4501 S Alameda St, Los Angeles; admission free; ⏲ 10am-7pm Mon-Fri; 9am-7pm Sat & Sun; ♿

EAT & DRINK
El Tepeyac Café
This might have been where the whole "burritos as big as your head" thing started. ☎ 323-267-8668; 812 N Evergreen Ave, Los Angeles; mains $4-12; ⏲ 6am-9:45pm

El Zarape
Fresh seafood – including lobster and scallops – stuffs the burritos here. ☎ 619-692-1652; www.elzarape.com; 4642 Park Blvd, San Diego; mains $4-12; ⏲ 6am-9:45pm

Lolita's Taco Shop
Greasy and heavenly, this is a great stop for a french fry–filled burrito. ☎ 858-874-7983; 7305 Clairemont Mesa Blvd Ste A, San Diego; mains $3-12; ⏲ 10am-9pm

Papalote
The classiest of San Francisco's burrito shops, with colorful art and a mystifying house salsa. ☎ 415-970-8815; www.papalote-sf.com; 3409 24th St, San Francisco; mains $5-12; ⏲ 11am-10pm Mon-Sat, 11am-9pm Sun; ♿

South Beach Bar & Grill
A killer happy hour gets you ready for the California Burrito. ☎ 619-226-4577; www.southbeachob.com; 5059 Newport Ave, Ocean Beach; mains $6-12; ⏲ 11am-2am

Taqueria Castillito
It might be a little rough around the edges, but the impeccable tubes at Castillito are short-listed among San Francisco's best. ☎ 415-621-6971; 2092 Mission St, San Francisco; mains $3-15; ⏲ 10am-2am; ♿

Taqueria El Farolito
The late-night scene at this tiny Mission juggernaut can get pretty wild. ☎ 415-826-4870; 2779 Mission St, San Francisco; mains $3-10; ⏲ 10am-2:45am Sun-Thu, 10am-4am Fri-Sat

Taqueria San Francisco
From their smoky, spicy chorizo to the super carne asada burrito, they make savory masterpieces. ☎ 415-641-1770; 2794 24th St, San Francisco; mains $3-10; ⏲ 10am-9:30pm; ♿

SLEEP
Elements Hotel
Part sleek hotel, part hostel, this is in *taquería* central. ☎ 415-440-1125; 2524 Mission St, San Francisco; r $25-70

Figueroa Hotel
Locals mingle at the bar at this Moroccan-themed hotel. ☎ 213-627-8971; www.figueroahotel.com; 939 S Figueroa St, Los Angeles; r $140-180

USEFUL WEBSITES
www.burritoeater.com
www.tacohunt.blogspot.com

LINK YOUR TRIP
www.lonelyplanet.com/trip-planner

TRIP
41 Dusty Trails on Highway 99 p259

NORTHERN CALIFORNIA TRIPS

San Francisco is the anchor of California's most diverse region, even if earthquakes have shown it isn't rock solid. From hiking the secluded trails of the Lost Coast to floating down the isolated bends of the Russian River, from poking around (and through) the redwoods to surmounting volcano summits, there's no shortage of natural places to explore. And sure there's the iconic Napa Valley for food and wine, but you can also sip equally impressive vintages in Alexander Valley and Livermore, try surprising microbrews in places that seem perfectly brewed themselves, like Boonville and Fort Bragg, pick apples in Sebastopol or go organic in Bodega Bay. Some might say such notions are for the birds...and they could be right. Alfred Hitchcock – and many other directors – have found ideal locations in San Francisco (*Vertigo*) and beyond (*The Birds* was shot in Bodega Bay). Search for your own ideal location, whether it be around Big Sur, Santa Cruz or high in the Sierras at Lake Tahoe.

PLAYLIST From Otis Redding's dock, to Tony Bennett's heart, to Jefferson Airplane's rabbit, Northern California has been a huge inspiration for music. Let these tunes inspire you down the road.

- "(Sittin' on) The Dock of the Bay," Otis Redding
- "Darkstar," Grateful Dead
- "Everyday People," Sly & The Family Stone
- "I Left My Heart In San Francisco," Tony Bennett
- "White Rabbit," Jefferson Airplane
- "Yay Area," E-40
- "The Book of Right-On," Joanna Newsom
- "Longview," Green Day

NORTHERN CALIFORNIA'S BEST TRIPS

NORTHERN CALIFORNIA TRIPS

48 Hours in San Francisco

WHY GO Flower power, Beatniks, blue jeans, biotech...what will SF dream up next? Get to know the world capital of weird inside out, from mural-lined alleyways named for poets to hilltop parks where wild parrots curse their hellos. Ditch your car, come as you are, and find your niche in San Francisco.

Snow globe of a city that it is, San Francisco is small, easy to grasp and likes nothing better than shaking things up and getting coated with glitter. In two days you can do up this 7 x 7-mile city, mingle with pirates and graffiti artists, shop with drag queens and brunch amid top chefs in a working kitchen.

San Francisco slackers have the right idea at the Ferry Building, the transport hub turned gourmet emporium where no one's in a hurry to get anywhere. Why rush when you can linger over poached eggs with local Dungeness crab and sesame oil, watching chefs prep the evening meal at ❶ **Boulette's Larder**? Once you're good and ready you can roll up the waterfront Embarcadero to Union St, where you'll cross the plaza named for the local entrepreneur without whom the city would be permanently half-naked: Levi Strauss.

Passing pet rocks and Zen gardens, head up Filbert St Steps. You'll know you're getting close to the top of Telegraph Hill (named for San Francisco's proto-internet invention) when you start getting heckled by the flock of trash-talking wild parrots who have taken over the tree-tops. Finally you'll reach ❷ **Coit Tower**, with wall-to-wall 1930s murals honoring San Francisco workers, which were almost painted over during the communist-baiting McCarthy era. The tower is capped by 360-degree top-floor panoramas revealing the Golden Gate Bridge in all its glory.

TIME
2 days

BEST TIME TO GO
Sep – Nov

START
Ferry Building

END
Castro Theatre

BEST TRIP

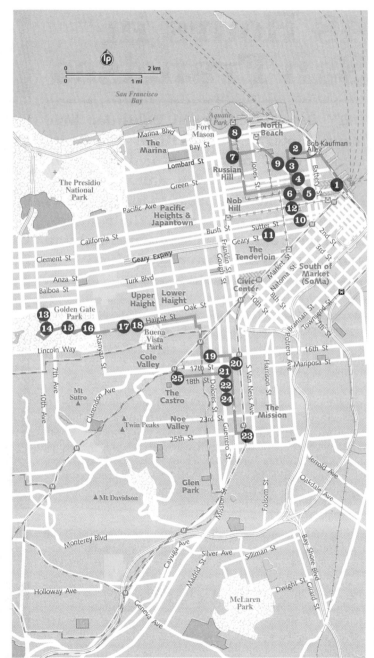

Downhill from Telegraph along Greenwich and Grant is North Beach, the Italian neighborhood where the US Navy dumped insubordinate sailors during WWII. It became a magnet for 1950s rebels: jazz musicians, civil rights agitators, topless dancers, Beat poets and dharma bums. One individual who defied all categories and conventions now has a street named after him: Bob Kaufman, the bebop-jazz-poet-voodoo-anarchist-Jewish-biracial-African-all-American-street-corner-prophet.

On Grant St you'll pass Boho boutiques and bars on your way to ❸ **Caffe Trieste**, the legendary Beat poet hangout with opera on the jukebox and accordion jam sessions on weekends. Throw back an espresso to power you two blocks to Columbus and the landmark ❹ **City Lights** bookstore, which fought charges of "willfully and lewdly" publishing Allen Ginsberg's epic *Howl and Other Poems* in 1957 and won a ground-breaking court ruling against book banning. Celebrate your freedom to read willfully and lewdly in the upstairs poetry section or downstairs in free-form non-fiction sections dedicated to Muckracking and Stolen Continents.

Turn right out the door to Jack Kerouac Alley, the mural-covered byway named for the *On the Road* author, with his thoughts on San Francisco embedded in the sidewalk: "The air was soft, the stars so fine, and the promise of every cobbled alley so great..." Walk across the pavement poetry to Chinatown's Grant St, where phone booths are topped with tiled pagodas and the smoky-rich aroma of roast duck wafts out deli doors. Hungry yet? Follow Grant past souvenir shops packed with butterfly kites and chirping toy crickets, turn left onto Clay St, with its fierce chess games in progress in Portsmouth Sq, and turn right one block south to Commercial St. In the

DETOUR Duck into the Bob Kaufman Alley in North Beach and enjoy a moment of profound silence in tribute to the poet who refused to speak for 12 years, beginning at the assassination of John F Kennedy. On the day the Vietnam War ended, he walked into a café and recited "All Those Ships That Never Sailed": "Today I bring them back/Huge and transitory/And let them sail/Forever."

19th century, this was one of the most notorious brothel byways in the Wild West, conveniently located close to waterfront saloons and bawdy Jenny Lind Theater, which with a few modifications became San Francisco's first City Hall. Today the greatest temptations on this block are the dim sum (dumplings) at ❺ **City View**, where servers narrowly avoid collisions between trolleys loaded with fragrant bamboo steamers during the lunch rush.

Indulge at your leisure, then walk one flat block down Kearny and one very steep block up Sacramento St to Waverly Pl, where prayer flags flap and incense wafts from 4th-floor temple balconies. When Chinatown crumbled and burned in the 1906 earthquake and fire, residents fled for their lives, and opportunistic real estate speculators urged City Hall to relocate Chinatown south of the city. But even before the smoke had cleared, Chinatown residents returned to pray in these temples, and if you visit **6 Tien Hou Temple** you can see the charred altar that has become a symbol of community endurance against the odds.

Revolution is only a block away, left on Clay St and right on Spofford Alley, where Sun Yat-sen plotted the overthrow of China's last emperor. The 1920s brought bootleggers and gun battles, but Spofford has mellowed with age, and in the evenings you'll hear the shuffling of tiles as octogenarians plot winning mah-jongg moves and an *erhu* (two-stringed Chinese fiddle) warms up with a plain-tive note. Head right on Jackson half a block and left onto Ross, where color-ful murals mark the entry to a street with a colorful history. SF's oldest alley was formerly known as Manila, Span-ish and Mexico Street after the origins of the women who once worked this block – until the 1906 fire tore through the alley, trapping the women and their clients behind locked bordello doors.

PLAYLIST Eclectic doesn't begin to describe San Francisco's music scene, or the unlikely hits local bands have produced. Listen for yourself and, for the ultimate SF DJ challenge, try mashing them up into one freakified song…

- "Take Five," Dave Brubeck
- "Sugar Magnolia," Grateful Dead
- "California Uber Alles," Dead Kennedys
- "San Francisco Anthem," San Quinn
- "Enter Sandman," Metallica
- "Lights," Journey
- "Me and Bobby McGee," Janis Joplin
- "Thank You (Falletinme Be Mice Elf Agin)," Sly and the Family Stone

On Jackson and Powell you can catch the Powell–Hyde cable car, which is not equipped with seat belts or air bags – for safety you just grab a leather strap and pray. You'll notice these vintage trolleys emit mechanical grunts on uphill climbs, and require burly brakemen and bionic brake-women to keep from careening down Russian Hill – for a city of risk takers, this is the perfect joyride. Leap on for a rickety ride uphill to **7 Sterling Park**, named for San Francisco's "King of Bohemia," poet and 1920s free-love advocate George Sterling, who loved verse, women, men, nature, opium and San Francisco, though not necessarily in that order. The Golden Gate Bridge and Pacific stretch past the wind-sculpted pines in this hilltop park and anyone not moved to poetry by sunsets here must've already left a heart elsewhere in San Francisco.

To keep the romance going, head downhill and splash out for dinner with a view at **8 Gary Danko**, winner of multiple James Beard awards and inventor of tasting menus San Francisco foodies swear are the culinary equivalent of Via-gra. For crowd-pleasing, family-friendly fare, head down zigzagging Lombard to Columbus and walk four blocks to **9 Cinecittá Pizzeria** for the capricciosa, loaded with artichoke hearts, prosciutto, olives, fresh mozzarella and an egg.

The next morning while the fog's still clearing, take public transit from your downtown digs at funky artist-decorated ❿ **Hotel des Arts**, designer-fabulous ⓫ **Hotel Adagio** or certified green ⓬ **Orchard Garden Hotel** to the ⓭ **MH de Young Memorial Museum** in Golden Gate Park (best options: N Judah streetcar or bus 71 from Powell and Market). Follow Andy Goldsworthy's simulated sidewalk earthquake cracks into the museum, which celebrates artists from Oceania to California. Blockbuster temporary shows range from Hiroshi Sugimoto's haunting time-lapse photographs of drive-ins to Dale Chihuly's bombastic glass sculpture. Access to the tower is free; catch the elevator by Ruth Asawa's mesmerizing meshwork sculptures, which dangle from the ceiling and cast psychedelic shadows around the gallery.

The copper-clad de Young is a shy landmark that's just trying to blend in – architects Herzog & de Meuron (of Tate Modern fame) treated the copper exterior to oxidized green to match the park. Across the plaza, Pritzker Prize–winning architect Renzo Piano has taken camouflage to the next level, capping the ⓮ **California Academy of Sciences** with a "living roof" of California wildflowers. The Academy houses 38,000 weird and wonderful animals in custom habitats: a white alligator stalks the swamp, butterflies flutter through the four-story rainforest dome, and balding Pierre the Penguin paddles his massive new tank in a custom-made wetsuit (shhh, don't mention the molting; he's sensitive).

> **ASK A LOCAL**
>
> "Movies in San Francisco are a spectator sport. San Francisco crowds don't realize the movie is not about them – audiences will hiss, yell and backtalk at the screen like it's going to change the ending. We have the best audiences in the world, period."
>
> *Peaches Christ, drag diva and San Francisco movie maven*

Stroll through the redwoods of the ⓯ **National AIDS Memorial Grove**, where volunteers have brought life back to a forgotten corner of the Golden Gate Park and created a haven of peace. Emerge in ⓰ **Sharon Meadow**, better known as the site of the Summer of Love. Spelunk through the faux-cavern tunnel to Haight St, where the parade of nonconformists has continued for 40 years.

Browse your way along five blocks of skate shops and tattoo parlors to the Victorian storefront with fishnet-clad legs kicking out the window. This is ⓱ **Piedmont**, the legendary drag supply store where counter staff call everyone "baby doll" and no one obeys the sign that reads: "No Playing in the Boas."

All that glamour is bound to make you hungry and possibly in need of a drink and, right across the street, ⓲ **Magnolia Brewpub** obliges. Make yourself at home at the communal table, consult your neighbors on the all-local, organic menu (bet they'll recommend the Prather Ranch burger) and work your way through the beer sampler. You may have to peel yourself off your chair

CITY

to continue your long, strange trip down Haight St, past flamboyant gilded Victorians, windswept Buena Vista Park and painfully punning storefronts: Haight Mail, Love & Haight, Lower Haighter.

Pass the medicinal marijuana club (sorry dude, 30-day waiting period), hang a right on Steiner and an immediate left onto Victorian-lined Laussat, which includes a Rasta house painted red, gold and green. Turn right on Fillmore, walk 2.5 blocks to Hermann, go left and walk two blocks to Church. Follow Church four blocks south across Market to 16th street and turn right – you'll see the spectacular cake-frosting churrigueresque towers of **19 Mission Dolores**. Duck inside to peek at spectacular stained-glass windows depicting California's 21 missions and San Francisco's gentle namesake saint, and pay respects to the native Miwok and Ohlone who built this mission at the memorial hut.

The Mission District has more than 250 murals hidden on side streets, and two blocks up on Valencia between 17th and 18th St is San Francisco's best open-air graffiti art gallery, **20 Clarion Alley**. Only the strong murals survive here: anything that fails to inspire gets peed on or painted over. Half a block further down Valencia, you'll spot San Francisco's biggest mural, **21 Maestrapiece**, a show of female strength that wraps around the trailblazing Women's Building.

Comic-artist Chris Ware's mural marks **22 826 Valencia**, the non-profit youth writing program and purveyor of pirate supplies. Pick up eye patches, tubs of lard and tall tales for long nights at sea, published by McSweeney's. Stop by the Fish Theater to see Otka the pufferfish immersed in Method acting. He's no Sean Penn but as the sign says: "Please don't judge the fish."

"…stop by the Fish Theater to see Otka the pufferfish immersed in Method acting."

Everyone in the Mission has strong opinions about burritos, Cal-Mex feasts wrapped in tortillas and tinfoil. At **23 La Taqueria** they don't mess around with debatable rice or tofu but stick to mesquite-grilled meats, plump beans, fresh salsa, and optional cheese and housemade spicy pickles. If you prefer to remain neutral on the great burrito debate, head to **24 Range**, where the menu is seasonal Californian, prices are reasonable, and style is repurposed industrial chic – think fan-belt lamps and blood-bank refrigerators for beer.

End your 48 hours in San Francisco with a roar at the historic **25 Castro Theatre**, where the crowd goes wild when the giant organ rises from the floor (no, really) and pumps out show tunes until the movie starts. Fingers crossed you'll get a Bette Davis double feature, where the crowd shouts lines like: "Fasten your seat belts, it's going to be a bumpy night!" Now that you know San Francisco, you should expect nothing less.

Alison Bing

TRIP INFORMATION

GETTING THERE
San Francisco is the capital of the breakaway republic of Northern California, a convenient 70 miles from Santa Cruz and a safe 381 miles north of Los Angeles.

DO

826 Valencia
Pirate supply sales fund 826's after-school programs, and a heartfelt, pirate-to-pirate "Arrrr!" is free with any booty purchased here. ☎ 415-642-5905; www.826valencia.org; 826 Valencia St; ☾ noon-6pm

California Academy of Sciences
Creature features and wild scenes unfold under the flower-topped roof of Renzo Piano's ground-breaking green building. ☎ 415-321-8000; www.calacademy.org; Concourse Dr; adult/senior & student/under 7 $24.95/19.95/free, 3rd Wed of month free; ☾ 9:30am-5pm Mon-Sat, 11am-5pm Sun

Castro Theatre
Independent cinema, silver-screen classics and cult-hit double features, plus the Gay/Lesbian/Bi/Trans Film Festival in June. ☎ 415-621-6120; www.castrotheatre.com; 429 Castro St; adult/child & matinee $9/6

City Lights
Purveyor of poetry and inspiration since 1953. The sign by the door paraphrases Dante: "Abandon All Despair, Ye Who Enter Here" – without that bummer baggage, there's more room for books. ☎ 415-362-8193; www.citylights.com; 261 Columbus Ave; ☾ 10am-midnight

Coit Tower
This monument to San Francisco's firefighters was named after firefighter benefactor and eccentric millionaire Lillie Hancock Coit, who had fire department logos sewn on her sheets. ☎ 415-362-0808; Telegraph Hill Blvd; adult/senior & child $3/2; ☾ 10am-6pm

MH de Young Memorial Museum
Travel around the world and back through the international collection of arts in this landmark copper building. ☎ 415-863-3330; www.thinker.org/deyoung; 50 Hagiwara Tea Garden Dr; adult/senior/student/under 12 $10/7/6/free, 1st Tue of month free; ☾ 9:30am- 5:15pm Tue-Sun, 9:30am-8:45pm Fri

Mission Dolores
Our Lady of the Sorrows doesn't look a day over 225 years, with original Ohlone ceilings and an adjoining basilica aglow with stained-glass scenes of California missions. ☎ 415-621-8203; 3321 16th St; adult/child $3/2; ☾ 9am-4pm

Piedmont
Glam up or get out at this emporium of inch-long eyelashes, feather boas and Day-Glo pleather hot pants designed on the premises. ☎ 415-864-8075; 1452 Haight St; ☾ 11am-7pm

Tien Hou Temple
Dedicated in 1852 to the Buddhist Goddess of Heaven, this survivor of the 1906 earthquake and fire is a Chinatown icon. **125 Waverly Place; admission free but offerings appreciated;** ☾ 10am-5pm

EAT & DRINK

Boulette's Larder
Local and organic products become sumptuous breakfasts before your eyes at communal chefs' tables. ☎ 415-399-1155; www.bouletteslarder.com; 1 Ferry Bldg Marketplace; breakfast/brunch mains $8-15; ☾ 8-10:30am & 11:30am-2:30pm Mon-Fri, 10am-2:30pm Sun

Caffe Trieste
Powerful espresso, bathroom-stall poetry, free wi-fi, and jukebox opera at the Beats' favorite hangout. ☎ 415-392-6739; 601 Vallejo St; ☾ 6:30am-11pm Sun-Thu, 6:30am-midnight Fri & Sat

Cinecittá Pizzeria
Local Italians throng this hole-in-the-wall pizzeria for thin-crust pies, draft beer and sass from Roman owner Romina. ☎ 415-291-8830; 663 Union St; pizzas $8-13; ☾ 11am-10pm Sun-Thu, 11am-midnight Fri-Sat

City View

Flag down rolling dim sum carts for plump shrimp and leek dumplings, savory spare ribs and garlicky Chinese broccoli. ☎ 415-398-2838; 662 Commercial St; small plates $2-8; ⏱ 11am-2:30pm Mon-Fri & 10am-2:30pm Sat-Sun

Gary Danko

All the right moves: James Beard award-winning California cuisine, sweeping bay views, smart yet easy-going service and tiny cakes as parting gifts. ☎ 415-749-2060; www.gary danko.com; 800 North Point St; 5-course tasting menu $98; ⏱ 5:30-10:30pm, book ahead

La Taqueria

Pure burrito bliss: classic tomatillo or mesquite salsa, smoky meats and beans inside a flour tortilla, with housemade spicy pickles. ☎ 415-285-7117; 2889 Mission St; burritos $4-7 ⏱ 11am-9pm

Magnolia Brewpub

Organic pub grub and homebrews with laid-back, Deadhead service in the hippie heart of the Haight. ☎ 415-864-7468; www.magno liapub.com; 1398 Haight St; mains $8-18; ⏱ noon-midnight Mon-Fri, 10am-midnight Sat, 10am-11pm Sun

Range

Clean flavors, inventive veggie offerings, euphoric desserts and clever appliance-store decor at surprisingly fair prices. ☎ 415-282-8283; www.rangesf.com; 842 Valencia St; mains $20-25; ⏱ 5:30-10pm Sun-Thu, 5:30-11pm Fri-Sat

SLEEP

Hotel Adagio

Downtown designer chic, with chipper staff, killer bar, deco building and shopping-central location. ☎ 415-775-5000, 800-228-8830; www.thehoteladagio.com; 550 Geary St; r $179-239

Hotel des Arts

Shack up in an art installation piece by an emerging local artist. ☎ 415-956-3232, 800-956-4322; www.sfhoteldesarts.com; 447 Bush St; r/deluxe/suite $129/189/289

Orchard Garden Hotel

High style gets down to earth with this LEED-certified green hotel's roof gardens, non-chemical cleaners, fresh air indoors, and nature-friendly policies. ☎ 415-399-9807; www.theorchardgardenhotel.com; 466 Bush St; r $179-289

USEFUL WEBSITES

www.sfgate.com
www.sfbg.com
www.craigslist.org
www.7x7.com
www.lonelyplanet.com

LINK YOUR TRIP
www.lonelyplanet.com/trip-planner

Redwoods & Radicals

WHY GO Home to old-growth redwoods, old-school activists and the logging companies they love to hate, Humboldt and Del Norte Counties do have their tensions. But both hippies and loggers will agree this is one fine place to hang out and hug (or chop) a tree.

Long before Julia Butterfly Hill annoyed the Pacific Lumber Company by climbing a 180ft-tall redwood in 1997 and camping out for two years, coast redwoods *(Sequoia sempervirens)* lined the narrow, 450-mile-long strip along California's Pacific coast between and southern Oregon. Lush emerald ferns and redwood needles carpet the ground beneath these giants that can live for 2200 years, grow to 378ft tall (the tallest tree ever recorded) and achieve a diameter of 22ft at the base, with bark up to 12in thick. The tallest trees reach their maximum height some time between 300 and 700 years of age.

Ease into the nutty north at serene ❶ **Richardson Grove State Park**. The park's three camping areas are sequestered under 14,000 acres of virgin forest with many trees over 1000 years old and 300ft tall. The preternatural silence and calm under the high canopy make a great first chance to sojourn with the really, really big boys overnight.

Keep heading north on Hwy 101 to ❷ **Garberville**, the biggest town in southern Humboldt County and the primary jumping-off point to the Lost Coast and the Avenue of the Giants. Garberville looks like Main St USA – until you notice the range of folks cruising the sidewalks. If you've ever wondered where all of the San Francisco hippies went, look no further. The hippies – many of whom came in the 1970s to grow sinsemilla (potent, seedless marijuana) after the feds chased them out of Santa Cruz – rub shoulders (but not much more) with old-guard fisher-logger types. At last count, the hippies were

TIME
3 – 4 days

DISTANCE
160 miles

BEST TIME TO GO
Apr – Nov

START
Richardson Grove State Park

END
Jedediah Smith Redwoods State Park

ALSO GOOD FOR

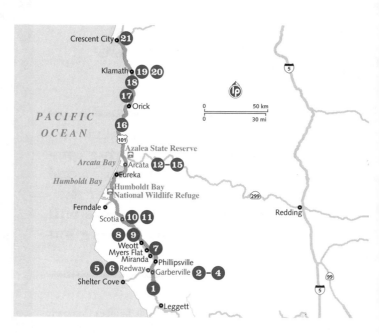

dominating the culture wars, with tie-dye shirts edging out fishing vests. But the war rages: a sign on the door of a local bar lays plain who is, and is not, welcome. It reads simply: "Absolutely NO patchouli oil!!!"

Drop in to ❸ **Woodrose Cafe** for fresh, organic breakfasts or lunches. Don't be surprised if a leather-clad Harley rider slides into a booth and orders the tofu ranchero and whole-wheat bagel. Appearances around here can be deceiving. The simple office of ❹ **Trees Foundation**, right around the corner, gives complete updates on where things stand with the fight for conservation and restoration. Staff can tell you how to get involved; after all, there are still people sitting in trees in this county…

Current-era radicals include the folks that make up the pot-growing industry. The ubiquitous weed has become quasi-legal via 1996's Proposition 215, allowing the cultivation of medical marijuana. Legal or not, the marijuana money that flows through these otherwise remote counties underwrites many of their institutions. On the purely nonfelony side, drop in to one of the hemp stores, where you can stock up on goods made from marijuana's sister plant.

Two miles west, Garberville's itsy-bitsy neighboring town of ❺ **Redway** is a stronghold for social organizations and alternative energy outfitters. Catch a dance at local institution ❻ **Mateel Community Center** to really see southern Humboldt let its hair down, or grab a bite at its café across the street.

Exit Hwy 101 when you see the sign for the **7** **Avenue of the Giants**, and travel parallel to Hwy 101. This incredible 32-mile, two-lane stretch of sun-dappled road winds beneath the biggest trees you may ever see.

Of all of California's redwood parks, **8** **Humboldt Redwoods State Park** is the most easily accessible. Over 100 miles of trails for hiking, mountain-biking and horseback riding crisscross 53,000 acres – 17,000 old-growth. The park protects some of the world's most magnificent trees, including 74 of the 100 tallest. Don't miss its **9** **Rockefeller Forest**, where you quickly walk out of sight of cars and feel like you have fallen into the time of dinosaurs. It's the world's largest contiguous old-growth redwood forest, and contains about 20% of all such remaining trees. Check out the subtly variegated rings, one per year of growth, on the cross sections of some of the downed giants that are left to mulch back into the earth over the next few hundred years.

PEACE, LOVE & HAPPINESS

Iconic local festival Reggae on the River has gone through some recent changes in management. At the time of writing, its reincarnation, **Reggae Rising** (www.reggaerising.com), is still a three-day extravaganza of tents, toking and irie feelings on the banks of the Eel River. Buy tickets early, and once you are on-site there is no re-entry, so settle in for excellent music, arts and crafts, and laid-back attitudes at the North Coast's hottest festival.

Who do the activists do battle with? Stop in at **10** **Scotia** to see the Pacific Lumber Company (Palco) and its company town. A bit spooky, hearing forklifts, smelling smokestacks, and seeing all the felled redwoods in piles, but this is how the state got its redwood hot tubs. Times are changing, though. The mill sawed its last big tree in 1997 and no longer has a blade big enough to cut giant redwoods. There's talk of the mill selling the town to its inhabitants. Find out more at the **11** **Scotia Museum & Visitors Center** or take a mill tour.

Once you've grasped Palco's party line about "forestry stewardship," log on to the website of the Bay Area Coalition for Headwaters Forest (www.headwaterspreserve.org) to learn about clear-cutting and the politics of the timber wars.

The North Coast's most progressive town, patchouli-dipped **12** **Arcata** appears to be a quaint little burg built around a pretty central square. It's also a bastion of alternative lifestyles and liberal politics that lean so far left the Green Party is considered moderate. In April 2003 the City Council not only voted to condemn the USA Patriot Act, but outlawed voluntary compliance with it. If you like to argue politics, you're gonna love it here.

Liberal or conservative, you'll appreciate the town's forward-thinking ecological practices. While the rest of America is only just starting to consider the idea of sustainability, Arcata has been living it for years: garbage trucks run on biodiesel, recycling gets picked up by tandem bicycle, wastewater gets filtered clean in marshlands, and almost every street has a bike lane. Many activist groups are headquartered here.

On the northeastern side of town, Humboldt State University anchors Arcata's counterculture. The ⑬ **Campus Center for Appropriate Technology** (CCAT) is a world leader in sustainable technologies. Take a self-guided tour of the CCAT House, a converted residence that uses only 4% of the energy of a comparably sized dwelling.

Great food abounds in restaurants throughout Arcata, but to see sustainable activism in action, forage for local organics in the aisles of the enormous ⑭ **Arcata Co-Op**. The brightly colored slips of paper in the kiosk out front advertise everything from cross-country rides to banjos for sale. ⑮ **Hotel Arcata** overlooks the central square so its simple, restored rooms make a great vantage for spying on the hippies, nerds, skaters, hikers, beggars, rednecks and squares trooping through the plaza below.

DRIVE-THRU NATURE

What better way to bond with a redwood than driving through its belly? Three carved-out (but alive!) redwoods await along Hwy 101: fold in your mirrors and inch forward through **Chandelier Drive-Thru Tree**, then cool off in the uberkitschy gift shop in Leggett; look up to the sky as you roll through **Shrine Drive-Thru Tree**, on the Avenue of the Giants in Myers Flat; or squeeze through **Tour Thru Tree**, then check out the emu off exit 769 in Klamath.

Suki Gear

Up the coast, ⑯ **Redwood National & State Parks** are made up of land spared from clear-cutting in the '60s, as part of the timber wars. These combined parks stretch along approximately 70 miles of coast – the national park was to absorb the state parks, but that never happened so they are jointly administered by the state and federal governments and include Redwood National Park, Prairie Creek Redwoods, Del Norte Coast Redwoods and Jedediah Smith Redwoods State Parks. Together, these parks have been declared an International Biosphere Reserve and World Heritage site.

Little-visited compared to their southern brethren, the world's tallest living trees have been standing here for time immemorial, predating the Roman Empire by over 500 years. Prepare to be impressed. In summer 2006, researchers found three new record-breaking trees in Redwood National Park. The tallest, Hyperion, measures a whopping 378ft – that's nearly 40 stories tall! Coming in a close second and third are Helios at 376ft and Icarus at 371ft. These just-discovered trees displace the old record holder, the 370ft-high

Stratosphere Giant in Rockefeller Forest. But the trees bear no signs, so you won't be able to find them – too many boot-clad visitors would compact the delicate root systems, so the park's not telling where they are.

At **17** **Prairie Creek Redwoods State Park**, fine treks include the truly spectacular 11.5-mile Coastal Trail and the 3.5-mile South Fork-Rhododendron-Brown Creek Loop, particularly beautiful in spring when rhododendrons and wildflowers blossom.

Coastal Dr follows Davison Rd to Gold Bluffs. Go west 3 miles north of Orick and double back north along a sometimes rough gravel road for 3.5 miles over the coastal hills to the fee station, then head up the coast to **18** **Gold Bluffs Beach**, where you can picnic or camp. One mile ahead, an easy half-mile trail leads to prehistoric-looking Fern Canyon, whose 60ft fern-covered sheer rock walls can be seen in Steven Spielberg's *Jurassic Park 2: The Lost World.* This is one of the most photographed spots on the North Coast – damp and lush, all emerald green – and totally worth getting your toes wet to see.

"…fern-covered sheer rock walls can be seen in Steven Spielberg's Jurassic Park 2: The Lost World."

Follow the winding road through beautiful inland forests with occasional views of the east and its layers of ridges and valleys, until you reach little Klamath with its bear bridge. If you're just passing through, grab a bite to eat at laid-back **19** **Klamath River Cafe,** where the fresh, basic food is home-cooked – a quality that's a bit hard to come by the further north you get. Charming **20** **Historic Requa Inn** overlooks the mouth of the Klamath River. Many of the cozy country-style rooms have mesmerizing views of the misty river, as does the dining room, where guests enjoy made-to-order breakfasts and dinners.

Wrap it all up at breathtaking **21** **Jedediah Smith Redwoods State Park**. The redwood stands here are so dense few trails penetrate the park, but the outstanding 11-mile Howland Hill Scenic Drive cuts through otherwise inaccessible areas (take Hwy 199 to South Fork Rd; turn right after crossing two bridges). It's a rough, unpaved road, and it gets graded only once a year in spring. The park's fabulous campground books up quickly. Beneath giant redwoods, the gorgeous sites are tucked along the banks of the Smith River. A true slice of heaven. That's what they've been fighting for.

Alexis Averbuck

TRIP INFORMATION

GETTING THERE
From San Francisco, take Hwy 101 195 miles north to Richardson Grove State Park.

DO

Campus Center for Appropriate Technology
Tour an energy-efficient home of the future; dig the pedal-powered TV! ☎ 707-826-3551; Buck House, Humboldt State University, Arcata; admission free; 🕑 9am-5pm Mon-Fri; 🚻

Humboldt Redwoods State Park
Volunteer-staffed visitor center lies between Myers Flat and Weott on Avenue of the Giants. ☎ 707-946-2263, campground reservations 800-444-7275; www.humboldtredwoods.org; day-use $6, campsites $15-20; 🕑 9am-5pm summer, 10am-4pm winter; 🚻 🎫

Mateel Community Center
This local mainstay organizes all manner of events and is a clearinghouse of southern Humboldt County information. ☎ 707-923-3368; www.mateel.org; 59 Rusk Lane, Redway; mains $11-24; 🕑 9am-5pm; 🚻

Scotia Museum & Visitors Center
At the town's south end, sign up for a free self-guided mill tour. ☎ 707-764-2222; www.palco.com; cnr Main & Bridge Sts, Scotia; 🕑 8am-4:30pm; 🚻

Redwood National & State Parks
No entry stations; pick up maps at the visitor center or park headquarters. ☎ 707-465-7765 visitor center, ☎ 707-465-7306 HQ; www.nps.gov/redw; Visitor Center, Hwy 101, Orick; HQ, 1111 2nd St, Crescent City; 🕑 9am-5pm; 🚻

Trees Foundation
Completely in the know, these folks also issue a quarterly newsletter loaded with conservationist information. ☎ 707-923-4377; www.treesfoundation.org; 439 Melville Rd, Garberville; 🕑 10am-4pm Mon-Thu

EAT

Arcata Co-Op
A local institution, it carries oodles of natural foods and supports local activities. ☎ 707-822-5947; cnr 8th & I Sts, Arcata; 🕑 6am-10pm; 🚻

Klamath River Cafe
Dig in to simple, fresh wraps or fish tacos, and homemade desserts. ☎ 707-482-1000; 164 Klamath Blvd, Klamath; mains $5-8; 🕑 6am-8:30pm Mon-Thu, 6am-4pm Fri, 7am-2pm Sat & Sun

Woodrose Cafe
The one place in town everyone can agree is great. ☎ 707-923-3191; 911 Redwood Dr, Garberville; mains $7-12; 🕑 8am-2:30pm Mon-Fri, to 1pm Sat & Sun; 🚻

SLEEP

Historic Requa Inn
After a day hiking, play Scrabble by the fire in the common area. ☎ 707-482-1425, 866-800-8777; www.requainn.com; 451 Requa Rd, Klamath; r incl breakfast $85-155; 🚻

Hotel Arcata
The 1915 brick Hotel Arcata anchors the plaza. Comfortable rooms have claw-foot tubs. ☎ 707-826-0217, 800-344-1221; www.hotelarcata.com; 708 9th St, Arcata; r $84-155; 🚻

Richardson Grove State Park
Inside a 1930s lodge, the visitor center often has a fire going during cool weather. ☎ 707-247-3318, campground reservations 800-444-7275; www.reserveamerica.com; day-use $6, campsites $15-20; 🕑 9am-2pm; 🚻 🎫

USEFUL WEBSITES
http://yournec.org
www.earthfirst.org

LINK YOUR TRIP
www.lonelyplanet.com/trip-planner

North County Eco Trip

WHY GO Californians have long been environmental pioneers. A trip through Sonoma and Mendocino Counties reveals ecologically sound work in action. Enjoy the many faces of sustainability: learn more about local ecosystems or sup on organically raised treats while keeping your own footprint small.

TIME
2 – 3 days

DISTANCE
95 miles

BEST TIME TO GO
May – Sep

START
Bodega Bay

END
Hopland

ALSO GOOD FOR

FOOD & DRINK

Begin at the windswept ❶ **Bodega Bay** coastal headlands to find a center of cutting-edge biological research at ❷ **Bodega Marine Laboratory & Reserve**. Run by UC Davis, the 263-acre spectacularly diverse teaching and research reserve surrounds the lab. Since the 1920s students have studied the waters off Bodega Bay, and among the many marine environments at their fingertips are rocky intertidal coastal areas, mudflats and sand flats, salt marsh, sand dunes and freshwater wetlands. On Friday afternoons docents give tours of the lab and its aquaria. If you happen to arrive at a different time, explore on your own at Bodega Head, part of the Sonoma Coast State Park, or at nearby Doran Beach.

Take Bodega Hwy inland, past tawny hillsides and grazing milk cows, to tiny, peaceful ❸ **Freestone**. Though it's a blink-and-you'll-miss-it kind of town, its one petite junction contains several ecologically friendly businesses. Best probably to start on an empty stomach at green-certified ❹ **Osmosis Day Spa Sanctuary** where a Zen-like tranquility prevails. Founder Michael Stusser built this exquisite place from the ground up with environmentally sensitive materials. The spa uses superefficient water filtration and ventilation systems and Stusser's next project is to create a wetland on the 5-acre property to recycle the spa's grey water. As a patron of the spa, though, these things remain invisible as you indulge in dry enzyme baths using aromatic cedar fibers, outdoor massages in a pagoda or its tea and meditation gardens.

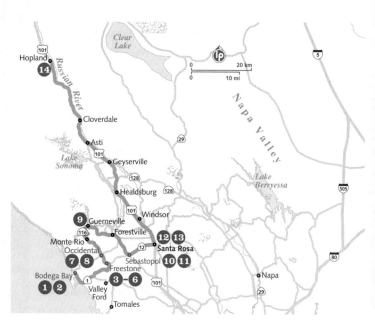

If the pampering works up your appetite, nip across the street to **5 Wild Flour Bakery**. Golden sunshine streams through the enormous windows in this restored Victorian brick building, illuminating the arms of the baker as he dispenses organic brick-oven breads, biscotti, scones and coffee.

Round out your gastronomic (yet responsible!) ecstasy at **6 Freestone Vineyards Guest Center**. Located in one of the rare spots in the area that produces excellent pinot noir, this vineyard practices environmentally friendly winemaking and maintains a real commitment to its 80 acres and the community of western Sonoma County.

ASK A LOCAL "There are great **farmers markets** in Marin, Sonoma, Santa Rosa, Sebastopol, Occidental and don't forget San Francisco at the Embarcadero. I think that these markets represent a really important niche in the sustainable, buy-local movement. They are fun and a great cultural experience…"

Reuben Weinzveg, Sebastopol

Wind along Bohemian Hwy to the top of the hill and **7 Occidental**. Surrounded by several longstanding communes, the town is an encampment of hotels, restaurants and shops making wares out of reclaimed materials, and home to **8 Occidental Arts & Ecology Center**. This wonderland (they call themselves a "nonprofit education and organizing center," but really it's a wonderland) in the moist, forested hilltops runs all manner of programs incorporating research, education and advocacy. Staff and volunteers teach in schools, grow heirloom seeds in a mother garden biodiversity project, fight for responsible water policy and run an arts program to boot. Activities for the public include medicinal plant walks and courses like Woodshop for Women. Or, help *them* out and volunteer in its elaborate gardens on Wednesdays.

Sleep over at secluded **9** **Creekside Inn & Resort** in Guerneville. It was recognized for "Best Practices in Environmental Impact" and awarded an EcoRing "Eco Hero" prize. Owner Lynn Crescione's dedication includes the use of chemical- and scent-free cleaning products and pesticide-free gardening at this rambling riverside compound of cottages and simple B&B rooms.

"…his techniques have led to many diverse and sometimes arguably bizarre plant-breeding scenarios…"

Located in a newly constructed green building, **10** **Peter Lowell's** in **11** **Sebastopol** prides itself on creating excellent organic meals with ingredients sourced from local sustainably minded farms. The menu changes with what's in season and the sleek dining room is as fresh and light as the food.

No tour of the region would be complete without picking up the *Sonoma County Farm Trails* (www.farmtrails.org) magazine and visiting some of these conscientious, food-lovin' farmers, horticulturalists and vintners yourself. Load up for your picnics with homemade local jams, cheeses, charcuterie, ciders, honeys…the list goes on and on. And your footprint stays small and local.

The trailblazer in local agriculture and plant wizardry was, of course, Luther Burbank (1849–1926), whose experimental farm is preserved and open for the public in Sebastopol. While his techniques have led to many diverse and sometimes arguably bizarre plant-breeding scenarios, a tour of the **12** **Luther Burbank Home & Gardens** in Santa Rosa will help you form your own opinions. Burbank developed many hybrid plant and tree species at his 19th-century Greek-revival home and was a buddy of Thomas Edison and Henry Ford. The phrase "to burbank," in the dictionary for a while, meant "to innovate."

State parks and reserves as well as **13** **Sonoma County Parks** throughout the region make for excellent camping and a small traveler footprint. Similarly, this part of the state is loaded with biodynamic wineries, animal rescue operations, organic eateries and green-minded businesses. But head up Hwy 101 to Hopland's **14** **Solar Living Institute** to get a primer on it all. Located in a spectacular 12-acre renewable energy and sustainable living demonstration site, it educates by example. Take a tour or attend a hands-on workshop on renewable energy, green building or organic gardening. Or volunteer there!

Don't want to burn fossil fuels on your trip? Do the whole thing by bike…
Alexis Averbuck

TRIP INFORMATION

GETTING THERE
From San Francisco, go north on Hwy 1 for 70 miles to Bodega Bay.

DO

Bodega Marine Laboratory & Reserve
One hundred UC Davis grad students and scientists study marine biology on a rugged bluff. ☎ 707-875-2211; www.bml.ucdavis .edu; 2099 Westside Rd, Bodega Bay; admission free; ☽ 2-4pm Fri; ♿

Luther Burbank Home & Gardens
The extensive gardens are lovely for lingering, and the house and museum showcase Burbank's life and work. ☎ 707-524-5445; cnr Santa Rosa & Sonoma Aves, Santa Rosa; garden admission free, house tour adult/child $4/free; ☽ gardens 8am-5pm, museum & house 10am-3:30pm Tue-Sun Apr-Oct; ♿

Occidental Arts & Ecology Center
Make an extra effort to get here – its work is extensive and based around community involvement. ☎ 707-874-1557; www.oaec .org; 15290 Coleman Valley Rd, Occidental; ☽ hours vary; ♿

Osmosis Day Spa Sanctuary
Massage, skincare, wellness? It's all good here. Make reservations, though, because a steady stream of folk throngs here from all around. ☎ 707-823-8231; www.osmosis .com; 209 Bohemian Hwy, Freestone; ☽ 9am-9pm

Solar Living Institute
Students and volunteers can camp on-site; register a week in advance. The annual SolFest in August adds great food and family fun. ☎ 707-744-2017; www.solarliving.org; 13771 S Hwy 101, Hopland; ☽ 10am-6pm; ♿

EAT & DRINK

Freestone Vineyards Guest Center
Get a warm welcome and sip the light fantastic at this tiny vintner's outpost. ☎ 707-874-1010; www.freestonevineyards.com; cnr Bodega & Bohemian Hwys, Freestone; tastings free; ☽ 11am-5pm Fri-Mon

Peter Lowell's
Locally owned and operated, it was conceived as a sustainable restaurant from the ground up. ☎ 707-829-1077; www.peterlowells.com; 7385 Healdsburg Ave, Sebastopol; mains $7-17; ☽ 7am-9pm Mon-Thu, to 10pm Fri, 10am-2pm & 5-10pm Sat, to 9pm Sun; ♿

Wild Flour Bakery
This one-room wonder gets packed with eager locals lining up for one of the 900 loaves baked per day. ☎ 707-874-3928; www.wildflour bread.com; 140 Bohemian Hwy, Freestone; ☽ 8.30am-6pm Fri-Mon; ♿

SLEEP

Creekside Inn & Resort
Across the river from downtown Guerneville, this resort's gregarious owner will fill you in on what's hot and ecologically conscious nearby. ☎ 707-869-3623, 800-776-6586; www.creeksideinn.com; 16180 Neeley Rd, Guerneville; r $90-175; ♿

Sonoma County Parks
Load up with information about regional parks and local camping possibilities at the Sonoma County Regional Parks Department. ☎ 707-565-2041; www.sonoma-county .org/parks; 2300 County Center Dr, Santa Rosa; ☽ 8am-5pm; ♿

USEFUL WEBSITES
www.slowfoodnation.org
www.sctransit.com

www.lonelyplanet.com/trip-planner

LINK YOUR TRIP

NorCal on the Big Screen

WHY GO Leave Hollywood behind and join us on a quickie tour of a few of the highlights of film in Northern California. We teamed up with George Baker, member of the Modesto Film Commission, to map out some of the north's homegrown silver-screen magic.

TIME
4 – 5 days

DISTANCE
380 miles

BEST TIME TO GO
Year-round

START
San Francisco

END
Mendocino

At the outset it is worth saying that whole books could be written about the movie sites of Northern California, and weeks of travel would not take you to each of the bucolic backdrops or sizzling city scenes that have snuck into film through the decades. Nevertheless, we constructed a trip, with George Baker's help, that gives but a wee sample.

Of course the belle of the silver screen, ❶ **San Francisco** inserts its pretty facades, steep hillsides and iconic bridges into all manner of flicks. Old black-and-white movies like 1941's *The Maltese Falcon,* starring Humphrey Bogart, took excellent advantage of the city's beautifully mysterious qualities.

One of SF's most photogenic neighborhoods is ❷ **Pacific Heights**. Its grand homes and exquisite views star in film upon film. The 1990 movie *Pacific Heights* showcased a gleefully crazed Michael Keaton terrorizing yuppie new-homeowners Melanie Griffith and Matthew Modine. Ironically, the actual house used in the movie was not located in Pacific Heights, but some of the street scenes were shot there.

Robin Williams got into drag to stalk Sally Field in *Mrs Doubtfire* (1993) at 2640 Steiner St, Pac Heights. A homegrown boy and originally a local comic, Williams still lives in San Francisco.

On a more sinister note, in *Basic Instinct* (1992) Michael Douglas and Sharon Stone played a murderously sexual cat-and-mouse game

throughout most of the city and even as far as Stinson Beach on the Marin coast. Stone's character's monster pad was located at 2930 Vallejo St at Baker St in Pac Heights. In SoMa, visit real-life Rawhide II at 280 7th St for the country-and-western bar that appears near the end of the movie. Classic ❸ **Tosca Café** in North Beach (serving since 1919) played the old-world-style bar where Douglas and the cops hung out jawin' all the time. San Francisco's hallmark Transamerica Pyramid seems to pop up in the background of most shots – perhaps a none-too-subtle symbol of the movie's themes.

> "...Michael Douglas and Sharon Stone played a murderously sexual cat-and-mouse game throughout most of the city..."

The city seems to be a favorite for some actors. Long before his instincts got the better of him with Sharon Stone, Douglas filmed the classic TV show *Streets of San Francisco* (1972–77) here with Karl Malden. Since then he has cropped up in many a SF movie, like *The Game* (1997), costarring Sean Penn. In this mind-bending thriller-mystery they chase each from the Presidio to Chinatown to the Ritz-Carlton Hotel. The freaky jump from the roof was shot at 1 Bush St.

❹ **The Presidio**, a very picturesque former army base, also had a movie named after it. Released in 1988 and starring Sean Connery and Mark Harmon, the film was shot throughout the park and included SF National Cemetery, the Officers' Club and Fort Point. But perhaps the most famous movie ever filmed at Fort Point (on the southern end of the Golden Gate Bridge) is Alfred Hitchcock's *Vertigo* (1958), starring James Stewart and Kim Novak.

Most of the Presidio has never been developed and remains wooded and green, as in its movie appearances. It's still a beautiful spot today to take a relaxing drive, walk or bike.

One of the Presidio's newer developments is **5** **Letterman Digital Arts Center**, created by Northern California filmmaker George Lucas. The campus, near Lombard Gate at the park's southern extent, is home to Lucas' Industrial Light and Magic – one of the biggest and most successful digital-effects companies in the world. About 1500 people work in the complex and visitors can roam the grounds or lunch at the excellent Lucas Cafeteria alongside a statue of wrinkled Jedimaster Yoda.

FESTS IN MODESTO

The **Northern California Film Festival** (www .norcalfilmfest.com) takes place in Modesto in August and aims to bring recognition to movies made by people from Northern California or films shot in this part of the state. In October the "Sundance of the Weird," **ShockerFest International Film Festival** (www.shockerfest.com), showcases independent sci-fi and horror flicks.

Next, jump south to Ocean Beach and the fantabulous ruins of the old **6** **Sutro Baths** (www.sutrobaths.com). The beach is a hardcore surfing site, but the tangled beams and girders of this weather-beaten semidemolished bathhouse were featured in 1971's *Harold and Maude* and still make for an exciting wander.

Every jail escape movie ever made might have been shot out in the middle of San Francisco Bay at **7** **Alcatraz**. From 1933 to 1963 the rocky island was home to the most notorious prison in the USA. Housing the brig of choice for serious offenders, "the Rock" was believed to be escape proof...until the Anglin brothers and coconspirator Frank Morris floated away on a self-made raft in 1962 and were never seen again. That enigmatic escape was made famous by the 1979 movie *Escape from Alcatraz,* starring Clint Eastwood.

The island also had a movie named after it: *The Rock* (1996). This time, though, Sean Connery and Nicolas Cage break *in* to nab Ed Harris, who has taken over the prison and is threatening the Bay Area with biological weapons.

Grab a bite to eat in North Beach at Cage's uncle, Francis Ford Coppola's place **8** **Café Zoetrope**. The filmmaker owns this little bistro bedecked with memorabilia, but he doesn't welcome diners at the door. Doesn't matter. You'll enjoy the pizzas (including the Sophia, named for his Oscar-winning daughter), and the Caesar salad is tops.

If you're ready for a rest, put your head down at nearby **⑨ Hotel Bohème**. Small and stylish, its updated gangster-era look makes subtle reference to the neighborhood's Beat history.

Or head to the **⑩ Castro Theatre**, where the building is as interesting as the mix of independent, foreign and classic films. Don't miss the Wurlitzer organ booming away before evening screenings. The theater is home to the Gay and Lesbian Film Festival and features in the 2008 film *Milk*, about former gay supervisor Harvey Milk.

Tear yourself away from the city and head south past Half Moon Bay (site of 2003's *House of Sand and Fog*, starring Oscar winners Ben Kingsley and Jennifer Connolly) to **⑪ Santa Cruz** (75 miles from San Francisco). The **⑫ Santa Cruz Beach Boardwalk** appeared in *Harold and Maude* and was a virtual costar of 1987's teen vampire hit, *The Lost Boy*s. The marauding bloodsuckers cavorted up and down the length of this old-school wooden boardwalk. Built in 1906, it is the oldest beachfront amusement park on the West Coast. If your nerves can take it, mimic the thrill of the chase by riding the rickety but marvelous Giant Dipper, a beloved wooden rollercoaster built in 1924.

> **DETOUR**
>
> Known as "The Movie Railroad," Railtown 1897 State Historic Park in **Jamestown**, 50 miles from Modesto, is home to one of America's last intact, still-operating railroad roundhouses. Its historic locomotives have featured in hundreds of film and TV productions, including *High Noon,* Viggo Mortensen's *Hidalgo* (2004) and *Petticoat Junction*. Pause for a refreshment at homey **Motherload Coffee Shop** in Main St, with its friendly folk, vintage counter and swivel stools. Nearby Sonora was the site of many old westerns like *The Virginian* (1929), starring a gangbusting Gary Cooper.

To feel like you are on a movie set yourself, sup at **⑬ Hula's Island Grill**, where '60s Vegas meets '50s Honolulu. The amazingly kitschy-yet-swanky tropical environment makes a perfect backdrop for tucking into fresh fish or sipping an umbrella-ed cocktail at the tiki bar.

You could easily while away a few days in Santa Cruz, surfing, sunning, soaking up the local customs and checking out locations from quintessential surfer flick, *The Endless Summer*. When you're done, head on to **⑭ Modesto**, 115 miles east of the Bay Area, to track down the sites of yesteryear's Hollywood westerns – like *Dodge City* (1939) starring ye olde swashbuckler Errol Flynn and Olivia de Havilland. Filmmaker George Lucas was raised in sleepy Modesto and the town is the subject (though not the location) of his breakthrough 1973 film, *American Graffiti*. George Baker points out that the counties around Modesto sport cornfields, rice paddies and all manner of terrain, so filmmakers regularly shoot movies set anywhere from Kansas to Vietnam (everything from *Cool Hand Luke* to *All the King's Men*) in this part of the state.

Surrounding towns like Oakdale were sites of movies like *Back to the Future*, part of which was shot at the ⑮ **Sierra Railroad**. Built in 1897 to connect the Central Valley to the Gold Country, it is the third-oldest railroad in North America. Take a ride on the Dinner Train, with its wacky range of themed events: murder mysteries, Wild West shows or romantic dinners. To reach Oakdale (15 miles), take Oakdale Rd north to Hwy 108 east.

Navigate back to Hwy 101 and continue north to up-and-coming ⑯ **Petaluma**. Formerly known for its chicken farms, the quaint downtown area has had a revival and is surrounded by serene rolling golden hills that undulate out to the coast. Historic downtown and the sun-swept ranches that surround it have been featured in movies from *The Zodiac* (2005) to *The Hulk* (2003) and *The Horse Whisperer* (1998), and *American Graffiti* was shot here. Maybe you missed *Flubber* (1997), but if you saw John Travolta in *Phenomenon* (1996) you probably remember all that warm light and peaceful countryside. Yep, Petaluma. Stop for a bite to eat at one of the many restaurants or stroll the new walking path along the Petaluma River, on Water St.

> **DETOUR**
>
> To sleep where some of *Cujo* (1982) was filmed – a possibly dubious choice – go to **Pine Beach Inn** (☎ 707-964-5603), between Mendocino and Fort Bragg. The tennis courts at this 12-acre motel complex were in the movie but the hotel itself is pretty basic and a bit more "Brady Bunch" in feel than *Cujo*. The cheapest rooms are near the highway, but go for a quieter "garden-view" room.

Zip north through wine country, which Baker points out was the setting for many movies and TV shows through the years, to the precious Victorian village of ⑰ **Mendocino**. This beautifully restored town festooned with blossoming gardens and dotted with weathered wooden water towers has become a filmmakers' darling for dramatic coastlines and old village settings. Among many others, Mendocino has starred in James Dean's *East of Eden* (1954), *The Majestic* (2001) with Jim Carrey, and *The Russians are Coming, The Russians are Coming* (1965), which was the first film shot entirely on the Mendocino coast.

Mendocino is packed with excellent B&Bs and fine restaurants. ⑱ **MacCallum House Inn & Restaurant** combines them both. Sit on the veranda for a romantic all-organic dinner of duck, gnocchi or salmon, or tipple scrummy cocktails at the hoppin' bar before resting your head in an 1882 refurbished barn.

In the morning pick up the "Films Made in Mendocino County" brochure to find the sites of 50 films shot up and down the coast – a great chance for photo ops posing as your favorite starlet.

Alexis Averbuck

HISTORY & CULTURE

TRIP INFORMATION

GETTING THERE
Not too tricky: start in San Francisco.

DO

Alcatraz Tours
Break into The Rock on an Alcatraz Cruises boat departing from Pier 33. Tickets include park admission. ☎ 415-981-7625; www .alcatrazcruises.com; adult/child 5-11yrs $26/16, night tour $33/19.50; ☒ 9am-4pm, with seasonal variations

Castro Theatre
Kick back and see a flick in the architectural highlight of Castro St. Who needs a cineplex when you've got a cool joint like this? ☎ 415-621-6120; www.castrotheatre.com; 429 Castro St, San Francisco

Santa Cruz Beach Boardwalk
Listen through the music from the classic calliope for the sound of vampire wings. ☎ 831-423-5590; www.beachboardwalk .com; admission free, rides $2-4; ☒ 11am-11pm daily summer, 11am-5pm Sat & Sun winter

Sierra Railroad
This classic short-line train continues to carry passengers, haul freight and make cameos in Hollywood movies. ☎ 800-866-1690; www .sierrarailroad.com; ☒ 8am-8pm Mon-Sat, 8am-5pm Sun, train times vary

EAT & DRINK

Café Zoetrope
Local-boy-done-good Francis Ford Coppola branches out into the culinary arts – with stellar success. ☎ 415-291-1700; www .cafecoppola.com; 916 Kearny St, San Francisco; mains $9-15; ☒ 11am-10pm Tue-Fri, noon-10pm Sat, noon-9pm Sun

Hula's Island Grill
Tropical glitz and glam set the mood for reliably fabulous food and cocktails. ☎ 831-426-4852; 221 Cathcart St, Santa Cruz; ☒ 11:30am-11pm Fri & Sat, 5-11pm Sun-Thu

Tosca Café
Step beyond the endearingly crusty facade to try this bar's famous jukebox loaded with opera records. ☎ 415-391-1244; 242 Columbus Ave, San Francisco; ☒ 5pm-late

SLEEP

Hotel Bohème
Hey Jack Kerouac… Spy on city life from one of the rooms bedecked in patterned textiles and facing the hopping avenue. ☎ 415-433-9111; www.hotelboheme.com; 444 Columbus Ave, San Francisco; r $175-195

MacCallum House Inn & Restaurant
All the cushy extras (robes, DVD players, plush linens) trick out this sweet Victorian spot. ☎ 707-937-0289; www.maccallum house.com; 45020 Albion St, Mendocino; r $175-325, suite $265-425, mains $12-37; ☒ meals 8-10:30am Mon-Fri, 8am-noon Sat & Sun, 5:30-10pm nightly; ☒

USEFUL WEBSITES
www.filminamerica.com
www.visitmodesto.com

LINK YOUR TRIP www.lonelyplanet.com/trip-planner

Finding Fault: Earthquake Sites

WHY GO Although earthquakes occur across California, the 1906 San Francisco quake remains a defining moment in the state's history. Unseen faults, such as the one responsible for the 1989 quake, crisscross the Bay Area. The evidence is there if you know where to look. So don your Sherlock hat and sleuth out some cracks in the earth.

The epicenter for the 1906 San Francisco earthquake is marked by mangy ❶ **Mussel Rock**, which sits like a turd amid the thrashing surf just offshore from Daly City. It was here on April 18 that the San Andreas Fault let a couple of centuries of built-up pressure rip. The resulting quake – estimated at 8.3 on the Richter scale – is among the most powerful of all time.

The site is overlooked by ❷ **Mussel Rock Park**, a grassy coastal expanse that easily stirs up images of geologic chaos. The sandy ground is unstable and surrounding streets are riddled with offshoot faults from the San Andreas. Many homes on Westline Dr have been undermined by the unstable earth. From here take Hwy 1 into ❸ **San Francisco**. For earthquake tourists, the entire city is a location, as most of it either tumbled down or went up in smoke during the raging fires that followed the quake. Two of the city's premier hotels, the ❹ **St Francis Hotel** and the ❺ **Fairmont**, are quake survivors. Both were virtually new in 1906 and had to be refurbished after being gutted by the flames.

Walk down Market St towards the iconic Ferry Building and pause where Kearney and 3rd Sts converge. ❻ **Lotta's Fountain** dates from 1875, and in 1906 was a meeting spot for survivors. Today people gather here on each anniversary of the quake at the fateful time of 5:12am. Continue to the end of Market and the ❼ **Ferry Building**, which figured in

TIME
2 days

DISTANCE
210 miles

BEST TIME TO GO
Mar – Oct

START
Daly City

END
Aptos

ALSO GOOD FOR

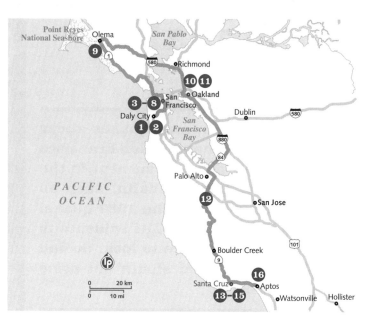

the 1989 Loma Prieta earthquake. The 7.1 temblor caused widespread damage in the Bay Area and fatally damaged a multi-level highway that ran like a scar down the middle of the Embarcadero. The eyesore freeway was eventually torn down, the lavish landscaping you now see was installed and the Ferry Building was turned into one of the nation's premier marketplaces for organic and artisan foods. **8 Mastrelli's Delicatessen** here has links to a deli that opened nearby in 1896.

FAULTY TOWERS

One of the region's biggest earthquake sites sits in the middle of the San Francisco Bay. The **Bay Bridge** (www.baybridgeinfo.org) was rendered useless during the 1989 quake, when a small segment of the east portion collapsed. Two decades later much of the structural steel on the suspension side has been restored, while the entire eastern portion is simply being replaced. The cost has shot past $6 billion and just keeps climbing.

Drive north across the Golden Gate Bridge to Sausalito and follow Hwy 1 north for 23 miles. After Stinson Beach the road follows the San Andreas fault, which runs through the rift valley like an arrow. Near Olema, look for the **9 Bear Valley Visitor Center** of the Point Reyes National Seashore, the national park that covers much of the peninsula. A short earthquake trail has reconstructed evidence of the 1906 quake, which caused local fences and buildings to move as much as 20ft.

Return to Olema and take Sir Francis Drake Blvd 15 miles southeast to San Rafael, where you can join I-580 and head to East Bay over the Richmond–

San Rafael Bridge. Go south to ⑩ **Oakland** and drive to ⑪ **14th St**. A large twisted metal sculpture on the corner of the Mandela Parkway recalls the destruction of the Cypress Structure, a double-decker concrete freeway that collapsed in the 1989 quake, killing 42 people. The lavishly landscaped parkway opened in 2005. Look for the wall bearing the inscription "15 seconds," which has a plaque with details of that horrible day.

Continue south on I-880 and cross the bay on the Dumbarton Bridge to Palo Alto. Take Page Mill Rd west 7 miles into the hills. ⑫ **Los Trancos Open Space Preserve** is a beautiful site that spans the San Andreas Fault as it bisects the tree-dotted rolling hills. A 1.5-mile earthquake trail is lined with stations explaining the movements of the fault.

"…much of the Pacific Garden Mall was destroyed or later had to be demolished."

Head for Hwy 9 and then 40 miles down into ⑬ **Santa Cruz**. The old brick buildings of the downtown area, which were built on dubious river sand, were no match for the 1989 quake, and much of the Pacific Garden Mall was destroyed or later had to be demolished. Yet Santa Cruz hung on and two thriving veteran businesses, ⑭ **Bookshop Santa Cruz**, which operated out of a tent in a parking lot for months after the earthquake, and ⑮ **Zoccoli's** deli, are proof of the town's rebirth.

The posh little village of Aptos, some 8 miles south of Santa Cruz, is the final stop on the tour. It sits at the base of the ⑯ **Forest of the Nisene Marks State Park**, where trails stretch through old logging camps and redwood groves all the way to the summit of the coastal mountains and the peak that gave the 1989 earthquake its name: Loma Prieta. A 3-mile trail goes from the end of the access road to the epicenter of the 1989 quake, where a sign gives the barest details of the events of 5:02pm, April 17. Pause in the quiet, surrounded by the impossibly green trees, and ponder when the San Andreas will next let rip.

Ryan Ver Berkmoes

ASK A LOCAL

"The **DeRose Winery** (www.derosewine.com) in Hollister is my favorite stop on a fault-finding tour of Northern California. The winery is in a beautiful valley that has been carved by the creeping San Andreas fault. The main building sits squarely on the fault – keeping the structure supported has been a challenge. But gosh, the wine is good. To me it serves as metaphor: Californians not just surviving, but thriving in earthquake country."

Susan Elizabeth Hough, author of Finding Fault in California, An Earthquake Tourist's Guide

TRIP INFORMATION

GETTING THERE
Take Hwy 1 10 miles south from San Francisco and exit at Palmetto Dr. Follow Westline Dr down to the ocean and Mussel Rock.

DO

Bear Valley Visitor Center
Displays in this vast and varied park are detailed and the earthquake trail is accessible. ☎ 415-464-5100; www.nps.gov/pore; **Point Reyes National Seashore, 1 Bear Valley Rd, Point Reyes Station; admission free;** ◷ 9am-5pm; ♿

Bookshop Santa Cruz
This landmark bookstore with many local titles operated out of a tent after the 1989 earthquake. ☎ 831-423-0900; **1520 Pacific Ave, Santa Cruz;** ◷ 10am-10pm; ♿

Forest of the Nisene Marks State Park
The site of the 1989 quake's epicenter in this 10,200-acre park is a vision of serenity. ☎ 831-763-7062; www.parks.ca.gov; **Aptos Creek Rd, Aptos;** ♿ ⊞

Los Trancos Open Space Preserve
Trails across the preserve's 274 acres tell the story of the San Andreas Fault, which is right under your feet. ☎ 650-691-1200; www.openspace.org; **Page Mill Rd, Palo Alto;** ♿ ⊞

Mussel Rock Park
The park overlooking the namesake rock that marks the epicenter of the 1906 quake is on shaky ground. **120 Westline Dr, Daly City;** ◷ **dawn to dusk;** ♿ ⊞

EAT

Ferry Building
The marketplace here occupies the entire ground floor and is popular throughout the day, while the weekend farmers market draws throngs. ☎ 415-693-0996; www.ferrybuildingmarketplace.com; **1 Ferry Building, San Francisco;** ♿

Mastrelli's Delicatessen
Salami sandwiches here are just as good as those wolfed down by earthquake survivors 100 years ago. ☎ 415-397-3354; **Marketplace Shop #47, 1 Ferry Building, San Francisco; sandwiches $7;** ◷ 9am-6pm; ♿

Zoccoli's
Long-running family-operated deli with great sandwiches and snacks. ☎ 831-423-1711; **1534 Pacific Ave, Santa Cruz; sandwiches $6;** ◷ 9am-7pm; ♿

SLEEP

Fairmont
High on Nob Hill, this grand hotel is surrounded by other 1906 survivors. It was set to open just days after the quake. ☎ 415-772-5000; www.fairmont.com; **950 Mason St, San Francisco; r from $250**

St Francis Hotel
The imposing southeast portion of this legendary hotel was rebuilt after 1906; it had only opened in 1904. ☎ 866-497-2788; www.westinstfrancis.com; **335 Powell St, San Francisco; r from $250**

USEFUL WEBSITES
www.earthquake.usgs.gov/regional/nca/1906/
www.sfmuseum.org/1906/06.html

LINK YOUR TRIP
www.lonelyplanet.com/trip-planner

NorCal Hop Spots

WHY GO With an enviable concentration of some of the country's best microbreweries, Northern California makes beer lovers swoon. We chatted with David Keene, owner of San Francisco's renowned Toronado beer pub, about his favorite places, though only a handful could fit here.

Ask a publican where to have lunch, and they'll steer you someplace serving beer – lots of really good beer. (Though of course it can't be *quite* as good as the selection they sell!) In San Francisco's Mission neighborhood, the ➊ **Monk's Kettle** focuses on craft beers from around the world and food that's organic, locally sourced and sustainably produced. Sample an artisan cheese plate with a gourmet sandwich or dive into the daily pot pie special, taking note of the menu's suggested beer pairings. To tour San Francisco without getting behind the wheel, walk over from the 16th St BART train station.

Book in advance to join the very sought-after tours at ➋ **Anchor Brewing** in the nearby Potrero Hill neighborhood. From the Monk's Kettle, the MUNI 22 bus stops a block away from the brewery. "It's the oldest microbrewery in San Francisco and one of the most beautiful breweries in the world," sighs Keene. On the extensive tours, wide-eyed enthusiasts swoon over the shiny copper brew kettles, spy on the open fermenters and inspect the bottling line. "IPA is probably the most popular style of microbrew beer at this time," he says, adding: "If you want some history, take a tour, drink some fresh Liberty, and see where West Coast IPA started in America." Naturally, the post-tour tasting in its sunny pub room remains its most popular feature.

Jump back on an eastbound 22 bus to 3rd St and catch the T train to Embarcadero station. From the Ferry Building, board the ferry to

TIME
3 days

DISTANCE
200 miles

BEST TIME TO GO
Year-round

START
San Francisco

END
Fort Bragg

Larkspur, where the ❸ **Marin Brewing Company**, a brewpub restaurant, sits a block from the boat. Keene notes that the brewer, Arne Johnson, has won many awards and currently makes some fantastic Belgian beers. You can see the glassed-in brewery behind the bar.

Sail back to the Ferry Building for dinner at the ❹ **Slanted Door**, a foodie hot spot with locally sourced modern Vietnamese cuisine and sweeping bay views. Savvy gourmands might not realize that besides the shaking beef and the clay-pot chicken, the beer list is divine. Can't rustle up a reservation? Jump a Powell-Mason cable car (from the Powell station) directly to North Beach's Belgian eatery ❺ **La Trappe**. Descend the spiral staircase to the brick-and-wood cellar dining room for mussels in white beer sauce with a side of *frites* (french fries) and excellent Trappist ale.

"The brewery's longstanding green credentials include a solar array that generates about half of its power."

The following day, tap a designated driver and drive an hour north on Hwy 101 to Santa Rosa. "Purely beer-wise, probably the hottest brewer in the country is Vinnie Cilurzo at ❻ **Russian River Brewing Company**," enthuses Keene. "He's kind of the father of double IPA. On one hand he's well-known for his hoppy beers – Pliny the Elder and Blind Pig IPA. Then on the other side of things he's very involved in wood-aged Belgian-style beers with *Brettanomyces* added to them, which is a bacteria that provides what's known as a horse-blanket aroma." Order a pizza from the kitchen in the back, and sigh in anticipation over the wooden barrels aging behind the bar. A tasting room is in the works at its new bottling facility.

From Santa Rosa, follow Hwy 101 north about 30 miles to Hwy 128 and go west another 30 miles to Boonville. Celebrating over 20 years of brewing, ❼ **Anderson Valley Brewing Company** sits on a large corner lot overlooking the valley, complete with a tasting room and beefy draft horses grazing the grounds. Keene remembers, "They were one of the first microbrews we had on draft here at Toronado. I used to go pick up the beer and drive it back down from Boonville." Perhaps to reward his long-standing loyalty, they make two beers named for him, and the Brother David's Double won a medal in the 2008 World Beer Cup. The grounds also include a Frisbee golf course, where players can buy beer to drink as they play. The brewery's longstanding green credentials include a solar array that generates about half of its power.

A mile away, Shaker-style furniture enlivens the 10 rooms of the countrified contemporary ❽ **Boonville Hotel**. Its excellent downstairs restaurant grows lots of its own greens and herbs, and in summer, diners migrate to garden deck tables shaded by an apple tree.

An hour up the coast on Hwy 1, Fort Bragg's ❾ **North Coast Brewing Company** has a small pub with tastings and a seafood- and steak-heavy food menu. Keene mentions that in addition to being makers of Belgian-style and organic beers (among others), their shop also carries exclusive special brewery bottlings. He counts the vintage Old Stock Ale, Red Seal Ale and the Old Rasputin stout as standouts.

Twelve miles south, the fifth-generation family-owned ❿ **Little River Inn** feels country-casual but elegant, with Victorian rooms in an 1850s house and others – including some perched on an ocean bluff – surveying rugged Pacific views. Fete the end of the trip with fresh seafood at the garden-view destination restaurant, and start planning the next.

Beth Kohn

BEER BIBLE

Before hitting the road, thumb through a copy of the **Celebrator** (www.celebrator.com) magazine. A national bimonthly guide to microbreweries and craft beers, it's available at good beer bars and brewpubs and publishes a comprehensive list of breweries, brewpubs and homebrew suppliers. Scheme another tasting vacation from its long list of Northern California locations.

DETOUR In Chico, east of I-5, the **Sierra Nevada Brewing Company** (www.sierranevada.com) has free tours daily without reservations needed. A state-of-the-art facility that's an homage to brewing, it contains gorgeous details like decorative hop-shaped tiling along the kettles and, as David Keene says, "every brewer drools when they go there." Frequent concerts rock the house at their 350-seat concert venue.

TRIP INFORMATION

GETTING THERE
Returning the 150 miles from Little River to San Francisco, go east on Hwy 128, and south on Hwy 101.

DO & DRINK
Anchor Brewing
The pride of San Francisco, this beautiful brewery does the most popular tours in town. ☎ 415-863-8350; www.anchorbrewing.com; 1705 Mariposa St, San Francisco; tours free; ⏱ tours by appointment Mon-Fri

Anderson Valley Brewing Company
This longstanding pastoral brewery beckons, complete with its own Frisbee golf course. ☎ 707-895-2337; www.avbc.com; 17700 Hwy 253, Boonville; tours $5; ⏱ tours 11:30am & 3pm, pub 11am-7pm

Marin Brewing Company
This great brewpub is easy to reach via the scenic ferry from San Francisco. ☎ 415-461-4677; www.marinbrewing.com; 1809 Larkspur Landing Circle, Larkspur; ⏱ 11am-midnight Sun-Thu, 11:30am-1am Fri & Sat

North Coast Brewing Company
A coastal brewery with a popular brewpub, and no reservations necessary for tours. ☎ 707-964-2739; www.northcoastbrewing.com; 455 N Main St, Fort Bragg; tours free; ⏱ tours noon Sat, taproom noon-10pm daily

Russian River Brewing Company
Email for tours of this cutting-edge brewery. ☎ 707-545-2337; www.russianriverbrewing.com; 725 4th St, Santa Rosa; tours free; ⏱ tours by appointment, pub 11am-midnight Sun-Thu, to 1am Fri & Sat

EAT
La Trappe
Lovers of Belgian beer and Belgian food find a happy marriage of both at this North Beach restaurant. ☎ 415-440-8727; 800 Greenwich St, San Francisco; mains $9-24; ⏱ 6pm-midnight Tue-Sun

Monk's Kettle
A new Mission District eatery, it showcases craft beers and organic and sustainably produced food. ☎ 415-865-9523; 3141 16th St, San Francisco; mains $11-20; ⏱ noon-2am Sun-Thu, 11:30am-2am Fri & Sat

Slanted Door
Book in advance to dine at this perennially popular Vietnamese eatery on the bay. ☎ 415-861-8032; 1 Ferry Building #3, San Francisco; mains $12-35; ⏱ 11am-10pm Sun-Thu, to 10:30pm Fri & Sat

SLEEP
Boonville Hotel
With a contemporary American-country style that would make Martha Stewart proud, it makes a pleasant retreat from city stress. ☎ 707-895-2210; www.boonvillehotel.com; 14050 Hwy 128, Boonville; r $125-275; 🛁 ❄

Little River Inn
With rooms overlooking the ocean, and an amazing restaurant, this family-owned resort is a lovely getaway. ☎ 707-937-5942, 888-466-5683; www.littleriverinn.com; 7901 N Hwy 1, Little River; r $130-365; 🛁 ❄

USEFUL WEBSITES
www.nchfinfo.org
www.whatalesyou.com

LINK YOUR TRIP
www.lonelyplanet.com/trip-planner

For the Birds: Hitchcock's California

WHY GO Alfred Hitchcock always preferred Northern California to Hollywood; he shot some of his most accomplished films within a 90-mile radius of San Francisco. From the ominous ocean vistas used for The Birds to his grand tour of moods in Vertigo, Hitchcock found a palette for his every vision.

TIME
2 – 3 days

DISTANCE
245 miles

BEST TIME TO GO
Feb – Nov

START
Bodega Bay

END
San Juan Bautista

ALSO GOOD FOR

❶ **Bodega Bay** is an otherwise unremarkable stop on a remarkable stretch of Hwy 1. However, it does have one enduring claim to fame: it was the setting for *The Birds*. Although the layout of the town was altered radically by special effects, you can get a good feel for the bay and its western shore, supposed site of Mitch Brenner's (Rod Taylor) farm. The ❷ **Tides Restaurant**, where much avian-caused havoc occurs, is still there but has been transmogrified since 1962 into a vast tourist-processing plant – no iota of the charming seaside restaurant of the movie remains. But venture 5 miles south of Bodega Bay on Hwy 1 to the tiny town of ❸ **Bodega** and you'll find two *Birds* icons: the schoolhouse and the church along Bodega Lane. Both are barely altered: if you see a crow you might share Tippi Hedren's sense of doom (though the house where Suzanne Pleshette gets fatally beaked was a set).

The next Hitchcock location is only 14 miles east on Hwy 12. ❹ **Santa Rosa** is a sun-dappled gem of a city, which served as the main location for 1943's *Shadow of a Doubt*. The train station where Uncle Charlie (Joseph Cotton) arrives in a swirl of sinister smoke still stands on Railroad Sq downtown. It's now the ❺ **California Welcome Center**, with info for tourists. Right across Wilson St, the ❻ **Hotel La Rose** has been in operation for over 100 years. It can be seen in numerous shots as the ever-less-genial Uncle Charlie shuttles around town one step ahead of suspicions that he's a serial killer.

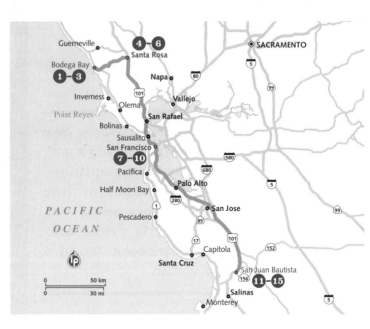

Hitchcock's love for ⑦ **San Francisco**, 60 miles south of Santa Rosa, was genuine, from its restaurants to its shops to its posh hotels. Although SF appeared in *The Birds, Family Plot* and more, it will always be most closely associated with the 1958 psychological masterpiece *Vertigo*. In its own dark way, the movie is a big wet kiss to the city by the bay. There are scores of locations still in existence but one of special note includes ⑧ **Mission Dolores**. Here Jimmy Stewart (Scotty) follows Kim Novak (Madeleine) and looks on as she visits the grave of Carlotta Valdes. The cemetery seen in the film is still here but, sadly, the tombstone used in the movie is gone (it actually remained in place for many years after 1958).

DETOUR Hitchcock turned to the San Joaquin Valley for two classic scenes. A three-hour drive southeast of San Juan Bautista takes you on I-5 to Hwy 46 in featureless Kern County. Drive east 4 miles to flat-as-a-board Corcoran Rd, head north and add a homicidal crop duster to complete the classic scene with Cary Grant in *North By Northwest*. Another 25 miles east brings you to the stretch of Hwy 99 Janet Leigh battles in the rain in *Psycho*.

Madeleine gets wet at ⑨ **Fort Point**, at the base of the Golden Gate Bridge, and Scotty plunges into the bay to save her. Although the scenes with the stars were filmed here, a stunt double actually jumped off the wall (the water scenes were shot in Hollywood). The old fort is no less imposing now as it was in VistaVision five decades ago. The dark plot twists in Vertigo are coming with abandon by the time we see Scotty obsessed with Judy, a working girl who reminds him of Madeleine (and with good reason!). The Empire Hotel where Judy bunks is on Sutter St. Renamed through the years, the hotel is now called (we're not making this up) the ❿ **Hotel Vertigo**! Obviously the owners would have been psycho not to take advantage of this angle. Rooms 501 and 502 are kept as they were in 1957 when they were used as models for the studio set in which Scotty creepily gets Judy to change her hair and clothes for him.

"In its own dark way, Vertigo *is a big wet kiss to the city by the bay."*

Just like Scotty and Madeleine/Judy, head south of San Francisco on Hwy 101 for 90 miles to ⓫ **San Juan Bautista.** (You may first want to go a little further south because just past Hwy 156 on Hwy 101 you pass through the majestic eucalyptus grove the pair drive through in *Vertigo.*) The centerpiece of the town is ⓬ **Mission San Juan Bautista**, which is death to Scotty's blondes. There's just one problem: there's no bell tower for the fatal plunges. It was a special effect and studio set. Still, you can sense Scotty's panic as you wander the familiar grounds. Nearby is ⓭ **San Juan Bautista State Historic Park**, which has several buildings used in *Vertigo*, including the Plaza Stables. During filming, Kim Novak took a liking to ⓮ **La Casa Rosa**, a restaurant that's changed little since it opened in 1935

ASK A LOCAL

"My favorite Hitchcock location is the **Brocklebank** [corner of Mason and Sacramento Sts] because it looks like a place where rich people would live. It seems glamorous and, when Kim Novak is shown leaving in her car, with a doorman at her wait, we are brought back to another world of glamour. Her outfits help fit the role, too."

Ruthe Stein, film writer for the San Francisco Chronicle

(the pink-hued building dates to 1858). Enjoy sweet dreams at ⓯ **Posada de San Juan,** which is close to the mission. If you hear a woman who sounds like she's falling, just put a pillow over your ear.

Ryan Ver Berkmoes

TRIP INFORMATION

GETTING THERE
Bodega Bay is 65 miles north of San Francisco on Hwy 1.

DO

California Welcome Center
Although the tracks are gone, the old depot never looked better and it's filled with useful info. ☎ 800-404-7673; www.visitsantarosa.com; 9 Fourth St, Santa Rosa; ☼ 9am-5pm

Fort Point
The fort was built as a defense during the Civil War and never fired a shot in anger. ☎ 415-556-1693; www.nps.gov/fopo; Marine Dr, the Presidio, San Francisco; ☼ 10am-5pm Thu-Mon; ☉

Mission Dolores
The current church dates to 1782. Note how Hitch managed to get the cross on the steeple in most shots. ☎ 415-621-8203; www.missiondolores.org; Dolores & 16th Sts, San Francisco; adult/child $5/3; ☉

Mission San Juan Bautista
The evocative 200-year-old cloisters are unchanged since Kim Novak ran down them in 1957. ☎ 831-623-4528; www.oldmissionsjb.org; off 2nd St; donation requested; ☼ 9:30am-4:45pm; ☉

San Juan Bautista State Historic Park
Many of the old wooden buildings here date to the mid-1800s, when this was on the main route north from LA; most appear in *Vertigo*. ☎ 831-623-4526; www.parks.ca.gov; adult/child $2/free; ☼ 10am-4:30pm; ☉

EAT

La Casa Rosa
This restaurant is almost as old as the mission and serves a variation on old California cooking: lots of tasty casseroles and fruit preserves. ☎ 831-623-4563; 107 Third St, San Juan Bautista; meals from $12; ☼ lunch Wed-Mon

Tides Restaurant
Tourists flock to this big seaside eatery like, er, birds. There are gift stores, a fresh counter and more. ☎ 707-875-3652; 835 Hwy 1, Bodega Bay; meals $10-25; ☼ lunch & dinner; ☉

SLEEP

Hotel La Rose
In the heart of the gentrified train station area, this small hotel is not a good place to make a new friend named Charlie. ☎ 707-579-3200; www.hotellarose.com; 308 Wilson St, Santa Rosa; r $120-280

Hotel Vertigo
This pretentiously hip hotel has taken the *Vertigo* plunge right down to the orange color palette from the film's titles. ☎ 415-885-6800, 800-553-1900; www.hotelvertigosf.com; 940 Sutter St, San Francisco; r from $250

Posada de San Juan
This mission-style hotel has 34 atmospheric rooms in the historic center of town. ☎ 831-623-4030; 310 Fourth St, San Juan Bautista; r $90-250

USEFUL WEBSITES
www.hitchcockwiki.com
www.footstepsinthefog.com

SUGGESTED READ
Footsteps in the Fog, Alfred Hitchcock's San Francisco – Jeff Kraft & Aaron Leventhal

LINK YOUR TRIP

www.lonelyplanet.com/trip-planner

Calistoga Cycle

WHY GO Up-valley doesn't mean snob valley when you're talking Calistoga, 45 minutes north of Napa. As local bike-shop owner Brad Suhr will attest, this mellow town is best explored by cycling through the sun-dappled vineyards, wood-slatted footbridges, and cruise-worthy back roads without Silverado Trail traffic.

Brad Suhr has ridden the Silverado Trail and Route 29 no fewer than 100 times. He believes Calistoga, founded in 1859 as a hot-springs resort beneath colossal, volcanic Mount St Helena, is really the last Old West town in Napa Valley. He's designed a bike route just around town and recommends you see it now, before the old-school spas turn into chichi ones. Though famous for water (geysers, spas and the bottled variety), the town also has unpretentious small wineries rivaling those down valley. Here's a cycling tour based on Brad's favorites.

Cyclists get their bikes and bearings at his ❶ **Calistoga Bike Shop**, where the staff will let you borrow a GPS unit or four-bottle wine carrier (if you buy more, the shop will pick it up for you). The shop outfits all kinds of riders and does a 24-hour-turnaround repair service, too.

Once saddled up, Washington St leads you off the main drag. Where the road ends, the bike path begins: the landscape falls open like a book, with vineyards stretching out on either side and a handsome view of the Palisades, the volcanic black-rock cliffs, on your left-hand side. Traffic noise is all but gone, replaced by the twittering of birds in the trees. Before long you'll cross two wood-slatted bridges. Take care on the second, as the wood slats have wider gaps.

When you come to a T-junction, turn right on Dunaweal St to begin a 5-mile loop to the Silverado Trail. Just past Twomey Vineyards you'll

TIME
1 – 2 days

DISTANCE
20 miles

BEST TIME TO GO
May – Oct

START
Calistoga

END
Calistoga

ALSO GOOD FOR

FOOD & DRINK

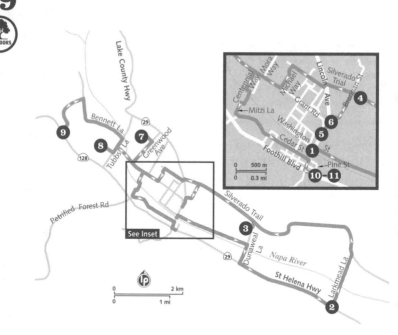

see a right-hand turnoff to ② **Castello di Amorosa.** "Crazy money spent on a crazy project," says Brad about the excessively grandiose re-creation of an Italian medieval castle (plus winery) built on the hilltop. The place was hand-built over 14 years with every period detail you can imagine, from fresco murals to brickwork in the catacombs to an actual torture chamber, complete with impaler and iron maiden. Look for it in Adam Sandler's *Bedtime Stories,* shot here in June 2008.

"…remember Brad's guidance to 'spit and cycle,' lest you start weaving on your own."

As you pedal around the loop on Larkmead and head left on the Silverado Trail, you'll notice the road bending in lazy curves, with a couple of wineries appearing on the right. Stop in if you like, but remember Brad's guidance to "spit and cycle," lest you start weaving on your own. At the corner of Silverado and Dunaweal it's impossible to miss ③ **Clos Pegase** winery and its cubist-geometric architecture; note the impressive sculpture garden. Inside, however, you may need to sweep aside a rack of sweatshirts to examine the Francis Bacon.

You'll be ready for a break at this point, so just past August Briggs winery and the Rosedale junction, stop off at the Solage resort and its chic ④ **SolBar.** The mostly organic gourmet menu doesn't diss a cheeseburger, and you can relax on the desert-minimalist patio with its sandy-sage-y tones and long horizontal planes (boccie ball courts, an extra-long lap pool, flat glassy-topped fountains). Back in town, take note of ❺ **Dr Wilkinson's Hot Springs Resort** on your right. You'll want to come back here later in the evening for "The Works," which includes a mud bath in a concrete tub filled with detoxifying peat moss and volcanic ash, mined here. It's strangely buoyant and soothing, despite the occasional mud-flecks you'll find in your hair afterwards.

Backtrack past bungalow rooms across the street at the ❻ **Indian Springs Resort**. Plan to return at the end of your ride if you crave a supercomfy bed. Continuing through Lake View, Morey and Michael Sts, you'll find a mix of old-California-style summer-houses and fancier moneyed ones. A right on Grant turns into Myrtledale; turn right again on Greenwood to cross a 1904 narrow stone bridge (watch for traffic) and you'll come across another of Brad's favorites, ❼ **Vincent Arroyo Winery**, on your

DETOUR An old stagecoach route provides a steep, techni-cal 9-mile ride up to Oat Hill and glorious views of Calistoga. In the 1800s it was used to haul supplies and ore; now, it's open to mountain bikers and hikers up for a challenge. The trail-head is where Hwy 29 and the Silverado Trail intersect, across from the pizza joint.

left. Happy dogs might greet you first; expect a warm welcome and personal-ized tour, perhaps from Vincent himself, in his garage-turned-tasting room.

The wine may leave you feeling a little loopy, but you're not imagining things if you spot a steamy jet stream shooting high in the air just off the intersection at Tubbs Lane. "It's not Yellowstone," Brad says of the rather wimpy ❽ **Old Faithful Geyser**, the epitome of kitsch Americana in a roadside attraction, "but it's one of only three in the world with regular eruptions." While you wait for one you can picnic, check out the darling goats at the petting zoo, and bask in the views of Mt St Helena.

True thrill seekers will love ❾ **Bennett Lane Winery**, a jog north on its namesake road off Tubbs Lane (the entrance is actually on Hwy 28, at the intersection). The winery sponsors Nascar racers, and if you're lucky you can see one of the cars down in the cellar (as of this writing, the owner's two cars had totaled each other in the last race!)

Making your way back into the town center, cruise back down Myrtledale and then follow what is mostly a dedicated bike path along Centennial and Mitzi Lane. Turn left at the Homeplate Café and follow Cedar St back to the bike shop to return your rental. Then it's just a few blocks' walk to the ❿ **Vallarta Market**, which Brad says makes "the best burritos in the upper valley," and the ⓫ **Wine Way Inn** next door, a charming B&B with a gener-ous, delicious breakfast.

Dominique Channell

TRIP INFORMATION

GETTING THERE
Calistoga is 74 miles from San Francisco on Hwy 80 and Hwy 29. Hwy 29 becomes Lincoln Ave in Calistoga.

DO
Calistoga Bike Shop
Bike rentals, cool self-guided tours, fast repairs. ☎ 707-942-9687, 866-942-2453; www.calistogabikeshop.com; 1318 Lincoln Ave, Calistoga; rental prices vary with bike type; ☺ 10am-6pm; ⛄

Castello di Amorosa
Re-created 12th-century European castle/winery, complete with torture chamber. ☎ 707-967-6272; www.castellodiamorosa.com; 4045 N St Helena Hwy, Calistoga; tasting fee $10-20, tour & tasting by reservation $25-40; ☺ 9:30am-6pm, to 5pm Dec-Feb 15; ⛄

Dr Wilkinson's Hot Springs Resort
Submerge yourself in glorious-feeling mud (from volcanic ash, mined here) at this detoxifying spa. ☎ 707-942-4102; www.dr wilkinson.com; 1507 Lincoln Ave, Calistoga; mud-bath package $89; ☺ 8:30am-3:45pm

Old Faithful Geyser
Pure kitsch roadside Americana: pet goats; watch geyser blow! ☎ 707-942-6463; www .oldfaithfulgeyser.com; 1299 Tubbs Lane, Calistoga; adult/under 6yr/6-12yr $8/free/$3 (check website for coupon); ☺ 9am-5pm, to 6pm summer; ⛄ 🐾

EAT
Solbar
Poussin *a la plancha* or double cheeseburger with fried pickles? Your choice, in chic decor with mountain views. ☎ 866-942-7442; www.solagecalistoga.com; 755 Silverado Trail, Calistoga; mains $14-26; ☺ 7am-3pm & 5pm-11pm

Vallarta Market
Mexican laborers crowd into this real-deal *taqueria* market. ☎ 707-942-8664; 1009 Foothill Blvd, Calistoga; mains $6-8; ☺ 9am-8pm; ⛄

DRINK
Bennett Lane Winery
Fancy yourself a winemaker? Blend your own against a mountainous backdrop at the top of the valley. ☎ 877-629-6272; www.bennett lane.com; 3340 Hwy 128, Calistoga; tasting fee $10; ☺ 10am-5:30pm

Clos Pegase
Winery with cubist architecture and an astounding art collection (Alexander Calder, Jean Dubuffet, Henry Moore). ☎ 707-942-4981; www.clospegase.com; 1060 Dunaweal Lane, Calistoga; tasting fee $10-25; ☺ 10:30am-5pm

Vincent Arroyo Winery
Taste small-production, big-reputation wines with friendly owners – in their garage, with their family dogs. ☎ 707-942-6995; www .vincentarroyo.com; 2361 Greenwood Ave, Calistoga; tasting free (appointment only); ☺ 10am-4:30pm; ⛄ 🐾

SLEEP
Indian Springs Resort
Stand-alone bungalows, much like a 1950s Florida retirement community, but bright and fresh with comfy beds. ☎ 800-572-0679, 707-942-4913; www.indiansprings calistoga.com; 1712 Lincoln Ave, Calistoga; r $185-290

Wine Way Inn
Simple, cozy craftsman-style B&B with romantic antiques and the innkeeper's handmade mini-quilts; fabulous, multicourse, truly gourmet breakfast. ☎ 800-572-0679, 707-942-0680; www.winewayinn.com; 1019 Foothill Blvd, Calistoga; r $100-200

LINK YOUR TRIP

www.lonelyplanet.com/trip-planner

Hidden Wineries, Hidden Valleys

WHY GO A patchwork of vineyards, orchards and gnarled oak trees covers toast-colored hills in these pastoral valleys. We teamed up with renowned vintner Kent Rosenblum of Rosenblum Cellars to fall off the beaten path and into boutique, family-run wineries throughout these two gorgeous, lesser-traveled wine regions.

TIME
2 days

DISTANCE
35 miles

BEST TIME TO GO
Year-round

START
Alexander Valley

END
Healdsburg

ALSO GOOD FOR

East of Hwy 101, serene Alexander Valley abuts the Mayacamas Mountains – cross the ridgeline and you're in Napa. Summers are hot here so you'll find cabernet sauvignon, merlot and warm-weather chardonnay, but there's fine sauvignon blanc and zinfandel too. The wines you'll be tasting are hard to find elsewhere, except at a few restaurants and in some specialty shops in San Francisco, Los Angeles and New York.

Photo ops abound as you meander through the valley's southern reaches, where the rolling hills and wide-open vineyards are postcard perfect.

One of Rosenblum's first stops is ❶ **Field Stone Winery**, owned and operated by the Staten family. Up on a rise, and surrounded by vineyards (of course!), the picturesque little winery is tucked in a special underground space carved into the oak-covered hillside. Rosenblum suggests trying its delicious sauvignon blanc.

Just up the road, ❷ **Hanna Winery** looks like a Tuscan-style train depot. It also has stellar views; consider buying a bottle and tucking into a picnic here. At the wine bar, look for estate-grown merlot and cabernet, and big-fruit zins and syrah. But Rosenblum loves their sauvignon blanc. On weekends tuck into an appointment-only sit-down reserve wine-and-cheese tasting.

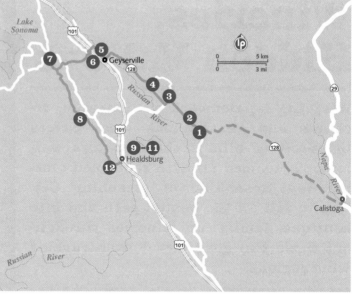

If you forgot picnic supplies, pop into the locally famous ❸ **Jimtown Store**. Touring cyclists line up for the sandwiches made using housemade spreads, like artichoke or fig and olive. Behind the deli and café, browse antique bric-a-brac, candles and Mexican oilcloths.

DETOUR Diminutive, laidback **Calistoga**, half an hour south on Hwy 128, drops out of the wine country chichi hunt with its small-town feel. Cruise quaint storefronts packed with restaurants, shops and galleries, or drop into one of the ubiquitous hot springs.

Giraffes in wine country? You bet! Nearby **Safari West** (www.safariwest.com) wild animal preserve covers 400 acres and protects zebras, cheetahs, giraffes and other exotic animals, which mostly roam free. Take a tour or sleep in one of its tent-cabins.

Check out the view from ❹ **Stryker Sonoma's** modern concrete-and-glass hilltop tasting room. The juxtaposition of the sleek winery and the rolling hills is impressive. Bring your Jimtown sandwiches! Their standout wines are fruit-forward zinfandel and sangiovese. Once you've reached your max on wineries, plan for a dinner at ❺ **Santi**. Among the region's best, Santi cooks *bellissima* rustic northern-Italian dishes, like *spaghetti calabrese*, well worth the 10-minute drive north. On balmy evenings, hold hands by candlelight on the big wooden deck out back.

If you're traveling in a pack, the five-bedroom, five-bath *luxe de luxe* ❻ **Alexander Valley Lodge** sleeps 14. Party like a rock star on 53 acres with views all around to Mt St Helena and the Russian River. The vistas from the sparkling pool, Jacuzzi, tiki bar and waterfall will blow your mind. If you don't have an entourage, drop down Hwy 101 to Healdsburg for its plethora of B&Bs.

Start your next wine-hoppin' day in the Dry Creek Valley. Nighttime fog doesn't usually ascend the 2000ft-high mountains west of Dry Creek, so the warmer weather is ideal for sauvignon blanc, zinfandel and cabernet sauvignon. West Dry Creek Rd is an undulating, winding country lane with no center stripe and one of Sonoma County's great back roads, ideal for cycling.

"On balmy evenings, hold hands by candlelight on the big wooden deck out back."

At the north end of the valley, Lou Preston runs homey **7** **Preston Vineyards** on a 19th-century organic farm. He bakes his own bread and, Rosenblum says, grows the "greatest tomatoes in the world." In the tasting room, candy-colored walls and tongue-in-groove ceilings set an inviting country mood. Its signature wine is citrusy sauvignon blanc, but try the Rhône varietals and small-lot wines: mourvèdre, viognier, cinsault and the cult favorite, barbera. Picnic in the shade of the walnut tree, then play boccie. Next, wisteria-draped **8** **Lambert Bridge Winery** has a motto: "Great wine served with great food shared by great friends." Rosenblum enjoys the ambient setting and wood-fired pizzas. A family-owned operation, it specializes in small lots of artisanal Bordeaux blends and varietals.

Rosenblum declares with zeal that perhaps the "best restaurant in the whole country!" hides away in **9** **Healdsburg**. With an inventive menu, **10** **Cyrus** has earned two Michelin stars for its wonderful food, excellent wine list and "the best service in America." The emphasis is on luxury foods prepared with a French sensibility and flavored with global spices. It's got one menu exclusively for champagne and caviar and another with an exciting array of courses like soft-shell crab with smoked soba noodles and oolong broth. The staff moves as if in a ballet, ever intuitive of your pace and tastes. For a more low-key setting, and to hang with the local viniculture crowd (Healdsburg is also home to one of Rosenblum Cellars' tasting rooms), head to **11** **Bistro Ralph**, Rosenblum's longstanding favorite for down-to-earth French country-style cooking.

If you love country inns and stately manor houses, the regal 1881 **12** **Madrona Manor** exudes Victorian elegance. Slip out of the modern world as you enter the 8 acres of dense woods and blooming gardens that enfold the famous hilltop mansion. A "painted lady" with its astonishing yet harmonious array of colors outside, the interior is decked out with many of its original furnishings. A separate carriage house, cottage and former schoolhouse contain some of the lavish rooms and suites as well. It makes a perfect place to relax and compare notes on your favorite wines of the day.

Alexis Averbuck

TRIP INFORMATION

GETTING THERE

From San Francisco, take Hwy 101 north. South of Windsor go east on Chalk Hill Rd to Hwy 128 north.

DO & DRINK

Field Stone Winery

This unique little winery is built into a hillside surrounded by its own family-run vineyards. ☎ 707-433-7266; www.fieldstonewinery .com; 10075 Hwy 128, Healdsburg; tastings free; ☇ 10am-5pm

Hanna Winery

Everyone loves this one-of-a-kind place. Wines cost $20 to $40 and it has an annual case production of 37,000. ☎ 707-431-4310, 800-854-3987; www.hannawinery.com; 9280 Hwy 128, Healdsburg; tastings free; ☇ 10am-4pm

Lambert Bridge Winery

A scrumptious stop in the middle of the Dry Creek Valley. Its top "flight" comes paired with cheeses. ☎ 707-431-9600, 800-975-0555; www.lambertbridge.com; 4085 W Dry Creek Rd, Healdsburg; tasting fee $10-25; ☇ 10:30am-4:30pm

Preston Vineyards

Enjoy the family feel here. The annual case production is only 5000. ☎ 707-433-3327, 800-305-9707; www.prestonvineyards.com; 9282 W Dry Creek Rd, Healdsburg; tasting fee $5, refundable with purchase; ☇ 11am-4:30pm

Stryker Sonoma

Great views surround the sleek new building. Bottles cost $18 to $48 and annual case production is 7000. ☎ 707-433-1944; www.strykersonoma.com; 5110 Hwy 128, Geyserville; tastings free; ☇ 10:30am-5pm

EAT

Bistro Ralph

Rub shoulders with winemakers tucking into classic dishes like chicken *paillard*. Also serves great martinis. ☎ 707-433-1380; 109 Plaza St, Healdsburg; lunch mains $10-15, dinner mains $17-27; ☇ 11:30am-2:30pm & 5:30-9pm Mon-Sat

Cyrus

Absolutely elegant, from the caviar cart to the cheese course, this is one meal to remember. Make reservations. ☎ 707-433-3311; www.cyrusrestaurant.com; 29 North St, Healdsburg; 3/4 courses $78/90; ☇ 5:30-9:30pm

Jimtown Store

Much more than a roadside stand, here cyclists, wine connoisseurs and soccer moms line up for their goodies. ☎ 707-433-1212; www.jimtown.com; 6706 Hwy 128, Healdsburg; mains $7-10; ☇ 7:30am-5pm, with seasonal variations

Santi

An Alexander Valley standard – Italian food as it is meant to be. ☎ 707-857-1790; www .tavernasanti.com; 21047 Geyserville Ave, Geyserville; lunch mains $12-18, dinner mains $20-35; ☇ 11:30am-2pm Wed-Sat & 5:30-9pm nightly

SLEEP

Alexander Valley Lodge

A full-on house decked out in safari-modern decor. The palatial rooms look out on world-class views. ☎ 707-756-2400; www.alex andervalleylodge.com; 20507 Geyserville Ave, Geyserville; per night $695-850

Madrona Manor

Brides book years in advance to be wed on this gorgeous estate. Two-night minimum most weekends. ☎ 707-433-4231, 800-258-4003; www.madronamanor.com; 1001 Westside Rd, Healdsburg; r & suites $195-445

LINK YOUR TRIP

TRIP
14 North County Eco Trip p123
19 Calistoga Cycle p145
22 Apples & Antiques in Sebastopol p157

www.lonelyplanet.com/trip-planner

Along the Russian River

WHY GO During summer, the lazy Russian River meanders through vineyards and down into redwood groves. Rare nesting ospreys fly overhead as you float slowly along toward the river's dramatic end at the Pacific Ocean, populated by surfers, sea gulls and seals.

Don't even dare to tame the beast of the river in winter when it fills to flood levels and often inundates low-lying homes. But when summer hits and the river level drops, it becomes an easy float, and the trails in the area stop sliding off the hills, and make for excellent hiking. Don't want to get your toes wet? You can also follow River Rd, which quickly leaves the bustle of Santa Rosa behind, narrowing as it approaches the dusky green river and winds along its tree-filled edges.

If you're river-running, either bring your own tubes, canoes and kayaks to launch from town or drop in to ❶ **Burke's Canoe Trips** to slip directly out onto the sunny water. Glimpse osprey, hawks and herons on the 10-mile paddle downriver from the Burke's to Guerneville, which takes about four hours. Burke's will shuttle you back from Guerneville to reclaim your car, or camp under their stand of riverside redwoods.

The county's wineries rival those of nearby Napa, so continuing on River Rd, when you emerge into a gorgeous valley of chardonnay and pinot noir vineyards surrounded by pine-covered hills, stop for audaciously bubbly refreshments at ❷ **Korbel Champagne Cellars**. About 2.5 miles east of central Guerneville, the ivy-draped brick winery gets jammed on weekends as folks come from all around to sip the excellent champagnes it's been making since 1882. The fascinating 45-minute winery tour teaches you Champagne Making 101. Winery maps at the visitor center make it easy to chart a world-class wine-tasting tour through other winding back roads.

TIME
2 days

DISTANCE
25 miles

BEST TIME TO GO
Jun – Sep

START
Forestville

END
Jenner

ALSO GOOD FOR

ROUTE

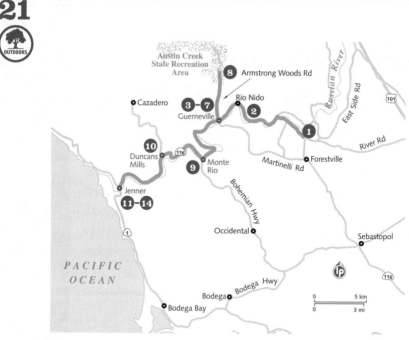

The colorful, oddball main street of ❸ **Guerneville** bustles with life, as tourists and locals alike cruise the storefronts and galleries and dip in to the cafés, restaurants and bars. Known for its openness to all (don't be surprised to spy chaps alongside polo shirts), the town is set up for easy walking.

Arrange float or fishing trips to the river's mouth at one of the outfitters in town or head to ❹ **Johnson's Beach** to rent kayaks and canoes that you launch from and return to the beach. A swinging scene for sunbathing city folk, it also hosts the Russian River Jazz Festival (September) and its companion Blues Festival (June). There's nothing quite like floating in the cool river on a scorching summer day while the sinuous notes of Wayne Shorter tickle your ears. When Dr John brings his signature zydeco/blues/jazz to town, revelers form full New Orleans–style second lines, complete with umbrellas and waving hankies.

Formerly Fife's (the booming gay resort), ❺ **Dawn Ranch Lodge**, restaurant, spa and pool are now patronized by everyone. Hummingbirds and butterflies flit through 15 acres along the riverbank, and the larger cottages overlook an emerald glade surrounded by quiet apple orchards. Nearby quintessential cozy American diner ❻ **Pat's Restaurant** comes complete with Naugahyde-padded booths and saucy waitresses. "Pat's Stack," a tower of pancakes, is good fuel for river-running. Or stock up for a river picnic at ❼ **Food for Humans**, where shiny pyramids of fresh organic produce taste as good as they look.

Soaring redwood trees and carpeted forest floor create a profound silence that spreads for 805 acres just a few miles to the north at **8** **Armstrong Redwoods State Reserve**. The *Return of the Jedi* Ewok village chase scene was filmed here; speed-pods zoomed between the trunks of these 265ft giants.

The tranquil, disabled-accessible Discovery Trail passes Armstrong Tree, a 1400-year-old behemoth. Strenuous longer routes climb deep into the forest, or you can giddyup with a guided horse trip from the pack station.

The river continues through the bucolic hillsides of West County, passing the venerable, and slightly odd, old-boys' club The Bohemian Grove. From the river the Grove looks like little more than a densely forested hillside with a dock, but it hides a constellation of cabins. Next, the river winds into tiny **9** **Monte Rio**. Festooned with a sign declaring it "Vacation Wonderland," it's really just best to stop in for a bite to eat, rent a kayak or swim at the beach. In the evening, catch a flick in the renovated airplane hangar. Likewise, the fine restaurants, bakery and shops in **10** **Duncans Mills** make a restful pit stop before the upcoming austere drama of the coast. Little more than a restored railway depot, this itsy-bitsy burg lies in a tranquil valley with galloping horses.

The river broadens as it ends its journey in tawny, oceanside hills dotted with cattle and sheep. Merging with the ocean at the small village of **11** **Jenner**, the mouth turns brackish and seals splash on its edges. The North Jenner Headlands Trail traverses sere bluffs, sprinkled with a surprising array of hardy succulents and grasses. The often empty trail along the crags affords views to Goat Rock and beyond. Or walk inland on the Shell Beach to **12** **Pomo Canyon trail** to emerge into wildflower-studded meadows with exquisite views of the Russian River and south as far as Pt Reyes. Just over the ridge to the east, pitch a tent at the walk-in **13** **Pomo Canyon Campground** under a cathedral-like grove of second-growth redwoods.

"…emerge into wildflower-studded meadows with exquisite views of the Russian River and vistas south…"

Unwind in style at the picture-perfect **14** **River's End** restaurant, perched on a cliff overlooking the grand sweep of the Pacific Ocean. While it serves world-class meals at world-class prices, consider simply sharing an appetizer paired with an award-winning glass of wine. Or tuck into a dessert like their unique chocolate cardamom ice cream, and watch the sun set in silent, gentle harmony.

Alexis Averbuck

RAINBOW FLAGS EVERYWHERE

You'll know it's Lazy Bear Weekend (August) because every establishment displays a hand-hewn bear statuette or a sign greeting the Bears. Who are the Bears, you may ask? Seven thousand gay men, prerequisite burly, coming to kick back *rio* style. Other gay gatherings like Women's Weekend (May) and Leather Weekend (November – it's colder…better for leather) maintain Guerneville's reputation as one of the most gay-friendly resorts in California.

TRIP INFORMATION

GETTING THERE
From San Francisco, shoot up Hwy 101 for 57 miles, take the River Rd/Guerneville exit and go west.

DO
Armstrong Redwoods State Reserve
Some of the closest old-growth redwoods to the Bay Area. ☎ 707-869-2015, 707-887-2939 horseback ride reservations; 17000 Armstrong Woods Rd, Guerneville; pedestrians/cars free/$6, horseback rides ½-/1-day $70/175-225; ☷ day use 8am-1hr after sunset, visitor center 11am-3pm; ♿ 🐾

Burke's Canoe Trips
A no-nonsense outfitter on the banks of the river, it will shuttle you back from Guerneville. ☎ 707-887-1222; www.burkescanoetrips.com; 8600 River Rd, Forestville; canoe per day incl shuttle $59; ☷ 9am-6pm; ♿

Johnson's Beach
Your one-stop shop for beach, campground, cabins and kayak/canoe rental. ☎ 707-869-2022; www.johnsonsbeach.com; 16241 First St, Guerneville; admission free, kayak & canoe per hour/day $8/25, campsites/cabins $14/50; ☷ 10am-6pm, closed Oct-Apr; ♿

EAT
Food for Humans
Friendly folks dispense fresh organic and bulk foods, right next to big ol' Safeway. It's David and Goliath! ☎ 707-869-3612; 16385 First St, Guerneville; ☷ 10am-9pm; ♿

Pat's Restaurant
Waitresses slinging hash will give you a little something to stick to your ribs before you hit the river. ☎ 707-869-9904; 16236 Main St, Guerneville; mains $6; ☷ 6am-3pm; ♿

River's End
A peaceful restaurant-lounge hanging off the edge of a cliff. ☎ 707-865-2484; www.rivers-end.com; 11048 Hwy 1, Jenner; mains $14-34; ☷ noon-3:30pm & 5-9pm Thu-Mon, with seasonal variations

DRINK
Korbel Champagne Cellars
Delicious, light and dry champagnes go well with gourmet deli snacks. It offers excellent garden and winery tours. ☎ 707-824-7000; www.korbel.com; 13250 River Rd, Guerneville; tours free; ☷ 10am-3:45pm

SLEEP
Armstrong Redwoods/Austin Creek State Recreation Area
A few of these bare-bones sites require a 3- to 5-mile backcountry hike. No reservations. ☎ 707-869-2015; www.parks.ca.gov; 17000 Armstrong Woods Rd, Guerneville; campsites $15; ♿ 🐾

Dawn Ranch Lodge
Party at the poolside bar or wander the tranquil groves and mellow out along the river. ☎ 707-869-0656; www.dawnranch.com; 16467 River Rd, Guerneville; r $149-350

Pomo Canyon Campground
Part of Sonoma Coast State Beach; walk-in camp at a beautiful spot near the trailhead. ☎ 707-875-3483; access on Willow Creek Rd off Hwy 1, Jenner; campsites $6; ☷ Apr-Nov

USEFUL WEBSITES
www.russianriver.com
www.gayrussianriver.com

LINK YOUR TRIP
TRIP   www.lonelyplanet.com/trip-planner

Apples & Antiques in Sebastopol

WHY GO Sebastopol was built on the abundant produce of its apple orchards, but now you can't go more than a mile without seeing a few antique stores. Both are part of the appeal (no pun intended). Come anytime, but especially in late summer, for a winning combo of sun, wholesome food and eclectic culture.

TIME
2 days

DISTANCE
8 miles

BEST TIME TO GO
May – Oct

START
Sebastopol

END
Sebastopol

ALSO GOOD FOR

HISTORY & CULTURE

The main road into town, Gravenstein Hwy is named after the sublime local heirloom apple variety. It is useful in an array of eats because of its fine balance of sweet and tart, and folks make it into pies, sauce, juice and vinegar, or just plain eat it straight. The twisted trunks of these old trees line the road in row upon row, even as upstart trendy vineyards try to supplant them. Despite originating in Denmark in 1669, and making the journey to California with Russians at Fort Ross in 1820, these formerly ubiquitous Gravensteins have now become a fought-for specialty because of the financial pressure to change over orchards to more lucrative crops like wine grapes.

Nevertheless, a dozen commercial growers and two processors remain in Sonoma County, literally holding their ground and ripening their sweet charges from a light lime green to their ultimate robust dark red stripes. The local fruit is still feted at the popular Apple Blossom Festival (April) and the Gravenstein Apple Fair (August).

Meanwhile, as you approach ❶ **Sebastopol** from the south on Gravenstein Hwy/Hwy 116, goofy little fly-by-night antique shops start cropping up alongside some of their more established brethren. ❷ **Antique Society** packs over 125 separate vendors into a 20,000-sq-ft former door factory. A stroll through this remarkably well-organized place might get you drooling for finely wrought end tables you never knew you needed. Or maybe it's the aromas drifting in from the

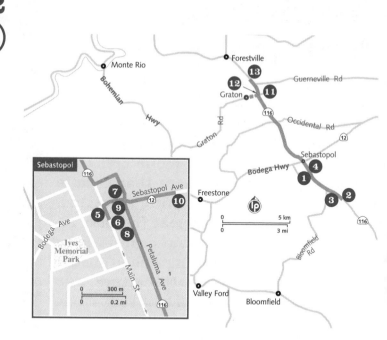

on-site Italian café and bakery. Shoppers refuel on fresh-cooked *pizzettas* and coffee that puts hair on their antique-lovin' chests.

Half a mile north, muscle trucks line the road on weekends, belching as they turn into booming ❸ **Midgley's Country Flea Market**. Booth upon booth of mom-and-pop vendors fill what amounts to a dusty park. So if you're not in the mood to make it all the way to Tijuana for your velvet Elvis painting, you can pick one up here for a song. Dig through piles of old silver, teetering stacks of out-of-print books and anything else your deepest garage-sale heart can imagine. Verdant piles of fresh produce, including apples, fill one section.

Almost in downtown, Mark at ❹ **Ashley's West County Vintage** holds down the area's thriving "resale" market with 20 years' experience selling high-end vintage clothes. This tiny shop overflows with cool old-school rayon dresses in bodacious colors, surf shirts that would make Don Ho proud and original-model Levi's. Mark has a brisk business shipping these hot jeans over to Japan, where the original indigo dyes are said to have powerful properties. Slip on a pair, see how they make your tush look, and buy 'em on the spot.

Shops line Main St in town, and make for good walkin'. The plain dining room of ❺ **East West Cafe** thrums steadily with a churn of hippies, hikers and ranchers, who dig in to fluffy French toast and apple and pork sausages, or hearty macrobiotic burritos. Healthy *and* delicious, who can beat that?

The fabulous hole-in-the-wall Michelin-starred ❻ **K&L Bistro** creates inventive provincial Cal-French concoctions. Two perfectly cooked homemade *boudin blanc* sausages, hard to find outside of France or Louisiana, come with a radicchio and (you guessed it!) apple salad. Tables are tight, but the crowd is friendly and fun.

Top off a shopping trip or meal with rich homemade ice cream made from local ingredients at ❼ **Screamin' Mimi's.** You'll know it by the big party-pink ice-cream cone hanging out front and the lines of kids at the counter ogling the goodies.

Down the block, newly minted ❽ **Hopmonk Tavern** and juke-jointy ❾ **Jasper O'Farrell's** get jamming when they have live music. The tavern has a full restaurant, including a late-night menu on weekends, and specializes in boutique beers, but they both make concession to the local fruit and serve seasonal ciders as well.

> **DETOUR** Jaunt a few minutes west on Graton Rd to tiny, vibrant **Graton**. Arts co-ops, antique shops and the Sonoma Wine Company jam-pack the miniscule main street. The exquisite sister restaurants Willowwood Market & Cafe and Underwood Bar & Bistro draw people to town for great eats and positively slurpable cocktails.

Right near downtown and tucked behind the historic Gravenstein train station, tidy ❿ **Sebastopol Inn** festoons comfortable rooms in Americana. Take advantage of the clear country skies in the hot tub and sparkling pool. Just north of town off Hwy 116, the ⓫ **Vine Hill Inn** has only four antique-filled rooms in a restored 1897 Victorian farmhouse, with gorgeous vineyard views. A B&B, the inn's delicious breakfast is made with fresh eggs from the barn's chickens.

Stock up on all things apple on the north side of town. The cavernous, green tin warehouse just as you leave the village of Sebastopol on Gravenstein Hwy contains Ace Cider. It brews delicious fruit ciders for its little ⓬ **Ace-in-the-Hole Pub**, which hosts raucous live music on weekends.

In the produce stands along the road, fresh produce abounds in addition to Gravensteins and Granny Smiths. Pick up the free *Sonoma County Farm Trails Guide* (www.farmtrails.org) to visit the farms and orchards that grow them.

In the end, though, it ain't an apple vacation without apple pie! For 24 years, roadside and orchard-tucked ⓭ **Mom's Apple Pie** has been cooking up Gravensteins from August to November and Granny Smiths from November to July. It offers a host of other flaky-crusted pies and if you want to go "sugar free" they'll add apple juice concentrate instead of cane sugar. But why would you?
Alexis Averbuck

FOOD & DRINK

TRIP INFORMATION

GETTING THERE
Northbound on Hwy 101, take the Rohnert Park/Sebastopol exit to Hwy 116 and go west.

DO

Antique Society
One of the *grand dames* of North Bay antiques; there's something for everyone here. ☎ 707-829-1733; www.antiquesociety.com; 2661 Gravenstein Hwy S, Sebastopol; ☾ 10am-5pm

Ashley's West County Vintage
Clothes, skateboards and household implements flow into the street in front of the oldest vintage shop in the county. ☎ 707-823-5048; 851 Gravenstein Hwy S, Sebastopol; ☾ 10am-5:30pm Thu-Mon

Midgley's Country Flea Market
The region's largest flea market overflows on weekends. It's a social scene in its own right. ☎ 707-823-7874; 2200 Gravenstein Hwy S, Sebastopol; ☾ 6:30am-4:30pm Sat & Sun; ⅍

Mom's Apple Pie
Apple is predictably good, but wild blueberry is worth trying. Yum, that flaky crust! ☎ 707-823-8330; www.momsapplepieusa .com; 4550 Gravenstein Hwy N, Sebastopol; whole pies $6-14; ☾ 10am-6pm; ⅍

EAT

East West Cafe
An unpretentious café serving grass-fed beef and blue-corn pancakes, it does steady business all day. ☎ 707-829-2822; 128 N Main St, Sebastopol; mains $7-14; ☾ 8am-9pm

K&L Bistro
Make reservations for top-flight French food in a comfortably elegant dining room. ☎ 707-823-6614; 119 S Main St, Sebastopol; mains $9-30; ☾ 11:30am-3pm Mon-Sat, 5-9pm Mon-Thu, to 10pm Fri & Sat

LINK YOUR TRIP
TRIP

Screamin' Mimi's
Sold by weight; get everything from a tiny kid-cone to a hot fudge fresh lavender sundae. ☎ 707-823-5902; www.screaminmimis icecream.com; 6902 Sebastopol Ave, Sebastopol; ☾ 11am-10pm; ⅍

DRINK

Ace-in-the-Hole Pub
This unpretentious roadside tavern draws a crowd for fresh apple and pear ciders and hoppin' music. ☎ 707-829-1223; 3100 Gravenstein Hwy N, Sebastopol; ☾ 11am-7pm Sun-Wed, 10am-9pm Thu-Sat

Hopmonk Tavern
A welcoming, straightforward tavern with a delish menu too. ☎ 707-829-7300; www .hopmonk.com; 230 Petaluma Ave, Sebastopol; ☾ 11:30am-9:30pm

Jasper O'Farrell's
There's pub grub and nightly entertainment at this Irish-style bar. Tuesday is open-mic night. ☎ 707-823-1389; www.jasperofarrells pub.com; 6957 Sebastopol Ave, Sebastopol; ☾ 11am-2am

SLEEP

Sebastopol Inn
It's easy to relax in the light, breezy rooms of this quiet and well-kept independent, non-cookie-cutter hotel. ☎ 707-829-2500, 800-653-1082; www.sebastopolinn.com; 6751 Sebastopol Ave, Sebastopol; r $110-300

Vine Hill Inn
Blossoming gardens surround a charming four-room 1897 Victorian farmhouse, with gorgeous vineyard views. ☎ 707-823-8832; www.vine-hill-inn.com; 3949 Vine Hill Rd, Sebastopol; r incl breakfast $170

USEFUL WEBSITES
www.sebastopol.org
www.slowfoodfoundation.com

www.lonelyplanet.com/trip-planner

Of London, Kerouac & Twain

WHY GO The three literary vagabonds left behind plenty of evidence of their love for Northern California. This trip chases the ghosts of our traveling bards from the fog-touched hills of Sonoma to the sun-soaked hills of Gold Country. For, like Kerouac says, "road is life."

TIME
2 – 4 days

DISTANCE
260 miles

BEST TIME TO GO
Year-round

START
Glen Ellen

END
Sonora

"I ride over my beautiful ranch. Between my legs is a beautiful horse. The air is wine. The grapes on a score of rolling hills are red with autumn flame. Across Sonoma Mountain, wisps of sea fog are stealing. The afternoon sun smolders in the drowsy sky. I have everything to make me glad I am alive." These are the words of Jack London, talking about his Sonoma County ranch, just outside the slumberous village of Glen Ellen. Except for the horse, it'd be just as accurate if it were written today.

The tranquil afternoon at ❶ **Jack London State Historic Park** is a scene in stark contrast to London's tales of tempestuous seafaring men. Of the three docent-led hikes through the ranch, "The Adventurer" highlights London's wanderlust, ending at the heavy volcanic rock that marks his grave, but the most eerie and quietly dramatic shrine is the charred crust of his so-called "dream ranch." London was the most successful writer in the States and still in his mid-30s when his home, weeks from completion, burned down – a story befitting an author whose heroes struggled against the malicious force of fate. So begins our tour of California's trio of literary travelers.

From London, this trip's eldest writer, we venture next to ❷ **San Francisco** for sites of the trip's most fleeting: Jack Kerouac. Head south on Hwy 101, across the Golden Gate and into North Beach, where Kerouac and the scrappy band of Beats left their indelible mark. Feeling a little bit unstudied? Get your reading at ❸ **City Lights** bookstore, where you can shuffle across the same creaking floors that Jack did.

HISTORY & CULTURE

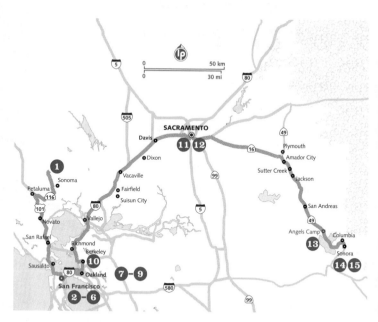

A step across Jack Kerouac Alley stands **4 Vesuvio**, where would-Beats still clack away on laptops while sipping beers. From the balcony, peer down on the North Beach characters who amble in the door and stagger out. If the books and bevies awake the desire for a Kerouac bobble-head figurine, take a few steps to **5 The Beat Museum**. The collection is a bit scrappy, though made up for by the enthusiasm of the staff.

> *"From the balcony, peer down on the North Beach characters who amble in the door and stagger out."*

Return to Columbus and walk another block up the hill to the **6 Hotel Bohème**, a cozy haunt with mosquito netting over the beds that was a favorite of Allen Ginsberg. To hit the pavement for even more Beat haunts, try the hotel's self-guided walking tour.

Kerouac himself advises to "lean forward to the next crazy venture beneath the skies," so head to Oakland over the Bay Bridge, passing 3rd St and Brannan en route, where London was born. The plaque isn't a great homage to Mr *Call of the Wild,* but it sets the mood for **7 Jack London Square**, just off I-880 (south of downtown Oakland). The yachting set and tourists make it hard to imagine the rough-and-tumble seaport that London chronicled in his great works, but the reconstructed London cabin and crooked rafters of **8 Heinold's First and Last Chance** recall the untamed yesteryear. Wander the surrounding streets to catch the smell of smoking meat at **9 Everett and Jones** and bury your face in a plate of smoky, sweet tri-tip before taking I-80 east.

A San Francisco newspaper eulogized London by saying no man ever had a more romantic life, "with the exception of Mark Twain." The gateway to Twain's California starts at UC Berkeley's Bancroft Library, which houses the remarkable ❿ **Mark Twain Project and Papers.** The keenest scholars get hushed over piles of little-known notebooks, letters and manuscripts – an allegedly complete collection of everything written in Twain's hand. When the gallery hosts other exhibits, the material is open by request.

In Sacramento, an hour east, Twain appeared as a newspaper contributor. Entering town you'll see the ramshackle revival of the ⓫ **Old Sacramento** historical district, where taffy

> **ASK A LOCAL**
>
> "Finding a frog that'll jump takes work. You'd think the big ones would go furthest, but I had a monster one time – it scared my cat – and it couldn't jump a foot. The real trick is just looking in their eyes and then giving 'em a big scare so – pow! – they really fly."
>
> *Audrey Olsen, Murphys*

shops and Harley-driving boomers come alive on weekends. Find the brightly lit Delta King riverboat and wander through its Mark Twain Salon, enjoying the balmy Sacramento summer night – a dryer, sweeter, no less intoxicating wine than the one London describes in Sonoma.

Save your appetite for the five-minute drive across town to ⓬ **Mulvaney's Building And Loan,** where chef Patrick Mulvaney changes the menu every single night to reflect the most seasonal ingredients. Lucky diners will open the menu to find the lamb shank, as soft as melting butter. Then take Hwy 49 south to get into the foothills where Twain first became a star, writing about the jumping frogs of Calaveras County. Every May, the Calaveras County Fair hosts a frog-jumping contest like the one Twain wrote about, near ⓭ **Angels Camp.** The sidewalks of the antique-riddled foothill village are impressed with the records of amphibious victors of yesteryear.

South 10 minutes is the ⓮ **Mark Twain Cabin** on Jackass Hill, where Twain actually wrote "The Celebrated Jumping Frog of Calaveras County". Twain lived here from December 1864 to March 1865, as the guest of the Gillis Brothers, who were miners. The cabin is a replica, though is apparently still worthy of protection behind a wrought iron fence. The fieldstone fireplace is said to be original; some say it's the place where Twain heard the jumping frog story. Another 10 minutes down Hwy 49, the ⓯ **Mark Twain Walking Tour,** carried out by a dedicated Twain impersonator, departs from various locations within Sonora. The guide also spends ample time on the region's other historical legends – gunslingers and cutthroats like Joaquin Murietta and Kit Carson. If the characters seem dicey, heed Twain's advice for the traveler and enjoy the spirit of danger: "Sail away from the safe harbor. Catch the trade winds in your sails. Explore. Dream. Discover."

Nate Cavalieri

HISTORY & CULTURE

TRIP INFORMATION

GETTING THERE
From San Francisco go up Hwy 101 45 minutes to Glen Ellen, in the heart of Sonoma County.

DO
The Beat Museum
On the block dominated by adult theaters, the $5 entrance fee gets you access to films of rare Beat readings. ☎ 800-537-6822; www.thebeatmuseum.org; 540 Broadway, San Francisco; admission $5; ⏱ 10am-10pm; ⚥

City Lights
Creak over the crooked floors of the Beats' favorite shop to stock up on California's literate travelers. ☎ 415-362-8193; www.citylights.com; 261 Columbus Ave, San Francisco; ⏱ 10am-midnight

Jack London State Historic Park
Visit London's grave and tour the grounds of his ranch. ☎ 707-938-5216; www.jacklondonpark.com; 2400 London Ranch Rd, Glen Ellen; admission $6; ⏱ 10am-5pm; ⚥ ✿

Mark Twain Cabin
While sitting around the fieldstone fireplace, Twain heard the story of a jumping frog. **Hwy 49 at Jackass Hill Rd, Sonora; admission free;** ⏱ dawn-dusk; ⚥ ✿

Mark Twain Project and Papers
Everything ever written in Mark Twain's hand is on display at the UC Berkeley's Bancroft Library. ☎ 510-642-6481; University of California, Berkeley; admission free; ⏱ 8am-10pm with seasonal variations

Mark Twain Walking Tour
A Twain impersonator walks through historic sites of Sonora. ☎ 888-881-3309; Sonora; admission $20, under 14yr free; ⏱ 10am, 11am & 1am, Sat & Sun; ⚥

EAT & DRINK
Everett and Jones
The portions are huge, but you'll still want the take-home sauce. ☎ 510-441-6022; www.eandjbbq.com; 126 Broadway, Oakland; mains $15-18; ⏱ 11am-10pm Mon-Thu, 11am-midnight Fri, noon-midnight Sat, noon-10pm Sun

Heinold's First and Last Chance
The floors haven't been square since London belly'd up to the bar. He has been replaced by a crew of surly office workers and tourists. ☎ 510-839-6761; www.heinoldsfirstandlastchance.com; 48 Webster St, Oakland; ⏱ noon-11pm Tue-Thu & Sun, 3-11pm Mon, noon-1am Fri & Sat

Mulvaney's Building And Loan
The menu changes every single day at Midtown Sacramento's exciting seasonal dining spot. ☎ 916-441-6022; www.culinaryspecialists.com; 1215 19th St, Sacramento; mains $31-50; ⏱ 11:30am-2pm & 5-10pm Tue-Sat

Vesuvio
Neil Cassidy and Jack Kerouac tipped back cold ones here. ☎ 415-362-3370; www.vesuvio.com; 255 Columbus Ave, San Francisco; ⏱ 6am-2am

SLEEP
Hotel Bohème
Perched above the busy streets of Beat central, it offers simple rooms with a writerly vibe. ☎ 415-362-6292; www.hotelboheme.com; 444 Columbus Ave, San Francisco; r $174-194

USEFUL WEBSITES
www.beatmuseum.org

LINK YOUR TRIP

www.lonelyplanet.com/trip-planner

Bay Area Bizarre

WHY GO If you build it, they will come, and the Bay Area is trying pretty damn hard to get your attention. With mind-bending architecture and quirky interior design, there are plenty of places to alter your consciousness, or at least get a good belly laugh.

Start the scavenger hunt of all things weird and wonderful with a few hours at San Francisco's ❶ **Exploratorium**, a touchy-feely science museum where you won't get wrist-slapped for trying to handle everything. But the boffo draw here is the tactile dome, a pitch-black geodesic dome you crawl and bump through and experience by touch, texture and temperature. Not for the claustrophobic, it's a groovy place to imagine what it's like to be swallowed by a whale or waiting around in the womb.

A nifty coastal art piece just past the Golden Gate Yacht Club, the ❷ **Wave Organ** is the creation of artist Peter Richards, and – not surprisingly – the Exploratorium. As the tide filters in and out, it produces odd gurgles and sloshing sounds. An acoustic sculpture built on a jetty, it has lots of nooks to investigate and sit in and contemplate. So, watery symphony or amplified bayside flatulence? You decide.

Another unusual sound space is the ❸ **Audium**, an aural overload that has the effect of ferrying listeners into a mildly dreamlike state. Others profess to going batty with boredom. A labor of love by composer Stan Shaff, this "sound sculpture" has been revving up the mood synthesizers since the 1960s.

As close as you can get to dining in a dollhouse, ❹ **Sam Wo** is an upright shoebox of a restaurant, with a width of no more than 12ft across. Slip through the kitchen of this Chinatown institution, past

TIME
3 days

DISTANCE
200 miles

BEST TIME TO GO
Year-round

START
San Francisco

END
San Francisco

ALSO GOOD FOR

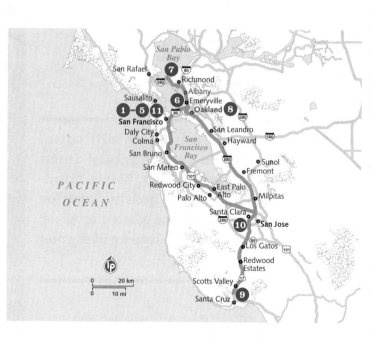

flames jumping around pans of frying noodles, and climb steep stairs to dining rooms stacked neatly on the two floors above. When the buzzer sounds, a hand-cranked dumbwaiter vaults the food upstairs so the waitstaff don't have to do a Stairmaster routine. Beat icon Jack Kerouac supposedly learned to use chopsticks here.

SCAVENGE & BUILD

Want to wallpaper your pad with vintage maps, or construct a giant fish from tossed-out CDs? The whacked-out art circus of Burning Man only happens once a year, but eccentric art and recycling are a way of life at Oakland's **East Bay Depot for Creative Reuse** (www.creativereuse .org), a favorite Bay Area spot to pick up inexpensive raw materials or just rummage around for that special decorating idea.

A time machine to the era of Flower Power, the '60s live on at the peaceful ❺ **Red Victorian B&B**. A comfortable respite in the buzzing Haight, themed choices here include the idealistic, rainbow-muraled Flower Child room and the carnival merry-go-round feel of the Playground Room. Lavalamp devotees should request a room called the Summer of Love. The shared Aquarium bathroom jiggles a cistern of goldfish whenever the toilet flushes.

Cross the Bay Bridge for breakfast at ❻ **Rudy's Can't Fail Café**, a modern diner with tables crafted from board games and strange toys under glass. There's a goofy punk-rock feel, possibly because the bassist from Green Day is a co-owner. Show up for yummy huevos or tofu rancheros anytime of the day, or just chow down on a big burger. Wipe that plate clean – there's an army of Barbie dolls encased in the back room, and they don't take kindly to leftovers.

Wanna get away from it all – and be trapped there? If you're an overnight guest at the ❼ **East Brother Light Station**, you'd better not sleepwalk too far. The little-known B&B in this historic lighthouse building sits on a speck of an island off the East Bay's Point Richmond, and you're not heading home until after daybreak, hon. Not that you'd want to. From October through April, bring earplugs if you're bothered by foghorns.

Head south to Oakland's Jack London Sq, and watch that first step at ❽ **Heinold's First and Last Chance Saloon**. Keeled to a severe slant during the 1906 earthquake, the wooden floor of the 1883 bar might make you feel self-conscious about stumbling before you even order.

DETOUR A scenic former landfill brought to life by surreal sculptures and DIY structures, the **Albany Bulb** is a spit of land in the East Bay whose admirers are fighting for it to be left alone. For years, homeless people and outside-the-box artists have come here to live and create on this wild semi-industrial coastside strip. From I-80, take the Buchanan St exit in Albany, but it may be leveled or sanitized soon, so watch the documentary **Bum's Paradise** (www.bumsparadise.com) if you're too late…

Continue south to the redwoods of Santa Cruz to see the ❾ **Mystery Spot**, perhaps best known statewide by its ubiquitous yellow-and-black bumper stickers. Hyped as a wrinkle in the laws of physics and gravity, it's a wooden structure skewed to vertigo-inducing angles so it's hard to tell which way is up. Check your equilibrium at the door, as dizziness is practically guaranteed.

Once you've regained your balance, reverse course and head north to San Jose. An odd structure purposefully commissioned to be that way by the heir to the Winchester rifle fortune, the ❿ **Winchester Mystery House** is a ridiculous Victorian mansion with 160 rooms of various sizes and little utility, with dead-end hallways and a staircase that runs up to a ceiling all jammed together like a toddler playing architect. Apparently Sarah Winchester spent 38 years constructing a mammoth white elephant because the spirits of the people killed by the rifles told her to. It's west of central San Jose and just north of I-280.

"…a wooden structure skewed to vertigo-inducing angles so it's hard to tell which way is up… "

Back in San Francisco, check your head at the boutique celebrity suites at the ⓫ **Hotel Triton**. Music fans can request the Carlos Santana "Black Magic Bedroom," with walls of concert memorabilia. Or ask for the suite honoring ice cream, with a free freezer-full, and a "special smell" wafting through the vents.

Beth Kohn

TRIP INFORMATION

GETTING THERE
From San Francisco, take I-80 for the East Bay, Hwy 101 for San Jose, and Hwy 17 for Santa Cruz.

DO
Audium
This '60s-throwback "sound sculpture" will either trip you out or have you edging to the exits. ☎ 415-771-1616; www.audium.org; 1616 Bush St, San Francisco; admission $15; ☼ 8:30pm Fri & Sat

Exploratorium
Book the tactile dome to crawl, touch and climb in utter darkness. ☎ 415-561-0360; www.exploratorium.edu; 3601 Lyon St, San Francisco; adult/child $14/9, tactile dome $17; ☼ 10am-5pm, extended summer hours ♿

Mystery Spot
The laws of gravity seem to go MIA at this dizzying building. ☎ 831-423-8897; www.mysteryspot.com; 465 Mystery Spot Rd, Santa Cruz; admission $5; ☼ 9am-5pm, extended summer hours ♿

Winchester Mystery House
A nonsensical Victorian mansion and white elephant constructed by an eccentric heiress. ☎ 408-247-2101; www.winchestermysteryhouse.com; 525 S Winchester Blvd, San Jose; adult/child $24/18; ☼ 9am-5pm, extended summer hours

EAT
Rudy's Can't Fail Café
Open until late, this hip diner has wacky game-themed decor, great breakfasts and $1 beers after 9pm. ☎ 510-594-1221; 4081 Hollis St, Emeryville; mains $6-10; ☼ 7am-1am ♿

Sam Wo
With good-n-greasy Chinese food, it's open after last call and you can almost touch both walls if you need steadying. ☎ 415-982-0596; 813 Washington St, San Francisco; mains $4-6; ☼ 11:30am-3am Mon-Sat, to 5:30pm Sun

DRINK
Heinold's First and Last Chance Saloon
Hoist a drink at this bar wrenched by the 1906 quake. ☎ 510-839-6761; www.heinoldsfirstandlastchance.com; 48 Webster St, Oakland; ☼ noon-11pm Tue-Thu & Sun, 3-11pm Mon, noon-1am Fri & Sat

SLEEP
East Brother Light Station
Happily strand yourself at this historic lighthouse B&B on a tiny bay island, reached via the light station's boat. ☎ 510-233-2385; www.ebls.org; Richmond; r incl breakfast & dinner Dec-Feb $284-374, Mar-Nov $315-415; ☼ Thu-Sun

Hotel Triton
Upgrade to the Jerry Garcia or Carlos Santana suites for some unique boutique hotel bliss. ☎ 415-394-0500, 800-800-1299; www.hoteltriton.com; 342 Grant Ave, San Francisco; r from $180 ♿

Red Victorian B&B
Feel the love of an era gone by at this friendly peace-themed lodging near the park in the Haight-Ashbury neighborhood. ☎ 415-864-1978; www.redvic.com; 1665 Haight St, San Francisco; r $99-229; ♿

USEFUL WEBSITES
www.sfgate.com/offbeat/whome.html
www.makerfaire.com/bayarea

LINK YOUR TRIP
www.lonelyplanet.com/trip-planner

Marin Fling

WHY GO Crossing north to Marin County on the windswept passageway of the Golden Gate Bridge, the scenery turns untamed. Home to grazing deer, herds of Tule elk, circling hawks and breaching whales, Marin County's undulating hills, redwood forest and crashing coastline prove a welcome respite from urban living.

TIME
3 days

DISTANCE
185 miles

BEST TIME TO GO
Apr – Oct

START
Sausalito

END
San Rafael

After driving over the turret-topped Golden Gate Bridge, pop your eyes back in their sockets and watch the road for the Alexander Ave exit, located just after the Vista Point area, and bear left before swinging back under the highway to ascend up, up, up the bay-view ridgeline of Conzelmen Rd. Keep an eye out for cyclists in low gear, pumping the pedals as they conquer it little by little.

Near echo-y WWII battery tunnels where the road becomes one-way, birders should make a mandatory stop to hike up ❶ Hawk Hill. Thousands of migrating birds of prey soar here from late summer to early fall, straddling a windy ridge with views of Rodeo Lagoon all the way to Alcatraz. On weekends in season, you can join volunteers to count and identify raptors such as red-tailed hawks, golden eagles and peregrine falcons.

Stay west on Conzelmen Rd, and in about a mile, turn your gaze to Bonita Cove. In season, hundreds of harbor seals haul out onto the rocks offshore, sunning their furry brown-and-gray-speckled bodies. The third lighthouse built on the West Coast, the ❷ Point Bonita Lighthouse was completed in 1855, but after complaints about its performance in fog, was scooted down to the promontory about 20 years later. During three afternoons a week you can cross through a dark rock tunnel – carved out with hand tools only – and traverse a

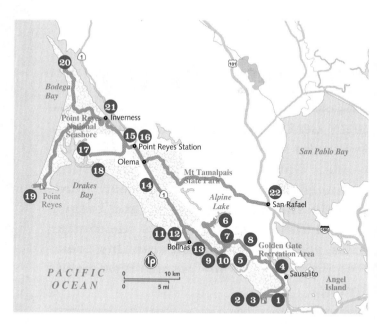

steep half-mile trail to inspect the lighthouse beacon. A bouncy suspension bridge delivers you to the Fresnel lens tower. To go one step better, come when the lighthouse opens its doors for monthly full-moon tours under the chilly cloak of night. Offshore to the northeast, take note of iced-white Bird Island, a speck of land wholly splattered by guano.

Continue 1 mile to the ❸ **Marin Headlands Visitor Center** to find excellent field guides and maps. The information station, in a historic military chapel, also has exhibits on the Headlands' natural and human history, including a shelter typical of the land's first inhabitants, the Coastal Miwok. Spotting deer in the Marin Headlands isn't difficult. Their subtle, trodden-down paths lace through the forest brush, and they're often seen grazing in open fields. They also tend to amble onto the roadway at dusk, so it can be more a matter of driving slowly enough so you don't see them *that* close.

"Gaze up at these hulking giants and feel dwarfed, but mind those slimy banana slugs underfoot."

Duck into Sausalito for lunch at ❹ **Fish**, and chow down on seafood sandwiches at redwood picnic tables facing Richardson Bay. A local leader in promoting fresh and sustainably caught fish, it has wonderful wild salmon in season, and refuses to serve the farmed stuff. To get there from the visitor center, go east on Bunker Rd, through the timed one-way tunnel and then north on the Sausalito Lateral Rd, which feeds into Bridgeway. At a traffic light about 1.5 miles past the ferry terminal, go right on Harbor Dr.

After lunch, sidle up to some very tall trees. Follow Hwy 101 north to Hwy 1 and then Panoramic Hwy, and look for signs to **5** **Muir Woods**. President Theodore Roosevelt designated this old-growth redwood grove as a national monument in 1908, after naturalist William Kent bought the land to save it from logging and donated it to the government. Gaze up at these hulking giants and feel dwarfed, but mind those slimy banana slugs underfoot.

Continue north on Panoramic Hwy to Pan Toll Rd, which turns into E Ridgecrest Blvd. At the very end, the East Peak of **6** **Mt Tamalpais State Park** rises to a commanding 2571ft. From the parking lot, climb the short trail up to the Gardner fire lookout, an active fire-spotting cabin perched on a base of locally gathered stone. Panoramic views take in the entire San Francisco Bay Area off into the Pacific Ocean.

Without the glow of a thousand city streetlights, the parks of Marin are a great place to view the stars and revel in the occasional meteor shower. Once a month, bundle up and bring a flashlight to one of the free **7** **Mt Tamalpais astronomy programs** at the Mountain Theater, a 1930s stone amphitheater built by the Civilian Construction Corps. The talks have been happening here for 20 years, with university professors presenting eclectic presentations, and telescope viewing to follow.

Grab your honey – or a good book to curl up with – and backtrack 4 miles to the upscale yet down-to-earth **8** **Mountain Home Inn** on Panoramic Hwy. A small rural retreat resting on a redwood and pine ridge, its 10 unfinished timber rooms – some with wood-burning fireplaces – gaze east out over the bay. A lack of televisions and the positioning of a good local trail map on the dresser make it clear that it's a place to breathe and unwind. For dinner, treat yourself to an exquisite prix fixe extravaganza in the elegant log-columned restaurant, featuring organic American cuisine and picture windows to survey the scenery.

> **DETOUR**
>
> Built in 1904 as a stopover for the Mill Valley and Mt Tamalpais Scenic Railway – 281 zigzags gave it the nickname "Crookedest Railroad in the World" – the **West Point Inn** (www.westpoint inn.com) is now a rustic hike-in lodge with simple rooms, cold-water cabins and no electricity. From its high south slope of Mt Tam, dreamy vistas embrace the bay and the Marin Headlands. Climb on up for a tranquil overnight or one of the fun monthly pancake breakfasts.

After the complimentary full breakfast in the morning, continue west on Panoramic Hwy and wind north along the sinuous S-curves of Hwy 1. A mile south on Hwy 1, cruise by to get a gander at the spectacular site of **9** **Steep Ravine Environmental Campground**. It has a series of beachfront campsites and several fanatically coveted rustic cabins overlooking the ocean; reservations can be booked seven months in advance, and usually are. Park on the side of the highway and walk down past a locked gate to see tidal pools studded with stunning orange and deep blue sea stars.

Continue north on Hwy 1, but stop for a bracing splash in the Pacific at sandy ❿ **Stinson Beach**, a 3-mile-long stretch that's also a popular surf spot. Then trace the shore of Bolinas Lagoon, where waterfowl prowl during low tide and harbor seals often frolic.

Next stop is Bolinas, but don't look for any signs directing you there. Residents from this famously private town tore the road sign down so many times that state highway officials finally gave in and stopped replacing it years ago. Turn off at the very first left after the lagoon. At the next block, go left onto Olema-Bolinas Rd. Then, past the opposite side of the lagoon and wooden fences veiled by ripe summer blackberries, go right on Mesa Rd about 2 miles later. The two-lane country road starts through a residential cluster thick with eucalyptus trees, but the ocean soon comes into view across wide open fields often dotted with deer.

ITCH ATTACK!

Common throughout Marin, poison oak exposure starts as a rash that makes you want to scratch your skin off, then explodes into huge weepy blisters that last for weeks. If not washed off properly, the plant's insidious oil remains on fabric for months or longer and can spread again. So learn to identify these shrubs or vines with three scalloped leaves, and wash with Tecnu or similar cleansers if you tangle with this nasty plant.

A bit more than a half mile after the pavement turns to gravel, you'll run across the Palomarin Field Station of ⓫ **PRBO Conservation Science** (originally the Point Reyes Bird Observatory). A working research facility, it has bird-banding and netting demonstrations, monthly guided walks, a visitors center and nature trail. During the 2007 *Cosco Busan* disaster, when an oil tanker spilled 58,000 gallons of toxic bunker fuel oil into San Francisco Bay, staff mobilized its Oil Spill Response Team to monitor and rescue affected seabirds.

At road's end is the Palomarin Trailhead, the tromping-off point for coastal day hikes into the Point Reyes National Seashore and some of the best backpacking an hour out of San Francisco. Pack some water and a towel and hightail it out to ⓬ **Bass Lake**, a pastoral and popular freshwater swimming spot reached by way of a 45-minute hike skirting the coast. Another 1.5 miles of walking brings you to the spectacular Alamere Falls, which tumbles down to the beach below.

Nip into town and peek behind the community center to find the ⓭ **Bolinas People's Store**, an awesome little co-op grocery store selling Fair Trade coffee, organic produce, fresh soup and yummy tamales. Relax and eat at the shady courtyard tables, and have a rummage through the Free Box, a shed full of clothes and other waiting-to-be-reused items.

Returning to Hwy 1, continue about 6 miles north to explore the landscape on horseback with a trail ride at ⑭ **Five Brooks Stables**. In addition to private hires, it has frequent daily rides for all riding levels. Take a slow amble through a pasture, or ascend over 1000ft to Inverness Ridge for views of the Olema Valley. If your butt can stay in the saddle for six hours, ride along the coastline to Wildcat Beach via Alamere Falls. Follow Hwy 1 north to Point Reyes Station for an organic coffee break at the ⑮ **Bovine Bakery**. Though it proudly refuses to do espresso drinks, the baked goods and fresh pizza are divine even without a cappuccino in hand. So scoop up a bear claw or a blueberry scone and then saunter a block and a half away to small-scale artisanal cheese-maker ⑯ **Cowgirl Creamery**. Reserve a spot in advance for its weekly tour, where you can watch the curd-making and cutting and then sample a half dozen of its fresh and aged cheeses. All of its milk is local and organic, with vegetarian rennet in the cheese.

Zigzag a little over a mile southwest to Limantour Rd, which leads to the ⑰ **Point Reyes Hostel**. Isolated and simple bunkhouses have warm and cozy front rooms with big windows,

ASK A LOCAL Want to see wildlife in Marin? Here are a few choice spots suggested by Anne Bauer, Director of Education at the **Marine Mammal Center** (www.tmmc.org):

- Gray whales at Point Reyes National Seashore (Chimney Rock & Point Reyes Lighthouse)

- Harbor seals at Bolinas (Duxbury Reef, Bolinas Lagoon), Marin Headlands (around Point Bonita) and Point Reyes National Seashore (Limantour Estero)

- Sea lions at Point Reyes National Seashore (Sea Lion Overlook)

as well as outdoor areas with hill views. If it's not too cold, and you find yourself longing for a quiet night under the stars, reserve a spot at the ⑱ **Coast Campground**, where a dozen walk-in tent sites sit on a grassy valley just 200yd away from the beach. Two trails lead here from the hostel, and cyclists can load up their gear for a flat and easy 2.7-mile ride in via the Coast Trail.

The next day, set aside some time for prowling on and around the ⑲ **Point Reyes Lighthouse**. At the very end of Sir Francis Drake Blvd, and jutting 10 miles out into the Pacific, this wild tip of land endures ferocious winds that can make it feel like the edge of the world. The lighthouse sits below the headlands at the base of over 300 stairs. Not merely a beautiful beacon site, it's also one of the best whale-watching spots along the coast, as gray whales pass the shore during their annual Alaska to Baja migration. Gray whale sightings tend to peak in mid-January and mid-March, with the season lasting from about January through April. However, the occasional spout or spy-hop of humpbacks and minkes can occur year-round.

From December through March, go to Elephant Seal Overlook to spy on a breeding colony of elephant seals near Chimney Rock, above gorgeous Drakes Bay. Note that on weekends and holidays from late December through mid-April, the road to Chimney Rock and the lighthouse is closed to private vehicles, and visitors must take a shuttle from Drakes Beach.

Fancy a walk on the really wild side? Backtrack to Pierce Point Rd and follow it north past historic dairy farms to the ❷⓿ **Tule Elk Reserve**. Park at the weathered Pierce Point Ranch complex, and bring a windbreaker to hike the spectacular Tomales Point Trail. A 9.5-mile out-and-back expedition to the slender northern corner of Point Reyes, the path meanders through dramatic (and often fog-swept) headlands that protect a population of over 400 Tule elk. With guaranteed elk-spotting and unrivaled views of the Pacific Ocean, Tomales Bay and Bodega Bay, it's one of the best hikes in Marin.

To more closely investigate some of that watery landscape, rejoin Sir Francis Drake Blvd going southeast and stop at Inverness to rent a kayak from ❷⓵ **Blue Waters Kayaking**. Located right on Tomales Bay, one of the top kayaking spots in the state, you can grab a paddle and aim for the sandy oasis of Heart's Desire Beach or sign up for a full day tour of Drakes Estero, where you'll see harbor seals galore.

Then go east on Sir Francis Drake Blvd, and in San Anselmo, continue straight toward downtown San Rafael via Red Hill Rd. At an electric-green corner, your last stop on the trek is the lush dining room of ❷⓶ **Sol Food Puerto Rican Cuisine**. Lazy ceiling fans, a profusion of tropical plants and the pulse of Latin rhythms create a soothing atmosphere for delicious dishes like a *jíbaro* sandwich (thinly-sliced steak served on green plantains) and other island-inspired mains concocted with *plátanos* (plantains), organic veggies and free-range meats. Sip on a coconut drink at the family-style tables and prepare your psyche for heading home.
Beth Kohn

TRIP INFORMATION

GETTING THERE
From San Francisco, take Hwy 101 over the Golden Gate Bridge to Sausalito. Return via Hwy 101 from San Rafael.

DO

Blue Waters Kayaking
Rent a kayak to explore Tomales Bay, or join a guided tour. ☎ 415-669-2600; www .bwkayak.com; 12938 Sir Francis Drake Blvd, Inverness; kayak rental 2/4hr $30/45; ⏱ 9am-5pm ⚐

Five Brooks Stables
Saddle up and explore the Point Reyes area year-round by horseback on these pony and trail rides. ☎ 415-663-1570; www.fivebrooks .com; Hwy 1, Olema; trail ride from $40; ⏱ 9am-5pm; ⚐

Marin Headlands Visitor Center
Pick up park information and learn about the rich human and natural history of the land. ☎ 415-331-1540; www.nps.gov/goga/ marin-headlands.htm; cnr Field & Bunker Rds, Sausalito; ⏱ 9:30am-4:30pm

Mt Tamalpais Astronomy Programs
Listen to the expert talk about the solar system and other cosmic concepts at this monthly event. ☎ 415-455-5370; www .mttam.net; Mountain Theater, Mill Valley; admission free; ⏱ variable

Mt Tamalpais State Park
Hike the scenic heights of Marin, and see the splendor of the Bay Area and Pacific Ocean. ☎ 415-388-2070; www.parks.ca.gov

Muir Woods
Walk through an awesome stand of the world's tallest trees – and feel very, very small. ☎ 415-388-2595; www.nps.gov/muwo; Mill Valley; admission $5; ⏱ 8am-sunset

Point Bonita Lighthouse
See the Pacific Ocean, Golden Gate Bridge and San Francisco skyline from a different perspective at this headlands viewpoint; call in advance to reserve a spot on a free full-moon tour. ☎ 415-331-1540; www.nps .gov/goga/pobo.htm; Fort Barry, Sausalito; ⏱ 12:30-3:30pm Sat-Mon

Point Reyes Lighthouse
Pack a windbreaker and whale-spotting binoculars to visit this weather-battered beacon jutting off the coast. ☎ 415-464-5100; www.nps.gov/pore; ⏱ lens room 2:30-4pm Thu-Mon, visitor center & other chambers 10am-4:30pm Thu-Mon

PRBO Conservation Science
Learn about the area's rich birdlife at this active field station. ☎ 415-868-0655; www .prbo.org; Mesa Rd, Bolinas; admission free; ⏱ 9am-5pm

EAT

Bovine Bakery
Possibly the best bakery in Marin; don't leave town without sampling one of its buttery creations. ☎ 415-663-9420; 11315 Hwy 1, Point Reyes Station; baked goods $2-5; ⏱ 6:30am-5pm Mon-Thu, 7am-5pm Sat & Sun

Bolinas People's Store
Pick up some local organic produce, a cup of coffee or some hot picnic food at this small community co-op. ☎ 415-868-1433; 14 Wharf Rd, Bolinas; ⏱ 8:30am-6:30pm

Cowgirl Creamery
Another foodie hotspot in Marin, this organic artisan cheese-maker does weekly tours. ☎ 415-663-9335; 80 4th St, Point Reyes Station; tour $3; ⏱ tour 11:30am Fri, store 10am-6pm Wed-Sun ⚐

Fish
Situated on the bay north of the ferry, this casual seafood restaurant is all about promoting and serving sustainably harvested fish. ☎ 415-331-3474; 350 Harbor Dr, Sausalito; mains $12-25; ⏱ 11:30am-8:30pm ⚐

Sol Food Puerto Rican Cuisine
Savor a scrumptious taste of island life at this colorful family-style eatery utilizing

many organic ingredients. ☎ 415-451-4765;
901 Lincoln Ave, San Rafael; mains $7-11;
🕒 11am-10pm

SLEEP

Coast Campground
Hike or bike in to this peaceful oceanside
campground on Drakes Bay in the Point
Reyes National Seashore. ☎ 415-663-8054;
www.nps.gov/pore/planyourvisit/camping
.htm; Point Reyes; campsite $15 ♿

Mountain Home Inn
Escape to this exemplary retreat with comfortable rooms, an excellent restaurant, and
hiking trails just outside the door. ☎ 415-
381-9000; www.mtnhomeinn.com; 810
Panoramic Hwy, Mill Valley; r $195-345

Point Reyes Hostel
Bunk down in a friendly multi-generational
hostel located in the wild heart of the park.
☎ 415-663-8811; www.norcalhostels
.org/reyes; 1390 Limantour Spit Rd, Point
Reyes; dm/r $20/58 ♿

Steep Ravine Environmental
Campground
Book months in advance to snag one of
these evocative cabins or a coastal campsite.
☎ reservations 800-444-7275; www
.reserveamerica.com; Hwy 1 near Stinson
Beach; campsite/cabin $15/60 ♿

USEFUL WEBSITES
www.bahiker.com/northbay.html
www.ggro.org

LINK YOUR TRIP

www.lonelyplanet.com/trip-planner

TRIP
14 North County Eco Trip p123
16 Finding Fault: Earthquake Sites p133

Mendocino Art Hop

WHY GO Rocks and windswept head-lands line the coast of Southern Mendoci-no County, and idiosyncratic hamlets dot a sparsely populated landscape, which manages to be both serene and rough at the same time. It's perfect country for artistic introspection and free-thinking live-and-let-live attitudes.

TIME
3 days

DISTANCE
60 miles

BEST TIME TO GO
Year-round

START
Gualala

END
Fort Bragg

Look one way and see the rocky shoreline of the breathtaking Pacific coast. Look the other and see the dynamic and varied work of local artists: both established and up-and-coming. The Mendocino coast is loaded with original art, and the drive is easy on the eyes, too. Word on the street is that Mendocino County has the highest number of resident artists per capita in the state.

The first tiny town you happen upon on Hwy 1, ❶ **Gualala**, is actually a hotbed of creativity, though you wouldn't know it if you zipped straight through. The enormous ❷ **Gualala Arts Center** was entirely built by volunteers on 11 acres to the southeast of town, and functions almost as a de facto community center. Follow the signpost off Hwy 1, wind down narrow Gualala Rd, and enter the clearing in the redwoods. The Gualala Arts nonprofit was established in 1961 and hangs rotating exhibits of work by local artists in the spacious atrium and the rear gallery. The center's beautiful outdoor amphitheatre hosts live performances.

Helpful staff arm you with all the news of arts events up and down the Mendocino coast, and also run an outpost in town at the Dolphin Arts Gallery. The center sponsors the August Arts in the Redwoods Festival, and offers ongoing workshops from mosaics to knitting.

Another highlight of the year's events is the late-summer/early-fall Studio Discovery Tour, which gives open access to a vast range of artists'

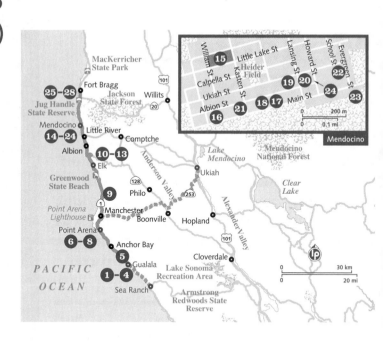

workspaces. Travel from the impeccably designed studios of financially successful artists living on prime oceanfront real estate, to the funky, hippy digs of artists tucked back behind the hills.

DETOUR Only 6 miles south of Gualala (and technically in Sonoma County), **Sea Ranch Lodge** (www.searanchlodge.com) is a marvel of modern California architecture. On a seaside bluff and part of the Sea Ranch planned community (all houses must be built of weathered wood), the lodge has cozy ocean-view rooms, serves internationally inspired California cuisine using the freshest local ingredients, and hosts rotating art exhibitions in its lobby to boot.

The Arts Center can provide a list of local galleries, most of which dot the main drag, all of which hold openings on the second Saturday of the month.

Also in the middle of this tiny town, beloved restaurant ❸ **Pangaea** is not only bedecked with local original art, but also brings culinary art to your plate. People come from all over the coast to feast on its delicacies, like organic halibut with corn succotash. Or, for a funkier scene, follow the sweet scent of pulled pork across the street to ❹ **Bones Roadhouse,** where tin mobiles hang from the ceiling and rustic Americana make the place a living sculpture.

Just north of town, the gorgeous ❺ **St Orres Inn** looks like a luxurious Russian dacha (in honor of the Russian settlement at nearby Ft Ross) and embodies the best of local arts. Festooned with watercolors by local painter Heidi Endemann, and serving world-class haute cuisine, the inn has been slowly expanding over the last 80 years, and now encompasses the elegant main lodge and two strings of perfect little cottages tucked beneath the redwoods.

Wind your way 15 miles north, where Hwy 1 swings into "downtown" ⑥ **Point Arena**. The offbeat ⑦ **Think Visual Art Gallery** makes a perfect pit stop. Idiosyncratic exhibits run the gamut from Western landscape photography to Native American modern sculpture. While you're in town, be sure to jaunt down the street to ⑧ **Franny's Cup and Saucer**, which is like entering a real-word version of the patisserie in the movie *Chocolat*. Franny and her mother, Barbara, handcraft exquisite concoctions in a cheery small storefront trimmed with artsy knickknacks. Try the key-lime torte topped with fresh blackberries.

> **DETOUR** The **Grace Hudson Museum** (www.gracehudsonmuseum.org), inland in Ukiah, is chock-full of Western art, especially the work of the Pomo Indians and the eponymous Grace Hudson. Exhibits thoughtfully combine art with history and anthropology. About 4.5 miles north of Point Arena, go west on Mountain View Rd for 26 miles, and connect to Hwy 253 in Boonville, which you follow west for 17 miles to Hwy 101 N and Ukiah.

Hwy 1 passes out of town and along the coast, cutting through expansive fields studded with grazing dairy cows – the local organic Stornetta dairy has many herds here and recently donated a 1132-acre chunk of headlands to the Bureau of Land Management (BLM) for public hiking and bird-watching. Looking inland you may be able to spot the occasional bobcat, prowling the open grasses on the hunt for field mice.

Have a decadently bucolic rest at ⑨ **Victorian Gardens**, a lovingly restored 1904 farmhouse on 92 exquisitely situated acres just north of Manchester. For larger groups, the owners can prepare 5-course authentic Italian dinners with carefully paired wines.

Nine miles along, the itsy bitsy town of ⑩ **Elk** has a good thing going, and knows it. Perched on the brink of the cliffs, it overlooks some of the most dramatic coastline in California and many artists and writers call the area home. The ⑪ **Elk Studio Gallery & Artist's Collective** charges no commission, since it is run entirely by the artists on display. Tucked into a tiny clapboard house looking across the road to the sea, the gallery contains everything from carvings and pottery to photography and jewelry. Peek upstairs into the working print-and-photo studio and minigallery.

Everyone swears by ⑫ **Queenie's Roadhouse Cafe**, next door, for a creative range of breakfast (wild rice waffles!?) and lunch treats. Local artist Kendrick Petty just sold the ⑬ **Greenwood Pier Inn**, but his painstakingly made psychedelic collages still line the walls of this eclectic collection of cottages overlooking the ocean.

Of course, the pièce de résistance of any Mendocino art trip is the quaint town of ⑭ **Mendocino** itself, packed from end to end with galleries, shops and restaurants. Perched on a wide promontory and surrounded by Mendocino Headlands State Park, the town was founded in the 1850s by transplanted New Englanders. The Victorian village thrived into the late 19th century based on the profits from redwood timber shipped south to San Francisco. The mills closed in the '30s and the town fell into disrepair until it was re-discovered and rejuvenated by artists and bohemians in the '50s. Abundant floral gardens line fantastically preserved Mendocino and it is listed on the National Register of Historic Places.

Like Gualala, Mendocino has its own ⑮ **Mendocino Art Center**, which is a hub for visual, musical and theatrical arts. Everything else in town is within easy walking distance.

The Art Center takes up an entire tree-filled block on Little Lake St. Walk up the stone path, through the colorful blooms and the iron-work sculptures, to its on-site galleries, which are open to the public. They feature everything from high-end one-of-a-kind paintings to modestly priced handmade prints and photographs. The center is nationally recognized for its classes, workshops and artist-in-residence programs. Check its website before you come and you may be able to get in on learning flame-work glass beading, oil painting with a knife or how to set a precious gem (among countless other workshops).

ASK A LOCAL

"With openings on the first and second weekends of the month, up and down the coast, you are guaranteed to have something interesting happening almost whenever you come."
Barbara Pratt, Gualala

Check out the *Mendocino Arts Showcase* brochure (also available at the Gualala Arts Center), which lists that quarter's goings-on around town and along the coast. The calendar is packed with seasonal events like The Whale and Jazz Festival and Mendocino Film Festival in April, Mendocino Music Festival in mid-July, or the Arts Center's very own Arts and Crafts fair, also in July. It also publishes the extensive *Mendocino Arts* magazine, which goes in-depth on the biographies and styles of individual local artists.

The center is also home to the Mendocino Theatre Company (www.1mtc.org), which stages contemporary plays in the 81-seat Helen Schoeni Theatre.

The town itself is loaded with galleries, all of which host openings on the second Saturday of the month. Doors are thrown open to strolling connoisseurs of both art and wine, and Mendocino buzzes with life. From time to time, the gorgeously rough-hewn, light-filled Oddfellows Hall, in the center of the village, hosts art shows – they're a real treat.

Private galleries run the gamut from straight-up visual arts to one fellow who works with sound, crafting bespoke speakers that look like furniture. The galleries mentioned here give you a taste of what's in store, but just wander the tiny roads and you will discover many a new artist.

Walk four blocks south on William St and turn right on Main St to reach the ⑯ **Artists' Cooperative of Mendocino.** Upstairs from Ocean Quilts in the white clapboard Sussex Building, with a splendid ocean-view balcony, this airy gallery is entirely run by 22 local artists, and charges no commission. Work includes everything from watercolors to ceramics and there is always a loquacious local artist in attendance.

Up Main St, ⑰ **Highlight** stands out for its exquisite wood artists. The local woodworkers guild established a fine woodworking program 27 years ago at nearby College of the Redwoods and these first-rate artists train new generations in furniture design, carving and building. The impeccable creations on display use materials like black walnut and canary wood and many incorporate delicate inlays. One can only imagine the work involved! Some weave in Pacific maple and mahogany that is quilted – a rare naturally occurring phenomenon which creates undulations in color and grain in the woods. These tables, chairs and chests are functional sculpture at its best.

Head over one block to Albion St to find the entrance to ⑱ **Reflections,** a gallery specializing in handmade kaleidoscopes. Made from glass, wood or ceramics, the carefully crafted pieces show that these sparkly viewers are more than just toys. One block inland on Ukiah St, ⑲ **Lark in the Morning** carries all manner of musical instruments. Have you always longed for a handmade tom-tom or lute? Here's your chance. Often a craftsperson is at work in the shop, and can answer your questions as you browse the bows, bodies and bongos. The store imports instruments from all over the world, like bamboo flutes from China called *dizi*. If playing isn't your bag, pick up a book or CD instead.

Mendocino offers a stunning array of culinary options. For a casual, tasty meal drop into the ⑳ **Mendocino Cafe.** Its diverse menu of fresh goodies weaves together Mexican, Asian and American cooking, with everything from fish tacos and Thai burritos to straight-up steak. It's especially lovely on a sunny day when you can dine alfresco with views of its rose garden and the sea beyond. Or step it up a bit at the excellent ㉑ **Moosse Cafe.** The ideal spot for a lingering lunch, bright and airy Moosse Cafe serves creamy-delicious mac-n-cheese, housemade pâté and Niçoise salads. At dinner, roast chicken and cioppino are the standouts. Save room for chocolate pudding.

Or blow it out at renowned ㉒ **Cafe Beaujolais.** Mendocino's iconic, much-beloved country-Cal-French restaurant occupies an 1896 house restyled into a monochromatic urban-chic dining room, perfect for holding hands by candlelight. The refined, inspired cooking draws diners from San Francisco, who make this the centerpiece of their trip.

When you are ready to rest your head for the night, Mendocino offers an equally extensive group of B&Bs and small inns, dripping with charm. Prices are strong, especially on weekends and during summer – they know how beautiful Mendocino is. One perfect romantic hideaway is ㉓ **Alegria**. The rooms have ocean-view decks and wood-burning fireplaces, and coastside there's private beach access, a rarity in Mendo. The ever-so-friendly innkeepers also rent cottages and rooms across the street at "Quartet," formerly McElroy's Cottage Inn, a 1900s Craftsman-style house with a simpler feel. Or try ㉔ **Headlands Inn**, where you pass through a lush, flowering garden to get to the cozy saltbox with feather beds and fireplaces. They even serve you breakfast in your room!

Many people overlook the next big town north, Fort Bragg, but when it comes to arts, this is a mistake. Not nearly as charming in architecture as Mendocino, the city has lower property values and has become a haven for artists who have been priced out of Mendo-proper. Galleries hold openings on the first Friday of the month and are mostly concentrated in the downtown area. Drop in to the ㉕ **Northcoast Artists Gallery** on Main St to see another excellent local arts cooperative and pick up a copy of its *Fort Bragg Gallery & Exhibition Guide,* which directs you to other galleries around town. Founded in 1986, Northcoast Artists is a collective of 20 local painters, sculptors, jewelers, photographers and ceramicists. A part of the gallery is devoted to a month-long exhibit, and the rest holds rotating installations by its membership.

Across the street and down the block, in the Company Store, the ㉖ **Mendocino Coast Photography Guild & Gallery** is the one gallery in the area exclusively dedicated to the medium. The members of the guild photograph, print and frame all of the work, mostly shots taken on the north coast, and offer classes too. It's a great place to find a memento of the crashing waves and ocean-scored bluffs.

Around the block, on Franklin St, do not miss ㉗ **Partners Gallery**. It stands out from the masses as a true contemporary art gallery. Recently relocated to this beautifully designed space, the gallery has a distinctly modern feel, and the pieces are hung with painstaking care so that each work sings.

Has seeing all of this homegrown art gotten your creative juices flowing? If so, cross the street to ㉘ **Racines Office & Art Supplies** and pick out a kit of materials to start a masterwork of your own.

Alexis Averbuck

HISTORY &
CULTURE

TRIP INFORMATION

GETTING THERE
From San Francisco, take Hwy 1 north for 115 miles to Gualala.

DO

Artists' Cooperative of Mendocino
Browse in an airy, light-filled space upstairs with views to the ocean. Chatty artists explain their work. ☎ 707-937-2217; www .artgallerymendocino.com; 45270 Main St, Mendocino; ⊘ 10:30am-4:30pm

Elk Studio Gallery & Artist's Collective
This diminutive clapboard house packs in a wide range of local art. ☎ 707-877-1128; www.artists-collective.net; 6031 S Hwy 1, Elk; ⊘ 10am-5pm

Gualala Arts Center
A central clearinghouse for arts along the coast, with rotating exhibits and helpful staff. ☎ 707-884-1138; www.gualalaarts.org; 46501 Gualala Rd, Gualala; ⊘ 9am-4pm Mon-Fri, noon-4pm Sat & Sun

Highlight
This oceanfront gallery shows a full range of artists, but you should spend extra time perusing the exquisite handmade wooden furniture. ☎ 707-937-3132; www.thehigh lightgallery.com; 45052 Main St, Mendocino; ⊘ 10am-5pm

Lark in the Morning
Need a sitar? Or a bagpipe? This is your place! Or just pick up a fabulous guitar. ☎ 707-937-5275; www.larkinthemorning.com; 45011 Ukiah St, Mendocino; ⊘ 10:30am-6pm Mon-Sat

Mendocino Art Center
Sprawling over an entire block, the campus encompasses extensive galleries, private classrooms and a contemporary theatre. ☎ 707-937-5818, 800-653-3328; www .mendocinoartcenter.org; 45200 Little Lake St, Mendocino; ⊘ 10am-4pm

Mendocino Coast Photography Guild & Gallery
Artist-owned and dedicated to fine-art photography on the north coast. ☎ 707-964-4706; www.mcpgg.com; 301 N Main St, Fort Bragg; ⊘ 10am-4pm Mon, noon-6pm Thu-Sun

Northcoast Artists Gallery
This first-rate, spacious gallery brings together top-notch art of many mediums from around the area. ☎ 707-964-8266; www .northcoastartists.org; 362 N Main St, Fort Bragg; ⊘ 10am-6pm

Partners Gallery
This excellent contemporary art gallery has an enduring reputation for staging beautifully hung international and group shows. ☎ 707-962-0233; www.partnersgallery.com; 335 N Franklin St, Fort Bragg; ⊘ 10am-5pm Thu-Mon

Racines Office & Art Supplies
Stock up on professional-grade arts supplies and make your own magic. ☎ 707-964-2416; www.racinesfortbragg.com; 344 N Franklin St, Fort Bragg; ⊘ 9am-5:30pm Mon-Fri, 10am-4:30pm Sat

Reflections
Enter on Albion St for fabulous one-of-a-kind handmade kaleidoscopes. Members of Brewster Kaleidoscope Society get a discount! ☎ 707-937-0173; www.reflections-kaleido scopes.com; 45050 Main St, Mendocino; ⊘ 10am-5pm Thu-Mon

Think Visual Art Gallery
Delve into the storefronts of Point Arena to find this idiosyncratic gallery owned by photographer Jeffrey Hillier. ☎ 707-882-4042; 215 Main St, Point Arena; ⊘ 10am-3pm

EAT

Bones Roadhouse
Smoked meats and Texas-style, wood-pit barbecue are the specialties. If you're riding a Harley, you'll fit right in. ☎ 707-884-1188; 38920 S Hwy 1, Gualala; mains $9-18; ⊘ 11:30am-9pm

Cafe Beaujolais
The best of the best; you can't go wrong here. Reservations essential. ☎ 707-937-5614; www.cafebeaujolais.com; 961 Ukiah St, Mendocino; lunch mains $9-20, dinner mains $27-40; ⏱ 11:30am-2:30pm Wed-Sun, 5:45-9pm nightly

Franny's Cup and Saucer
For top-quality pastries and killer ginger snaps, seek out this oasis of goodness. Even her savories are a treat. ☎ 707-882-2500; 213 Main St, Point Arena; pastries $1-5; ⏱ 8am-5pm Wed-Sat

Mendocino Cafe
If it's warm, breathe the fresh ocean air from the deck of this cream-colored Victorian. ☎ 707-937-6141; 10451 Lansing St, Mendocino; lunch mains $9-14, dinner mains $11-20; ⏱ 11:30am-4pm & 5-10pm

Moosse Cafe
Enjoy top-shelf California-French cuisine in a sunny, relaxed atmosphere with ocean views. ☎ 707-937-4323; www.theblueheron.com; 390 Kasten St, Mendocino; lunch mains $12-16, dinner mains $22-28; ⏱ noon-2pm & 6-10pm

Pangaea
The hands-down best restaurant on the coast south of Mendocino. Make reservations as this tiny, brightly painted house fills quickly. ☎ 707-884-9669; www.pangaeacafe.com; 39165 S Hwy 1, Gualala; mains $27-30; ⏱ 6-11pm Wed-Sun

Queenie's Roadhouse Cafe
Always-good Queenie's is the top choice for breakfast or lunch, with terrific omelets, scrambles, salads and sandwiches. ☎ 707-877-3285; 6061 S Hwy 1, Elk; mains $6-10; ⏱ 8am-3pm Thu-Mon

SLEEP

Alegria
Hide away in a secluded oceanside cottage, and enjoy fresh-baked cookies in the afternoon. A path leads to a private beach. ☎ 707-937-5150, 800-780-7905; www.oceanfrontmagic.com; 44781 Main St, Mendocino; r $140-300

Greenwood Pier Inn
Datura blossoms hang from outside lights. If you like a New Agey feel, try one of its well-placed ocean-view cottages. ☎ 707-877-9997; www.greenwoodpierinn.com; 5928 S Hwy 1, Elk; r $150-325

Headlands Inn
Try to reserve a room with one of the dormer windows for the best views in this B&B. ☎ 707-937-4431; www.headlandsinn.com; cnr Albion & Howard Sts, Mendocino; r $130-230

St Orres Inn
The main hotel, with luxurious shared bathrooms, has copper domes. Cottages are an indulgence. ☎ 707-884-3303, dining room 707-884-3335; www.saintorres.com; 36601 Hwy 1, Gualala; r $90-350

Victorian Gardens
Hidden on 92 acres on a bluff back from the ocean, exquisite Victorian Gardens' four beautifully appointed guest rooms have spectacular views all around. ☎ 707-882-3606; www.innatvictoriangardens.com; 14409 S Hwy 1, Manchester; r $240-310

USEFUL WEBSITES
www.mendocinoarts.org
www.mendocinocoast.com

LINK YOUR TRIP
www.lonelyplanet.com/trip-planner

Hiking the Lost Coast

WHY GO Secluded trails and tiny dirt roads crisscross this pristine slice of California coast. We joined up with local photographer and environmental professional Douglas Fir to track his favorite hikes and lookouts. On the way we earned mountaintop views of ocean and deep forest, and rubbed shoulders with majestic Roosevelt elk.

TIME
3 – 4 days

DISTANCE
100 miles

BEST TIME TO GO
May – Aug

START
Usal Beach Campground

END
Ferndale

ALSO GOOD FOR

ROUTE

California's gorgeous "Lost Coast" extends from just north of Rockport, where Hwy 1 cuts inland, to the town of Ferndale in the north. One of the state's most untouched coastal areas, the region became "lost" when the highway system bypassed it early in the 20th century. The central and southern stretches fall respectively within the King Range National Conservation Area and the Sinkyone Wilderness State Park. Steep, rugged King Range, less than 3 miles from the coast, rises over 4000ft, with near-vertical cliffs plunging to the sea. High rainfall causes frequent landslides; the area north of King Range is more accessible, but the scenery less dramatic.

A resident of southern Humboldt County for the past 40 years, Douglas Fir has explored and documented the length and breadth of this remote, craggy shoreline, which gives way to gentle streams, river valleys and inland peaks. Fir's favorite spots dot the entire length of the coast, and he recommends many hikes: some strenuous and multiday, others a quick day walk.

Usal Rd breaks off from Hwy 1 north of Rockport and runs inland along Timber Ridge and Jackass Ridge to a junction called Four Corners. The road is often only passable with a 4WD vehicle with high suspension, especially in winter, so drive it at your own risk! Slide off the beaten path and into ❶ **Usal Beach Campground**, at the

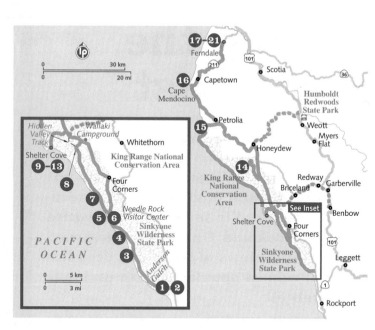

southernmost point of Sinkyone Wilderness, along tranquil Usal Creek. The southern terminus of the ② **Lost Coast Trail**, the bedraggled pier down at the beach was used for the transport of redwood at the turn of the century.

BUREAU OF LAND MANAGEMENT

We explored the Lost Coast from many different points, which often required backtracking by car or planning for a pick-up and shuttle back to our vehicle. The Bureau of Land Management office at Whitethorn (☎ 707-986-5400; www .blm.gov/ca; 768 Shelter Cove Rd) lists approved shuttle services, posts road and trail conditions and closures, manages the King Range National Conservation Area and is a useful spot to pick up maps. It's open daily between Memorial Day and Labor Day, and weekdays between September and May. Alternatively, take a guided hike with a group like Sanctuary Forest (www .sanctuaryforest.org).

A day hike 2 miles up-coast brings you within sight of a sparkling seasonal waterfall but Fir recommends the strenuous (about 20-mile) hike on the Lost Coast Trail leading from Usal to Needle Rock. Anderson Gulch is only 7.5 miles from Usal but has no beach access, so aim to camp at the ③ **Wheeler Campground**, 12 miles up the coast, if you can. Alternatively, since climbs can be extreme in the southern part of Sinkyone, drive along Usal Rd to the Needle Rock visitor center via Shelter Cove or Whitethorn and arrive at this part of the park from the north.

Another excellent place to rest your aching limbs, ④ **Bear Harbor Campground**, lies at the southern terminus of Briceland Rd. Little more than a wide track, the twisting 2.7 miles of Briceland Rd leading to the campground from the Needle Rock visitor center are closed in winter to protect the dirt roadbed, but the whole thing is part of the Lost Coast Trail. One of Fir's favorite spots, Bear Harbor was used by smugglers during prohibition – hard to get caught here! You are more likely to be surrounded by majestic Roosevelt elk, which pass through in quiet, munching herds. Don't feed them. Though they are peaceful, they are wild animals, and we are visitors on *their* land.

"One of Fir's favorite spots, Bear Harbor was used by smugglers during prohibition..."

5 Needle Rock and the **6** Needle Rock visitor center afford gorgeous views up and down the coast. Ocean mist clings to the faces of the mountainside and the setting sun glows warmly across the secluded landscape. The friendly volunteer rangers sell maps and provide helpful information, especially about road conditions. If you feel like tempering your camping experience, rent their Barn Camp, which gives you oceanfront shelter on a platform in a quaint weathered wooden barn.

A great day hike goes from Needle Rock to **7** Whale Gulch (4.5-mile round-trip), where a small lagoon is studded with piles of driftwood. Either continue north on foot about 6 miles to **8** Chemise Mountain and the King Range National Conservation Area or, if you are in a car, head north to the junction at Four Corners, and take Chemise Mountain Rd to reach the Chemise Mountain Trail (drive to the back of Wailaki Campground to reach the head of the trail). This quick ascent of just over half a mile winds steadily through redwoods, madrones and tan oaks, and brings us to an overlook where ridge after ridge of the King Range stretch off into the distance, undisturbed by humankind.

To the northwest, isolated **9** Shelter Cove is the main community on the Lost Coast. An unincorporated town 25 long miles west of Garberville, the area is a patchwork of government-

DETOUR

A monument to 1920s rustic elegance, **Benbow Hotel & Resort** (www.benbowinn.com) is a national historic landmark and the Redwood Empire's first luxury resort. Hollywood's elite once frolicked in the Tudor-style mansion's lobby, where you can play chess by the crackling fire and enjoy a complimentary afternoon tea and evening hors d'oeuvres. Rooms have comfy beds and antique furniture. Dig in to excellent Euro-Cal cuisine or Sunday brunch in their shade-dappled dining room.

owned land and private property. In the late 19th and early 20th centuries it used to be the departure point for shipping the bark of the locally occurring tan oak. As the name suggests, the bark was used as a natural tanning agent before chemical agents were developed in the 1920s. Fifty years ago, southern California fast-talkers subdivided the land, built an airstrip, and flew potential investors in, convincing them to buy seaside plots for retirement houses. But they didn't tell buyers that a steep, winding, one-lane dirt road provided the only access. Today, there's still only one route in, but it is now paved. Nevertheless, take care when it's foggy out.

An encampment of restaurants and inns makes this a great spot for a break or a convenient base from which to explore. The best place to stay, hands down, is the sparkling oceanfront ❿ **Shelter Cove Bed & Breakfast**, managed by supercool, design-savvy owners. Every room is a tiny labor of love and the breakfast has nothing to do with roughing it. Or arrange for a kitchen suite at ⓫ **Oceanfront Inn & Lighthouse**. Even the tidy, modern smaller rooms have microwaves, refrigerators and balconies overlooking the sea.

> **DETOUR** From the intersection of Wilder Ridge Rd and Mattole Rd, follow Mattole Rd northeast for half an hour to primeval **Rockefeller Forest**. This preserved 10,000-acre tract of contiguous, uncut coastal redwoods appears as it did a century ago. It is part of **Humboldt Redwoods State Park** (☎707-946-2409), which covers 53,000 acres – 17,000 of which are old-growth – and contains some of the world's most magnificent trees.

The ocean-view ⓬ **Cove Restaurant** cooks up abundant salads, rich soups and succulent steaks. ⓭ **Shelter Cove RV Park, Campground & Deli** has hot showers and outdoor tables. Don't miss the crunchy fish and chips when they've just brought in a fresh catch.

Head further north into the King Range to one of Fir's favorite spots at ⓮ **King's Peak**. From the trailhead to the summit (round trip 4 miles) climb to a height of 4000ft and reap the benefits of your labor with vistas in all directions. To the west, of course, you have the Pacific and Big Flat River Creek. To the east see as far as the Yolla Bolly Wilderness on a clear day.

One way to traverse the King Range National Conservation area is to hike the whole way from Black Sands Beach, just north of Shelter Cove to the ⓯ **mouth of the Mattole River** and the BLM campground there. The Lost Coast Trail stays along the beach the 24.5 miles north, passing the abandoned Punta Gorda Lighthouse along the way. Plan for it to take two or three days. There are no designated campsites on this stretch of trail, but you are allowed to simply pitch your tent wherever you like. Best bets are the more sheltered areas near the mouths of the creeks. The mouth of the Mattole River marks the end of the Lost Coast Trail.

Alternately, to drive from Shelter Cove to the mouth of the Mattole River, follow King Peak Rd or Wilder Ridge Rd to Mattole Rd. Go west to the coast on Lighthouse Rd which will drop you down to the BLM campground.

Drive northwest to wind-swept ⓰ **Cape Mendocino** – take Lighthouse Rd to Mattole Rd to get there. Some claim that Cape Mendocino is the westernmost point in the contiguous USA. It's not (that honor belongs to Cape Alava, Washington).

Mattole Rd finally drops you back into the lap of civilization at quaint, Victorian **17** **Ferndale**. Ferndale has so well preserved its architecture that the entire town is listed as a state and federal historical landmark. Stroll along the shop fronts of Main St and visit galleries, antiquarian bookshops, quaint emporia and soda fountains.

Pamper yourself at the old-fashioned **18** **Victorian Inn**. The bright, sunny rooms inside this 1890 two-story, former bank building are cozily furnished with thick carpeting, fine linens and specially chosen antiques.

Fir's pick for dinner in Ferndale is **19** **Curley's Grill**. Curley's whips up everything from steak sandwiches and meatloaf to braised lamb shank and Niçoise salads, all served on brightly colored Fiestaware. Or sidle up to the old-style bar for one of their excellent cocktails. For Italian-American food and prime rib hop across the street to **20** **Hotel Ivanhoe**.

FERNDALE FESTIVALS & EVENTS

This wee town has a packed social calendar. In May cheer on the famous moving sculptures at the Kinetic Sculpture Race or the sweaty bicyclists riding the Tour of the Unknown Coast. The Scandinavian Mid-Summer Festival ramps up the folk dancing and feasting in June and the Humboldt County Fair gets hopping in mid-August. Let out your inner German at the Victorian Village Oktoberfest & Harvest Day in October or deck the halls at Ferndale's very merry Christmas celebrations.

Swing back into cultural life at the **21** **Ferndale Repertory Theatre**. This terrific company produces shows year-round. If you have a chance to see one, be sure to go.

Part of what Fir loves about having the Lost Coast as his back yard is the many faces it can have. In fall the weather is clear, if cool. Wildflowers bloom from April through May, and gray whales migrate from December through April. The warmest, driest months are June to August, but days are foggy. Before heading out on the trails, grab a map and be sure you are prepared: to purify water, to layer up your clothes and shelter from the rain (weather can change quickly, and mostly, there is no cell phone service). Head out to get lost in nature, not literally lost!

Alexis Averbuck

TRIP INFORMATION

GETTING THERE
Take Hwy 101 north to Hwy 1, then follow it south to milepost 90.88. Take County Rd 431 north to Usal Campground.

DO
Ferndale Repertory Theatre
This top-shelf local rep company produces excellent contemporary theater in the historic Hart Theatre Building. ☎ 707-786-5483; www.ferndale-rep.org; 447 Main St, Ferndale

Needle Rock visitor center
Register for campsites and get maps and information from this visitor center in Sinkyone Wilderness State Park. ☎ 707-986-7711; www.parks.ca.gov; sites/Barn Room $15/20; ⏱ staffed 4 hours per day

EAT
Cove Restaurant
Sup on excellent salads and fresh fish at this oceanfront eatery. A treat after the trail. ☎ 707-986-1197; 10 Seal Ct, Shelter Cove; mains $8-25; ⏱ 10am-2pm & 5-9pm Thu-Sun

Curley's Grill
Downstairs at the Victorian Inn, pretend like you're in the upscale Old West. ☎ 707-786-9696; 400 Ocean Ave, Ferndale; mains $10-25; ⏱ 11:30am-9pm

Hotel Ivanhoe
Hearty portions of pasta and prime rib will stick to *your* ribs. They also have a bang-up bar. ☎ 707-786-9000; 315 Main St, Ferndale; mains $10-20; ⏱ 5-9pm Wed-Sun

SLEEP
Oceanfront Inn & Lighthouse
Spartan decor lets you see the view; the best rooms are upstairs, with peaked ceilings and giant windows. ☎ 707-986-7002; http://sheltercoveoceanfrontinn.com; 10 Seal Ct, Shelter Cove; r $125-175

Shelter Cove Bed & Breakfast
Recently renovated, each room has ocean views. Breakfasts are works of art. ☎ 707-986-7161; www.sheltercovebandb.com; 148 Dolphin Dr, Shelter Cove; r $145-195

Shelter Cove RV Park, Campground & Deli
Decidedly *un*sheltered, this basic campground has unobstructed views of the ocean. ☎ 707-986-7474; 492 Machi Rd, Shelter Cove; tent/RV sites $25/35

Victorian Inn
Fluffy pillows and floral wallpaper await you in this venerable, comfortable hotel. ☎ 707-786-4949, 888-589-1808; www.a-victorian-inn.com; 400 Ocean Ave, Ferndale; r $105-245

USEFUL WEBSITES
www.lostcoasttrail.com
www.victorianferndale.org/chamber

SUGGESTED READS
- *Heydays in Humboldt: The True History of the Mattole Valley and the Lost Coast of Humboldt County*, Ken Roscoe
- *Backwoods Chronicle: A History of Southern Humboldt, 1849–1920*, Mary Anderson
- *Totem Salmon: Life Lessons from Another Species*, Freeman House
- *Cash Crop: An American Dream*, Ray Raphael

LINK YOUR TRIP
www.lonelyplanet.com/trip-planner

Livermore's Fine Vines

WHY GO Napa Valley isn't the only grapey hot spot near San Francisco. In-the-know wine lovers venture an hour east of the foggy city to tour the warm rolling hills and fertile vine-staked valleys of the Livermore Valley, where more than 40 wineries invite you to taste their wares.

TIME
2 – 3 days

DISTANCE
32 miles

BEST TIME TO GO
Year-round

START
Pleasanton

END
Livermore

ALSO GOOD FOR

OUTDOORS

One of the oldest wine-producing regions in the country, these oak-dotted hills and farmlands of grazing cows are best sashayed through on weekends, when tasting rooms fling open their doors and giddy visitors can sample tasting flights until their designated drivers cut them off.

Start in the town of ❶ **Pleasanton** on a Thursday or Friday afternoon, and make a beeline for the ❷ **Mitchell Katz Winery**. Established on the site of the historic Ruby Hill Winery, a shady palm-studded driveway leads to a stately replica of the original 1887 brick building, set off by endless rows of grapevines and a horizon of distant hills. Inside, sidle up to the lengthy bar under a dramatic cathedral ceiling, and tickle your tongue with the light and drinkable sangiovese and the amply full-bodied Fat Boy cabernet sauvignon.

With your first tasting under your belt, duck back into downtown Pleasanton for dinner. The historic town has weathered a number of fires, but a number of interesting period buildings still stand, including the ❸ **Pleasanton Hotel Restaurant**. Rebuilt after two unfortunate conflagrations, the current edifice dates from 1898. Enter by way of a creaky wooden boardwalk and dine on fresh fish under old-fashioned chandeliers. Monthly winemaker dinners give the local folks a chance to shine, though regional wine pairings always grace the menu.

On the same block, the lovely ❹ **Rose Hotel** is newer accommodations, though a gallery of historic town photographs, an airy cherry-paneled

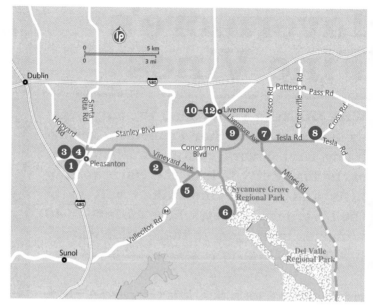

atrium and wrought-iron banisters give it a veneer of maturity. Rooms, which start at a cartwheel-compatible 450 sq ft, have a romantic European flavor, with custom cabinetry and overstuffed sea green chairs, and Jacuzzi-tub bathrooms. Fresh fruit and fragrant roses in the hallways are ripe for picking, and the full continental breakfast is a bracing start for a full day at the vineyards.

> **DETOUR** For a refreshing nearby dip, check out the lake at **Del Valle Regional Park** (http://ebparks .org/parks/del_valle), a 5-mile-long oasis surrounded by low hills. You can camp and swim there – the water's reliably bathtub warm in summer – or rent a boat or kayak on-site to explore the shoreline. From Tesla Rd, it's about 3.5 miles south on Mines Rd and then another 3 miles on Del Valle Rd.

The following day, head east again for the day's first stop at the ⑤ **Fenestra Winery**. With a utilitarian tasting room in the midst of its production facilities, you can sip flights surrounded by stacks of wine barrels and a wall of fluttering prize-winning ribbons that testify to its prestigious 30-year-plus history. A number of its wines come from obscure Portuguese verdelho, alvarelhao or touriga grapes, and since 2008, about 80% of the facility's electricity has been solar-generated.

In business for over 125 years and now turning out a hefty 350,000 cases a year, Wente Vineyards is the largest wine producer in the region as well as California's oldest winery continuously operated by the same family. The

6 **Restaurant at Wente Vineyards** is a local special-occasion favorite, with gourmet dishes almost exclusively composed of locally obtained ingredients, and herbs grown on-site. On select weeknights from June through September, big-name bands play in an outdoor garden amphitheater.

7 **Wente Vineyards'** wine is made at another site on Tesla Rd, Livermore's main winery row. Here, its Estate Tasting Room serves a number of tasting flights and offers four free daily tours of the facilities. Try to visit during harvest time, when truckloads of grapes come in from the fields and you can watch them get poured into the crusher-destemmer and bladder press.

"… talk terroir as Rhode Island Reds peck the ground under flowing California pepper trees."

For the night, prepare to be pampered at the **8** **Purple Orchid Inn**, located a bit further east off Tesla Rd. A rural B&B with a full spa, it's a popular destination for weddings and romantic weekends. Each of the guest rooms has a gas fireplace and whirlpool tub, and the frilliness level varies room to room. After a full breakfast, a couples' massage and a leisurely swim in the inn's outdoor waterfall pool, head towards central Livermore by way of rustic **9** **Retzlaff Vineyards**. A smaller organic estate vineyard with a devoted following, almost all of its bottles are sold on-site. Meet the owner and pull up a chair to hear her talk *terroir* as Rhode Island Reds peck the ground under flowing California pepper trees.

10 **Livermore's** downtown has seen a renaissance since a major highway was rerouted from the middle of town, and the restored brick compound of **11** **Blacksmith Square** shelters a group of small tasting rooms around a pretty courtyard where there's often live music and special events. One standout is Battaion Cellars, a new sparkling-wine producer with a scrumptious list of bruts made with grapes from the Champagne region.

End the day a few blocks away under the gleaming pressed-tin ceiling at **12** **Movida**, where menus are as hefty as coffee-table design tomes. Feast on

ASK A LOCAL To tour the region by pedal-power, rent bicycles at **Livermore Cyclery** (www.livermorecyclery.com) in downtown Livermore. Owner Steve Howard points out that cooler fall temperatures make it the best time to ride, and it's also harvest time. He recommends the following routes: Sycamore Grove; S Livermore Ave to Greenville Rd, by way of the Tesla Rd wineries; a loop using Cross Rd and Patterson Pass Rd; Vineyard Ave and the Ruby Hills area; and Mines Rd.

creative small plates in a sexy room of saucy red banquettes and eye-popping black-and-white wall hangings, and bliss out over a final dose of local flavor from an oversized wine glass.

Beth Kohn

TRIP INFORMATION

GETTING THERE
From Oakland, take I-580 and go 30 miles east to Pleasanton's Santa Rita Rd exit; return via I-580 from Livermore.

DO
Blacksmith Square
A historic brick complex in downtown Livermore, it has six tasting rooms in one easily-accessible location. www.black smith-square.com; 21 S Livermore Ave, Livermore; ☽ variable hours Thu-Sun

EAT
Movida
A slick and stylized contemporary dining room serving tapas, shared small plates and cocktails. ☎ 925-373-1002; 2417 1st St, Livermore; tapas $8-16; ☽ 4-10pm Mon-Thu, 4-11pm Fri, 10:30am-11pm Sat, 10:30am-9:30pm Sun

Pleasanton Hotel Restaurant
Pair fresh fish with local wines in this historic hotel setting. ☎ 925-846-8106; 855 Main St, Pleasanton; mains $10-25; ☽ 11:30am-2pm & 5:30-8:30pm Tue-Sat, 10:30am-1:30pm & 4:30-7:30pm Sun

Restaurant at Wente Vineyards
Reservations recommended on weekends and are required for special concert events. ☎ 925-456-2450; 5050 Arroyo Road, Livermore; lunch mains $15-27, dinner mains $29-39; ☽ lunch & dinner daily, plus brunch Sunday

DRINK
Fenestra Winery
Sample unique varietals in the no-frills tasting room of an award-winning winery operating primarily on solar power. ☎ 925-447-5246; www.fenestrawinery.com; 83 Vallecitos Rd, Livermore; tasting fee $5; ☽ noon-5pm Fri-Sun

Mitchell Katz Winery
An exciting new winery and tasting room located on the historic Ruby Hill site. ☎ 925-931-0744; www.mitchellkatzwinery.com; 1188 Vineyard Ave, Pleasanton; tasting fee $5; ☽ noon-5pm Thu-Sun, to 6pm Fri

Retzlaff Vineyards
A friendly estate winery, it grows organic grapes in a picnic-friendly setting. ☎ 925-447-8941; www.retzlaffwinery.com; 1356 S Livermore Ave, Livermore; tasting fee $5; ☽ noon-2pm Tue-Fri, to 4:30pm Sat & Sun

Wente Vineyards
Wente's Estate Winery location gives free winery tours and contains its main tasting room. ☎ 925-456-2305, ext 4; www.wente vineyards.com; 5565 Tesla Rd, Livermore; tasting fee $1-10; ☽ 11am-6:30pm

SLEEP
Purple Orchid Inn
Views of rolling hills and farmland complement this romantic rural B&B with a pool and full spa. ☎ 925-606-8855, 800-353-4549; www.purpleorchid.com; 4549 Cross Rd, Livermore; r Sun-Thu $170-360, Fri & Sat $200-420

Rose Hotel
A 38-room downtown B&B awash in fresh roses, its luxurious rooms and suites are supremely comfortable. ☎ 925-846-8802, 800-843-9540; www.rosehotel.net; 807 Main St, Pleasanton; r $260-290, suites $510-710

USEFUL WEBSITES
www.livermorewine.com
www.trivalleycvb.com

LINK YOUR TRIP
www.lonelyplanet.com/trip-planner

Tahoe Snow Trip

WHY GO From wintertime through spring, Lake Tahoe woos powder-hungry skiers and boarders worldwide with scores of slopes embracing a hypnotic bowl of sapphire blue. Downhill and cross-country aficionados will salivate over the more than 500 trails that ring and tower over the water, with sublime lake views amid hushed pine forest.

TIME
3 – 4 days

DISTANCE
155 miles

BEST TIME TO GO
Dec – Apr

START
South Lake Tahoe

END
Soda Springs

Without a filling breakfast, those slopes will quickly wear you down to a jittery knock-kneed invertebrate. Get an early start in South Lake Tahoe at ❶ **Ernie's Coffee Shop**, a sun-filled local institution that dishes out filling four-egg omelets, hearty biscuits with gravy and bottomless cups of locally roasted coffee. Toddlers can happily munch the ears off the Mickey Mouse pancakes decorated with syrup, and cool caricatures of the restaurant staff – some who've been working here for over 20 years – hang over the entrance to the kitchen.

Start your slopeside romp at ❷ **Kirkwood**, 35 miles southwest (via Hwy 89) on Hwy 88. An amazing combination of both alpine and cross-country terrain, it easily satisfies in both departments. Because the resort is a tad more remote than others, the downhill crowds tend not to be as fierce as other places, and because there's less development nearby, the mountain vistas seem more wild and pristine. Also, Kirkwood's high-elevation valley location means that it's blessed with tons of deep, dry snow that sticks around a long, long time. Encompassing 14 lifts, 2000 vertical feet and 68 runs, the tree-skiing is great, as are the gullies and chutes.

Another cool downhill option at Kirkwood is the availability of cat skiing runs. For a premium, treaded snowcat vehicles (generally used for trail grooming) will chauffeur you up to untrammeled backcountry

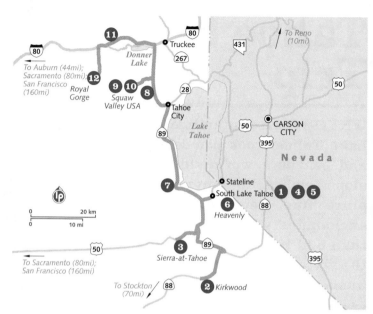

areas where no one else goes. In other parts of the country, heli-skiers pay three to four times as much to access this kind of gorgeous remote powder. Kirkwood also offers a number of backcountry training classes, covering subjects from the basics of backcountry awareness all the way to avalanche transceiver training.

Definitely not a jogging trail, Kirkwood's cross-country network has sections that are very challenging and where you can actually gain some elevation. The groomed track and snowshoe trails stretch 80km, and views from the higher slopes are phenomenal. You can even bring dogs on one ridgeline loop called the High Trail.

Want to catch some air instead? Aim a bit closer to town, and go 12 miles south on Hwy 50 to ❸ **Sierra-at-Tahoe**, also known as snowboarding central. Freestylers will want to check out the 17ft Zaugg superpipe and the six terrain parks with gnarly jumps, rails and boxes galore. Dude! In addition, five backcountry gates can set you sailing off on hundreds of acres of steep off-piste areas via Huckleberry Bowl. Parents will appreciate that in addition to an excellent ski school for kids as young as three, the resort has a licensed daycare center for tykes 18 months to five years old.

At closing time, peel yourself away from the pipe and head back to South Lake Tahoe. Settle in at the ❹ **Deerfield Lodge at Heavenly**, a boutique inn at a respectful distance from the kitschy chain motel clusters so well-represented in this bustling lakeside town. It's a 12-room establishment with kitchenettes, blissfully comfortable beds, and amusing details like coat racks crafted from skis and snowboards, and all rooms have a patio or balcony facing out onto a pretty courtyard. Suites have bathroom Jacuzzi tubs. Make sure you arrive in time to recharge with complimentary afternoon wine and snacks.

With only seven tables, a reservation is a level-headed necessity at **5** **Café Fiore**, located just across the street. This upscale yet unpretentious Italian eatery resides in a cozy cabin bedecked with its award-winning collection of wine offerings, and encircled by a graceful grapevine mural. It's romantic and convivial, and locals rave about the perfect garlic bread, scrumptious pasta and the homemade white-chocolate ice cream. In summer, the patio opens and a few more tables become available.

> **DETOUR** For many people, the I-80 drive to Lake Tahoe is incomplete without a burger and bathroom break at **Ikedas** (www.ikedas.com) in Auburn. A family fast-food restaurant, farm stand and bakery that's been in business since 1970, it's located right next to the highway about 30 miles east of Sacramento. It seems like everyone drops by to eat on the way out or back – break up the trip over an inexpensive burger, a mountain of spicy curly fries and a slice of fresh raspberry pie.

If luck courses through your veins, spend some time – and a giddy stack of coins or chips – at one of the big casinos a few minutes away across the border in Stateline, Nevada. The gambling palaces of Harrah's, Harvey's, MontBleu and the Horizon conveniently vie to offload your unneeded cash, with nightclubs and 24-hour restaurants to keep you entertained and amped to play until the ski lifts start in the morning.

In the morning, properly fed with a hearty continental breakfast at the hotel, today's the day to explore **6** **Heavenly**, the evocatively and appropriately named South Shore ski behemoth. From the hotel, the mountain's California Lodge base is just a few blocks away. The largest resort in the state, 4800-acre Heavenly straddles the California–Nevada border and bristles with superlatives. It has Lake Tahoe's highest summit, and California's longest vertical drop, with 29 lifts and four base lodges. It can't be stressed enough that the views are divine. From the top, you're right on the spine of the Sierras and on the cusp between mountains and desert flatlands of Nevada.

"Pull over to gaze at Emerald Bay, a resplendent teardrop cove leaking from the lake…"

For the most dramatic rise, ascend the steep gondola from Heavenly Village in Stateline, and watch the lake views unfold and blossom. From mid-mountain, reach the oxygen-gulping altitude of 10,040ft via the Sky Express lift, and cruise down the Skyline Trail.

Unless the road's temporarily closed after a heavy snowfall, set course for the North Shore on scenic lakeside Hwy 89. Pull over to gaze at ❼ **Emerald Bay**, a resplendent teardrop cove leaking from the lake, where the deep blue-green waters frame the impeccably placed Fannette Island. This uninhabited granite speck, the only island in Lake Tahoe, holds the remains of a tiny 1920s house formerly used as a "tea house" for heiress Lora Knight. After Vikingsholm (her enormous Scandinavian-style castle on the bay, which you can tour in the summer months) was completed in 1929, she would occasionally motor-boat guests to the island, though modern vandals have destroyed most of the building. Visitors can reach the island by boat from July through December, as Canadian geese take up residence during the rest of the year.

Half an hour north on Hwy 89, at the entrance to the Alpine Meadows resort, icicles dangle from the eaves of the ❽ **River Ranch Lodge**, a charming inn that backs up against the Truckee River. Rooms feature either elegant antiques or classy lodgepole-pine furniture, and upstairs rooms have soothing river-view balconies. At night, snuggle up and get cozy under a down comforter, and listen to the chilly river rushing by. Dinner at its restaurant is a meat-heavy gourmet affair, with rotating standouts like filet mignon and roasted duck, and a blazing fireplace to set the mood.

The following day, continue the adventure at one of the best downhill resorts in the world. ❾ **Squaw Valley USA** hosted the 1960 Winter Olympics, and the flame still burns boldly at the entrance from two-lane Hwy 89. With 4000 acres, 34 lifts, 2850 vertical feet and over 170 runs, Squaw is one of the largest ski and snowboard playgrounds in Lake Tahoe. It's also the shining star of the region, with an Olympics-caliber infrastructure and so much mountain area that you could spend the whole weekend and not ski the same run twice. With the summits of KT-22, Squaw Creek, Emigrant and Granite Chief splayed along the ridge, it's almost like four mountains wrapped up in one.

Before queuing for a vertiginous ride up the mountain, fuel up with a "bisk-wich" from the counter in the lobby of the cable-car building. The stuffed homemade buttermilk biscuits are tasty handheld to-go breakfasts, and good to grab when fresh powder awaits. Then hold on tight as the cable car rises 2000 vertical feet over granite ledges to High Camp, depositing riders at a lofty 8200ft. Nonskiers can execute an alpine twirl (or the popular wobbly-ankle wall-clenching circuit) at the outdoor ice rink, soaking up the wide-open vistas of the lake so, so far below.

From this staging area, snap on those bindings, and head for some intermediate or black diamond runs off the back side. Or explore the expansive front face, with family-friendly beginner trails to adrenaline-explosion black diamonds and lots of adventures in between. Starting at High Camp, the longest trail, Mountain Run, winds down a glorious 3.2 miles, and is floodlit for night skiing until early spring. If you can stand up that long (and still walk the next day), it's possible to pack in a 12-hour downhill day.

Whenever you decide to call it quits, the slopeside ⑩ **Le Chamois** has all the comfort food you're jonesing for après-ski. Sidle up to this popular and social spot sandwiched between the rental shop and the cable car, and re-energize on gooey pizza, delicious beer on tap and dreamy views of the mountain you conquered.

On Donner Pass Rd about a mile west of the Sugar Bowl resort, and tucked a short hike up a hill, the 1934 ⑪ **Clair Tappaan Lodge** is a textbook example of what a classic ski lodge should be. A cozy and well-maintained rustic mountain lodge owned by the Sierra Club, it has wooden A-frame dorms and family rooms, family-style meals and small chores expected of guests.

SNOWSHOEING UNDER THE STARS

A crisp quiet night with a blazing glow across the lake. What could be more magical than a snowshoe tour under a full moon? Reserve ahead of time, as these ramblings are very popular:

- Northstar at Tahoe (www.northstarattahoe.com), to the north near Tahoe Vista

- Ed Z'Berg-Sugar Pine Point State Park (www.parks.ca.gov/?page_id=510), to the southwest

- Kirkwood, to the south on Hwy 88

- Squaw Valley USA, to the north near Tahoe City

The library has excellent materials to keep you lingering in front of the woodburning stove. Though the lodge puts you near all the major North Shore ski resorts, you can cross-country ski right out the door or careen down the sledding hill out back. And even though it's a simple place, it doesn't skimp on the (obligatory) hot tub.

For the final day of the trip, cross-country fans should prick up their ears because ⑫ **Royal Gorge** is the largest cross-country resort in North America. With eight heated warming huts and four trailside cafés along 191 miles of groomed track, it's a beautiful place to explore, and all trails have great skating lanes and two diagonal stride tracks. Telemark skiers and snowshoeing fans are also welcome. If you can spend one more day, consider overnighting at one of its two cozy lodges.

Beth Kohn

TRIP INFORMATION

GETTING THERE & AWAY
From San Francisco, take I-50 to South Lake Tahoe. Return from Tahoe City via Hwy 89 and then I-80.

DO
Heavenly
The Siren of the south, this resort straddles the California–Nevada border. ☎ 775-586-7000, 800-432-8365; www.skiheavenly.com; cnr Wildwood & Saddle, South Lake Tahoe; adult/child $78/39; ☽ 9am-4pm Mon-Fri, 8:30am-4pm Sat & Sun; ♿

Kirkwood
Venture further south to see fewer people at this excellent alpine and cross-country resort. ☎ 209-258-6000, 877-547-5966; www.kirkwood.com; Hwy 88, Kirkwood; downhill adult/child $69/14, cross-country adult/under 10yr $22/free; ☽ 9am-4pm; ♿

Royal Gorge
Get (happily) lost in the largest groomed cross-country resort in North America. ☎ 530-426-3871; www.royalgorge.com; Soda Springs; adult/child weekend $29/16, midweek $25/15; ☽ 9am-5pm Mon-Fri, 8:30am-5pm Sat & Sun; ♿

Sierra-at-Tahoe
Get excited about the gnarly terrain parks, an awesome superpipe and easy backcountry access. ☎ 530-659-7453; www.sierraattahoe.com; 1111 Sierra-at-Tahoe Rd, Twin Bridges; adult/child/teen $65/16/55; ☽ 9am-4pm Mon-Fri, 8:30am-4pm Sat & Sun; ♿

Squaw Valley USA
This huge world-class North Shore resort hosted the 1960 Winter Olympic Games. ☎ 530-583-6985, 888-736-9740; www.squaw.com; off Hwy 89; adult/child/teen $73/10/55; ☽ 9am-9pm Mon-Fri, 8:30am-9pm Sat & Sun; ♿

LINK YOUR TRIP

EAT
Café Fiore
For fine dining, reserve ahead and snag a table at this tiny Italian eatery with an oversized wine list. ☎ 530-541-2908; 1169 Ski Run Blvd #5, South Lake Tahoe; mains $16-31; ☽ 5:30-10:30pm

Ernie's Coffee Shop
Bask in the morning sunshine as you sip your coffee and rev up for a day on the slopes. ☎ 530-541-2161; 1207 Hwy 50, South Lake Tahoe; mains $7-10; ☽ 6am-2pm; ♿

Le Chamois
Kick off your gear a few steps from the mountain and dig in to some end-of-the-day beer and pizza. Squaw Valley USA, off Hwy 89; pizzas from $10; ☽ 11am-7pm Mon-Fri, 11am-8pm Sat & Sun

SLEEP
Clair Tappaan Lodge
Turn back the clock and bed down at this historic Tahoe lodge. ☎ 530-426-3632, 800-629-6775; www.sierraclub.org/outings/lodges/ctl; 19940 Donner Pass Rd, Norden; dm members/nonmembers Easter-late Nov $46/51, Dec-Easter $55/60; ♿

Deerfield Lodge at Heavenly
Escape the chain-hotel scene at this small independent boutique hotel in the shadow of Heavenly. ☎ 888-757-3337; www.tahoedeerfieldlodge.com; 1200 Ski Run Blvd, South Lake Tahoe; r/suites $229/329; ♿

River Ranch Lodge
Drift off to dreamland as the Truckee River tumbles below your window. ☎ 530-583-4264, 866-991-9912; www.riverranchlodge.com; Hwy 89 at Alpine Meadows Rd, Tahoe City; r $115-200; ♿

USEFUL WEBSITES
www.skilaketahoe.com
www.slidingonthecheap.com

www.lonelyplanet.com/trip-planner

Volcano Hikes: Lassen to Shasta

WHY GO Sparkling streams, labyrinthine caves, deep forests and dramatic peaks abound in this little-visited part of California. One of the state's best-kept secrets, the chain of volcanoes that makes up the Southern Cascade range harbors true wilderness and a few creature comforts to boot.

TIME
2 – 3 days

DISTANCE
140 miles

BEST TIME TO GO
Jul – Sep

START
Lassen Volcanic National Park

END
Weed

Driving east from Red Bluff across rolling fields studded with volcanic boulders, the austere mountains of ❶ **Lassen Volcanic National Park** loom in the distance. Lassen rises 2000 dramatic feet over the surrounding landscape to 10,457ft above sea level. Its dome has a volume of half a cubic mile making it one of the world's largest plug-dome volcanoes. The lava that formed the dome had a high volume of silica, which made it thick and unable to flow far – this created the dome shape. Classified as an active volcano, its most recent eruption was in 1915, when it blew a giant billow of smoke, steam and ash 7 miles into the atmosphere.

Approaching the peaks, the road begins to climb, entering corridors of dense forest and emerging at the brand-new green-certified ❷ **Kohm Yah-mah-nee Visitor Facility**. Stop in to pick up maps and the handy newspaper outlining campsites and facilities throughout the park, and wander its xeriscape gardens, designed to conserve water.

The variegated crags of the lower mountains emerge above the tree line into valleys that remain snowpacked even in summer. Sparkling runoff feeds waterfalls and bright sprays of yellow wildflowers. The park's 150 miles of hiking trails begin right away but many are only open in summer. Roam through the tawny stone slopes of burbling ❸ **Sulfur Works** – you'll know it by the ripe scent in the air and the gaseous bursts hissing over the roadway. The moderate 1.5-mile hike to ❹ **Bumpass Hell** traverses an active geothermal area festooned with

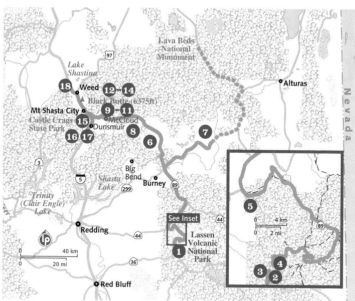

otherworldly colored pools and billowing clouds of steam. Nearby Brokeoff Mountain provides an alternative to the more technical Lassen Peak Trail (both trailheads are marked from the road), but even the climb up Lassen is empty when compared to similar routes in the Sierras. Check in at the visitor facility to find out about trail conditions before hiking.

Follow Hwy 89 27 miles through the park (the road closes in winter) and circle east of Lassen. Ice floats on the highland ponds, and the occasional fly fisher casts a line in green glades strewn with snowpack. Emerge at **5** **Manzanita Lake**, an emerald gem. A bit lower, it is swimmable in summer and makes a refreshing final sojourn before following Hwy 89/Shasta Volcanic Scenic Byway north. Six miles northwest of Four Corners, the crossroads where Hwy 89 intersects Hwy 299 from Redding, swing in to **6** **McArthur-Burney Falls Memorial State Park**. Fed by a spring, the splashing 129ft waterfalls flow at the same temperature, 42°F, year-round. Clear, lava-filtered water surges over the top and also from springs in the waterfall's face. Hiking trails include a portion of the Pacific Crest Trail, which continues north to Castle Crags State Park.

About 10 miles northeast, **7** **Ahjumawi Lava Springs State Park** encompasses abundant springs, aquamarine bays and islets, and jagged flows of black basalt lava. It is truly off the beaten path, and only reached by boat; make arrangements for primitive camping through McArthur-Burney Memorial State Park.

Bump along the tiny, partially paved McCloud River Loop, which begins off Hwy 89 about 11 miles east of McCloud, to find the lovely trail at **8** **Three Falls** on lower Mt Shasta. The easy, 1½-mile trail passes gorgeous, secluded falls, and a riparian habitat for bird-watching in the Bigelow Meadow. Old logging town **9** **McCloud** sits on the southern slopes of Shasta, under the looming peak. It's a mellow place from which to explore the bodacious wilderness. Antique train cars are still used for the **10** **Shasta Sunset Dinner Train**, a superscenic, open-air ride through Mt Shasta's forested southern reaches. Looking to rest your head? The grand, elegant, butter yellow **11** **McCloud Hotel** first opened in 1916 and has been lovingly restored. Sumptuous breakfasts of fluffy eggs and rich muffins prep you for taking on epic Mt Shasta.

Classified as an active volcano, **12** **Mt Shasta** remains a mecca for mystics, attracted to the peak's reported cosmic properties. Native Americans have long considered it to be no less than the Great Spirit's wigwam. Reach its highest drivable point by heading through Mt Shasta City to Everitt Memorial Hwy, which leads to **13** **Bunny Flat** (6860ft). Numerous trails lead out across the mountain and have spectacular views. Some trails connect to the Pacific Crest Trail – the ranger station has excellent maps. In late summer the road stays open and you can drive to Everitt Vista Point (7900ft), where a short walk leads to a stone-walled outcropping with exceptional views of Lassen Peak, the Mt Eddy and Marble Mountains and the whole Strawberry Valley. It feels like Mars on the 2½-mile trail to the top of **14** **Black Butte**, a striking, treeless ebony cone rising almost 3000ft.

> **DETOUR**
>
> **Lava Beds National Monument** (www.nps.gov/labe), perched on yet another crater, is a truly remarkable 72-sq-mile landscape of volcanic features – lava flows, craters, cinder cones, spatter cones, shield volcanoes and amazing lava tubes. Nearly 750 caves have been found in the monument and they remain a comfortable 55°F no matter what the outside temperature. Spy Native American petroglyphs throughout the park too.

Nine miles southwest of Lake Siskiyou on Castle Lake Rd, dive into shimmering **15** **Castle Lake**, an easily accessible yet pristine mountain pool surrounded by granite formations and pine forest. Just south, cheery **16** **Café Maddalena** put the wee village of Dunsmuir on the foodie map. Though original owner Maddalena Sera no longer runs the café (rumor has it she is now Francis Ford Coppola's personal chef), Bret LaMott maintains its stellar reputation. Moist, pan-roasted sea bass comes paired with chard, oranges and tomatoes. **17** **Sengthongs Restaurant & Blue Sky Room** serves up sizzling Thai, Lao and Vietnamese food and books first-rate jazz, reggae, salsa or blues most nights. Half an hour north, wind down at the weathered bathhouse of **18** **Stewart Mineral Springs Resort**, which bubbles with heated mineral springs. Its soothing dry-wood sauna heals the body at the end of a long hike.

Alexis Averbuck

TRIP INFORMATION

GETTING THERE
Cruise I-5 north of San Francisco to Red Bluff, and jog east on Hwy 36 for 40 miles.

DO
Ahjumawi Lava Springs State Park
The name for this lava- and spring-strewn park comes from Pit River Native Americans and means "where the waters come together."
☎ 530-335-2777; www.parks.ca.gov

Lassen Volcanic National Park
The supergreen new Kohm Yah-mah-nee Visitor Facility has educational exhibits, bookstore, auditorium, gift shop and restaurant.
☎ 530-595-4444; www.nps.gov/lavo; park entrance $10; ☾ 9am-6pm Jun-Sep, with seasonal variations; ⚐

McArthur-Burney Falls Memorial State Park
The park's campgrounds have hot showers and are open year-round, even when there's snow on the ground. ☎ 530-335-2777; summer reservations ☎ 800-444-7275; www.parks.ca.gov; day-use/campsites $6/20; ⚐

Mt Shasta
The Mt Shasta ranger station issues wilderness and mountain-climbing permits, good advice, weather reports and everything else you need for exploring. ☎ 530-926-4511; www.fs.fed.us/r5/shastatrinity; 204 W Alma St, Mt Shasta City; ☾ 8am-4:30pm

EAT
Shasta Sunset Dinner Train
Clickety-clack along the slopes of Mt Shasta aboard 1916-vintage cars. ☎ 530-964-2142; www.shastasunset.com; Main St, McCloud; adult/child $12/8, 3hr dinner ride $80; ☾ Thu-Sat summer, with seasonal variations

Café Maddalena
Welcoming spot for southern European and North African specialties. The wine bar is stocked with rare Mediterranean labels.
☎ 530-235-2725; 5801 Sacramento Ave, Dunsmuir; mains $20-26; ☾ 5-10pm Thu-Sun

Sengthongs Restaurant & Blue Sky Room
Heaping bowls of noodle-iciousness combine with rockin' live music. ☎ 530-235-4770; www.sengthongs.com; 5843 Dunsmuir Ave, Dunsmuir; mains $11-20; ☾ 11am-2pm Mon-Fri, 4-9:30pm Mon, Tue, Thu-Sat

SLEEP
McCloud Hotel
Snuggle down in an antique four-poster bed and listen for the train whistle across tiny Main St. ☎ 530-964-2822, 800-964-2823; www.mccloudhotel.com; 408 Main St, McCloud; r $100-235

Stewart Mineral Springs Resort
Relax at an old-world clothing-optional western bathhouse along Parks Creek with dry-wood sauna and heated mineral baths.
☎ 530-938-2222; www.stewartmineralsprings.com; 4617 Stewart Springs Rd, Weed; tepee $30, r $65-85; ⚐ ⚑

USEFUL WEBSITES
www.mtshastachamber.com
www.shastacascade.org

LINK YOUR TRIP
www.lonelyplanet.com/trip-planner

Along Highway 1 to Santa Cruz

WHY GO California's river of tourism, Hwy 1, is best known for its curvaceous charms south of Carmel and Big Sur. But those in the know will tell you that the most jaw-dropping stretch of this iconic road starts south of San Francisco and runs down to Santa Cruz.

Often fog bound, ❶ **Pacifica** is home to thousands of commuters, whose cookie-cutter homes snake across the hillsides. It is also the place where one of the most famous stretches of Hwy 1 begins in earnest. The divided four-lane highway peters out at an intersection overlooking pounding waves, a portent of things to come.

The road narrows to two lanes and then jogs inland through some thick eucalyptus groves before turning back to the coast. On your left you won't be able to miss a massive construction site consisting of a soaring bridge that plunges the road into twin tunnels. Why the huge project? Drive another 500yd and you'll see, as Hwy 1 enters a Martian wasteland of rubble known as the ❷ **Devil's Slide**. Highly unstable, the rocky hillsides here are crumbling in slow motion. Huge wire fences and bulldozers stand ready to deal with falling boulders. Meanwhile, the road is regularly closed as parts drop into the ocean below – something that's been going on since it was completed in 1937. Constant closures propelled locals to demand a more geologically stable replacement, due to open some time after 2011 when the original will remain open for exploration as a walkway.

The road stabilizes from here south, which is good, as you'd rather be enjoying the views of the surf hitting the rocks at ❸ **Montara State Beach** than watching out for a yawning chasm of doom. Watch for the small, usually fog-bound, community of ❹ **Moss Beach**. Just south (and right before a small airport) look for Cypruss Rd, which goes

TIME
2 days

DISTANCE
65 miles

BEST TIME TO GO
Year-round

START
Pacifica

END
Santa Cruz

ALSO GOOD FOR

OUTDOORS

west. Follow the road down along the airport out to Pigeon Point. This is as close as you can get to **5** **Mavericks**, the legendary surf break about half a mile offshore. Although it was only popularized in the 1990s, the break's fame is driven by wintertime waves, which top 50ft.

Another 4 miles brings you to **6** **Half Moon Bay** (HMB), a once sleepy coastal town of farms and fog lovers that's now a popular bedroom community. Turn inland one block from Hwy 1 and cruise Main St, a tree-lined series of blocks with knick-knackeries, used bookstores, antique shops and cafés. At the north end, the **7** **Half Moon Bay Coffee Company** has excellent baked goods and a patio where you're more likely to be warmed by the coffee than any feeble rays of sun.

"Vistas of pounding surf, unspoiled shores and dramatic rock outcrops stretch for miles."

South of HMB, you'll spot the coast's many farms and vast greenhouses filled with ferns, ficuses and other potted plants hoping for a good home. For the next 15 miles, Hwy 1 gently follows the contours of the coast and is the string to a series of pearls that are the succession of beaches and coves. Vistas of pounding surf, unspoiled shores and dramatic rock outcrops stretch for miles. The state beaches here include **8** **Pescadero State Beach**; look for Pescadero Rd just south of the marshlands, which heads east to – you guessed it – **9** **Pescadero**. Little more than a crossroads, it could be called "lunch-seekers heaven." Besides some groceries with good deli counters, it's home to **10** **Duarte's Tavern**, an unadorned veteran that serves some of the freshest fish on the coast. Or duck into the humdrum-looking **11** **Taqueria Y Mercado De Amigos** for spectacular Mexican fare. Take it back to the state beach for a picnic (aka feast for the gulls).

PLUMBING FOR PUMPKINS

Starting at Half Moon Bay and heading south, look for farms selling their produce. In the fall, many explode with orange as the pumpkin harvest nears. You can stroll the fields looking for your own vision of the Great Pumpkin. Other crops hawked from barns and the roadside include artichokes, brussels sprouts and squash. About 2 miles north of Davenport, **Swanton Berry Farm** (www.swantonberryfarm.com) lets you pick your own strawberries and enjoy other berry delights, including baked treats.

Returning to Hwy 1, the world-class views continue; fortunately the constant variation means that those with short-attention spans won't start eyeing the DVD player. After about 5 miles look for the large **12** **Pigeon Point Lighthouse** on the right. Now a state park (like much of the coast), the precursor to today's structure was first switched on in 1872 to reduce the maritime carnage along the treacherous rocks. There are nature hikes along the cliffs and down to the tidepools below. If you are especially charmed you can bunk down for the night in the **13** **Pigeon Point Lighthouse Hostel**. Beds are in the old keeper's quarters, which has walls deeply imbued with the smell of the sea.

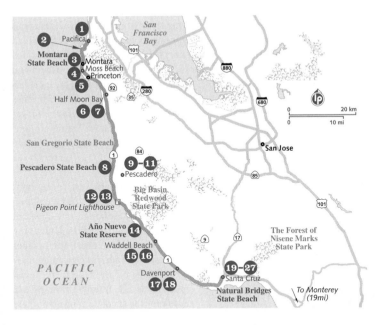

Another 5 miles of road and one stunning bay brings you into a grove of trees. Watch for the entrance on the right to ⑭ **Año Nuevo State Reserve**. Here during winter and early spring you'll find the rock stars of the coast: hundreds of enormous elephant seals mating, giving birth, learning to swim, carousing and often just lying prone in the sand. Join rangers for nature hikes (book in advance) through the dunes for views of the huge pinnipeds (adults top 1600lb).

Over the next 6 miles, Hwy 1 again follows the coast. As you descend a long hill bordered by a sheer cliff face

SAVING THE WHALES

Centered on the Monterey Bay, but stretching north to the Golden Gate and south well down the central coast, the **Monterey Bay National Marine Sanctuary** (www.montereybay.noaa.gov) protects one of the richest aquatic habitats in the world, including 276 miles of coast and 5322 sq miles of ocean.

that harkens back to the Devil's Slide, look for ⑮ **Waddell Beach** on your right. A good parking area overlooks breaks that are usually alive with windsurfers and other daredevils inventing new ways to use wind and waves to produce adrenaline. Wander the chilly sands, get blasted by the winds and you'll quickly understand that without a wet suit, you won't be hankering to don a swimsuit. Across the road is the trailhead for a popular hike that descends from the redwoods of Big Basin Sate Park, some 12 miles uphill inland. Look for the ⑯ **Rancho del Oso Nature and History Center**, which has two interpretive trails through the marshlands behind the beach.

At this point, Hwy 1 begins slowly moving away from the rocky shoreline as the coast becomes dominated by high limestone and sandstone cliffs, which regularly shed chunks into the white waters below. Eight miles from Waddell Beach, ⑰ **Davenport** was for decades a dusty home to farmers, fishers and folks toiling away at the cement plant. Like other minor coastal burgs, it has had a bit of a spiff-up. Day traders watch the markets move on CNBC in cafés while they buy and sell using their laptops. Across Hwy 1, there are movements almost as weighty. Whales pass Davenport's cliffs while migrating or heading to the Monterey Bay for an anchovy feast. Depending on the season you may see blue, gray or humpback whales.

The urge to eat your vegetables could strike south of Davenport. Those alien-looking stalks you see are brussels sprouts, a nightmare for finicky children and a delight for pint-sized-cabbage connoisseurs. Although not apparent from Hwy 1, numerous sandy coves dot the base of the cliffs. Unlike the beaches to the north, which are on exposed stretches of coast, the beaches south of Davenport are sheltered by cliffs and on sunny days can actually get slightly balmy. One of the most popular is ⑱ **Bonny Doon Beach**. Look for the small parking area where the road of the same name meets Hwy 1. Scuttle across the train tracks and small dunes to the cliffs and then clamber down the marked path to the beach. At the north end of the cove clothing is optional by tradition.

> **DETOUR**
>
> Head inland for almost 4 miles from Hwy 1 on Bonny Doon Rd and gird your liver and your palette for the surprising wines of **Bonny Doon Vineyard** (www.bonnydoonvineyard.com). Run by wine radical Randall Grahm, it features small vintages made with grapes and techniques overlooked by most of the wine world. After a few of his wines with names like Cardinal Zin hit the big time, Grahm sold them so he could concentrate on the unusual and provocative.

After 10 more miles you reach ⑲ **Santa Cruz**, the popular beach town that combines lots of folks intent on alternative lifestyles, millionaires from Silicon Valley and a whole lot of university students. Its downtown, the ⑳ **Pacific Garden Mall**, is a pedestrian's dream, where you can while away the hours in lots of non-chain shops and excellent bookstores.

After a day of reveling on the coast, you'd be adrift if you didn't bed down for the night within earshot of the sonorous surf. The ㉑ **Sea & Sand Inn** sits right on the cliff overlooking Santa Cruz's wharf and the north end of the Monterey Bay. Across the street, ㉒ **Seaway Inn** is a touch more upscale. From both you can stroll W Cliff Dr, which follows the city's picture-perfect clifftop for about a mile past the aptly named Lighthouse Point. Join the gawkers on the cliffs peering down at the floating kelp beds, hulking sea lions, playful sea otters and black-clad surfers. ㉓ **Steamers Lane** here is one of the top surf spots on the coast. You needn't go far for a fine briney meal:

24 Dolphin Restaurant, at the end of the wharf, has been serving fresh local fish and fine chowder for generations.

The next day, ditch the car and walk the Santa Cruz cliffs. Continue past Lighthouse Point for about 2 miles until you reach **25 Natural Bridges State Beach**. Named for a jutting precipice that had large arches hollowed in it by the constant surf (though it has mostly collapsed), this is where you can spot marine life at the opposite end of the size spectrum from whales. Starfish, anemones, crabs and more are found in the myriad tidepools carved into the limestone rocks. Just above Natural Bridges, learn more about local sea creatures great and small at the **26 Seymour Marine Discovery Center**, a public lab run by the University of California at Santa Cruz (UCSC).

Finally, after all the bracing pure air, fresh local foods and jaw-dropping natural beauty, it's time for something completely different. Head to the **27 Santa Cruz Beach Boardwalk**, where you can gorge yourself on low-brow corndogs before setting off on one of the many rides, including the iconic wooden rollercoaster, the Big Dipper, and the old-school Cave Train. Who says you have to get all your thrills from nature?

Ryan Ver Berkmoes

TRIP INFORMATION

GETTING THERE
Pacifica is easily reached in under 30 minutes, depending on traffic. Go south on Hwy 1 from San Francisco.

DO

Año Nuevo State Reserve
Enormous elephant seals pound the sand during breeding season. ☎ 650-879-2025; www.parks.ca.gov; Pescadero; admission $6; ☼ daylight, tour times vary; ♿

Rancho del Oso Nature and History Center
Walk down marked nature trails on the coast. ☎ 831-427-2288; 3600 Hwy 1, Davenport; admission free; ☼ displays noon-4pm Sat & Sun; ♿

Santa Cruz Beach Boardwalk
Why go to Coney Island when you can have a Coney Island dog here and then run amok on the bumper cars? ☎ 831-423-5590; www.beachboardwalk.com; Santa Cruz; admission free, rides cost extra; ☼ 11am-11pm summer, 11am-5pm Sat & Sun winter; ♿

Seymour Marine Discovery Center
Enjoy the interactive exhibits, aquariums and a blue whale skeleton. ☎ 831-459-3800; near Delaware Ave & Swift St, Santa Cruz; adult/student $6/4; ☼ 10am-5pm Tue-Sat, noon-5pm Sun; ♿

EAT

Dolphin Restaurant
Eat inside or plop down at a picnic table with your new friends, the seagulls. ☎ 831-426-5830; Municipal Wharf, Santa Cruz; meals $9-18; ☼ breakfast, lunch & dinner; ♿

Duarte's Tavern
Cioppino, abalone and more grace the menu at this timeless old tavern that gets jammed on weekends. ☎ 650-879-0464; www.duartestavern.com; 202 Stage Rd, Pescadero; mains $12-30; ☼ 7am-9pm

Half Moon Bay Coffee Company
There's a full café menu but the real allure awaits in the bakery displays. ☎ 650-726-3664; 20 Stone Pine Rd, Half Moon Bay; meals $7-12; ☼ 7am-5pm; ♿

Taqueria Y Mercado De Amigos
It's what's inside that counts. This burrito bar inside a corner store has perfectly piquant *al pastor* and heavenly salsa. ☎ 650-879-0232; 1999 Pescadero Creek Rd, Pescadero; mains $5; ☼ 10am-6pm

SLEEP

Pigeon Point Lighthouse Hostel
Book ahead for a bunk in the old lighthouse keeper's quarters. ☎ 650-879-0633; www.norcalhostels.org; 210 Pigeon Point Rd, Pescadero; dm $20-24, r $55-65; ♿

Sea & Sand Inn
Perched pleasantly on the cliff, some of the 20 rooms have whirlpools and fireplaces. ☎ 831-427-3400; www.santacruzmotels.com; 201 W Cliff Dr; r $100-400

Seaway Inn
Many of the brightly furnished rooms have views across the road to the bay. ☎ 831-471-9004; www.seawayinn.com; 176 W Cliff Dr; r $100-250; ♿

USEFUL WEBSITES
www.parks.ca.gov
www.santacruzca.org

LINK YOUR TRIP
www.lonelyplanet.com/trip-planner

Steinbeck Country

WHY GO From Salinas farmhands to Monterey cannery workers, the sun-crisped Central Valley hills to the fishing coastline, author John Steinbeck drew a perfect picture of his intimate landscapes and the communities he knew. See the land and people through his eyes, and follow this trail through the area he called home.

TIME
2 – 3 days

DISTANCE
42 miles

BEST TIME TO GO
Year-round

START
Salinas

END
Monterey

ALSO GOOD FOR

Observing the contemporary lovefest surrounding ❶ Salinas' favorite son, it's jolting to recall that the local library once burned *The Grapes of Wrath*. Inside the large, modern ❷ **National Steinbeck Center**, facing downtown from the foot of Main St, a map points out the settings for many of his books, which come to life through hands-on exhibits and minitheaters. Kids can climb on a red pony or touch the fuzzy mouse Lenny kept in his pocket in *Of Mice and Men,* while adults can listen to Steinbeck's 1962 Nobel acceptance speech. An adjunct agriculture museum showcases the local economy, incorporating historical labor struggles, water politics and the stories of immigrant farmworkers.

A few blocks west, visit ❸ **Steinbeck House**, the author's birth site and childhood home. A classic Queen Anne Victorian with dainty bird-patterned lace curtains, it's an interesting minimuseum and restaurant, where waitstaff in quasi-period dress serve lunch and high tea. An excellent downtown brewpub with an old industrial feel, ❹ **Monterey Coast Brewing** dishes up a selection of seafood salads, grilled sandwiches and burgers in a red brick room facing gleaming brew vats. The wine list has a great selection from local wineries, but it's the Scottish Red Ale and Irish Stout that keep the patrons coming back. Another good food option is ❺ **Hullaballoo**, a few blocks south on Main in shaded historic Oldtown. Locals love its "bold American cooking," white tablecloths and intimate lighting, making it a popular spot

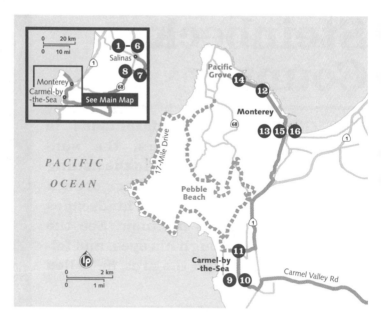

for both first dates and company dinners. Many Steinbeck pilgrims come to pay their respects at the **6 Garden of Memories Cemetery**, 2 miles southeast at Romie Lane. An iron sign points the way to the Hamilton family plot, where a simple grave marker identifies Steinbeck's ashes. He died in 1968.

Continue another 2 miles south on Abbott St until the city gives way to farms, and follow the sign for **7 Spreckels**, a former sugar-company town, where Steinbeck worked as a chemist's assistant and which he used as a backdrop for *Of Mice and Men*. Heavy trucks churn up dust and gravel along the road, and stooped-over farmworkers handpick strawberries. The 1898 Spreckels Emporium, at the corner of Hatton Ave, is worth a wander inside. Clusters of 1950s advertisements climb the soaring walls, surveying sparsely stocked shelves with cans spaced a foot apart and unused antique coolers. You can easily envision the company store Steinbeck once knew.

Drivers rejoining Hwy 68 may be startled to see farmworkers of Brobdingnagian proportions looming on the horizon. John Cerney's celebrated cutout murals depict past and present employees of **8 The Farm**, a quirky organic farm with a petting zoo, field tours and a lovely produce stand. Climb and descend the pleasantly winding Laureles Grade – mentioned in *The Pastures of Heaven* – to Carmel Valley Rd and continue toward the coast. Reaching Hwy 1 at **9 Carmel-by-the-Sea**, go slightly south to take a leap back in time. Established in 1769, the arched basilica and restored garden courtyard of the ➓ **Mission San Carlos Borromèo de Carmelo** make visitors feel as though they've landed in Spain. Wind 1 mile north through leafy residential streets to central Carmel. If you have a pooch in tow, you're both gonna love the ⓫ **Cypress Inn.** In this elegant and pet-friendly – no, pet-ecstatic – 1929 inn owned by Doris Day, it can feel like there are more (well-behaved) canine guests than human ones. Airy, colorful terra-cotta hallways give it a Mediterranean feel, and rooms facing the courtyard dazzle with light. Wait till the time feels just right, and then settle down on the veranda to read *East of Eden* or *The Long Valley.*

Head 6 miles north (via Hwy 1) to visit what was, in Steinbeck's time, the largest sardine cannery in Monterey. The ⓬ **Monterey Bay Aquarium** mesmerizes adults and kids with exhibits of rescued sea otters and stealthy giant octopuses, and a living kelp forest in a three-story, 343,000-gallon tank.

> **DETOUR**
>
> Once promoted as "Mother Nature's Drive-Thru," **17-Mile Drive** (www.pebblebeach.com) is a spectacularly scenic private toll road that loops around the Monterey Peninsula, connecting Pacific Grove, Pebble Beach and Carmel-by-the-Sea. If you have time to spare, meander by car or bicycle through this route of postcard vistas, gawking at Monterey cypress trees, world-famous golf courses, and the site where Spanish explorer Gaspar de Portolá dropped anchor in 1769 on the way to Monterey Bay.

Walk south along ⓭ **Monterey's** Cannery Row, evading the junk-food emporiums, to see the one-room shacks of former cannery workers on Bruce Ariss Way. On the way back, stop at an unpainted wooden building across the street (number 800), which was the biology lab (and occasional home) of Steinbeck's close friend Ed Ricketts. At the corner of Prescott Ave, pause to snap a photo with a bust of the bard himself. From Cannery Row, it's just over a mile to Pacific Grove, where Steinbeck's family had a summer cottage. In a minimalist dining room, feast on sustainably harvested seafood at ⓮ **Passionfish,** where the dessert menu includes an impressive list of loose teas. Then head 3 miles back to central Monterey to sneak a peek at the ⓯ **Old Monterey Jail,** mentioned in *Tortilla Flat.* Turn in at the ⓰ **Monterey Hotel,** a restored

KELP DIVING

Steinbeck's best friend, and the model for Doc in *Cannery Row*, marine biologist Ed Ricketts studied the ecosystem of Monterey Bay, and you can explore it too. Swathe yourself in some supersexy neoprene and take that 50°F plunge. Monterey Bay is renowned for its undulating forests of giant kelp, which can grow to 175ft in size and up to 2ft per day. Gaze up at the sunlight percolating through the fronds, creating brilliant beams called "god rays." The **Monterey Bay Dive Center** (www.mbdcscuba.com) rents out equipment and oxygen tanks.

1904 Victorian in the center of historic Old Monterey, with genteel plantation shutters, white ceiling fans and hand-carved furniture. Pull out one of your dog-eared Steinbeck novels and live his world all over again.

Beth Kohn

HISTORY & CULTURE

TRIP INFORMATION

GETTING THERE
From San Francisco, take Hwy 101 south to Salinas. From Monterey, return on Hwy 101 via Hwy 1 to CA-156.

DO
The Farm
A nifty organic farm with kids' activities and a yummy farm stand. ☎ 831-455-2575; www.thefarm-salinasvalley.com; Hwy 68 & Spreckels Blvd, Salinas; tours adult/child $6/4; ☺ tours 1pm Tue & Thu; ⓑ

Mission San Carlos Borromèo de Carmelo
The second-oldest California mission, it's also one of the most attractive and complete. ☎ 831-624-1271; www.carmelmission.org; 3080 Rio Rd, Carmel-by-the-Sea; adult/child $5/1; ☺ 9:30am-5pm

Monterey Bay Aquarium
A world-class aquarium, Monterey's biggest attraction contains exquisite displays of regional marine life. ☎ 831-648-4800; www.mbayaq.org; 886 Cannery Row, Monterey; adult/child $25/16; ☺ 10am-6pm, extended summer hours; ⓑ

National Steinbeck Center
The works and life of author John Steinbeck are illustrated and celebrated in this modern museum. ☎ 831-775-4720; www.steinbeck.org; 1 Main St, Salinas; adult/child $11/6; ☺ 10am-5pm; ⓑ

Old Monterey Jail
No one ever escaped from this thick-walled granite and adobe building, built in 1854. ☎ 831-646-5640; www.monterey.org/museum/jail.html; Dutra St btwn Madison & King Sts; ☺ 10am-4pm

Steinbeck House
Steinbeck's childhood home is open for summer tours and year-round viewing. ☎ 831-424-2735; www.steinbeckhouse.com; 132 Central Ave, Salinas; tours adult/child $4/2; ☺ tours 1pm & 3pm Sun Jun-Aug, restaurant 11:30am-2pm Tue-Sat year-round

EAT & DRINK
Hullaballoo
A lively, artistic feel and a seasonally changing menu makes for an eclectic and popular downtown eatery. ☎ 831-757-3663; 228 Main St, Salinas; mains $11-28; ☺ 11:30am-9pm Mon-Thu, 11:30am-10pm Fri & Sat

Monterey Coast Brewing
A brewpub slinging excellent victuals and pouring dynamite housemade beers. ☎ 831-758-2337; 165 Main St, Salinas; lunch mains $8-11, dinner mains $10-19; ☺ 11am-11pm Tue-Sun, 11am-4pm Mon

Passionfish
One of the finest fish restaurants in the region, it serves fresh, sustainable seafood in any number of inventive ways. ☎ 831-655-3311; 701 Lighthouse Ave, Pacific Grove; mains $17-24; ☺ 5-9pm

SLEEP
Cypress Inn
Dog (and cat) owners will adore this beautiful pro-pet hotel done up in Spanish colonial style. ☎ 831-624-3871; www.cypress-inn.com; Lincoln St & 7th Ave, Carmel-by-the-Sea; r $150-445; ⓖ

Monterey Hotel
This well-located 1904 hotel is grand in the traditional manner, with rooms furnished in old-world style. ☎ 831-375-3184, 800-727-0960; www.montereyhotel.com; 406 Alvarado St, Monterey; r $100-240

USEFUL WEBSITES
www.montereyinfo.org
www.mtycounty.com

www.lonelyplanet.com/trip-planner

LINK YOUR TRIP

All Wet in Big Sur

WHY GO Nestled up against mossy, mysterious-looking redwood forests, the rocky Big Sur coast is a secretive place. So, you'll need help getting to know it like the locals do, especially if you want to find hidden hot springs, waterfalls and beaches. Show up in spring, when waterfalls peak.

Beyond Carmel-by-the-Sea, the northern gateway to Big Sur country, Hwy 1 pulls out all the stops when it comes to dramatic scenery. You'll snake along a winding coastal road, carved out of giant cliffs that rise above storm-tossed Pacific beaches. At times, the ocean looks far away, and impossible to reach. But it's not – you just have to know where to pull off the road and stop.

Big Sur is more a state of mind than a place you can pinpoint on a map, to tell the truth. The fearlessly arched ❶ **Bixby Bridge** lets you know you've arrived. It was this bridge, a keystone of the Pacific Coast Hwy, that finally unlocked this remote stretch of coast starting in the era of the Great Depression. Few can resist stopping on the north side of the bridge to snap at least a few photos.

With such gorgeous ocean vistas, you're probably eager to hit the beach by now. Twenty miles south of Carmel, ❷ **Andrew Molera State Park** is forgotten by most visitors. Walk the peaceful, mile-long trail out to where the Big Sur River meets the rocky beach, and you might be lucky enough to have the sand and surf all to yourself. Also keep an eye out for California condors, as these endangered creatures are making a brave-hearted comeback along the coast.

Something about the salty sea air might make you ravenous. On Big Sur's main drag, nothing more than a chockablock stretch of Hwy 1,

TIME
2 days

DISTANCE
65 miles

BEST TIME TO GO
Dec – May

START
Bixby Bridge

END
Salmon Creek Falls

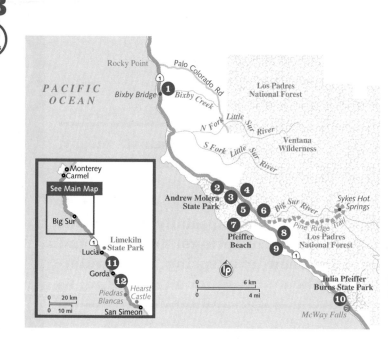

3 **Big Sur Burrito Bar** wraps up San Francisco–sized burritos and wraps and blends real fruit-juice smoothies at the back of a well-stocked general store. If you've quickly fallen under Big Sur's charms, snap up a room at **4** **Glen Oaks**, a rustic-chic motel renovated with recycled and renewable stone and bamboo elements; it also has organic bath goodies. Just five minutes down the road is the Latin-flavored **5** **Big Sur Roadhouse**, run by talented chefs who once worked at Sierra Mar, the Post Ranch Inn's hoity-toity dining room.

The biggest all-natural draw on the Big Sur coast is **6** **Pfeiffer Big Sur State Park**. Hike through tall redwood groves and loop around 60ft-high Pfeiffer Falls, a delicate cascade hidden deep in the forest that usually runs from December through May, then climb to Valley View vista. The gigantic campground lies in a redwood valley; facilities include showers and laundry. Summer crowds are the only drawback. On the west side of Hwy 1, **7** **Pfeiffer Beach** has a huge arched rock formation through which waves crash with life-af-firming power. It's often windy, and the surf is too dangerous for swimming. But dig down into the wet sand – it's purple! That's because manganese garnet washes down from the steep, craggy hillsides above. To get here, make a sharp right onto Sycamore Canyon Rd, marked by a small brown sign that says "narrow road" at the top, about a quarter-mile south of Big Sur Station.

"...dig down into the wet sand – it's purple!"

After climbing back onto Hwy 1, traffic streams south past the turnoff for the famous **8 Ventana Inn**, catering to honeymooning couples and paparazzi-fleeing celebs, who pad from private yoga classes to the Japanese baths and the clothing-optional pool. If the weather turns stormy, you can hole up all day next to the wood-burning fireplaces in the inn's rustic-style cottages. Further south, **9 Nepenthe** restaurant gets the thumbs-up from locals and out-of-towners alike. The name comes from a Greek word meaning "isle of no sorrow," and indeed, it's hard to feel at all blue while sitting on its cliff-top terrace, the vast ocean spread out before you.

DETOUR Ocean beaches, forest streams and waterfalls aren't the only places to get wet in Big Sur. The Santa Lucia Mountains hide all-natural hot springs, too. The best known is **Sykes Hot Springs**, reached via a challenging 20-mile round-trip trail starting from Big Sur Station. Next to the Big Sur River, its small boulder-lined pools filled with 100°F waters are free and always open. Plan on camping overnight, and don't expect solitude during peak tourist season (roughly April to September).

If your appetite for chasing waterfalls still burns, pass up Partington Cove and instead swing into **10 Julia Pfeiffer Burns State Park**, where the short Overlook Trail rushes downhill toward the sea. What's the hurry, you ask? Everyone wants to see McWay Falls, which gushes year-round over granite cliffs and free-falls into the ocean – or the beach, depending on the tide. This is the classic Big Sur postcard shot, with tree-topped rocks jutting above a golden, crescent-shaped beach next to swirling blue pools and crashing white surf. It's truly a spectacular sight.

Settle in for the half-hour drive south past a string of gemlike beaches and coves. Warmed by gas fireplaces and country quilt-covered beds, **11 Treebones Resort** offers a collection of yurts perched on an ocean-view hilltop property above Gorda. If you have any slivers of sunlight left, keep trucking down the highway to **12 Salmon Creek Falls**, which usually runs from December through May. Tucked up a canyon in the Los Padres National Forest, this double-drop waterfall can be glimpsed from the road, but that's missing the point. Take a short hike to the falls and splash around in the pools at the base, where kids shriek and dogs happily yip and yap.

ASK A LOCAL "Limekiln State Park (☎ 831-667-2403; www.parks.ca.gov) is priceless. Get out of your car and walk into the redwood forest groves, with the oohs-and-aahs payoff of a year-round waterfall, looking like a sheet of water in winter. Then go over to the other part of the park, where the sheer power and awesome beauty of a boutiquey beach just draws you in. It's a two-in-one park, with drama in both corners."
Rich L, Big Sur

Sara Benson

TRIP INFORMATION

GETTING THERE
From San Francisco, drive south on Hwy 101 past Gilroy. Take Hwy 156 west toward Monterey, then Hwy 1 south.

DO

Andrew Molera State Park
Ideal for beachcombing and coastal nature walks; campsites are first-come, first-served. ☎ 831-667-2315; www.parks.ca.gov; Hwy 1; day-use fee $8; ☽ 30min before sunrise-30min after sunset; 🚹

Julia Pfeiffer Burns State Park
Popular but petite park named after a Big Sur pioneer. ☎ 831-667-2315; www.parks.ca.gov; 47225 Hwy 1; day-use fee $8; ☽ 30min before sunrise-30min after sunset; 🚹

Pfeiffer Beach
Hidden down a side road to the sea, this dog-friendly beach is worth the trouble of getting to. ☎ 831-667-2315; www.fs.fed .us/r5/lospadres; Hwy 1; day-use fee $5; ☽ 9am-8pm; 🚹 🅿

Pfeiffer Big Sur State Park
Entrance is half a mile north of ranger-staffed Big Sur Station. ☎ 831-667-2315; www .parks.ca.gov; 47225 Hwy 1; day-use fee $8; ☽ 30min before sunrise-30min after sunset; 🚹

Salmon Creek Falls
Hwy 1 shoulder parking can be very crowded at the hairpin turn, marked by a tiny trail-head sign. ☎ 831-385-5434; www.fs.fed .us/r5/lospadres; Hwy 1; admission free; ☽ 24hr; 🚹 🅿

EAT

Big Sur Burrito Bar
Next to the Big Sur River Inn, this made-to-order burrito and deli-wrap counter is a quick

hunger fix. ☎ 831-667-2700; Hwy 1; mains $4-6; ☽ 11am-7pm; 🚹

Big Sur Roadhouse
Woodsy restaurant with a Latin twist glows from the copper-top bar and fireplace, with riverside patio tables out back. ☎ 831-667-2264; www.bigsurroadhouse.com; Hwy 1; mains $12-25; ☽ 5:30-9pm Wed-Mon

Nepenthe
Though tasty, the California cuisine takes a back seat to ocean views. At night, stay toasty round the fire pit. ☎ 831-667-2345; www.nepenthebigsur.com; Hwy 1; mains $12-36; ☽ 11:30am-10pm

SLEEP

Glen Oaks
Hip, eco-conscious San Francisco design dramatically transforms this snug 1950s redwood-and-adobe motor lodge. ☎ 831-667-2105; www.glenoaksbigsur.com; Hwy 1; r $155-225

Treebones Resort
Rustically furnished hillside yurts are a short walk from the common bath and shower house. ☎ 877-424-4787; www.treebones resort.com; off Willow Creek Rd, 71895 Hwy 1; r $155-235; 🚹

Ventana Inn
Grab a deluxe fireplace room or villa with a view, or pitch a tent in a private camp-ground. ☎ 831-667-2331, campground 831-667-2712; www.ventanainn.com; Hwy 1; campsites $35-65, r from $450; ☽ campground May-Oct; 🚹 🅿

USEFUL WEBSITES
www.bigsurcalifornia.org
www.parks.ca.gov

www.lonelyplanet.com/trip-planner

LINK YOUR TRIP

Bay Area Day Trips

With the exception of Alcatraz, San Francisco is easy to escape. In half an hour you're in secluded Pacific coves or towering redwood groves. Even at a South Bay goat ranch or inner-city Oakland gallery, the beach and memorable meals are never far away.

BERKELEY

Even if you missed out on the radical '60s here, you're just in time for lunch at Chez Panisse, plus maybe a protest, some provocative art and punk bands afterwards. Chef Alice Waters started the movement for local, sustainable food here back in the '70s, and her converted Craftsman cottage still serves up exciting Bay Area flavors in the French manner – call ahead for prix-fixe dining at Chez Panisse or à la carte at the upstairs café. You're bound to find a war protest or at least a consciousness-raising session in progress near Sproul Hall at University of California Berkeley, and the nearby Berkeley Art Museum and Pacific Film Archive both have stellar collections and international reputations thanks to their university connections. Students shop for new personas at the vintage boutiques, bookstores and music stores on Telegraph Ave, but to see Berkeley's homegrown youth culture in pogo-ing action head to 924 Gilman, the historic all-ages punk venue that helped launch the likes of Green Day and Rancid. **Take BART (Bay Area Rapid Transit) Richmond line to Downtown Berkeley station, or drive Hwy 80 east across the Bay Bridge, take the University Ave exit onto 24, and take the Telegraph Ave exit downtown.**

see also **TRIPS 7 & 24**

OAKLAND

Gritty and quaint at the same time, Oakland has pastel Victorians and paddleboats on Lake Merritt but also street dance videos at the Oakland Museum of California and tattoos of Hells Angels insignia and West Coast rapper Tupac Shakur (he grew up here). The operative Oakland phrase is "keeping it real," meaning real prices, real diversity and real talent. Oakland's idea of Friday night is the historic art-deco Paramount for jazz or classic R&B, or the Parkway, a 1926 cinema that serves pizza and beer to moviegoers splayed out across living-room furniture. San Franciscans actually cross the Bay to eat at Camino, a converted furniture-store-turned-dining-room featuring two neighborly, 30ft redwood chefs' tables and former Chez Panisse chef Russell Moore. Oakland's Chinatown offers sweet deals on Cambodian and Cantonese eats, and downtown boasts tasty Korean BBQ and Vietnamese *pho* (noodle soup). Since artists can still afford to live in Oakland, collectors discover emerging talents at downtown artists' spaces and galleries at First Friday openings (see www.oaklandartmurmur.com for listings). **Take BART (Bay Area Rapid Transit) to Oakland 19th St or Lake Merritt stops. By car, take Hwy 80 across the Bay Bridge and follow signs for downtown Oakland.**

See also **TRIP 16**

MARIN HEADLANDS

The most amazing thing about the Headlands is not the unspoiled stretch of parkland right across the Golden Gate Bridge from San Francisco, nor the inspired conversion of a military base into an art center and nature preserve, nor even the spectacular views of rugged coastline and crashing surf. It's the smell. Sea breezes blowing through aromatic hillsides with 119 native plant species and *yerba buena* (good herbs) clear the city right out of your system and make it that much easier to take on the Tennessee Valley Trail (marked off Hwy 1 to Stinson Beach). Picnics seem to taste better here, and you can enjoy a fabulous organic dinner among sculptors and dancers in the renovated barracks at Headlands Center for the Arts (for reservations, call ☎ 415-331-2787, ext 28). Residencies here draw art stars from around the globe, and the kitchen's no slouch either: two former *Top Chef* contestants started their careers here. The nearby Marine Mammal Center is a major draw for kids, as is the hands-on Bay Area Discovery Museum. **Take MUNI bus #74, or drive Hwy 101 and take either the last Sausalito exit or the Hwy 1/Stinson Beach exit.**

See also **TRIP 14**

SAUSALITO

Like a dollhouse version of a bayside town, Sausalito is almost too picturesque to be true. Down at the marina, fanciful houseboats built by hippies and moguls range from a converted 1889 Pullman car called "The Train Wreck" to the three-story, 4000-sq-ft Oyama Wildflower Barge, complete with Japanese tea ceremony room, indoor hot tub and high-tech media room. Uphill, picture windows let you mentally rearrange the furniture in houses scattered across steep slopes (don't say "earthquake" out loud here). The tiny downtown is packed with boutiques and temptations: wind-up toys at Sausalito Ferry Company Gift Store, bottled *yuzu* citrus and sake cocktails at the Sake 2 Me outlet, and handcrafted haute-minimalist dinnerware at Sausalito's own Heath Ceramics at 30% off retail. Rent a bike at A Bicycle Odyssey to explore town, until you work up an appetite for Avatar's savory, genre-bending Indian-Mexican enchiladas, or the classic pancakes-and-bacon brunch combo at Fred's Coffee Shop. **Take Hwy 101 across the Golden Gate Bridge and the Alexander Ave exit right after Vista Point. Follow the winding downhill road to the downtown waterfront.**

See also **TRIP 25**

MUIR WOODS

Other cities' backyards can't compare to San Francisco's Muir Woods. This stand of 600- to 1200-year-old redwoods is one of the world's last old-growth forests, with 250ft trees that could give San Francisco skyscrapers an inferiority complex. So how do they reach such grand old ages and staggering heights? Surprisingly shallow roots spread out and intertwine across the forest floor, forming a strong support network. Visiting world leaders saw a metaphor here and, in 1945, pivotal meetings to form the UN were held in the stately Cathedral Grove. If Muir Woods puts you in a meditative mood, head down the road to the Tassajara Zen Center for tea in the organic Zen garden. Over the hill lies secluded Stinson Beach, where you can beachcomb and chow down with the surfers at Sand Dollar Restaurant. **Take Hwy 101 north across Golden Gate Bridge, exiting at Hwy 1/Stinson Beach. Drive half a mile to the stoplight, turn left, and drive 2.7 miles to the crest of the hill. Turn right towards Muir Woods/Mount Tamalpais, go almost a mile to the four-way intersection and turn left towards Muir Woods.**

See also **TRIP 14**

BOLINAS

The Wild West's hippie surfer town of Bolinas has tried to discourage its cult following. You won't find a highway sign for it, because the citizens of Bolinas have allowed no signage to remain intact for more than 36 hours since 1993, and the highway department has given up on replacements. There are no police in town – Bolinas residents prefer conflict resolution – and "shopping spree" here means buying local handicrafts or taking and leaving stuff at the famous Free Box. Behind the post office is 2 Mile Surf Shop, which offers surf lessons and sweatshirts emblazoned with the "Bolinas 2 Miles" highway sign that mysteriously turned up here. Bolinas beach has graffitied driftwood and gentle waves, but surfing here takes nerve – this cove is a shark feeding area. For beach reading, the unstaffed bookstore by the post office works on an honesty system: put what you think books are worth into the cashbox, from $2 for passable pulp to $20 for masterpieces. Coast Cafe serves surfer-size portions of organic eats and local fish, and Smiley's Schooner Saloon has raucous Open Mic nights and occasional appearances by local Tom Waits. **From northbound Hwy 101, take the Stinson Beach exit and drive straight through Stinson Beach along Bolinas Lagoon. Take the first unsigned left, hang another left at Horseshoe Hill Rd, and drive 1 mile to downtown Bolinas.**

See also **TRIP 8**

PESCADERO

With windblown trees and weathered gingerbread houses, Pescadero could be just another cute coastal California town – but wait until you get a taste of it.

Artichokes grown on these coastal lowlands are the not-so-secret ingredient in Arcangeli Bakery's garlicky artichoke bread, best devoured warm from the oven with petal-strewn Van Goat cheese from up the street at Harley Farms Goat Dairy. Bucktoothed Bart the guard llama keeps a watchful eye on the herd but lets visitors close enough to pet the kids on pre-arranged dairy tours, which end in goat-cheese tastings. Duarte's Tavern features fresh fish cooked as you like it – grilled, blackened or pan-fried in cornmeal – and a legendary ollalieberry pie baked to Grandma Duarte's exacting specifications. To walk it all off, take the half-hour historical walking tour of the Pigeon Point Lighthouse bluff, or a longer hike to see male sea lions who missed out on mating season at Losers' Beach at nearby Año Nuevo reserve. **Drive Hwy 101 or 280 south from San Francisco to Hwy 92, heading east to Half Moon Bay. Take Hwy 1 south through Half Moon Bay about 14 miles to Pescadero Beach, and turn left at the sign.**

See also **TRIP 31**

Alison Bing

CENTRAL CALIFORNIA TRIPS

Central California's greatest charm is what it's not: north or south. Not only have the mindsets of the state's poles not taken root, neither have the populations. The middle of California has its own personality, which, though overshadowed by the Bay Area and LA's megalopolis, has distinct charms waiting to be explored. But before you start maybe you should have a drink – wines from Amador County and Paso Robles win raves. Or perhaps a little therapeutic parboiling of the soul in a Sierra hot spring? The region bursts with bounty you can choose yourself at U-Pick farms. Or maybe your real high should actually be elevated: Hwy 395 traces a sinuous course along the top of the state, bumping up against backcountry and approaching wonders like Mammoth Lakes. Look for traces of gold and remnants of ghost towns on Hwy 49 or, for those who like their road a little straighter, Hwy 99 shoots like an arrow up the San Joaquin Valley, picking up cowboy twangs from Sacramento to Bakersfield. Finally, let unparalleled Yosemite take you to another place entirely.

PLAYLIST ♫ The airwaves of Central California put out a lot of country. You might think you're in Nashville, but really you're in Bakersfield. Other classic tunes have enough metal to fill a garage.

- "A Hundred Years from Now," Tommy Collins
- "It's Such a Pretty World Today," Wynn Stewart
- "The Way it Is," Tesla
- "Short Skirt/Long Jacket," Cake
- "I've Got a Tiger by the Tail," Buck Owens
- "I Think I'll Just Stay Here and Drink," Merle Haggard
- "One More Dollar," Gillian Welch
- "La Banda Del Carro Rojo," Tigres Del Norte

⭐ **BEST TRIP**

CENTRAL CALIFORNIA'S BEST TRIPS

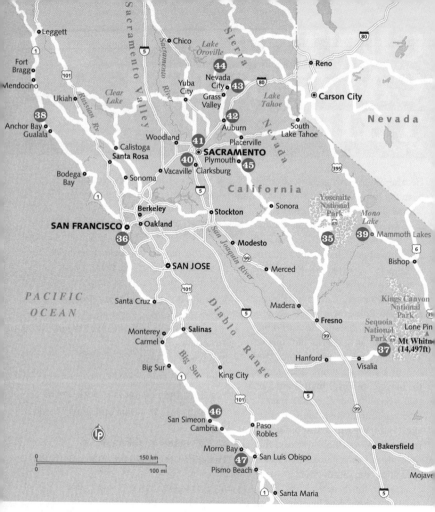

CENTRAL CALIFORNIA TRIPS

High Altitudes on Highway 395

WHY GO A straight shot along California's arched geological backbone, Hwy 395 is a refreshing alternative to Hwy 1 or I-5. With high-altitude vistas, crumbling Old West ghost towns and endless recreational distractions, it's also the launching pad for some of the state's best backcountry.

The diminutive town of Lone Pine stands as the southern gateway to the craggy jewels of the Eastern Sierra. The superstar draw here is the celestial granite giant of ❶ **Mt Whitney**, at 14,496ft the loftiest peak in the Lower 48 and the obsession of thousands of high-country hikers every year. Desperately coveted permits (assigned by advance lottery) are your only passport to the summit, though drop-in day-trippers can swan up to Lone Pine Lake – about 6 miles round-trip – and kick up some dust on the iconic Whitney Trail.

Just outside of Lone Pine on the Whitney Portal Rd, an orange otherworldly alpenglow makes the ❷ **Alabama Hills** a must for watching a slow-motion sunset. A frequent backdrop for movie Westerns and the *Lone Ranger* TV series, the rounded earthen-colored mounds stand out against the steely gray foothills and jagged pinnacles of the Sierra range, and a number of graceful rock arches are within easy hiking distance of the roads.

Swagger back into town after your successful summit – or at least damn fine gaze into the heavens – and fuel up at the ❸ **High Sierra Café**, an essential 24-hour diner where breakfast's served around the clock. In the center of Lone Pine and within walking distance of everywhere, the ❹ **Dow Villa Motel** has small but inexpensive rooms in a "historic hotel" building, as well as larger modern motel rooms with kitchenettes, comfy furniture and oodles of mountain light.

TIME
4 – 5 days

DISTANCE
260 miles

BEST TIME TO GO
Jun – Sep

START
Lone Pine

END
Reno

ALSO GOOD FOR

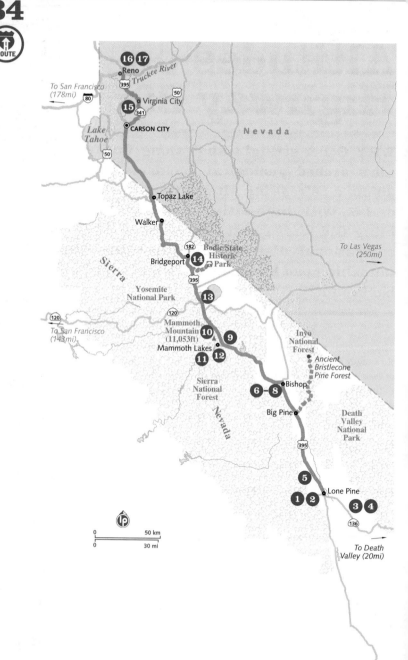

In the morning, continue a few miles north until you see an incongruous military-style watchtower on the side of the road. It marks the middle-of-nowhere remains of the **5** **Manzanar National Historic Site**, a concentration camp where Japanese Americans from the West Coast were interned during the height of WWII. Often mistaken for Mt Whitney, the peak of 14,375ft Mt Williamson looms above this flat, dusty plain, a lonely expanse that bursts with yellow wildflowers in spring. Pick up a map for a self-guided tour of the foundations and landscaping ponds. An excellent interpretive center tells the stories of individuals wrenched from their communities and jailed here merely for having Japanese ancestry.

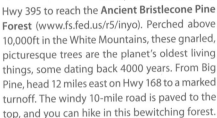

DETOUR For giddy oxygen-scarce views, drive an hour off Hwy 395 to reach the **Ancient Bristlecone Pine Forest** (www.fs.fed.us/r5/inyo). Perched above 10,000ft in the White Mountains, these gnarled, picturesque trees are the planet's oldest living things, some dating back 4000 years. From Big Pine, head 12 miles east on Hwy 168 to a marked turnoff. The windy 10-mile road is paved to the top, and you can hike in this bewitching forest.

About a third of the way north from Lone Pine to Reno is Bishop, the second-largest town in the Eastern Sierra. A low-key place, its older section has covered sidewalks and classic 1950s neon signs. Time your arrival for the afternoon wine and cheese at **6** **Joseph House Inn Bed & Breakfast**, a beautifully restored ranch-style home with homey flowery decor and a patio spilling out onto a tranquil 3-acre garden. For piled-high sandwiches, stop by the roadside mecca of **7** **Erick Schat's Bakkery** before you leave town. It's filled to the rafters with cooling racks of crusty fresh bread, and has been making its signature sheepherder loaf and other buttery baked goodies since 1938.

Off Hwy 6, 4.5 miles northeast of town, the **8** **Laws Railroad Museum & Historical Site** is the last remaining station from the narrow-gauge Carson and Colorado railway line. Dozens of historic buildings from the region have been reassembled here with period artifacts to create a time-capsule village. Train buffs will hyperventilate over the collection of antique railcars, and kids love exploring the 1883 depot and clanging the brass bell.

"… superheated water filters through seismic vents, and simmering sulfurous pools bubble madly… "

Back on Hwy 395, continue 35 miles north to witness the unleashed geothermal power at the **9** **Hot Creek Geological Site**. In the midst of a cold, crystal blue creek, super-heated water filters through seismic vents, and simmering sulfurous pools bubble madly on the shore. Until recently a popular (if toe-scalding and potentially treacherous) alpine swimming hole, it's now closed for dips, but definitely worth seeing. A short trail leads you down to the smoking water framed by gorgeous Sierra views. From the highway, turn east and go 3 miles on Hot Creek Hatchery Rd.

Splendidly situated at a breathless 8000ft, Mammoth Lakes is an active year-round outdoor-recreation hub buffered by alpine wilderness and punctuated by its signature 11,000ft Mammoth Mountain. When the snow finally melts, the mountain resort does a quick costume change to become the massive ❿ **Mammoth Mountain Bike Park**. With more than 100 miles of single-track trails, it's a Siren's song for fat tires and the thrill-seeking riders who love them. Snow-dappled peaks contour the horizon, and daredevils can scorch through a free-ride network of bouncy berms and jaw-clenching jumps.

Keep the car parked at Mammoth Mountain and catch a mandatory shuttle from the Gondola Building to one of the area's coolest geological marvels, the evocatively named ⓫ **Devils Postpile**. Like a wobbly stack of warped organ pipes, the accordion-like formation is composed of multisided columns of blue-gray basalt that were created about 10,000 years ago. Hoof up the hillside trail for a view from above, where you can see a distinct hexagonal honeycomb design.

DETOUR

Thirteen miles of graded unpaved road lead to **Bodie** (www.parks.ca.gov/bodie), one of the West's best-preserved ghost towns. Gold was discovered here in 1859, and the place grew from a bare-bones mining camp to a lawless boomtown of 10,000. Fights and murders occurred almost daily, fueled by liquor from 65 saloons, some of which doubled as brothels, gambling halls or opium dens. When production plummeted, Bodie was abandoned, and about 200 weather-beaten buildings now sit frozen in time in this cold, barren and wind-swept valley.

For dinner and a bucolic night's stay, head back into town and venture southwest along Lake Mary Rd to the ⓬ **Tamarack Lodge & Resort**, a charming year-round hideaway on the forested shore of Lower Twin Lake. In the lodge building, cozy homespun rooms with creaky floors date back to 1924, and the wood-beamed lobby is a spiffy setting for a nighttime book by the fireplace. Privacy-seekers can choose between a few dozen detached cabins ranging from the very simple to simply deluxe. For a romantic meal, the resort's destination dining room, the 10-table Lakefront Restaurant, gazes out over the lake and boasts French-California specialties like elk medallions *au poivre* and heirloom tomatoes with Basque cheese.

Back on Hwy 395, the ancient pool of ⓭ **Mono Lake** (*mow*-no) unfolds for 695 sq miles between the Sierra Nevada range and the Great Basin Desert. With no showers lakeside, the salinity and alkaline levels are unfortunately too high for a pleasant swim. Instead, paddle a kayak around the weathered towers of tufa, drink in wide-open views of the Mono Craters volcanic field, and discreetly spy on the ospreys and water birds that live in this unique habitat.

For those who get limp at the knees when contemplating a steaming alfresco soak, a dip at ⓮ **Travertine Hot Springs** in Bridgeport is one of the prime reasons to explore the back roads of the Eastern Sierra. Around a half mile south of town, turn east on Jack Sawyer Rd and then follow a dirt road for approximately 1 mile until the road ends. Perched on a hill with commanding views of the snow-crested Sierras, a streaked-orange travertine rock formation feeds a trio of divine mud-bottomed pools of varying temperatures. It's a relaxing place to watch the sun sizzle out for the night and handy for soothing achy hiking muscles.

During the 1860s gold rush, ⓯ **Virginia City** was a high-flying, rip-roaring Wild West boomtown. Mark Twain spent time in this raucous place during its heyday, and his eyewitness descriptions of mining life were published in *Roughing It*. The high-elevation town is a National Historic Landmark, with a main street of Victorian buildings, wooden sidewalks and some hokey but fun knickknack museums. To get there from Bridgeport, head 80 miles north on Hwy 395, 8 miles east on Hwy 50, and then another 7 miles via Hwy 341 and Hwy 342.

Wind through a spectacular 13 miles of high desert along Hwy 341 to rejoin Hwy 395, and another 7 miles to reach ⓰ **Reno**, the second-largest city in Nevada. Cursed with a holdover reputation as a Las Vegas wannabe, word's slowly getting out that it's carved a noncasino niche as an all-season outdoor recreation spot. The Truckee River bisects the heart of Reno, and in the heat of summer, the Truckee River Whitewater Park teems with urban kayakers and swimmers bobbing along on inner tubes.

Completing the scenic trek, spend your final night at the Italian-themed ⓱ **Siena**, Reno's only contemporary boutique hotel. One of the city's most luxurious addresses, it boasts warm and contemporary riverside rooms and a casino with a European feel, with a building topped off by a Tuscan-style clock tower and scores of dramatic arches. If you have a trying day in the casino, the spa's ever-so-tranquil "serenity room" will put everything in perspective.

Only have two days to see the sights? From Lone Pine, take a stroll in the Alabama Hills, stop for lunch in Bishop, and then wind your way north to Devils Postpile and spend the night in Mammoth Lakes. The following day, rent a kayak to cruise Mono Lake and then shoot west to San Francisco by way of Hwy 120 through Yosemite National Park.

Beth Kohn

TRIP INFORMATION

GETTING THERE
From I-5 in Los Angeles, it's 200 miles (approximately four hours) to Lone Pine via Hwy 14 and Hwy 395.

DO

Devils Postpile
This unique volcanic rock formation lies just outside of Mammoth Lakes, within the Ansel Adams Wilderness. ☎ 760-934-2289; www.nps.gov/depo; mandatory shuttle adult/child $7/4 or per car/bicycle $20/free; ☼ 7am-7pm Jun–mid-Sep

Laws Railroad Museum & Historical Site
An entire village re-created around the last stretch of an antique rail line. ☎ 760-873-5950; www.lawsmuseum.org; Silver Canyon Rd, Laws; donation requested $5; ☼ 10am-4pm; ♿

Mammoth Mountain Bike Park
After the snow melts, this resort becomes a mountain-biking hot spot. ☎ 760-934-0706; www.mammothmountain.com; SR 203, Mammoth Lakes; 1-day pass adult/child $39/20; ☼ 9am-6pm late Jun-Sep; ♿

Manzanar National Historic Site
A solemn place, it commemorates the Japanese-American internment camp located here during WWII. ☎ 760-878-2194; www.nps.gov/manz; admission free; ☼ interpretive center 9am-4:30pm Nov-Apr, 8:30am-5pm May-Oct

Mt Whitney
The Eastern Sierra InterAgency Visitor Center is the epicenter of the Mt Whitney permit lottery. ☎ 760-876-6222; www.fs.fed.us/r5/inyo; cnr Hwy 395 & SR 136, Lone Pine; ☼ 8am-6pm summer, to 5pm otherwise

EAT

Erick Schat's Bakkery
It's worth the wait to scoop up a loaf of its steamy fresh bread. ☎ 760-873-7156; 763 N Main St, Bishop; sandwiches $5-7; ☼ 6am-6pm Sat-Thu, 6am-7pm Fri

High Sierra Café
Refuel with a big plate of fried chicken or grab a sandwich for the road. ☎ 760-876-5796; 446 S Main St, Lone Pine; breakfast & lunch mains $4-7, dinner mains $9-13; ☼ 24hr

SLEEP

Dow Villa Motel
With lots of amenities, this centrally located motel is where you want to lay your head. ☎ 760-876-5521, 800-824-9317; www.dowvillamotel.com; 310 S Main St, Lone Pine; r $45-142

Joseph House Inn Bed & Breakfast
Relax in this comfortable B&B with a glorious garden. ☎ 760-872-3389; www.josephhouseinn.com; 376 W Yaney St, Bishop; r incl full breakfast $143-178; ☼ closed Jan; ♿

Siena
Reno's only contemporary boutique hotel is also one of its most luxurious addresses, with cozy, nicely appointed riverside rooms. ☎ 775-337-6260, 877-743-6233; www.sienareno.com; 1 S Lake St, Reno, NV; r from $80

Tamarack Lodge & Resort
Atmospheric lodge rooms and comfortable cabins make this a coveted night's stay. ☎ 760-934-2442, 800-626-6684; www.tamaracklodge.com; Lake Mary Rd, Mammoth Lakes; lodges r $89-149, cabins $149-589; ♿

USEFUL WEBSITES
www.395.com
www.scenic395.com

www.lonelyplanet.com/trip-planner

LINK YOUR TRIP

Yosemite Aquatic

WHY GO One of the most iconic national parks in the country, Yosemite is a playground of valleys and peaks, all enhanced by the cycle of water. Its waterfalls leap to life in springtime and during the brief lazy summer, lakes offer a chilly but merciful respite from the heat.

Setting off from the South Entrance station in the Wawona area, start your exploration of ❶ **Yosemite National Park** with a hike to the soothing white water of ❷ **Chilnualna Falls**. From the trailhead at the end of Chilnualna Falls Rd, follow Chilnualna Creek to a series of tumbling cascades, before the path rises through open, mixed-conifer forest. Along long, sweeping switchbacks, take in views of Wawona Dome and the Chowchilla Mountains before reaching the 6200ft top of Chilnualna Falls. Total mileage out and back is just under 9 miles.

With their massive stature and multimillennium maturity, the chunky high-rise sequoias of ❸ **Mariposa Grove** will make you feel rather insignificant. It's the largest grove of giant sequoias in the park: approximately 500 mature trees towering over 250 acres, with a number of mammoths hanging tight in the parking lot. A few walking trails wind through this very popular grove, but you can hear yourself think if you come during the early evening. Notwithstanding a cruel hack job back in 1895, the walk-through California Tunnel Tree continues to survive, so pose the family in front and snap away. Though the tree is fun to scale, don't bother looking for the more famous Wawona Tunnel Tree; it collapsed in a heap decades ago.

Before dusk, linger for cocktails on the whitewashed veranda of the ❹ **Wawona Hotel** and listen for frogs croaking from the lawn fountain in a goofy staccato chorus. Then usher in the evening with dinner

TIME
3 – 4 days

DISTANCE
165 miles

BEST TIME TO GO
Apr – Sep

START
South Entrance Station

END
Harden Lake

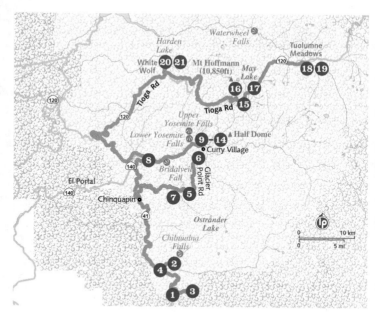

in the Victorian-era hotel dining room, a classy white-tablecloth affair with high-backed wooden chairs and picture windows, lit by the warm glow of hand-painted sequoia-themed lamps. Organic produce and sustainably farmed meats highlight a menu of creatively classic American cuisine. A National Historic Landmark dating back to 1879, the hotel's rooms flaunt a flowery period style, with no distracting televisions or phones.

The next day, edge further north to the Glacier Point Rd area, and lace up your hiking shoes for a five-star out-and-back ramble to **5 Ostrander Lake**. A scree-framed granite bowl cut into evergreen forest, its waters make a fine place to refresh yourself after the 6-mile hike. A stone ski hut is closed for the warmer months, but kindles the spark for cross-country ski adventures in the winter.

Brush off any lingering trail dust and drive to **6 Glacier Point**, at the end of Glacier Point Rd. You'll find the entire eastern Yosemite Valley spread before you, from Yosemite Falls to Half Dome, as well as the distant peaks that ring Tuolumne Meadows. Half Dome looms practically at eye level, and if you look closely you can spot ant-sized hikers on its summit, though the cable ladder isn't visible. At the tip of the point is Overhanging Rock, a huge granite slab protruding from the cliff edge like an outstretched tongue, defying gravity and providing a scenic stage for daredevil extroverts in the late 19th and early 20th centuries.

When the day ends, retreat to your tent at ❼ **Bridalveil Creek Campground**, a first-come first-served spot with nicely spaced sites shaded by a pretty pine forest. Unless it's a busy weekend, you can usually snag a space if you show up in the morning. At 7200ft, the nights here are much crisper than they are in the valley, and a summer sleeping bag just won't cut it.

In the morning, percolate some cowboy coffee over the stove and then set out for Yosemite Valley. Right after the exit from the Wawona Tunnel, pull over at the parking lot of ❽ **Tunnel View** to get your first look at the spectacular end point of the creek you camped at.

A 620ft ribbon of water, Bridalveil Fall is most stunning in springtime, when it thunders down to earth and soaks the ground with spray. By late summer, it's a mere whisper, often lifted and blown aloft by the wind. Looking left you see the lush green valley, iconic Half Dome and the almost 3600ft sheer face of El Capitan.

If you and your knees don't mind conquering four dozen switchbacks (in each direction, mind you) and a sizeable chunk of elevation, hike to the top of ❾ **Yosemite Falls**.

WET WINTER WONDERLAND

When the temperature drops and the white stuff falls, there are tons of groovy outdoor activities to choose from: strap on some skis or a snowboard at the Badger Pass resort; snow tube down the hill at Crane Flat; plod around on a ranger-led snowshoe tour; try to stay standing on ice skates at Curry Village; or cross-country ski to winter huts at Ostrander Lake, Glacier Point and Tuolumne Meadows.

You'll be rewarded with splendid valley views and an up-close look at this lengthy three-tier falls with a 2425ft drop. Also in sight from the top are Glacier Point, North Dome and the photographic all-time favorite, Half Dome.

❿ **Mirror Lake** is another excellent valley hike without any punishing increase in elevation. Reflecting Mt Watkins and Half Dome upon its tranquil surface, shallow Mirror Lake is one of the valley's most photographed sites. It dries to a puddle as summer proceeds – spring is an optimal time to walk there because the lake is full and the dogwoods are in full bloom. The trail starts near shuttle stop 17 and crosses Tenaya Bridge, from where a partially paved trail heads to the lake.

"...spring is optimal because the lake is full and the dogwoods are in full bloom."

In the height of summer, get wet and do a little drifting as you raft the ⓫ **Merced River**. A serene 3-mile stretch between Stoneman Bridge and Sentinel Beach is gentle enough for kids, and you can rent a raft at Curry Village or bring your own vessel. A return shuttle brings you back to the beginning.

For those who want to laze the day away, there's also an option of paying to swan around the lodging's **12** **swimming pools**. The round pool at the Ahwahnee and the old swimming tank at the Wawona Hotel are only open to overnighters, but nonguests can cool off at the outdoor pools at the Curry Village and Yosemite Lodge.

As well-stocked as (but more expensive than) your hometown grocery store, the **13** **Village Store** in Yosemite Village is the place to stock up on food and any camping supplies inadvertently left back on your doorstep. Transport your bounty to **14** **North Pines Campground**, a relatively quiet valley complex that encompasses some nice riverside sites, and break out the marshmallows.

The following day, leave the valley crowds behind and head to the high country on Tioga Rd. About 47 miles away from the campground, your first full stop should be **15** **Olmstead Point**, one of the best roadside viewpoints in the park. A lunar landscape of glaciated granite, you can see down Tenaya Canyon to the backside of Half Dome. To take in the scene without a parking lot full of people, stroll a quarter-mile down to the overlook, where you can get past the tree cover and see even deeper into the canyon.

ASK A LOCAL

"One of the only major waterfalls in Tuolumne Meadows is **Waterwheel Falls**. You pick up the Glen Aulin Trail right across from the Tuolumne Meadows store and go up Cold Canyon. Not a typical Yosemite fall from a cliff, it's more of a dramatic cascade. It falls into a series of pools and the water churns it up. Then it boils up and goes down to the next pool and happens again."

Kari Cobb, former campground ranger at Tuolumne Meadows

Backtrack a mile or so west on Tioga Rd and ditch the car for the exemplary hike to **16** **May Lake** and Mt Hoffmann. An easy (but not flat) trail climbs just over a mile to the knockout treeline basin of the lake, where the May Lake High Sierra Camp sits. Tracing the shore, the path continuing to Mt Hoffman enters a talus field marked by multiple routes. From the base of a large plateau, dodge nosy marmots as you scramble up the rocky summit to a substantial 10,850ft. From the geographical center of the park, the views are faraway and astounding, and you feel like you're at eye level to the surrounding peaks.

A few miles east of the trailhead, **17** **Tenaya Lake** might be a great place to splash – it all depends on how you feel about cold water. That said, a sandy half-moon beach wraps around the east end of the lake, tempting you to enjoy some of the most enjoyable swimming in the park. It's hard to resist a glistening lake with sapphire waters. Sunbathers and picnickers flock to the rocks that rim its north and west sides.

If it's not too late in the afternoon, make a pit stop a bit further east at the ⑱ **Tuolumne Meadows Grill**, and scarf down some ketchup-drizzled fries and a beef or veggie burger. A busy spot and a nostalgic summertime tradition for many, the hard-sided and tent-topped eatery closes around 5pm, so don't dillydally getting there. Slurp up some soft-serve ice cream at the picnic tables out front, and watch the people stream through.

Just around the corner, the ⑲ **Tuolumne Meadows Campground** is the place to settle in for the night. Though it's the park's biggest campground, the 300-plus sites are decently spaced over a large forested area. And if you didn't think to reserve ahead, it's reassuring to know that it keeps half of its sites available as first-come, first-served.

Heading back west on Tioga Rd in the morning, stop for a buffet breakfast at the small, rustic ⑳ **White Wolf Lodge dining room**. Fill up on eggs, fruit salad and cereal, plus rotating daily specials like breakfast burritos or pancakes. After a filling family-style meal inside or on the pleasant front porch, squeeze in one last hike.

From the back of the lodge parking lot, aim for ㉑ **Harden Lake**, following a section of the Old Tioga Rd running parallel to the Middle Fork of the Tuolumne River and then a footpath through Jeffrey and lodgepole pines. An unusually warm body of water for these parts, the lake evaporates rapidly during the summer and heats to a tepid temperature as it becomes more shallow. So bring a towel and splash around without feeling like a polar bear.
Beth Kohn

TRIP INFORMATION

GETTING THERE
From Los Angeles, arrive on Hwy 41 via Hwy 99; from San Francisco take I-580 to Hwy 120.

DO
Merced River
Float the day away on a raft and return via the concessionaire shuttle (children under 50lb not permitted in rental rafts). ☎ 209-372-4386; www.yosemitepark.com/Activities.aspx; Curry Village Recreation Center; rental per adult/child $26/16; ⏱ 10am-4pm; ♿

Swimming pools
Do chilly lakes give you goose bumps? Dive in at the outdoor pools at Curry Village or Yosemite Lodge. Adult/child $5/4; ⏱ mid-May–mid-Sep; ♿

Yosemite National Park
Glacier-carved valleys resting amid dramatic mountains make this one of the best national parks in the whole United States. ☎ 209-372-0200; www.nps.gov/yose; admission per car/motorcycle or bicycle $20/10

EAT
Tuolumne Meadows Grill
Fast, cheap and out-of-control fun, this manic summertime eatery serves yummy grilled food to eat on the picnic tables out front. ☎ 209-372-8426; mains $4-8; ⏱ 8am-5pm Jun–mid-Sep

Village Store
Whatever you want to eat, there's a decent chance that this medium-sized grocery and souvenir store will stock it. ☎ 209-372-1253; ⏱ 8am-10pm summer, 8am-8pm rest of year

White Wolf Lodge dining room
Tucked off the Tioga Rd, this cute historic building does a breakfast buffet and reservation-only family-style dinners. ☎ 209-372-8416; breakfast buffet $10, dinner $23; ⏱ 7:30-9:30am & 6-8pm summer

SLEEP
Bridalveil Creek Campground
A 110-site campground at 7200ft that's thankfully removed from the valley throngs and summer heat. Glacier Point Rd; site $14; ⏱ Jun-early Sep; ♿ 🐕

North Pines Campground
One of the nicest valley campgrounds, its 81 sites are slightly removed from development and adjacent to the horse stables. ☎ 877-444-6777, 518-885-3639; www.recreation.gov; site $20; ⏱ Apr-Sep; ♿ 🐕

Tuolumne Meadows campground
The park campground sitting closest to Hwy 395 has 304 well-spaced sites. ☎ 877-444-6777, 518-885-3639; www.recreation.gov; site $20; ⏱ Jul-Sep; ♿ 🐕

Wawona Hotel
Sleep the night in Victorian style inside one of these six graceful whitewashed buildings with period furniture. ☎ 209-375-6556, reservations 559-253-5635; www.yosemitepark.com; r shared/private bathroom $119/184; ⏱ Easter-Oct, weekends Nov-Mar

USEFUL WEBSITES
www.yosemite.org
www.yni.org

LINK YOUR TRIP
www.lonelyplanet.com/trip-planner

TRIP
36

HISTORY &
CULTURE

Pioneer Trails & Ghost Towns

WHY GO With Gold Rush boomtowns, wind-battered ghost towns, abandoned mines and spirited saloons, California's land-hungry homesteaders and starry-eyed prospectors made an indelible mark on the rugged landscape. Trace the stagecoach routes and freight-train lines to step back in history.

TIME
3 – 4 days

DISTANCE
1090 miles

BEST TIME TO GO
Jun – Sep

START
San Francisco

END
Goodsprings, NV

Start the trek in modern downtown San Francisco at the ❶ **Society of California Pioneers**, the state's oldest private historical society. Its exhibits are drawn from a voluminous collection of artifacts, which hail from the era of Mexican landholders up to the 1906 San Francisco earthquake. With photographs by Carleton Watkins, journals by 19th-century gold prospectors, and maps of early European settlements, it's a great place to get your bearings on this period of California history.

About an hour south of San Francisco and a mile east off coastal Hwy 1 is the ❷ **San Gregorio General Store**, an 1889 Mission-style trading post that once sat astride the major stagecoach route from Santa Cruz to San Francisco. You might not be in the market for cast-iron frying pans or a raccoon trap, but the café has tasty deli sandwiches, and stiff drinks can be had at a wooden saloon bar singed by ranchers' branding irons. On Friday and Saturday, foot-stomping bluegrass and R&B bands pack this middle-of-nowhere place with locals, spandex-clad cyclists and the occasional Harley rally.

Head back north on Hwy 1 to Half Moon Bay, take Hwy 92 over the San Mateo Bridge, and go north to meet up with I-80 to Sacramento. Considered by many to be the end of the California Trail, ❸ **Sutter's Fort State Historic Park** contains a collection of Gold Rush artifacts and the Bibles, diaries and other personal effects transported to California by European pioneers. In 1848, when gold was discovered

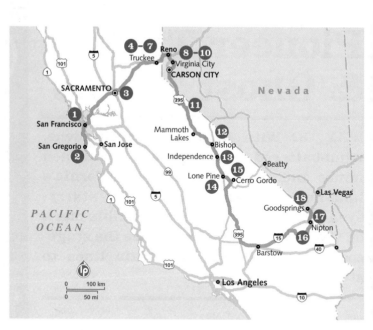

"…the grand Victorian hosted notables including President Ulysses S Grant and local newspaper writer Mark Twain."

further east at Sutter's Mill, hundreds of thousands of prospectors streamed through the fort, the only non-Indian settlement for hundreds of miles, on their way to search for riches.

Continue east on I-80 to the ④ **Emigrant Trail Museum** at Donner Lake, just before Truckee. Exhibits highlight local Native American history and overland emigration during the 1840s, though the site is probably best known as a camp for the Donner Party, a group of emigrant families who were trapped here in 1846–47, and who became infamous for eating their dead to survive. On the north side of Donner Lake, bunk up at the rustic ⑤ **Clair Tappaan Lodge**. A friendly mountain lodge owned by the Sierra Club, shared meals and cozy dorm and family rooms make for a social overnight. The hot tub isn't so utilitarian, but no one's complaining.

In the morning, take I-80 to wander through the historic district of central Truckee. With 200-pound doors and walls as thick as 32 inches, cells in the strongbox ⑥ **Truckee Jail Museum** housed rowdy detainees from 1875 until 1964. One of only a few surviving 19th-century jails in the state, George "Machine Gun" Kelly was reportedly held here for shoplifting at a local store.

In a historic 125-year-old hotel building a block and a half southeast, ⑦ **Moody's** oozes urbane flair. With a rotating gourmet menu made from fresh organic ingredients, and supper-club looks, it's one of the best restaurants in town.

From Truckee, rejoin I-80 to Reno, where you'll head south on Hwy 395, and then south on Hwy 341 to Virginia City. The 1859 discovery of the Comstock Lode caused a silver rush that made the town swell to a rough-and-tumble 30,000. A fair number of places have opened up whacky museums, charging a few bucks to showcase the artifacts found in the basement. It's a bit corny, but it's still worth coming here to walk the town's wooden arcade walkways and ponder its high-elevation views. A tour of the ⑧ **Chollar Mine**, which extracted gold and silver until WWII, lets you see the square-set timbers that supported excavation.

A mile south on Hwy 342 at the Gold Hill Hotel, the ⑨ **Crown Point Restaurant** serves meaty American dishes like elk filet and rib-eye steaks on proper white tablecloths. Back in town, the former mine office is now the antique-filled ⑩ **Chollar Mansion B&B**. Built in 1861, the grand Victorian hosted notables including President Ulysses S Grant and former Virginia City resident and local newspaper writer Mark Twain. Rejoin Hwy 341 to go west on I-50 and then south on Hwy 395. To the east, Hwy 270 takes you to big, bad ⑪ **Bodie**, California's best-preserved ghost town, once notorious for lawlessness and mining-camp mayhem. The discovery of gold lured almost 10,000 people here during its heyday,

 About face and eastward ho! Turning onto **Hwy 6** in Bishop, you might do a double-take at the roadside highway sign. The official marker states that it's 3205 miles east to Provincetown, Massachusetts. Also known as the Grand Army of the Republic Highway, Hwy 6 really is a transcontinental road – the second-longest highway in the country.

and approximately 200 wooden structures still stand, frozen in time in this high altitude valley. You can peer in the windows to see what was left, and a visitor center opens in the warmer months.

Drink in dreamy views of Mono Lake, the snow-tipped Sierras and the White Mountains as you shoot south 83 miles on Hwy 395. Approaching Bishop, turn east on Hwy 6 to reach the ⑫ **Laws Railroad Museum & Historical Site**, a remnant of the narrow-gauge Carson and Colorado rail line that closed in 1960. The *Slim Princess* rests on the last bit of track, with Engine No 9 and a handful of freight cars surrounded by restored historic structures recreating a village.

An excellent archive of the Eastern Sierra located in the small town of Independence, the ⑬ **Eastern California Museum** contains one of the most complete collections of Paiute and Shoshone baskets in the country, as well as historic photographs of local rock climbers scaling Sierra peaks like Whitney with huge packs and no harnesses. Ask the staff to point out the nearby home of Mary Hunter Austin, a turn-of-the-19th-century writer involved in the fight to keep the region's water supply from being diverted to Los Angeles.

Established with the collection of another museum once located in the Death Valley town of Darwin, Lone Pine's ⑭ **Southern Inyo Museum** has an incredibly rich trove of period artifacts tucked away in a small yellow building. Check out the rusting heavy mining equipment, and a display of local insects in the bug room. Besides town photos dating back to 1904, its most fascinating images of the Owens Valley were taken during the construction of the Los Angeles Aqueduct.

START YOUR CAMELS

It started as a practical joke, but the **Virginia City International Camel Races** (www.visitvirginia citynv.com) have now been going for 50 years. Movie director John Huston scooped up the honors as winner of the first race when he happened to be in the area filming *The Misfits* with Clark Gable and Marilyn Monroe. He rode a speedy specimen borrowed from the San Francisco Zoo. Watch the hopeful dromedaries galumphing towards the finish line and expect enormous crowds for this popular September event.

About $17 million worth of silver mined from the "fat hill" of ⑮ **Cerro Gordo** helped build up Los Angeles, since it was the closest and biggest city from which to buy goods. It's now a ghost town, reached via Hwy 136 from Lone Pine. Call ahead to tour restored buildings including the 1871 wooden hotel, a small museum of mining artifacts, and the former mine-owner's 1868 home, where you can also overnight. The main road in climbs almost 5000ft over 7.5 miles, but a 4WD isn't required.

From Hwy 395, head east on Hwy 58 to Barstow and then east on I-15 to Kelbaker Rd, and into the scrub, sand-dune and cinder-cone landscape of the Mojave National Preserve. In a town named by railway construction workers who drew names from a hat, 25 Union Pacific Railroad freight trains chug through daily at the recently restored ⑯ **Kelso Depot Visitor Center**. A grand 1924 Mission revival–style depot with exhibits including Native American, ranching and railroad history, visitors line up to jump in the seat of an old saddle, and to tinker with a manual railcar mover.

Continue to the northwestern corner of the preserve, where the ⑰ **Hotel Nipton** is "conveniently located in the middle of nowhere." With a wraparound porch for contemplating the night sky, this pint-sized 1910 adobe hotel has simple rooms available within or spacious tent cabins under the stars and you can hear the wail of freight trains racing across the desert. Finally, hoist a drink at the ⑱ **Pioneer Saloon** in Goodsprings, Nevada. A few miles from the California border via Hwy 161 (off I-15), this 1913 stamped-tin roadside shack with a potbellied stove is southern Nevada's oldest bar, and a bullet-riddled wall testifies to its raucous Wild West history.

Beth Kohn

TRIP INFORMATION

GETTING THERE & AWAY
Begin in downtown San Francisco; from journey's end in Goodsprings, swing over to Los Angeles via I-15 and then I-10.

DO

Bodie
Trek out to experience California's best-preserved ghost town, formerly a lawless mining settlement, now a state park. ☎ 760-647-6445; www.parks.ca.gov/bodie; Hwy 270, Bodie; adult/child $3/1; ☼ 8am-7pm Jun-Aug, 9am-4pm Sep-May

Cerro Gordo
Call ahead to tour or overnight at this privately owned ghost town east of Lone Pine. ☎ 760-876-5030; www.cerrogordo .us; off Hwy 136, near Keeler; donation requested; ☼ early May-Oct, weather variable

Chollar Mine
Take a tour to view this old silver and gold mine at the south end of F St. ☎ 775-847-0155; F St, Virginia City; adult/child $7/2; ☼ 1-4pm May-Oct

Eastern California Museum
Exhibits touch on numerous chapters in Sierra history, including the pioneer days and the Manzanar internment camp. ☎ 760-878-0364; www.inyocounty.us/ecmuseum; 155 N Grant St, Independence; donation requested; ☼ 10am-5pm Wed-Mon

Emigrant Trail Museum
Learn about the hardships faced by emigrants journeying to California, including the ill-fated Donner Party, at Donner Memorial State Park. ☎ 530-582-7892; www.parks .ca.gov/?page_id=503; Donner Lake; admission $6; ☼ 9am-4pm

Kelso Depot
Play with old trains and learn about the Mojave Preserve at this restored train depot that's now the main park visitors center.
☎ 760-252-6108; www.nps.gov/moja/plan yourvisit/visitorcenters.htm; Kelbaker Rd, Kelso; admission free; ☼ 9am-5pm

Laws Railroad Museum & Historical Site
Explore this historical railroad and recreated village, a few miles northeast of Bishop. ☎ 760-873-5950; www.lawsmuseum.org; Silver Canyon Rd, Laws; $5 donation requested; ☼ 10am-4pm; ♿

Society of California Pioneers
An immense archive of photos, maps and other media, with rotating exhibits and an appointment-only research library. ☎ 415-957-1849; www.californiapioneers.org; 300 4th St, San Francisco; admission $5; ☼ 10am-4pm Wed-Fri & 1st Sat of month

Southern Inyo Museum
Traipse through the region's mining and water history at this unexpectedly excellent small museum. ☎ 760-876-5052; www .newcosoheritagesocietyinc.org; 127 W Bush St, Lone Pine; admission free; ☼ 9am-4pm Thu-Sat mid-Apr–Oct

Sutter's Fort State Historic Park
See artifacts of white pioneers displayed inside a restoration of John Sutter's famous fort. ☎ 916-445-4422; www.parks.ca.gov/ default.asp?page_id=485; 2701 L St, Sacramento; adult/child $6/3; ☼ 10am-5pm

Truckee Jail Museum
In use until the 1960s, it's filled with relics from the wild days of yore. ☎ 530-582-0893; www.truckeehistory.org/jailmuseum.htm; cnr Jiboom & Spring Sts, Truckee; ☼ 11am-4pm Sat & Sun late May-early Sep

EAT & DRINK

Crown Point Restaurant
Tuck into an upscale meal at the Gold Hill Hotel; note that it shuts early if it's slow. ☎ 775-847-0111; Hwy 342, Gold Hill, NV; mains $15-38; ☼ 5-9pm

Moody's
A sophisticated supper club in the historic district, with live jazz four nights a week.

☎ 530-587-8688; 10007 Bridge St, Truckee; lunch mains $12-14, dinner $22-30; ⏱ 11am-10pm

Pioneer Saloon

Relive the Wild West spirit at this historically raucous bar, where they might stay open until daybreak if they like you. ☎ 702-874-9362; 310 W Spring St, Goodsprings, NV; ⏱ 8am-midnight

San Gregorio General Store

Kick up your heels at this landmark trading post with a bar and free music on the weekends. ☎ 650-726-0565; cnr Hwy 84 & Stage Rd, San Gregorio; ⏱ 9am-6pm

SLEEP

Chollar Mansion B&B

Formerly the town mine office, it's now filled with antiques and the views go on forever. ☎ 775-847-9777, 877-246-5527; www .chollarmansion.com; 565 S D St, Virginia City; r $135

Clair Tappaan Lodge

Catch the emigrant spirit at this rustic Sierra Club lodge with communal meals. ☎ 530-426-3632, 800-679-6775; www.ctl.sierra club.org; 19940 Donner Pass Rd, Norden; dorm incl meals member/nonmember from $46/51; ♿

Hotel Nipton

In the northeast corner of the preserve, this early 20th-century railroad town has all the peace you desire. ☎ 760-856-2335; www .nipton.com; 107355 Nipton Rd, Nipton; cabins/r $60/70; ♿

USEFUL WEBSITES

www.ghosttowns.com/states/ca
www.nps.gov/cali

LINK YOUR TRIP

www.lonelyplanet.com/trip-planner

Tree Time in Sequoia & Kings Canyon

WHY GO If you want to feel small, crane your neck to the heavens and marvel at the heft of these giant sequoias. Home of one of the deepest canyons in the US and some of the biggest trees on earth, these Sierra-straddling parks collect superlatives but not the Yosemite crowds.

TIME
3 – 4 days

DISTANCE
195 miles

BEST TIME TO GO
Jun – Sep

START
Big Stump Entrance

END
Mineral King

ALSO GOOD FOR

HISTORY & CULTURE

Two parks managed together like fraternal twins, the roads in ❶ Sequoia & Kings Canyon National Parks seem to barely scratch the surface of its beauty. To see its treasures, you'll need to get out and stretch your legs.

On Hwy 180, trace the path of Kings River and drop down into Kings Canyon on the 30-mile Kings Canyon Scenic Byway. With a maximum depth of 8200ft, this glacier-sculpted canyon boasts the deepest cleft in the contiguous US. Pull over at the sweeping ❷ Junction View overlook to get an eyeful of the river's Middle and South Fork and the steely peaks clustered nearby.

If the day's hot and your suit's handy when you reach Road's End, stroll from the wilderness permit office to ❸ Muir Rock. A large flat-top river boulder where John Muir gave talks during early Sierra Club field trips, it's a popular spot for shrieking cannonball dives and wet summer fun. Spend the night creekside at ❹ Sheep Creek Campground. Located a bit further from the Cedar Grove Village area than the three other area campgrounds, it's often less used.

For a sobering reminder of what the parks protect, reverse course and head back west 26 miles from Cedar Grove, making an easy detour to the ❺ Converse Basin Grove. Now a sequoia cemetery, it once held the world's largest grove of mature sequoias. The one colossus left to live was the Boole Tree, the eighth-largest known giant sequoia. On the

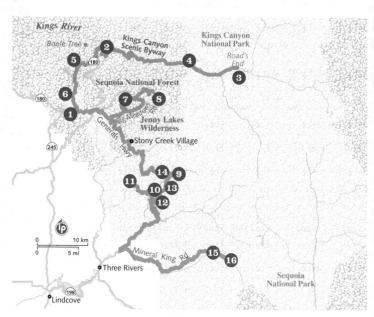

road in, stop at Stump Meadow to see the oversized vestiges of 19th-century logging. Check your park map to locate the unpaved Forest Service roads to the grove.

Continue about 4 miles south to the **6** **General Grant Grove**, where you'll see some of the big ones of yore. Saunter along the paved half-mile General Grant Tree Trail, an interpretive walk that visits a number of skyscraper-sized sequoias, including the 27-story General Grant Tree, the world's third-largest living tree. Kids will adore the Fallen Monarch, a massive, fire-hollowed walk-through trunk that's done duty as a cabin, hotel, saloon and horse stable.

To see one of the most evocative fire lookouts in the country, go south on the Generals Hwy, east on Big Meadows Rd and follow signs to the staffed **7** **Buck Rock Fire Lookout**. Built in 1923, a wooden panoramic-view cab lords over the horizon from 8500ft atop a granite rise, reached by 172 stairs.

DREAMS TO SAWDUST

Before Sequoia National Park existed, an idealistic organization of workers called the **Kaweah Cooperative Colony** began a utopian community in the pristine foothills below Giant Forest. They developed a labor-based currency, organized a school and farmed the land. But the 1890 victory of park designation wiped out their land claims and quashed their socialist dreams. Remaining Kaweah relics include the simple **Squatters Cabin** near Crescent Meadow and the one-room **Kaweah Post Office**, just north of Three Rivers.

A bit further east, hike a mile into the forest for ice water and gourmet meals at the **8** **Sequoia High Sierra Camp**. A luxurious off-the-grid tent-cabin resort perched at 8200ft, it's nirvana for active, sociable people who don't think "luxury camping" is an oxymoron.

The next day, rejoin Generals Hwy and motor south to Lodgepole Village. Duck into the visitor center to buy afternoon tickets for Crystal Cave and pick up a salad or wrap at the **9** **Watchtower Deli** for a picnic lunch outside. If you have curious little ones, head south to the Giant Forest Area and spend an hour or two at the indoor-outdoor **10** **Beetle Rock Education Center**, where activity stations let kids ogle and interact with bones, bugs and (fake) animal poop. Afterwards, continue 2 miles south and then about 7 miles northwest to take your tour of **11** **Crystal Cave**, a chilly otherworld carved by an underground river. Stalactites hang like daggers from the ceiling, and milky white marble formations 10,000 years old take the shape of ethereal curtains, domes, columns and shields.

Back in the daylight, backtrack 2 miles north on Generals Hwy to get schooled on sequoia ecology and fire cycles at the **12** **Giant Forest Museum**, and then have a gander at **13** **Giant Forest**, a mind-blowing throng of ancient giant sequoias. By volume, the largest living tree on earth, the massive General Sherman Tree rockets 275ft to the sky. Then return a few miles north to the **14** **Wuksachi Lodge**, the parks' most upscale lodging and dining. Spacious rooms have a southwestern feel, and the wood-paneled dining room enchants with a stone fireplace and forest views. Gourmet dinners and decadent desserts like chocolate mousse and ice-cream sundaes top off your day.

Continue south on Hwy 198 and, as you exit east before Three Rivers, clench the steering wheel for the hair-raising and winding 1½-hour ride to Mineral King, a remote and marmot-overrun section of the park and historic mining hamlet. *Almost* at the end, mop your brow and stop for pie and burgers at the **15** **Silver City Mountain Resort**, the only restaurant on the road. Situate your tent at **16** **Cold Springs Campground**, set along a peaceful creek with gorgeous ridge views. Trailheads to the high country begin at the end of the road, where historic private cabins dot the valley floor flanked by massive mountains and jagged peaks.

Beth Kohn

> **ASK A LOCAL**
>
> "I first went there in the summer of 1943 and I've gone most summers since. There are 67 cabins in all; mostly built by people's grandfathers or great-grandfathers. It's a historic and continuing community – the majority of us are descendants of those first miners. My family's cabin is one of the oldest, and we cook on an old wood stove that probably dates from the 1880s. Nobody has electricity."
>
> *Jane Coughran, Mineral King cabin owner*

TRIP INFORMATION

GETTING THERE
From Fresno, take Hwy 180 to the Big Stump Entrance. Return from Mineral King via Hwy 198 and Hwy 99.

DO

Beetle Rock Education Center
A bright and cheerful activity cabin run by the Sequoia Natural History Association, it's appropriate for kids aged three to 15. ☎ 559-565-4251; admission free; ☉ 10am-4pm summer; ♿

Buck Rock Fire Lookout
An active 1920s fire lookout, its long staircase leads to a dollhouse-sized wooden cab on a dramatic 8500ft granite rise. www.buckrock.org; admission free; ☉ 9:30am-6pm Jul-Oct

Crystal Cave
Buy tickets in advance and bring a sweater for this fantastical river-cave experience. ☎ 559-565-3759; www.sequoiahistory.org; Crystal Cave Rd; adult/child $11/6; ☉ tours 10:30am-4:30pm mid-May–Oct, with variations; ♿

Giant Forest Museum
A fun primer in sequoia ecology, this pint-sized museum has hands-on exhibits about some very big trees. ☎ 559-565-4480; admission free; ☉ 9am-7pm Jul-Aug, 9am-6pm Apr-Jun & Sep-Oct, 9am-4pm Nov-Mar; ♿

Sequoia & Kings Canyon National Parks
Towering trees and a deep, deep canyon are but two reasons to visit the parks. ☎ 559-565-3341; www.nps.gov/seki; per car $20, per motorcycle or bicycle $10; ♿ 🐾

EAT

Silver City Mountain Resort
Mineral King's only restaurant serves homemade pie and simple meals under a pleasant tree canopy. ☎ 559-561-3223; www.silvercityresort.com; Mineral King Rd; ☉ 8am-8pm Thu-Mon late May-early Oct; ♿

Watchtower Deli
Conveniently located in Lodgepole Village, this gourmet deli sells healthy to-go fare like foccacia sandwiches and prepared deli salads. Mains $6-8; ☉ 11am-6pm Apr-Oct

Wuksachi Lodge
The most upscale option in the parks, Wuksachi's dining room serves a breakfast buffet, soup-and-salad lunch fare, and all-out extravagant dinners. ☎ 559-565-4070; dinner mains $9-32; ☉ 7-10am, 11:30am-2:30pm & 5-10pm; ♿

SLEEP

Cold Springs Campground
Towards the end of a tortuous 25-mile road, these non-reservable tent sites sit by a creek near the ranger station. Mineral King Rd; campsites $12; ☉ late May-Oct; ♿ 🐾

Sequoia High Sierra Camp
Settle in for gourmet meals and comfy beds at this luxury tent cabin oasis. ☎ 866-654-2877; www.sequoiahighsierracamp.com; r incl meals per adult/child over 3yr $250/100; ☉ mid-Jun–early Oct; ♿

Sheep Creek Campground
In the Cedar Grove region at the bottom of Kings Canyon, choose from 111 well-spaced sites situated along pretty creekside loops. campsites $18; ☉ late Apr–mid-Nov; ♿ 🐾

USEFUL WEBSITES
www.sequoiahistory.org
www.sequoiaparksfoundation.org

LINK YOUR TRIP

www.lonelyplanet.com/trip-planner

Pick-It-Yourself Tour

WHY GO What's more satisfying – the crack that brings a perfectly ripe apple off the branch or the snap it makes when you sink your teeth into it? This trip cuts out the middlepeople between the soil of Northern California and your lunch, touring places to pick it yourself.

It's time to get up and get some breakfast. This fact is apparent because of the irregular exclamations of a rooster and because the sun is dancing through the east-facing windows in bright blotches on the refinished hardwood floor. Rustling out of the cotton sheets, you wander across the dewy yard to gather the fixings – a pile of fresh eggs in a hanging basket (thanks to some friends of the alarm clock), and seasonal vegetables and fruit, which you pull from the ground itself. This is morning at ❶ **Mar Vista Cottages**, a converted fishing village steps from the Pacific shore at Anchor Bay, an appropriate start for exploring the freshest farms and orchards of Northern California.

What hits your taste buds on this trip is a matter of season: spring has the puckering zing of stone fruit and fall brings the crunch of apples and squash. Although Northern California's hospitable climate and cultural emphasis on seasonal dining makes the trip possible year-round, the harvest of late summer is best.

Leave Mar Vista Cottages and head south along the salty cliffs of Hwy 1, past coastline pullouts that get crowded with the vehicles of abalone divers. Thirty minutes south is ❷ **Salt Point State Park**, where a grid of trails crisscross grasslands and wooded hills – from the foggy pygmy forests to the edge of sandstone cliffs that descend into the bursting surf. For a picnic head to Stump Beach, which has fire rings and access to wincingly cold, barefoot wandering in the Pacific. If you know what you're doing, you can even hunt for mushrooms.

TIME
2 – 4 days

DISTANCE
237 miles

BEST TIME TO GO
Jul – Oct

START
Anchor Bay

END
Sacramento

ALSO GOOD FOR

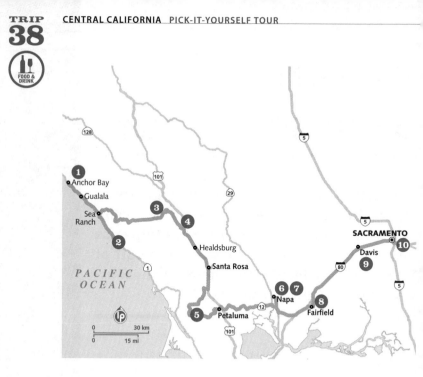

From Salt Point go inland, twisting under shady redwoods along Stewarts Point Skaggs Springs Rd until it crests over the coastal range near the edge of the **3** **Lake Sonoma State Recreation Area**. It has grassy, primitive hike-in camping within a stumble of the surrounding wine-tasting rooms, and a lake full of sunfish and perch for those who want to take the hunter-gatherer theme all the way. The route becomes Dry Creek Rd as it passes Sonoma County's rolling vineyards and the salty moisture from the coast dries out. After 15 minutes you'll reach downtown Healdsburg and **4** **Love Farms**, a sustainable, if comparably tiny, 6-acre organic farm under the pruning shears of Ron and Bibiana Love. They grow year-round, but the best season is mid to late summer, when you can pick some of the 30 varieties of fleshy heirloom tomatoes, which are perfect naked or dressed only with a sprinkle of salt.

"...chat with 90-year old John Hoffman, who's been farming here since before Napa was, well, Napa."

From Healdsburg, it's 30 minutes south on Hwy 101 to the exit for Hwy 116 (Gravenstein Hwy), and another 20 minutes through the rolling countryside to **5** **Chileno Valley Ranch**, a 600-acre farm that sits behind miles of white picket fence on the cow-dotted hills. Through summer and fall the farm offers painting and gardening workshops (a chance to learn to grow it, pick it and paint it yourself) and has a tidy orchard of apples, open for picking during harvest. Year-round it sells grass-fed beef, raised on the surrounding acres, by the quarter, half or whole cow.

Leaving the ranch, head east for an hour on CA 116 and then take CA 12/CA 121 into Napa County. Just outside of Napa visit **6 Hoffman Farms**, a family-operated plot that starts slowly in the spring, with peaches and figs, and explodes with a cornucopia of produce in August, with snappy, bright Bartlett pears and crimson sugar prunes. Make time to chat with 90-year old John Hoffman, who's been farming here since before Napa was, well, Napa.

You can't leave the area without investigating wine, so carve out half a day for the unmatched **7 Copia: The American Center for Wine, Food & Arts**, whose interactive exhibits focus on demystifying wine and sustainable growing techniques. Among the center's fascinating installations are ones that tackle the question "What Is American Food?" There is a sustainable garden on-site that supplies an outstanding restaurant and daily food demonstration classes, and there's even a plot for little ones to get their hands dirty learning the origins of food.

> **ASK A LOCAL**
>
> "The way to tell if your apple is ready, really ripe, is by color. A yellow apple will be ready and crunchy when the skin is almost completely changed from green to yellow. The reds – look for the part of 'em that isn't red, that should be yellow, not green. But there's only so much you can tell by looking. The real way to tell is by tasting."
>
> *Robbie Heath, Brentwood*

Enough with the fruit already! You need some spice! Leave Napa on CA 12 and head north on I-80, exiting immediately at Green Valley Rd for **8 Castañeda Brothers Produce**. Grab a cart at the dusty parking lot and wander the grounds for squash, tomatoes and watermelon. Best of all are the colorful spicy peppers that come in a dozen varieties.

From boysenberries to ollalieberries – just about every berry under the sun is available at **9 Impossible Acres**, 35 miles up I-80 (exit onto CA 113). Planted to offer picking experiences through an extended growing season, the wide open fields introduce the Central Valley's huge growing possibilities, with bing cherries in the spring through to late-season pumpkins.

Another 30 minutes up the road comes the reward for the labor. At **10 The Kitchen Restaurant**, Randall Selland and Nancy Zimmer give quality local and imported ingredients the gourmet treatment, with four- to five-hour demonstration dinners in their intimate dining space. In the late summer Selland's apple desserts keep diners reveling and, if you watch closely enough, you might even learn to transform that trunk full of veggies into a masterpiece of your own.

Nate Cavalieri

TRIP INFORMATION

GETTING THERE
Take the Golden Gate Bridge north from San Francisco and drive three hours up Hwy 1 to reach Anchor Bay.

DO

Castañeda Brothers Produce
Load up the wheelbarrow with tons of squash and fruit, and be sure to sample the hot peppers. ☎ 707-333-3982; www.casta nedabros.com; 4075 Green Valley Rd, Fairfield; ⏲ 9am-5pm Jun-Nov; ♿

Chileno Valley Ranch
Painting workshops take place on an organic beef and u-pick apple ranch. ☎ 707-765-6664; www.chilenobnb.com; 5105 Chileno Valley Rd, Petaluma; 4-day workshops $450; ⏲ by appointment

Copia: The American Center for Wine, Food & Arts
If you visit one place in Napa, this is it, an unmatched museum about the way food grows. ☎ 707-259-1600; www.copia.org; 500 First St, Napa; admission free; ⏲ 10am-6pm; ♿

Hoffman Farms
John Hoffman knows every tree of his orchard; he's been growing in Napa for 50 years. ☎ 707-226-8938; 2125 Silverado Tr, Napa; ⏲ 9am-5pm Aug-Dec; ♿

Impossible Acres
The long growing season of the Central Valley offers ollalieberries, tomatoes and peaches. ☎ 530-750-0451; www.impossible acres.com; 26565 Road 97 D, Davis; ⏲ 9am-6pm Wed-Sun; ♿

Love Farms
This 6-acre patch is truly a labor of the Loves, with 30 varieties of heirloom tomatoes. ☎ 707-433-1230; www.lovefarms.com; 15069 Grove St, Healdsburg; ⏲ 10am-5pm Sat & Sun, by appointment Mon-Fri; ♿

Salt Point State Park
Hike grassy hills to the sandstone coast and make use of abundant campsites. ☎ 707-847-3221; www.parks.ca.gov; 25050 Hwy 1, Jenner; day use $6, sites $15-25; ⏲ visitors center 10am-3pm Sat & Sun; ♿

EAT & SLEEP

The Kitchen Restaurant
Local produce gets transformed before your eyes in this demonstration kitchen. ☎ 916-568-7171; www.thekitchenrestaurant.com; 2225 Hurley Way, Sacramento; prix fixe $125; ⏲ 5-10pm Wed-Sun

Lake Sonoma State Recreation Area
Choose from hike-in, boat-in or drive-in sites, in Sonoma wine country. ☎ 877-444-6777; www.russianrivertravel.com; 3333 Skaggs Springs, Geyserville; sites $10; ⏲ 7am-10pm; ♿ 🐾

Mar Vista Cottages
A dozen fishing cabins come beautifully restored and appointed. ☎ 877-855-3522; www.marvistamendocino.com; 35101 S Hwy 1, Gualala; cottages $155-275; ♿ 🐾

USEFUL WEBSITES
www.pickyourown.org
www.localharvest.org

LINK YOUR TRIP
www.lonelyplanet.com/trip-planner

Mammoth Lakes Adventure

WHY GO A year-round whirlwind of outdoor activities, the High Sierra town of Mammoth Lakes never stops to catch its breath. Anchored by the Mammoth Mountain resort, it's a beehive of adventure sports and the stepping-off point for countless wilderness forays and geological and geothermal explorations.

As you enter town on Hwy 203, swing on in to the ❶ **Mammoth Ranger Station & Welcome Center** to get your bearings. At this dual purpose building, housing the Forest Service office and the Mammoth Lakes Visitors Bureau, you can load up on maps, wilderness permits, bear canisters and glossy brochures galore.

Hungry yet? Detour to the ❷ **Base Camp Café** for a bracing dose of organic tea or coffee with a filling breakfast or comfort food like Tex-Mex onion straws and pesto chicken fajitas. Decorated with various backpacking and mountaineering gear, the bathroom has a hysterical photo display of backcountry outhouses.

Unless you're overnighting at one of the half-dozen campgrounds in the Reds Meadow Rd area west of town, a shuttle in from Mammoth Mountain is mandatory from June until snow falls, and it's a tremendous help for one-way hikes like this recommended half-day ramble. From the back of the Soda Springs campground, walk south along the mostly shaded Pacific Crest Trail as it traces the Middle Fork of the San Joaquin River through the Ansel Adams Wilderness. After a log bridge, a short detour leads to the pretty cascades of Minaret Falls. At the junction with the John Muir Trail, go left to ogle ❸ **Devils Postpile**, a bizarre basalt formation that looks like a bundle of spaghetti noodles frozen upright and then fractured. When viewed from above, the columns form a groovy honeycomb pattern. Follow signs southeast

TIME
2 – 3 days

BEST TIME TO GO
Jun – Sep

START
Mammoth Lakes

END
Mammoth Lakes

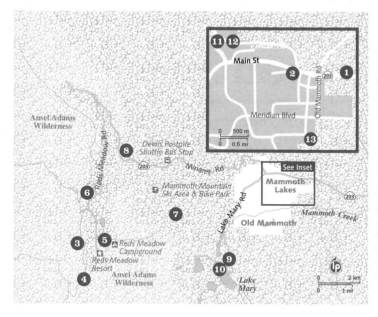

to ④ **Rainbow Falls**, where the river leaps 101ft, diffusing into a prism of mist. Shuttle north one stop from the Rainbow Falls trailhead to rinse off at the dreamy ⑤ **hot springs showers** at the Reds Meadow Campground (not the nearby resort). A half-dozen rustic (and pretty dim) private rooms let you take it all off and freshen up with water piped in from an adjacent natural hot spring. Brace yourself for the first blast – it's *really* hot and the temperature can't be moderated. Spend the night a few shuttle stops over at the tranquil willow-shaded ⑥ **Minaret Falls Campground**, a popular fishing spot where the best riverside campsites have views of the cascade.

Winter's a dream at ⑦ **Mammoth Mountain**, though it hardly dozes during summertime. Spotlighting an inactive 11,053ft volcanic peak, the ever-burgeoning resort complex has 3100 vertical feet – enough to whet any snow-sports appetite – a fine mix of tree-line and open-bowl skiing, and an enviably long season that often lasts from November to June.

In summer, the mountain becomes the massive Mammoth Mountain Bike Park, and with a slew of cyclists decked out in body armor, it could be mistaken for the set of an apocalyptic *Mad Max* sequel. With more than 100 miles of well-tended single-track trails and a crazy terrain park, it draws those who know their knobby tires. Noncyclists can forego elbow pads and warrior gear and ride the vertiginous gondola to the apex, where tricked-out cyclists careen down the gondola's exit stairs against a backdrop of snow-speckled mountaintops.

A mile west from Mammoth Mountain, it's worth backtracking by car to experience an alpenglow sunset at **8** **Minaret Vista**. Huge views take in the San Joaquin River valley, Banner Peak, Mt Ritter and the dramatic Minarets – named for their resemblance to mosque spires.

Hiking and mountain-biking not your thing? Saddle up a four-legged critter from the **9** **Mammoth Lakes Pack Outfit** and clip-clop out to the wilderness. More experienced riders can help with the herding on horse and mule drives at the beginning and end of the summer season. Or rent a canoe or kayak from the **10** **Pokonobe Marina** and paddle through nearby Lake Mary under the snow-skirted horn of Crystal Crag.

Across the street from the Village gondola, settle in at **11** **Petra's Bistro & Wine Bar** for seasonal California cuisine and wines recommended by its three sommeliers. In wintertime, the best seats in the house are the cozy fireside couches. Start the evening with a cheese course and choose from 28 wines available by the glass or 240 vintages by the bottle. If beer's your weakness, step downstairs to the adjoining **12** **Clocktower Cellar** in the basement of the Alpenhof Lodge. Choose from over 30 draughts and 50 bottled varieties (especially German brews) served under a ceiling tiled with bottle caps.

When it's time to hit the hay, the **13** **Mammoth Creek Inn** boasts unobstructed mountain views from the edge of a handy commercial strip of shops and restaurants. Warm colors brighten contemporary rooms with little luxuries like robes. Superspacious upstairs loft rooms are good for groups, and kitchen suites are available as well. Two comfortable lounges make good reading nooks, and a hot tub and sauna downstairs feel perfect after a day on the trail.

Beth Kohn

DETOUR

Nestled between the White Mountains and the Sierra Nevada near Mammoth is a tantalizing slew of natural pools with snow-capped views. When the high-altitude summer nights turn chilly and the coyotes cry, you'll never want to towel off. About 9 miles south of town, **Benton Crossing Rd** juts east off Hwy 395, accessing a delicious bounty of hot springs. For detailed directions and maps, pick up Matt Bischoff's excellent *Touring California and Nevada Hot Springs*.

ASK A LOCAL

"The Long Valley Caldera has several fairly obvious manifestations, and one of them is a geothermal plant that mines heat from magma. During the 1980s and '90s there were lots of recurring earthquakes around Mammoth Mountain and there are areas that show the results of carbon dioxide – magmatic gas – coming through. One of the most dramatic areas is the bunch of dead trees at the end of Horseshoe Lake."

David Hill, Scientist-in-Charge, US Geological Survey, Long Valley Observatory

OUTDOORS

TRIP INFORMATION

GETTING THERE & AWAY

From I-5 in Los Angeles, take Hwy 14 northeast to Hwy 395, and continue 160 miles north to Hwy 203.

DO

Devils Postpile

Amateur geologists go ga-ga over this exceptionally unusual and evocatively named basalt rock formation. **☎ 760-934-2289; www.nps.gov/depo; Reds Meadow Rd; shuttle per adult/child $7/4, car $20; ranger station 9am-5pm Jun-Oct;**

Mammoth Lakes Pack Outfit

Grab the reins and head for the hills on a horseback-riding trip to the backcountry. **☎ 760-934-2434; www.mammothpack.com; Lake Mary Rd, Mammoth Lakes; rides from $40;**

Mammoth Mountain

The southern Sierra's best ski resort transforms into a bike park in summer. **☎ 760-934-0745, 800-626-6684; 1 Minaret Rd, Mammoth Lakes; www.mammothmountain.com; 1-day bike pass adult/child $40/20, winter lift ticket $80/40;**

Mammoth Lakes Ranger Station & Welcome Center

This one-stop shop for wilderness, recreational and general info is located on the way into town from Hwy 395. **☎ 760-924-5500; Hwy 203, Mammoth Lakes; 8am-5pm**

Pokonobe Marina

Rent a boat from this resort on the north end of Lake Mary. **☎ 760-934-2437; Lake Mary Rd, Mammoth Lakes; canoe & single kayak rental per hour $16;**

EAT & DRINK

Base Camp Café

A casual outdoor-themed restaurant, it serves filling breakfasts and good grilled comfort food. **☎ 760-934-3900; 3325 Main St, Mammoth Lakes; mains $6-11; 7:30am-9pm Thu-Sun, 7:30am-3pm Mon-Wed**

Clocktower Cellar

Locals throng this half-hidden basement in the Alpenhof Lodge for the huge selection of draft and bottled beers. **☎ 760-934-2725; 6080 Minaret Rd, Mammoth Lakes; 5-11pm, with seasonal variations**

Petra's Bistro & Wine Bar

An upscale café with a large selection of vintages by the glass. **☎ 760-934-3500; 6080 Minaret Rd, Mammoth Lakes; mains $14-32; 5:30pm-late Tue-Sun, with seasonal variations**

SLEEP

Mammoth Creek Inn

Sleep and sauna at this pleasant mountain-view lodging on the edge of town. **☎ 760-934-6162, 866-466-7000; www.mammothcreekinn.com; 663 Old Mammoth Rd, Mammoth Lakes; r $165-193, ste $215-498;**

Minaret Falls Campground

Snooze by the side of the river at one of these lovely 27 first-come, first-served Forest Service campsites. **☎ 760-924-5500; Reds Meadow Rd; www.fs.fed.us/r5/inyo/recreation/camping/minaret-falls.shtml; campsites $16; Jun-Sep;**

USEFUL WEBSITES

www.fs.fed.us/r5/inyo

www.visitmammoth.com

LINK YOUR TRIP

www.lonelyplanet.com/trip-planner

TRIP
34 High Altitudes on Highway 395 p225
35 Yosemite Aquatic p231
36 Pioneer Trails & Ghost Towns p237

Lazy Delta Dawdle

WHY GO Slipping along the glassy waterways or shady levy roads of the Sacramento-San Joaquin River Delta brings you to an eccentric string of one-horse towns, where savory plates of steaming crawdads, scads of taxidermy and unexpected adventures are around every bend.

TIME
2 – 4 days

DISTANCE
103 miles

BEST TIME TO GO
May – Aug

START
Clarksburg

END
Port Costa

ALSO GOOD FOR

When exploring the network of channels and back roads of the 750,000-acre Sacramento-San Joaquin River Delta, consider one question before all others: by land or by sea? Each has advantages: the gently sweeping levy roads can excite any latent road warrior, while those who want to get wet – dawdling along on a houseboat, trolling for bass or gunning a powerboat – can explore a maze of endless channels.

The fields and arid heat surrounding West Sacramento offer little clue that the "Thousand Miles of Waterways" is near. Begin south on CA 84, following Gregory Ave until it connects with S River Rd (by boat, these directions get a lot simpler: follow the Sacramento River south). Near Clarksburg follow signs for ❶ **Old Sugar Mill** for the region's first surprise: a thriving community of winemakers. A jazz combo echoes through the huge space, a perfect accompaniment to the wines of the Carvalho family, who founded the community space and installed a custom crushing facility.

Continue south five minutes along the river, through Steamboat Landing and across one of the Delta's rusting bridges, and turn right onto Grand Island Rd. After 3 miles is the ❷ **Historic Grand Island Mansion**, an Italian Renaissance building built in 1917 for an orchard baron, which fills with taffeta-clad weddings most Saturdays and hosts a Sunday champagne brunch. The mansion has its own guest dock for those coming by water.

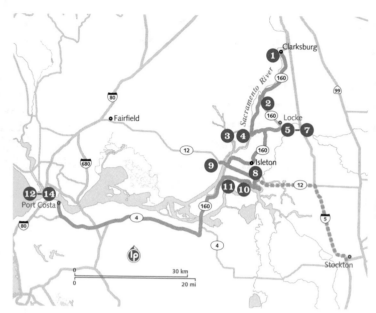

A few minutes south is the Hartland Nursery, home of **3** **Delta Ecotours**. Jeff Hart's tours are ideal for landlubbers wanting to travel the channels and learn about the area's unique environment and history. The nursery is filled with regional plants and is a worthy stop even if the tours aren't happening.

Following Grand Island Rd south, pass one of the delta's curious transportation features, **4** **Ryder Island Car Ferry**, which crosses Steamboat Slough into the delta's less-traveled back roads. Just south of the ferry stop, turn east on CA 220 to return to S River Rd, which has now joined CA 160 at the edge of a wide stretch of the Sacramento River. After five minutes north on CA 160, you'll pass Walnut Grove on the way to its sister city, **5** **Locke**. Declared a National Historic Landmark, Locke was founded by Chinese laborers, who built the levies. Its wild heyday was prohibition, when the lack of a police force and quiet nearby waterways made it a hotbed of boozing and gambling.

The shadowy main street parallels the river, lined with tightly packed rows of wooden structures with creaking balconies. Locke's wild days are evident in the **6** **Dai Loy Museum**, a former gambling house with exhibits on regional history, and **7** **Al the Wop's**, a magnet for amiable Harley crews. The draw isn't the food (the special is a peanut butter–slathered hamburger) as much as it is the ambience. Above the creaking floorboards, the ceiling's covered in crusty dollar bills and more than one pair of erstwhile undies.

Fifteen minutes south on CA 160 it seems more like the Mississippi Delta than California in Isleton, "Crawdad Town, USA." On hot weekends, the patio at ❽ **Isleton Joe's** is misted with water as patrons slurp up butter-soaked, ruby-red crayfish, drowned out by the live band. River trippers can get to Joe's: there are docks at Isleton, and it's a two-block walk.

Take CA 160 to Rio Vista, just 10 minutes by car or boat, for a creepy cold one at ❾ **Foster's Bighorn**. Doolittles beware – hundreds of game heads line the wall, collected by Bill Foster, a chillingly passionate hunter who bagged exotic game in every corner of the world. Frozen snarls abound: 300 trophies including Kodak bears,

> **DETOUR**
>
> When you find **Stockton** on a map, it hardly seems possible to reach it by sea, but the channels of the delta make it California's largest inland agricultural port. If you make the trip, pull in at Rough and Ready Island, a WWII-era naval supply base that was decommissioned in 1995, and stroll to the historic downtown. By boat or car, it's about an hour from Sacramento.

rhinos and big cats of every stripe. The centerpiece is a full-grown African elephant, whose trunk extends 13ft from the wall. There is a menu, but good luck finishing the steak.

Back in the sunlight, follow CA 12 east to the 12-mile ❿ **Delta Loop**. With marshy lowlands, wide horizons and afternoon watering holes, the drive is best taken at an unhurried pace. Marinas line the southern stretch, chartering anything that floats. The loop ends at the ⓫ **Brannan Island State Recreation Area**, where sandy picnic areas and grassy barbecue areas draw hard-partying campers. For families, a small nature center on-site has hands-on displays of delta wildlife (similar to Foster's Bighorn, but with a smaller menagerie and less beer) and there's a beach where a lifeguard watches little ones wade into the reeds.

In the morning, boaters will have the superior ride, navigating the wide channel south to the dazzling Suisun Bay. Those on land can take CA 160 south to connect with CA 4. Drive west for 30 minutes or float about an hour before reaching ⓬ **Port Costa**, on the expansive San Pablo Bay. Rest your heels at the ⓭ **Warehouse Café**. The talk on the porch revolves around the horse-power of the machines that brought them to the door. Inside, there's plenty on tap and an enormous stuffed polar bear encased behind glass.

Just across the dusty lot is the ⓮ **Burlington Hotel**, the best (and only) place to stay in town. The weather-beaten lodgings have loads of musty charm but belie its history as a five-star Victorian brothel. It caps the voyage with aptly surreal details, and as you open the window to let in the famed delta breeze, it seems like no other place on earth.

Nate Cavalieri

TRIP INFORMATION

GETTING THERE
From Sacramento, take I-5 south and exit at Pocket Rd. Go left on Pocket Rd, right on Freeport Blvd and right again at S River Rd to reach Clarksburg.

DO

Dai Loy Museum
This former gambling house – translated as "Big Welcome" – testifies to Locke's lucky past. ☎ 916-776-1661; 5 Main St, Locke; admission $2; ⊙ noon-3pm Sat & Sun; 🔥

Delta Ecotours
Excellent three-hour pontoon tours take you into the heart of the delta's wild waterways. ☎ 916-775-4545; 13737 Grand Island Rd, Walnut Grove; adult/child $40/20; ⊙ Sat by appointment; 🔥

Old Sugar Mill
With tasting rooms and live jazz, this is the center of the delta's wine region. ☎ 916-744-1615; www.oldsugarmill.com; 35265 Willow Ave, Clarksburg; admission free; ⊙ 11am-5pm Wed-Sun; 🔥

EAT & DRINK

Al the Wop's
Whet your whistle before trying the peanut-butter burger. ☎ 916-776-1600; 13943 Main St, Locke; mains $8-15; ⊙ 11am-9pm

Foster's Bighorn
A veritable museum of taxidermy – with beer – built by a frighteningly passionate game enthusiast. ☎ 707-374-2511; www

.fostersbighorn.com; 143 Main St, Rio Vista; mains $8-25; ⊙ 11am-9pm

Historic Grand Island Mansion
Stroll the elegant grounds after the Sunday champagne brunch. ☎ 916-775-1705; www.grandislandmansion.com; 13415 Grand Island Rd, Walnut Grove; brunch $22-26; ⊙ 10:30am-2pm Sun, Mon-Sat by appointment

Isleton Joe's
Wipe your chin after sucking down the crayfish on the breezy patio, which often hosts live bands. ☎ 916-776-1600; www.isletonjoes.com; 212 Second St, Isleton; mains $5-17; ⊙ 8am-9pm

Warehouse Café
Cyclists and boaters mingle over microbrews while gawking at the stuffed polar bear. ☎ 510-787-1827; 5 Canyon Lake Dr; ⊙ 11am-1am; 🔥

SLEEP

Brannan Island State Recreation Area
Reach campsites by boat or car, but the hike-in sites at the water are best. ☎ 916-777-7701; www.parks.ca.gov; 17645 State Highway 160, Rio Vista; sites $11-25; 🔥 🐾

Burlington Hotel
The rooms of this former brothel are a little dog-eared, but it's tall on quirky delta charisma. ☎ 510-787-1827; 5 Canyon Lake Dr, Port Costa; r $24-54

USEFUL WEBSITES
www.sacdelta.com
www.deltaloop.com

LINK YOUR TRIP
TRIP

www.lonelyplanet.com/trip-planner

Dusty Trails on Highway 99

WHY GO Tripping down sunbaked Hwy 99 offers a dusty tour of what some call the real California – where hungry appetites find fresh-picked fruit and veggies and mid-century roadside cafés. Those with hungry ears can gorge on the raucous twang of Bakersfield's famous country music kings, Merle Haggard and Buck Owens.

TIME
2 – 4 days

DISTANCE
305 miles

BEST TIME TO GO
Apr – Aug

START
Sacramento

END
Bakersfield

ALSO GOOD FOR

FOOD & DRINK

With the air-conditioning off and the windows down, the rush of heat through the window smells of tilled earth, pollen and, somehow, even sunshine. The neat rows of supersized homes in Sacramento suburbs give way to the orderly patchwork of supersized fields of fruit trees and cotton, begging for Buck Owens' 1958 single, "Second Fiddle."

The tune doesn't bear Owens' signatures as an architect of the "Bakersfield Sound" – absent is the rude telecaster twang and heart-shattering harmonies of longtime sidekick Don Rich – but when Owens swings back around to that chorus, asking in his aw-shucks tenor "why must I play second fiddle in your heart?" there is no better soundtrack for the trip down Hwy 99.

Traversing California's Great Central Valley, Hwy 99 doesn't offer the edgy dramatic thrills of its prettier sister, Hwy 1, or the lauded nostalgia of Route 66 that leads to Los Angeles. In fact, after the smoothly paved I-5 was completed in the 1970s, the indistinguishable chain restaurants and hell-bent rush of traffic may have dimmed its claim as "California's Main Street." But traveling Hwy 99 between Sacramento and Bakersfield reveals a part of California that few ever slow down to enjoy – birthplace of a raucous brand of country music and historic two-stoplight farm towns that continue to slowly fade under the 300-plus annual days of squint-bright sunshine.

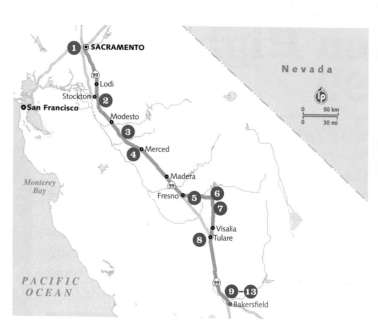

Taste the goods of the valley first at the sprawling **①** **Sacramento Central Farmers' Market**. In the summer, Sacramento has a market every day of the week, but the biggest and best is open on Sunday mornings year-round. It's held conveniently near the on-ramp to Hwy 99, under the elevated freeway at 8th and W St. Throughout the summer it sells many of the 300-odd crops hauled in from the valley, a colorful riot of fruits and veggies that left the vine hours earlier: corn and stone fruit, strawberries and leafy greens.

With the trunk full of vitals, start the voyage south, creeping out of the oft-jammed lanes of Elk Grove's suburban sprawl and into the sprawling valley.

"... a robotic cheese-making exhibit led by an animated cow is likely to thrill kids and creep out their parents...."

The agricultural prosperity of the region reveals itself slowly, showing its first signs with the billboards announcing the burgeoning wineries that have sprouted up surrounding Lodi. Soon, the air takes on the inimitable smell of the region, a mix of sweet pollen and pungent cattle that line the highway.

The best lunch on the route comes 13 miles south of Lodi, in Stockton at **②** **Manny's California Fresh Café**. Finding Manny's at the center of Stockton requires navigating the sun-tattered outskirts of the city to find the "Miracle Mile" – a strip of Bikram Yoga centers and old-world pharmacies that evidence a city at the crossroads of the region's changing identity. Shaded by Japanese maples, Manny's cool interior is filled with the smell of fresh rotisserie meats accompanied by crunchy salads, grown mostly on surrounding farms. A din of Sinatra accompanies black-and-white photos lining the walls, perfect to browse while waiting for artfully crispy fried chicken, fresh oysters, and burgers that come saddled under fat slices of avocado.

An hour south of Stockton, Hwy 99 leads to ❸ **Turlock**, a city that's become a kind of Grand Central Station of the Central Valley's cattle trade. Turlock is tiny, so it isn't hard to spot the stockyards near the center of town, where livestock auctions happen daily. A quick jog south on Rte 165 approaches the ❹ **Hilmar Cheese Factory**. Aptly on scale with the agri-industry of the valley, it processes a million pounds of cheese a day as the largest cheese-manufacturing site in the world. The product isn't gourmet (many of those million pounds are simple varieties of cheddar or jack); the stars of the expansive visitors center are "Squeakers," young curds of cheese with a texture that squeaks in your mouth as you chew them. A robotic cheese-making exhibit led by an animated Jersey cow, Daisy, is likely to thrill kids and creep out their parents.

PLAYLIST Driving down Hwy 99 requires getting on a first-name basis with Bakersfield's two drawling titans: Merle and Buck. Masters of twanging telecasters and hayseed heartbreak, they're country kings of the Central Valley.

- "I'm Gonna Break Every Heart I Can," Merle Haggard
- "I've Got a Tiger By the Tail," Buck Owens
- "Okie from Muskogee," Merle Haggard
- "Second Fiddle," Buck Owens
- "Swinging Doors," Merle Haggard
- "The Bottle Let Me Down," Merle Haggard
- "The Streets of Bakersfield," Buck Owens and Dwight Yoakam
- "Under Your Spell Again," Buck Owens

To taste more fresh goods, travel another hour and a half down Hwy 99 to Selma (the "Raisin Capital of the World"), where the ❺ **Circle K Ranch**, which sits just east of the highway amid orchards of peaches, plums and nectarines. The store has seasonal fruits and nuts from May to November, but the best deals are in the adjacent packing house, where, aided by some passable Spanish, it's possible to barter for a few bushels of freshly picked goods for a fraction of supermarket price.

Just east of Selma's sleepy downtown, is the downright comatose ❻ **Reedley** ("The World's Fruit Basket"). Reedley was the wheat transport hub during the late 19th century and hasn't changed much since. Strolling one end of the sun-beaten downtown to the other takes a few minutes, past the remodeled 1903 opera house in the shadow of the water tower. Nearby, the renovated 19-room ❼ **Hotel Burgess** has polished wood floors, modern amenities and quiet Victorian elegance. If traveling in spring, ask about a detour on the "Blossom Trail," where plum, peach and almond orchards explode into color.

Back out to Hwy 99 and 30 minutes further south is Tulare, another small agricultural hub and one-time headquarters of Southern Pacific railroad. Now the biggest news in town is the ⑧ **International Agri-Center** and its annual World Ag Expo, held in February. Native son David Watte offers half-day tours of local farms through the Agri-Center year around. Want to wander through fields of black-eyed beans or under shady almond trees? Watte is your man. He hosts groups of growers from other parts of the world and any city slickers looking to, in his own words, "stop and kick the tires a little bit." His own family farm – all 4000 acres of it – grows dairy feed and cotton.

Nearing Bakersfield, the landscape is dotted by evidence of California's *other* Gold Rush: rusting rigs alongside the route that continues to burrow into Southern California's vast oil fields. Oil was discovered here in the late 1800s, and Kern Country, the southernmost county on Hwy 99, still pumps more than some OPEC countries. In the 1930s the oil attracted a stream of "Okies" – farmers who migrated out of the dusty Great Plains – to work the derricks. The children of these tough-as-nails roughnecks minted the "Bakersfield Sound" in the mid-1950s. The poorly mannered child of western swing, Bakersfield's brand of country waved a defiant middle finger to the silky country that defined the Nashville establishment of its day.

The architects of this sound – Wynn Stewart, Bill Woods, Fuzzy Owen and TV variety show host Cousin Herb – paved the way for Merle and Buck, who, like the rock-and-roll rebels halfway across the south, peddled rebellion. No longer would jukeboxes weep with cheese-soaked Nashville crooners like Jim Reeves and Eddy Arnold; the Bakersfield Sound was full-volume electric twang, played loud enough to be heard over the working-class rowdies looking to drink, dance and brawl their way through a Friday night at (now demolished) landmarks like the Lucky Spot and the Blackboard.

ASK A LOCAL

"Some of the best places for music were surrounding towns like Farmersville – little places with no air-conditioning, no TV. Folks would come outside and drink beer and play guitar, and kids would play in the yard. You'd hear twangs from Texas, Oklahoma and Arkansas. That became the 'Bakersfield Sound.'"

Gerald Haslam, Oildale

Insight into this history and the region which birthed it can be found at the musty ⑨ **Kern County Museum**. Don't get distracted by the Roosevelt elk or the wildcat cubs in the large (fairly disturbing) display of taxidermy wildlife – on the 2nd floor waits a collection of pristine memorabilia from Bakersfield's musical heyday. Behind the glass is Cousin Herb's dazzling Nudie Suit, Fuzzy Owen's steel guitar and the gold lamé stage gear of Bonnie Owens, the first lady of Bakersfield. She chalked up marriages to Buck (who supplied her surname) *and* Merle Haggard.

Any blisteringly hot afternoon in **10** **Bakersfield** begs for a stop at the unimpeachable **11** **Dewar's Candy Shop**. Perched on the pastel stools at the counter, families dig into their homemade ice cream – dreamy flavors like lemon flake and cotton candy – all made from ingredients from surrounding farms; flavors change seasonally. For a slightly more somber afternoon, find the final resting place of the "King of Bakersfield," Buck Owens, who lies behind a pair of heavy cast-iron doors (shaped like guitars, of course) of a kingly marble monument at the **12** **Greenlawn Southwest Cemetery**, five minutes south of town. When he died from a heart attack in 2006, Bakersfield rightly shut down to acknowledge his legacy, and fans from across the world visit the mausoleum.

Perhaps a more fitting legacy for Owens is the joint that bears his name in brilliant neon: **13** **Buck Owens' Crystal Palace**. Part music museum, part honky-tonk, part steakhouse, the Palace has a top-drawer country act on stage every night, and locals in meticulous western wear tear up the dance floor. It's filled with bronze effigies of country greats from Bakersfield and beyond – Johnny Cash, George Jones and Willie Nelson among them – and memorabilia from Owens' estate. Buck himself took the stage here until he was well into his 70s. As the band begins the last set of the evening, the cowboys and cowgirls too spent for the electric-slide park it in front of the 1974 Pontiac convertible mounted behind the bar. Designed by rhinestone cowboy clothier Nudie Cohn, it's decorated with six-shooter door handles, hand-tooled leather interior and studded with silver dollars. According to lore Buck won it off Elvis Presley in a poker game. After enough 32oz beers, the ride has a lot in common with the dusty trip that began in Sacramento: a stunning one-of-a-kind, a reminder of a bygone era and a surprising treasure for the curious traveler.

Nate Cavalieri

TRIP INFORMATION

GETTING THERE
From Sacramento, head south on Hwy 99. Continue through the Great Central Valley to a sunny strut down the streets of Bakersfield.

DO

Circle K Ranch
The "Raisin Capital's" country store sells goods from surrounding orchards, but the deals are in the packing house next door. ☎ 800-362-9899; www.circlekranch.com; 8640 E Manning Ave, Selma; ☉ 8am-6pm Mon-Sat 🕭

Greenlawn Southwest Cemetery
Drop off some flowers for the "King of Bakersfield," Buck Owens, at his impressive marble resting place. ☎ 661-834-8820; 2739 Panama Lane, Bakersfield; admission free; ☉ sunrise-sunset Mon-Sun; 🕭

Hilmar Cheese Company Visitor Center
A cartoon cow talks to guests about cheese production, and the grounds are good for picnicking. ☎ 209-667-6076; www.hilmar cheese.com; 9001 North Lander Ave, Hilmar; admission free; ☉ 7am-7pm Mon-Sun; 🕭

International Agri-Center
David Watte leads tours year-round, but the February farm show is a huge annual event. ☎ 559-688-1751; www.farmshow.org; 4450 S Laspina St, Tulare; half-/full-day farm tours $15/$25; ☉ by appointment; 🕭

Kern County Museum
The 2nd floor of this community museum has jaw-dropping artifacts of the "Bakersfield Sound." ☎ 661-852-5000; www.kcmuseum .org; 3801 Chester Ave, Bakersfield; adult/child $8/5; ☉ 10am-5pm Mon-Sat, noon-5pm Sun; 🕭

LINK YOUR TRIP

TRIP
38 Pick-It-Yourself Tour p247
43 Gold Digging on Highway 49 p269

Sacramento Central Farmers' Market
Buy California goods at a pittance of the supermarket price. www.california-grown .com; cnr 8th & W St, under Hwy 80 overpass; admission free; ☉ 8am-noon Sun; 🕭 🕭

EAT

Buck Owens' Crystal Palace
Country bands play nightly in this neon-lit beer hall, music museum and steak house. ☎ 661-328-7560; www.buckowens.com; 2800 Buck Owens Blvd, Bakersfield; mains $8-25; ☉ restaurant 5pm-midnight Mon-Sat, 9:30am-2pm Sun

Dewar's Candy Shop
A classic, pastel-painted soda fountain with fresh-made ice cream and candies, all using ingredients from the surrounding valley. ☎ 661-322-0933; 1120 Eye St, Bakersfield; mains $3-10; ☉ 11am-9pm Mon-Thu, to 10pm Fri & Sat; 🕭

Manny's California Fresh Café
Shady patios and Sinatra accompany the freshest diner fare in the Central Valley. ☎ 209-463-6415; 1612 Pacific Ave, Stockton; mains $6-15; ☉ 10am-9:45pm Mon-Sun; 🕭

SLEEP

Hotel Burgess
It's advisable to book in advance, especially for the skylight rooms. ☎ 559-637-1793; www.hotelburgess.com; 1726 11th St, Reedley; r $90

USEFUL WEBSITES
www.california-grown.com
www.thatbakersfieldsound.com

SUGGESTED READS
- *The Other California*, Gerald Haslam
- *Proud to Be an Okie: Cultural Politics, Country Music, and Migration to Southern California*, Peter La Chapelle

www.lonelyplanet.com/trip-planner

Rafting the American River

WHY GO River guide Scott Armstrong has been exploring the canyon of the Middle Fork of the American River for 25 years. He leads us on a two-day adventure of white water, through a canyon famed for gold and dramatic scenery.

From the canyon floor, where the Middle Fork of the American River tumbles over granite and serpentine boulders in a white rush, it becomes obvious that all the dams controlling the water and the regulations governing the visitors don't matter; the place is untamed. As white water goes, this fork of the American isn't the biggest or baddest, but rushing past rusting mining relics and the untouched wilds of the vast Auburn State Recreation Area makes one of the best two-day rafting trips in the western states.

Start just north of Auburn by filling up at ❶ **Ikeda's California Country Market**. The SUVs rushing to Tahoe on the highway don't lend Ikeda's much ambience, but the burgers are a savory customizable mess. Don't fool around, go for the mushroom. Head up I-80 and exit at Canyon Way, taking it north to Iowa Hill Rd. Three miles further north is ❷ **Mineral Bar Campground**.

On the drive to Foresthill the next morning, cross the towering ❸ **Foresthill Bridge**, 730ft above the canyon floor. The tallest bridge in the state, it offers a bird's-eye view of the terrain that awaits. Ten minutes further, the ❹ **Forest Hill Ranger Station** offers permits and information for those exploring the area without a guide. If you visit Foresthill before the trip, blunt your nerves at the ❺ **Red Dirt Saloon**, where peanut shells crunch underfoot as patrons take in the collection of antique firearms. Across the street is ❻ **Worton's Grocery Store**, a family run stop for final supplies (don't forget the booze – All-Outdoors has a BYOB policy). A minute back out of town, turn on Sunset Dr to the meeting place of ❼ **All-Outdoors California Whitewater Rafting**.

TIME
2 – 3 days

DISTANCE
60 miles

BEST TIME TO GO
May – Jun

START
Auburn

END
Lotus

ALSO GOOD FOR

HISTORY & CULTURE

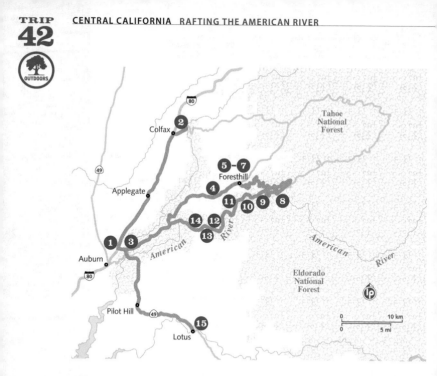

The All-Outdoors van shudders down Mosquito Ridge to the put-in point at the Oxbow Reservoir. There's a palpable sense of anticipation that rises in the gut at the sound of the rushing water you hear when you step from the dusty gravel ramp and into the numbing, emerald river. Scott Armstrong pushes off and it comes into sight: **8 Panic Alley**, the icy Class III drop that begins the trip. Between the adrenaline and the needlelike cold water, the descent is riveting.

"When you get through that," says Armstrong. "Its like, 'Ah…' The trip has begun. You're instantly able to focus."

Armstrong sits at the back of the taut gray raft and casually navigates the rapids like someone who grew up on this river; when he was a boy the company started by his father was the first commercial company making trips on the Middle Fork of the American River. Armstrong is 45, but looks 10 years younger, with dark curly hair that shows a touch of gray. He's hiked, rafted and explored every inch of the canyon and speaks passionately about the area's geology, wildlife and history.

"…you step from the dusty gravel ramp and into the numbing, emerald river."

For would-be rafters, his plan is simple: "Plan ahead, be willing to change and be adaptable when everything blows up in your face." Nothing blows up until we encounter the Middle Fork's unique feature, a rushing chasm of frothing water that blasts through a mining tube, called **9 Tunnel Chute**. On the way through the rush, one of the paddlers falls out and is rewarded by a challenging swim. "I try to downplay how much it sucks to fall in there," Armstrong says. "But it's not too pleasant. It's like getting flushed down a toilet."

In another hour, after the technical pass through **10 Kanaka**, a Class IV rapid that Armstrong calls the trip's most challenging, he leads a hike up **11 Dardanelle Creek**, topped with a trickling waterfall and deep water-worn pools. After a riverside lunch of sandwiches and fresh seasonal fruit, the afternoon passes lazily, with gentle Class II rapids twisting through remote canyons to **12 Ford's Bar** campground. The setting sun paints the riverbanks shades of orange as the crew prepares dinner: seasonal veggies and chicken on the grill followed by chocolatey concoctions from a Dutch oven. You can hike in and camp at Ford's Bar with a permit arranged through the Foresthill Ranger Station.

The next morning, after eggs and hair-raising coffee, the rafts point toward **13 Canyon Creek**, where rafters disembark for a demanding hike. "Anytime you're on a river and see a side creek," Armstrong advises, "you have to head up it. There's always a good swimming hole." Bouldering 1000ft up the creek, which is scented with California Bay trees and dotted with blackberries, Armstrong leads the group to a sparkling hidden pool surrounded by ferns at the base of a waterfall.

IT'S NOT JUNK – IT'S AN ANTIQUE

Along the riverbanks are plenty of reminders of the machinery that once scoured the hills for gold. Think twice about the impulse to clean up that decaying scrap heap – because of its historical significance and age, the rusty machinery on the sides of the river is covered by the Antiquities Act, created by Theodore Roosevelt to stop pot hunters from looting native American sites.

Back on the river, the frothing water crescendos until you reach the unraftable rocks of **14 Ruck-a-Chucky**. "It's the experience of being in a powerful place," Anderson says. "It can push at a person's comfort zone." After schlepping gear around the falls, the crew hits the water with another hour of moderate white-water navigating. "By the end of the second day you look back and say 'I really accomplished something.'"

The rafts are loaded onto the truck for a winding 30-minute ramble through the wooded hills along Ruck-A-Chucky Rd, connecting with Hwy 49. Twenty minutes south is Lotus, home of the **15 Café Mahjaic**. Here, enjoy a lunch enlivened by international fusions like the rich chocolate chipotle prawns and savory free-range fowl. It can all be perfectly paired with a glass from a nearby vineyard, a decidedly civilized way to toast the rushing wilds.

Nate Cavalieri

TRIP INFORMATION

GETTING THERE
From San Francisco or Sacramento take I-80 east and head to the hills, pulling over in Auburn at the exit for Auburn Revine/Foresthill Rd. Follow the signs east toward Foresthill.

DO

All-Outdoors California Whitewater Rafting
This family-run outfitter was the first on the river and is among only a few that lead adventuresome two-day wilderness ventures. Their burrito might be worth the trip alone. ☎ 800-247-2387; www.aorafting.com; Middle Fork tours depart 5845 Sunset Dr, Foresthill; ⓨ reservations 8am-7pm Mon-Fri, 8am-4pm Sat & Sun; 🐾

Foresthill Ranger Station
For souls venturing into the wilds without a guide, this is the stop for permits, maps and information. ☎ 530-367-2224; Middle Fork tours depart 5845 Sunset Drive Foresthill; ⓨ reservation line 8am-7pm Mon-Fri, 8am-4pm Sat & Sun; 🐾

EAT AND DRINK

Café Mahjaic
Quit roughing it with international fusions. The *saganaki* (fried Greek cheese) is the menu must-have. ☎ 530-621-4562; www.cafemahjaic.com; 1006 Lotus Rd, Lotus; ⓨ 5-10pm

Ikeda's California Country Market
This off-highway spot has juicy burgers with homemade hiker snacks and the best home-made fruit pies in Gold Country. ☎ 530-885-4243; www.ikedas.com; 13500 Lincoln Way, Auburn; ⓨ 8am-7pm Mon-Thu, 8am-9pm Fri, 8am-8pm Sat & Sun; 🐾

Red Dirt Saloon
Cheap swill, hell-raising locals and a display of antique firearms; an adjoining steakhouse serves 'em thick and rare. ☎ 530-367-3644; 24601 Foresthill Rd, Foresthill; ⓨ 10am-midnight

Worton's Grocery Store
This grocer supplies rafters heading into the canyon for white-water expeditions with pre-made picnic lunches. ☎ 530-367-4040; 23140 Foresthill Rd, Foresthill; ⓨ 7am-10pm; 🐾

SLEEP

Ford's Bar
On a sweeping bend of the Middle Fork this blackberry-dotted camp is accessible by a 2-mile hike or half-day raft. Get your permits in advance from the Foresthill Ranger Station. ☎ 800-444-7275; www.parks.ca.gov; 2-mile hike from Ruck-A-Chucky Rd, Auburn; permits $15

Mineral Bar Campground
The perfect staging area for the white-water adventure; bring your own water. Get your permits in advance from the Foresthill Ranger Station. ☎ 800-444-7275; www.parks.ca.gov; off Iowa Hill Rd, Colfax; permits $15; 🐾

USEFUL WEBSITES
www.theamericanriver.com
www.aorafting.com

LINK YOUR TRIP
www.lonelyplanet.com/trip-planner

Gold Digging on Highway 49

WHY GO A trip through Gold Country, more than any other region in California, shows off California's formative years, when hell-raising prospectors and Wild West ruffians rushed the hills for gold. There's still gold in them thar hills, and plenty of adventure along Hwy 49.

When you roll into Nevada City on a sunny day, the promise of adventure recalls the days when headlines screamed about gold in California and the state was born. Today the region offers a burden of different riches: exploring crumbling false-front saloons, rusting machines that moved mountains in search of gold, and an endless parade of greening bronze historical markers – making Hwy 49 one of the state's greatest historic byways.

Nevada City's main drag, Broad St, is dominated by the ❶ **National Hotel**, which claims to be the oldest continuously operating hotel west of the Rockies. The adjoining bar has a heavy pour on a hot afternoon, but skip the rooms upstairs, they need airing out. Strolling a few steps west to Union St, the shady ❷ **Calanan Park** is filled with rusty mining equipment. Just around the corner is Nevada City's 1861 fire house, where the ❸ **Fire House Museum** is run by the Nevada Country Historical Society. The most impressive stuff in the collection comes from Chinese laborers who often built, but seldom profited from, the mines.

Taking Hwy 49 – the so-called "Golden Chain" – south for 10 minutes, exit at Empire St for the ❹ **Empire Mine State Historic Park**. This was the biggest mother of the mother lode: the richest hard-rock mine in California produced 5.8 million ounces of gold between 1850 and 1956. The mine yard is littered with massive mining equipment and buildings constructed from waste rock. There are docent-led tours and sunny hiking, and the main shaft has plans to open for underground tours.

TIME
3 days

DISTANCE
152 miles

BEST TIME TO GO
Jun – Oct

START
Nevada City

END
Jamestown

ALSO GOOD FOR

HISTORY & CULTURE

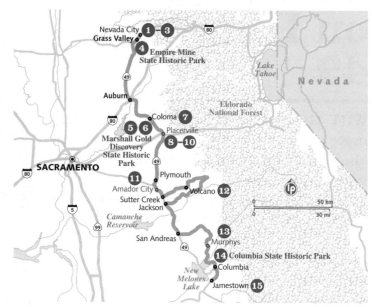

Back on Hwy 49, you'll enter the stretch of the "Golden Chain" that's among its most scenic. Patched with shade from oak and pine, it drifts along the foothills offering glimpses of the region's original beauty. A few minutes south of Auburn, stop at the **5** **Marshall Gold Discovery State Historic Park**. Unlike many of the fairly haphazard displays of hydraulic mining equipment that litter parks in the area, this is a pastoral, low-key affair. A simple dirt path leads to the place along the bank where Marshall made his discovery on January 24, 1848.

"…a simple dirt path leads to the place along the bank where Marshall made his discovery…"

Several buildings – including a reconstruction of the fateful mill – are within a stroll to the hill where the **6** **James Marshall Monument** marks Marshall's resting place. Ironically, he died a ward of the state. The park's many trails pass old mining artifacts and pioneer cemeteries. Panning for gold is popular – you can pay $3.50 to pan at nearby Beckeart's Gun Shop.

For a second day of panning, spend the night at the **7** **Coloma Country Inn**. Built by a prospecting family in 1852, the old farmhouse offers cute little rooms, excellent food (the berries that grow locally in profusion are used) and utter peace and quiet that is starkly different from the calamity of the area's past.

Fifteen minutes south things get more lively in "Old Hangtown," a name **8** **Placerville** earned when five men hung here in 1849. The El Dorado

County seat, the town has a thriving and well-preserved downtown with antique shops, outdoor activity stores, galleries and character-filled bars. Most buildings along Main St date back to the 1850s, and many places stock the good, free walking-tour brochure. The **❾ Placerville Hardware** is the oldest continuously operating hardware store west of the Mississippi River, where you can get maps of the region. Placerville's bars are akin to watering holes in the Midwest: they open around 6am, get an annual cleaning at Christmas and are great for people who want to soak up local color. Marked by vintage signs, the **❿ Hangman's Tree** is built over the stump of the eponymous tree.

⓫ Amador City is a quiet little village some 30 miles south of Placerville that was once home to the Keystone Mine – one of the most prolific gold holes in California. Now the town has shops, frilly B&Bs, and cafés along its shady streets. It's a great departure point for Amador Country's booming wine region. Traveling inland to Volcano, the **⓬ St George Hotel** has 20 rooms which vary in size and amenity. The restaurant (open for brunch on Sundays and for dinner from Thursday to Sunday) wins raves for its creative use of herbs and produce grown in the hotel's garden, and the accompanying bar serves a specialty called "Moose Milk" to anyone with a strong enough stomach to try it.

⓭ Murphys, is just east of Hwy 49 on Murphys Grade Rd. It is named for Daniel and John Murphy, who founded a trading post and mining operation on Murphy Creek in 1848. Main St has refined boutiques and galleries with at least one shop offering a sun-drenched Gold Country staple: ice cream.

CHASING THE ELEPHANT

Every gold prospector in the hills came to "see the elephant," a phrase that captured the adventurous rush for gold, and a central colloquialism of '49ers. Those on the Oregon Tail were "following the elephant's tracks" and when they hit it rich, they'd declare they'd seen the beast from "trunk to tail." Like seeing a rare beast, rushing the California hills was a once-in-a-lifetime risk, with potential for a jumbo reward.

Next, grab some suspenders and a floppy hat and hit **⓮ Columbia State Historic Park** in Columbia, near the so-called "Gem of the Southern Mines." Columbia is a compelling meeting of commercial and historic interests. Your costume will fit right in at the compelling collision of commercial and historical interests. Four blocks of the town are preserved as a State Historic Park, where the fudge and candle shops are restrained, and volunteers perambulate in vintage costumes and demonstrate gold panning. For the big bucks, try heading 8 miles south on Hwy 49 to Jamestown, where **⓯ Gold Prospecting Adventures** offers gold-finding outings involving much more elaborate methods. Since the vast majority of the gold is still said to be underground in the region, it's your best chance to pull out a little bit of gold for yourself.

Nate Cavalieri

TRIP INFORMATION

GETTING THERE
From Sacramento, take I-80 east to the exit for Grass Valley. Connect with Hwy 49, the "Golden Chain," and head north to Nevada City.

DO

Columbia State Historic Park
With volunteers in costume and a recreated village, its like a Gold Rush Disneyland. ☎ 209-588-9128; 11255 Jackson St, Columbia; admission free; ⏱ 8am-sunset; ♿ ❄

Empire Mine State Historic Park
A new train tour goes deep underground in a retired gold mine. ☎ 530-273-8522; www .empiremine.com; 10791 E Empire St, Grass Valley; admission $3; ⏱ 9am-6pm with seasonal variations; ❄

Fire House Museum
Native artifacts are joined by displays about Chinese laborers and Donner Party relics. ☎ 530-265-5468; www.nevadacounty history.org; 214 Main St, Nevada City; admission free; ⏱ 1-4pm Fri-Sun; ♿

Gold Prospecting Adventures
It offers courses to help you strike it rich, including some for college credit. ☎ 209-984-4653; www.goldprospecting.com; 18170 Main St, Jamestown; classes from $30; ⏱ by appointment; ♿

Placerville Hardware
This historic hardware is ideal for stocking up on gold-panning gear. ☎ 530-622-1151; 441 Main St, Placerville; ⏱ 8am-6pm Mon-Sat, to 5pm Sun; ♿

Marshall Gold Discovery State Historic Park
This serene spot once started an international Gold Rush; it's now marked by quiet monuments and gold panning. ☎ 530-622-3470; 310 Black St, Coloma; admission free; ⏱ 8am-sunset; ♿ ❄

DRINK

Hangman's Tree
This rough gold-country bar has a hanging dummy outside, and gets aptly rowdy after dark. ☎ 530-622-5339; 305 Main St, Placerville; ⏱ 10am-2am

SLEEP

Coloma Country Inn
The cottage suite is perfect for a quiet Gold Country retreat, where you can spend an afternoon floating on the pond. ☎ 530-622-6919; www.colomacountryinn.com; 345 High St, Coloma; r $150-245

St George Hotel
A simple, quiet hotel on the end of Main St in sleepy Volcano is just up the stairs from the area's best Gold Rush bar. ☎ 209-296-4458; www.stgeorgehotel.com; 16104 Main St, Volcano; r $98-115

USEFUL WEBSITES
www.historichwy49.com

LINK YOUR TRIP
www.lonelyplanet.com/trip-planner

Hot Springs & Swimming Holes

WHY GO From the frigid waters of the Sierra Nevada's mother lode to the soothing sulfuric hot springs of the Coastal Range, this trip will get you wet in California's most famous inland waters, winding through scenic and wild regions of Northern California along the way.

TIME
3 days

DISTANCE
171 miles

BEST TIME TO GO
Jul – Sep

START
Nevada City

END
St Helena

Take three big strides and that final gasp during the leap, 35ft down to the sky-blue reflection at the surface of the water. Plunging below, your nerves are shocked; suddenly so acutely aware of the icy temperature that it almost feels hot. You rise back to the surface of the water, legs kicking, heart thundering in your chest, hardly able to restrain the "Whooooo!" that bounces against the granite. As you pull yourself out of the water, the first thing that crosses your mind: let's do it again.

Once you muster the courage to take the leap at ❶ **Mushroom Hole**, it's hard to stop. The rollercoaster chills and the free fall, the frigid water that chills you to the bone until you lie out on a rock under unyielding summer sun. Surely one of the best swimming holes in the Sierra Nevada, this is the ideal way to start an exploration of California's wet spots – with a full-throated "Cannonball!"

In the middle of the ❷ **Tahoe National Forest**, just above the Middle Fork of the Yuba River, Mushroom Hole is named for the fungi-shaped rock that dominates the view. You'll know it when you see it but getting here isn't easy. It's 14 miles north of Nevada City on Hwy 49; when you go over the bridge that crosses the Middle Yuba River, keep your eyes peeled for a rough side road where you'll pull off for a poison oak–lined hike. There are lots of places to camp throughout the forest, and dispersed camping permits are available if you want to make it a two-day splash, but be sure to observe the restrictions for camping away from the water's edge.

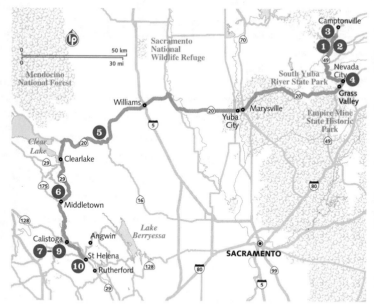

A more private plunge can be had upstream, by heading back to Hwy 49 and traveling a mile north. There's a turnout with space for two cars at the head of a path leading to ❸ **Oregon Creek**. The river rushes over smooth stones here, creating a tranquil spot for a swim, so secluded that suits are optional. Explore the big, square granite boulders upstream and you'll reach a pair of small falls that feed the pools, which make for excellent picnic spots.

A day of hiking and swimming can work up an appetite, so head back into Nevada City for dinner at the ❹ **New Moon Café**, where Peter Selaya's regularly changing menu keeps an organic, local bent. If you visit during the peak of the summer keep to the aquatic theme by trying the wild, line-caught fish or seared duck, prepared with a French-Asian fusion.

Drive two hours west through the winding scenery of CA 20, out of the Sierras and into the Costal Range Foothills. Twenty-two miles past Williams, turn right on Bear Valley Rd to reach ❺ **Wilbur Hot Springs**. A sign announces "Time To Slow Down" as you pull up to the spacious lodge that sits opposite Japanese-style, clothing-optional thermal pools. The lodge is a retreat from modern bustle, where the sounds of guests' impromptu acoustic jam sessions float along on the air, which smells sharply of the mineral waters. There's a stocked library and a communal, professionally appointed kitchen that takes on a festive atmosphere as bottles get uncorked during dinner. Trails around the lodge lead past closed mine shafts that once pulled copper, sulfur and gold.

Continue west from the sanctuary for half an hour before going south on CA 53, which turns into CA 29 and leads to Middleton. Just before the small downtown, take a right on Harbin Springs Rd to reach **6 Harbin Hot Springs**. It once hosted a druggie-hippie cult in the 1960s, but now the site draws yoga retreats, and patrons jar themselves into a Zen state by leaping between cold plunges and steaming mineral pools.

Be warned: the clothing-optional policy and facility's popularity combine in a way that might give a modest person the willies.

Head 20 miles south down CA 29 to Calistoga, a place so famous for its water that they bottle it. Pick up a smoky brisket lunch at **7 Buster's Southern BBQ & Bakery** before finding the palm-lined drive to the area's

ASK A LOCAL

"The best stretch of swimming holes is up and down Hwy 49. When you get near a river crossing, keep your eyes open for pullouts where cars have parked. Follow the path and never stop at the first place – that's the one that's going to get crowded. Nine times out of 10, there's a better swimming hole just upstream, and an even better one just upstream from that."

Jeff Schwartz, Nevada City

historic spa, **8 Indian Springs**. This might be the area's most family friendly hot springs, where groups lunch by an Olympic-sized thermal pool or sip on cucumber water by the quiet Buddah pool and spend long, slow weekends in the lovely Spanish colonial lodge.

Take the final dip at the rustic tub inside **9 Bothe-Napa Valley State Park**, which is fed by natural springs and surrounded by a network of mossy, fern- and redwood-lined trails. The best camping in the park comes at the shady walk-in sites, which lie under low-lying manzanita near the stony bed of Ritchey Creek.

"...a tranquil spot for a swim, so secluded that suits are optional."

Dry off and head into St Helena for dinner at the **10 Martini House**, one of Wine Country's handsomest dining rooms. Celeb chef Todd Humphries ensures the freshest in seasonal and regional fare with farm-raised meat and wild fish and game. After dinner, head downstairs for the final plunge – at the bar, where locals take in the house's signature drink.

Nate Cavalieri

TRIP INFORMATION

GETTING THERE
From Sacramento, head east on I-80 and north on Hwy 49 to reach Nevada City. Mushroom Hole is a 20-minute drive north.

DO
Harbin Hot Springs
Try not to blush at this classic, quiet NorCal clothing-optional hot-water retreat. ☎ 707-987-2477; www.harbin.org; 18424 Harbin Springs Rd, Middleton; day pass $25-35

Indian Springs
This historic Calistoga getaway has an Olympic-sized mineral-fed pool and sundry spa packages. ☎ 707-942-4913; www.indianspringscalistoga.com; 1712 Lincoln Ave, Calistoga; packages from $150, rooms from $210; 🐾

EAT
Buster's Southern BBQ & Bakery
Get your taste buds warmed up before hitting the steamy waters of Calistoga. ☎ 707-942-5605; www.busterssouthernbbq.com; Hwy 29 at Lincoln Ave, Calistoga; mains $5-21; 🕐 9am-11pm Mon-Sat, 11am-6pm Sun; 🐾

Martini House
The coziest dining room in Napa Valley, where organic local food is done in gourmet fusions. ☎ 707-963-2233; www.martini

house.com; 1245 Spring St, St Helena; mains $15-40; 🕐 4:30-10pm

New Moon Café
Fresh seasonal dishes make this the best lunch in Nevada City. ☎ 530-265-6399; www.thenewmooncafe.com; 230 York St, Nevada City; mains $13-30; 🕐 11:30am-2pm, 5-10pm

SLEEP
Bothe-Napa Valley State Park
Hike through redwood forests before cooling off with a dip in the natural, spring-fed pool. ☎ 707-942-4575; www.napanet.net; 3801 Saint Helena Hwy, Calistoga; sites $16, day use with pool access $6; 🐾 🐾

Tahoe National Forest
Dispersed camping can bring you within a stone's throw of your favorite Sierra swimming hole. ☎ 530-265-4531; free permits available at 631 Coyote St, Nevada City; 🕐 8am-5pm Mon-Fri, 8am-4:30pm Sun; 🐾

Wilbur Hot Springs
The sign on the road in says it all about this heavenly thermal springs retreat: time to slow down. ☎ 530-543-2306; www.wilburhotsprings.com; end of Bear Valley Rd, Wilbur; day use $45, campsites $56, r from $177

USEFUL WEBSITES
www.swimmingholes.org
www.running-water.com

LINK YOUR TRIP
www.lonelyplanet.com/trip-planner

Zins of Amador County

WHY GO Follow the gently winding roads through the untamed hills of the western Sierra Nevada to the least pretentious wine region in the state – where a cast of colorful locals grows zinfandels that are bold enough to punch you in the nose.

TIME
2 days

DISTANCE
49 miles

BEST TIME TO GO
Jun – Aug

START
Plymouth

END
Drytown

One of the most notorious local winemakers is at center stage, behind the drum kit of a makeshift country band, who are making a wobbly racket at the only bar in town. On the back patio, baby boomers keep watch on their brilliantly polished Harleys as they chat up a group of farmers who allude to harvesting something a bit more inebriating than grapes, and a slobbering 120lb mastiff chews through his leash and heads toward an unattended drink. Everyone is here for the wine, winding drives and one of the most scenic wine regions in the western states. In Amador County, Napa Valley seems about as far away as the moon.

Only 30 minutes from Sacramento and less than two hours from San Francisco, Amador County is an underdog of California's winemaking regions. Its thriving circuit of family wineries, Gold Rush history and local characters make for excellent wine touring without a whiff of pretension. The region lays claim to the oldest zinfandel vines in the United States and the surrounding country has a lot in common with this celebrated variety – bold and richly colored, earthy and constantly surprising.

The home base for exploring Amador County's narrow strip of land is ❶ Plymouth, where the Gold Rush history of the region is evident in its original name, Old Pokerville. European prospectors came to the Sierra Nevada by the scores in the mid-19th century and established the winemaking tradition, bringing cuttings from the old country that thrived in the heat and high elevation. Few card sharks haunt the slumbering main street today (the last census tallied less than 1000

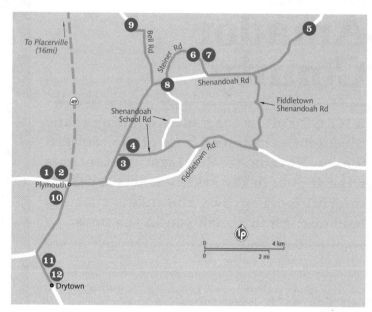

residents); it wakes up late when the streets fill with the smell of barbecue, a few strolling tourists and the occasional rumble of a motorcycle posse. Many of those hogs line up outside ❷ **Incahoots**, a scruffy barbecue place with a roadhouse vibe where bikers, ranchers and wine drinkers pack the rough-cut wooden tables. It ain't all that fancy – but for an opening meal in Amador, it's aptly unpretentious, and the huge piles of tangy beef ribs are ideal for those looking to buffer the sampling of local wine that awaits.

DETOUR ➤ Though the most remote, Amador isn't the only wine-producing region of the foothills. The hot temperatures and gentle terraces of its northern neighbor, El Dorado Country, also yield astonishingly good, bold reds. Take a detour up Hwy 49 into **Placerville**, where the main street has a handful of tasting bars. El Dorado Winery Association is a good place to start. If you get tired of drinking wine, roll into a dive bar for a cold one, like the Hangman's Tree or Liar's Bench.

To begin the circuit of Amador wineries, start by heading east out of Plymouth on Shenandoah Rd, which veers to the north just east of Hwy 49. One mile up the road, turn right on Shenandoah School Rd, lined on both sides with vines basking in the heat. This will be the sight out the window for most of the trip through Amador's wine region: hill after rolling hill covered with rocky rows of neatly pruned vines, soaking up gallons of too-bright sun, interrupted occasionally by the blotchy shade of oak trees. This vision would make the zinfandel in your cellar homesick.

The first, and one of the best family wineries along the road, is the ❸ **Wilderotter Vineyard**, whose stone- and wood-finished tasting room overlooks sweeping acreage to the south. Wilderotter pulled a big upset at the 2007 California State Fair when its 2005 barbera picked up the prestigious bragging rights for "Best Red" in the state (take *that* Napa!). The little statue of a golden bear in the tasting room is the pride and joy of the well-mannered women who run the tasting room, who are hardly able to conceal their delight. The king-making barbera is in short supply and likely to run out, but other excellent choices lie in their mourvédre and estate zinfandel.

A stone's throw east is ❹ **CG di Arie**, a spacious tasting room that sits on the opposite side of the road and is wont to draw the occasional limo bus of bachelorettes. Arie's Southern Exposure zinfandel is the most memorable – if you don't count his biography. A relative newcomer to the Shenandoah Valley, Turkish-born Arie immigrated to Israel as a teen, where he operated tanks during conscripted military service. Then he donned a lab coat for top commercial food makers, eventually helping to create processed gastronomic marvels like Power Bars, pudding cups and, perhaps most impressively, Cap'n Crunch. His artisanal reds employ some of the technological ingenuity behind these space-aged foods – look at the custom-made stainless steel tanks off the tasting room. Like most Amador County wineries, there's no charge for tasting.

"This vision would make the zinfandel in your cellar homesick."

This modernity is a striking contrast to the dust-covered barrels in the museum at the ❺ **Sobon Estate**, which is on the former D'Agostini Estate – go a few minutes up the Shenandoah School Rd, which becomes Fiddletown Rd, left at Fiddletown Shenandoah Rd and just east on Shenandoah Rd. It's thought to be the first place zinfandel was harvested in California. Today, the Sobon family keeps a tidy, if slightly mildewed, collection of artifacts in one of the original D'Agostini buildings, and has a tasting room pouring several zingy reds.

The Old Vines zinfandel – its flagship – has everything you want in a bottle from Amador: a medium-bodied wine with tons of character, with notes of dark plum and berry, and balanced with ashy earthiness. Best, the family-operated estate puts a great emphasis on sustainable growing practices; it's now run completely on solar energy.

Head back down Shenandoah Rd, turn north on Steiner Rd and drive for a few minutes till you find ❻ **Deaver Vineyards**, run by another historic winemaking family, who operate a tasting room at the shore of a large pond. If he's not in the fields, look for Ken Deaver, likely in muddy boots and overalls. He's the third generation of winemakers here; the Deavers first planted in

1853. Their "Mission Vines" were established in the years after the gold discovery. They've been producing their complex and celebrated Deaver Sierra Foothill zinfandel, a full-bodied blend tasting of berries, anise and leather, from the same vines since 1860. After all the reds its nice to get a little bubbly, and the Deavers pour excellent sparkling whites, the best of which comes with notes of almond.

The family also owns a cozy little four-room bed and breakfast across the property, the **7** **Amador Harvest Inn**. It's the place for wine-trippers to mingle in the common room and wake to the smell of home-cooked breakfast from the warmly hospitable innkeeper, Joan. The breakfast conversation leans toward how to make the visit to the affordable, pastoral corner of the foothills into more than a vacation.

As Steiner Rd horseshoes back to Shenandoah Rd, there are signs pointing out a quick detour to the **8** **Amador Flower Farm**, a spectacular 14-acre plot that explodes with color during the long growing season and has lots of shady picnic spots. A walk along the farm's crunching gravel paths and manicured grounds reveals themed demonstration gardens exhibiting daylilies, curious perennials and other colorfully diverse blooms that scent the warm, dry air.

If you want to keep exploring the wines of the area, drive in any direction. The corner of Steiner and Shenandoah Rds is in the middle of some of the best wineries in the county, so a few minutes of exploring will lead you across the searing, sun-dry foothills to excellent small tasting rooms. Driving west for a minute and north on Bell Rd brings you to one of these exciting small growers, **9** **Story Winery**, which has a modest tasting room shaded by oaks. Their Hilltop zin is grown at 1649ft in elevation, one of the higher wines of the country, and it retains a residual sweetness that makes it a bit more mellow than most of its neighbors.

> **ASK A LOCAL**
>
> "People think of Amador, and they think of one thing – the heat. There's this perception that it's hotter up here than Napa. But when you look at it, we might get hotter earlier, but it rarely gets as hot – it almost never gets over 100°F. When those days are followed by cool breezes off the Sierras, the grapes love it. It helps them lock in the acidity, which makes a balanced wine."
> *Jim Dunlap, Amador City*

With these last stops, sweet wine and flowers, it's time for a return trip to Plymouth for dinner at **10** **Taste**, the region's most exceptional (and possibly only) fine dining option. Pull on the oversized fork-shaped door handle and creak over the rough-cut floorboards to be greeted by smells of fresh, seasonally changing dishes, all artfully presented. Small and large plate options include earthy mushroom "cigars" wrapped in a flaky phyllo and conventional fancy favorites like Chilean sea bass. In addition to their extensive list of wines from the surrounding area, they also offer a well-structured flight of Amador zins for those who just can't decide.

Connect with Hwy 49 and travel south for five minutes. On the left, just past the interchange for CA 16, is ⓫ **Drytown Cellars**, which sits perched above a dusty driveway. Drytown's winemaker, Allen Kreutzer, is on hand to greet visitors with big pours, slaps on the back and a cluttered trophy shelf. With his mess of blonde hair and gregarious, unpretentious hospitality, Kreutzer typifies Amador's spirit just as much as his wines – daring takes on zinfandel and syrah, pinot and barbera and an excellent coffee-flavored dessert wine.

The best part is, Kreutzer's wine is only part of the entertainment: he plays drums in blues and country bands half a mile up Hwy 49 at the ⓬ **Drytown Club**, known wryly as "the only wet spot in Drytown." Bikes line up in front of the big front porch on weekends, where local growers and wags mix amiably with sun-pink tourists. The bands that come in are probably unlikely to graduate to the big time anytime soon, but when they hit a groove on a balmy summer evening, people start to dance. Chasing a day of wine tasting with an evening of cold beer, surrounded by a good-natured mix of locals and a big friendly dog, it seems like anything could happen. In Amador County, that's just the way it should be.

Nate Cavalieri

FOOD & DRINK

TRIP INFORMATION

GETTING THERE
From Sacramento, take CA 99 west to Watt Ave. Take Watt to CA 16, which rolls over foothills for 30 miles into Plymouth.

DO
Amador Flower Farm
The demonstration gardens will help you envision your thumb turning green. ☎ 209-245-6660; www.amadorflowerfarm.com; 22001 Shenandoah School Rd, Plymouth; admission free; ⊘ 9am-4pm

EAT
Incahoots
Nothing breaks up the wine tasting like gnawing on smoky ribs with a crew of bikers. ☎ 209-245-4455; 9486 Main St, Plymouth; mains $5-23; ⊘ 11am-8pm Sun-Thu, 11am-9pm Fri & Sat

Taste
Exceptional local wines are paired with Amador's only four-star fine dining. ☎ 209-245-3463; 9402 Main St, Plymouth; www .restauranttaste.com; mains $31-50; ⊘ 5-11pm Mon-Fri, 4:30-11pm Sat & Sun

DRINK
CG di Arie
After inventing Cap'n Crunch, making wine is simple for this Amador newcomer. ☎ 209-245-4700; www.cgdiarie.com; 19919 Shenandoah School Rd, Plymouth; tasting free; ⊘ 10am-4:30pm Thu-Mon

Deaver Vineyards
A family affair? Pretty much everyone who works here has the last name Deaver. ☎ 209-245-5512; www.deavervineyard .com; 12455 Steiner Rd, Plymouth; tasting free; ⊘ 10am-4:30pm Thu-Mon

Drytown Cellars
This is the most fun tasting room in Amador thanks to a gregarious host. ☎ 209-245-3500; www.drytowncellars.com; 16030 Hwy 49, Drytown; tasting free; ⊘ 11am-5pm Thu-Sun

Drytown Club
A shady foothills bar with friendly locals, messy blues and lots of shiny bikes. ☎ 209-245-6722; www.drytownclub.com; 15950 Hwy 49, Drytown; ⊘ 3pm-2am Thu-Fri, 1pm-2am Sat & Sun; ⊛

Sobon Estate
Taste wine from some of the oldest vines in the county and tour the museum. ☎ 209-245-4455; www.sobonwine.com; 14430 Shenandoah Rd, Plymouth; tasting free; ⊘ 10am-5pm

Story Winery
A stable of unique, full-bodied zinfandels, some grown from old vines, put Story on the map. ☎ 209-245-6208; www.zin.com; 10525 Bell Rd, Plymouth; tasting free; ⊘ 10am-5pm

Wilderotter
This winery brought home prestigious honors for California's best red at the state fair. ☎ 209-245-6208; www.wilderottervineyard .com; 19890 Shenandoah School Rd, Plymouth; tasting free; ⊘ 10:30am-5pm Fri-Sun, 11am-4pm Mon & Thu

SLEEP
Amador Harvest Inn
The four flowery rooms in this cozy bed and breakfast make you feel like you're staying with your favorite aunt. ☎ 209-245-5512; www.amadorharvestinn.com; 12455 Steiner Rd, Plymouth; r $100

USEFUL WEBSITES
www.amadorwine.com

www.lonelyplanet.com/trip-planner

LINK YOUR TRIP

Central Coast High Life

WHY GO Live the lifestyles of the rich and famous, California coastal style. From the opulent heights of Hearst Castle, where movie stars and tycoons cavorted during the Roaring Twenties, throughout the budding Paso Robles wine country, indulgence is your top priority, from epicurean delights at in-the-know restaurants to over-the-top hotels.

TIME
1 – 2 days

DISTANCE
70 miles

BEST TIME TO GO
Mar – Oct

START
San Simeon

END
Paso Robles

ALSO GOOD FOR

FOOD & DRINK

Lording over California's central coast, sprawling hilltop ❶ Hearst Castle is a must-see stop. Darkly fictionalized in Orson Welles' masterpiece *Citizen Kane,* this palatial mansion was once owned by newspaper magnate William Randolph Hearst. Designed by San Francisco architect Julia Morgan, yet never entirely finished, the castle is a time capsule of luxe life during the 1920s and '30s, when everyone from Hollywood starlets (notably Hearst's mistress, Marion Davies) to foreign heads-of-state such as Winston Churchill stayed here. Morgan based the design of the main building on a Spanish cathedral and, over a period of decades, catered to Hearst's every design whim, deftly integrating the spoils of his European shopping sprees (ancient artifacts, monasteries etc). On evening guided tours, costumed docents bring history to life. The estate sprawls across acres of lushly landscaped gardens, accentuated by shimmering pools, and fountains and statues from ancient Greece.

South of Hearst Castle and San Simeon, the village of ❷ Cambria is a lone pearl cast along the central California coast. A fave place for modern-day bigwigs to retire, money is no object here, just like at the castle. Exit Hwy 1 and drift south along Moonstone Beach Dr past idyllic seascapes and a wooden boardwalk that ambles atop the windy bluffs. If you fall in love with the spot, as so many people have before you, linger overnight at the ❸ FogCatcher Inn, a hospitable beachfront hotel. Its faux English Tudor–style cottages harbor modern

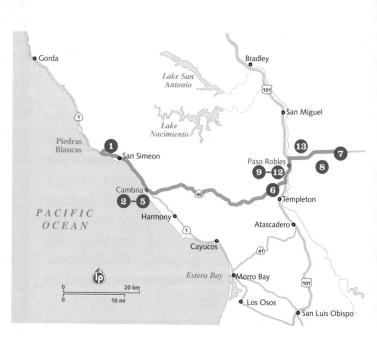

rooms, some with gas fireplaces that make bedding down on foggy coastal nights a sweet pleasure.

On the opposite side of Hwy 1, Main St winds through downtown Cambria into the East Village, stuffed with treasure-full antique shops, art galleries and European-style bakeries and coffee shops. En route, you might glimpse the amicable aficionados of the ❹ **Cambria Lawn Bowling Club**, who while away a few mornings here. Curious passersby are welcome to join in and learn this genteel medieval English sport on the green. Afterward, hobnob over lunch at ❺ **Indigo Moon**, an artisan cheese shop, wine bar and bistro, where chefs make fresh wine-country fare from bountiful produce grown nearby in the fertile inland valleys.

South of Cambria, Hwy 46 leads east into the emerging Paso Robles wine country. Franciscan missionaries brought the first grapes to this region in the late 18th century, but it wasn't until the 1920s that zinfandel vines took root here. In March, many of this blossoming viticultural region's 150 wineries throw open their doors – and more importantly, their rich cellars – for the Zinfandel Festival, followed by the Wine Festival in May and the Harvest Wine Tour in October.

Curvaceous Hwy 46 rises and falls through golden hills and green pasture lands where cows graze. Rural side roads off Hwy 46 lead north and south to family-owned vineyards and farm stands. Trust serendipity and follow any of them to discover the region's next break-out winery. Or make a bee-line along Hwy 46 to a time-tested, proven label: **6 Castoro Cellars.** Sporting a beaver as their mascot, these makers of "dam fine wine" have a tasting room shaded by cork trees and an arbor of grapevines. Outdoor summer concerts bring picnicking families rolling in.

Shortly thereafter, Hwy 46 runs into Hwy 101. If you haven't tasted your fill yet, jog north on Hwy 101 to pick up the continuation of Hwy 46 east

ASK A LOCAL

"What attracted me to living in Cambria was everything: the beauty of the ocean, a perfect climate, a forest that I love, and the peacefulness of it all. If you like to walk, take the Windsor Blvd exit off Hwy 1 and drive down to the waterfront. Where the road dead ends, a 2-mile round-trip bluff trail leads across **East West Ranch**. There's a feeling of serenity there, with no roads and no cars."
Sondra B, Cambria

past the big-shouldered giants of Paso Robles wineries: Martin & Weyrich, Firestone, EOS and Eberle. At the eastern edge of the vineyards, **7 Tobin James Cellars** lassos the region's Wild West angle – outlaw Jesse James' family once lived in the area – with its brassy, rule-breaking reds. Drive back west along Union Rd and follow the well-signed detour to zany **8 Clautiere Vineyard**, which has a tasting room worthy of a Tim Burton movie, piled high with Dr Seuss hats you can try on as you tipple rich Rhône-style red blends like "Mon Beau Rouge."

After a long afternoon spent wandering around sun-drenched vineyards, retreat to leafy downtown **9 Paso Robles**. Off Spring St, a grassy central park where kids are always at play is ringed by more wine-tasting rooms, gourmet food and wine shops and urbane boutiques. Specializing in Spanish-spiced cuisine, **10 Villa Creek** will win you over just with its bar menu, but it's in the tall-ceilinged dining room, which mimics an estate wine cellar, that chef

"...a tasting room worthy of a Tim Burton movie, piled high with Dr Seuss hats you can try on..."

Tom Fundaro really wows. Villa Creek's own heady vintages garnered a nod from Robert Parker. A few blocks away at more modern **11 Artisan**, chef Chris Kobayashi often ducks out of the kitchen just to make sure you like his contemporary renditions of classic American cuisine. Both chefs take advantage of organic produce, wild-caught seafood and sustainably farmed meats.

Then retire in style to downtown boutique **12 Hotel Cheval**, where you can cocoon with your lover in an art-splashed aerie, or live the winemaker's dream at **13 Villa Toscana Bed & Breakfast**, which imports a little bit of Tuscany to central California, with its cloistered walkways, sunny courtyard and sumptuous suites.

Sara Benson

TRIP INFORMATION

GETTING THERE
From San Francisco, drive Hwy 101 south to Paso Robles, then Hwy 46 west to Hwy 1 north. From Los Angeles, take Hwy 101 north to San Luis Obispo, then Hwy 1 north.

DO
Cambria Lawn Bowling Club
Call ahead to confirm lawn-bowling club hours. ☎ 805-927-3364; Joslyn Recreational Center, 950 Main St, Cambria; ☽ meet at 9:15am Mon, Wed, Fri & Sat

Hearst Castle
Reserve guided tours as far in advance as possible. ☎ info 805-927-2020, reservations 800-444-4445; www.hearstcastle.com; 750 Hearst Castle Rd, San Simeon; tours adult/child from $20/10; ☽ hours vary, 1st tour usually 8:20am

EAT
Artisan
New American cuisine shines, thanks to organic produce, wild-caught seafood and sustainably farmed meat. ☎ 805-237-8084; www.artisanpasorobles.com; 1401 Park St, Paso Robles; mains $12-30; ☽ 11am-10pm Mon-Sat, 10am-10pm Sun

Indigo Moon
Breezy patio tables complement market-fresh salads, toasted sandwiches and crunchy sweet-potato fries. ☎ 805-927-2911; 1940 Main St, Cambria; mains $6-25; ☽ 11am-4pm daily, 5-9pm Wed-Sun

Villa Creek
Dine like a don in the winery's formal restaurant, or perch casually at the bar for *carne asada* tacos made with Hearst Ranch beef. ☎ 805-238-3000; www.villacreek.com; 1144 Pine St, Paso Robles; mains $20-40; ☽ 5:30-10pm

DRINK
Castoro Cellars
Husband-and-wife team produce custom-crush wines, including some with organic grapes from Whale Rock Vineyards. ☎ 805-238-0725; www.castorocellars.com; tasting fee free-$5; 1315 N Bethel Rd, Templeton; ☽ 10am-5:30pm

Clautiere Vineyard
Don't let the whimsical, devil-may-care attitude fool you: serious Rhône-style blends and hard-to-find varietals delight connoisseurs. ☎ 805-237-3789; www.clautierevineyard.com; tasting fee $5; 1340 Penman Springs Rd, Paso Robles; ☽ noon-5pm

Tobin James Cellars
Boisterous Old West–styled saloon pours bold, teasingly named red varietals, like the "Liquid Love" late-harvest zinfandel. ☎ 805-239-2204; www.tobinjames.com; tasting free; 8950 Union Rd, Paso Robles; ☽ 10am-6pm; ♣

SLEEP
FogCatcher Inn
Seaside hotel delivers high-quality rooms; ask for a hand-drawn, helpfully annotated area map. ☎ 805-927-1400, 800-425-4121; www.fogcatcherinn.com; 6400 Moonstone Beach Dr, Cambria; r $110-360; ♿ ♣

Hotel Cheval
About a dozen rooms with California king beds and spa-worthy amenities fill this downtown hideaway. ☎ 805-226-9995, 866-522-6999; www.hotelcheval.com; 1021 Pine St, Paso Robles; r $195-375

Villa Toscana Bed & Breakfast
Move over, Napa: the winemaker's villa is tailor-made for romantic luxury. ☎ 805-238-5600; www.myvillatoscana.com; 4230 Buena Vista, Paso Robles; r $425-635

LINK YOUR TRIP

www.lonelyplanet.com/trip-planner

San Luis Obispo Wild Wildlife

WHY GO Kayak around Morro Rock, watch migratory birds on the Pacific Flyway, wander through an elfin forest and visit a beachfront monarch butterfly grove – it's nothing but all-natural fun here. Let California State Park Interpreter Michael Connolly show you where the wild things really are.

Happily stranded halfway between San Francisco Bay and LA, the laid-back college town of ❶ San Luis Obispo is a gateway to cool coastal adventures. Heading north or south along Hwy 1, you'll discover fishing is the backbone of the coastal communities ringed around San Luis Obispo and Estero Bays. These beach towns are also a haven for outdoor pursuits, both on land and in the chilly ocean water – and where there's natural beauty, there's also a cache of wildlife, from tiny tidepool creatures to ginormous gray whales. For this trip, we've teamed up with educational naturalist Michael Connolly to sniff out the coast's top wildlife-watching opportunities.

As you pull into Morro Bay, ❷ Morro Rock dominates the seascape. Connolly points out that "this geologic sentinel has been used as a landmark by mariners for hundreds of years." Drive north of the marina, with its small fishing fleet that is at the heart of this community, and out to the base of the rock. Indigenous Chumash tribespeople are the only ones who are legally allowed to climb the rock today, because peregrine falcons make their nests there. Bring binoculars to spy these aggressive flyers with gunmetal-gray wings, banded bellies and black-tipped tails.

Returning to the embarcadero, Connolly asks you to "take a minute to sniff the air, as it changes from the saltiness of the sea to the more organic aromas of the bay." Then get a different perspective

TIME
2 days

DISTANCE
85 miles

BEST TIME TO GO
Dec – Mar

START
San Luis Obispo

END
San Luis Obispo

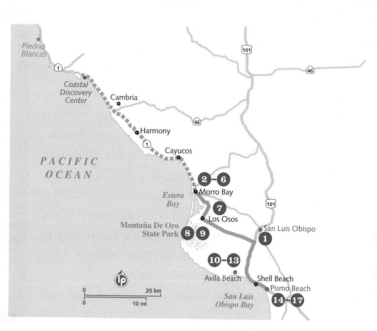

on the rock with ❸ **Sub-Sea Tours**. Their yellow semisubmersible tour boats have underwater viewing windows – just about the next best thing to scuba diving – so you can peek at underwater kelp forests where sea otters and fish dart about. In summer, humpback whales feed off Morro Bay. But you're more likely to see harbor seals and sea lions than a whale breaching as you paddle around the bay in a rental kayak.

"…underwater viewing windows (let) you peek at underwater kelp forests where sea otters and fish dart about."

In ❹ **Morro Bay State Park**, make time for the Museum of Natural History, where families can explore the estuary's ecosystem. Look over the stuffed models of common birds, including great egrets, cormorants, western gulls, short-billed dowitchers, long-billed curlews and more. You can join docent-guided tours of the park's great blue heron rookery, hidden in eucalyptus trees. In January, birders flock together for the Morro Bay Bird Festival, offering specialist-led tours of more diverse habitats, from woodlands to wetlands. Morro Bay's unique position on the Pacific Flyway, about halfway between San Francisco and LA, means that over 200 species can be spotted during the festival's long weekend.

For a good night's sleep in Morro Bay, Connolly recommends the garden-shaded ❺ **Inn at Morro Bay** for the "tranquillity of overlooking the calm end of Morro Bay." He adds: "Although a lot of motels say that their best feature is their ocean views, they're superlative here." From the outside, this two-story motor lodge with brick-paved driveway looks much smaller and simpler than it really is. Most renovated rooms have featherbeds and gas fireplaces to ward off gloomy coastal fog. Connolly eats further north on Hwy 1 at the **6** **Taco Temple**, where the exuberant California fusion flavors are reflected in the crayon-box colors on the seafood shack's exterior. At the next table, there might be fishers talking about the old days or a group of starving, dog-tired surfers. Connolly's fave dish is the chicken burrito: it "has an entire salad of vegetables wrapped up inside, and it's as big as my arm."

A small patch of wilderness that even many locals don't know of, **7** **El Moro Elfin Forest** hides in a residential subdivision of Los Osos. The town was named by Spanish explorer Gaspar de Portolá in 1769 after he encountered grizzly bears in the valley. (Don't be alarmed: the last grizzly was extirpated from California in 1922; the only ones seen hereabouts today are the ornamental statues on the bridge coming into town.) Inside this diverse ecological niche, traipse along a boardwalk through a pygmy forest of oak trees, and over ancient sand dunes sheltering a unique plant community, for impressive views of the Morro Bay estuary. Connolly advises walkers to "look carefully for coast horned lizards, which blend into the background to hide from predators, such as hawks and coyote, using cryptic coloration."

DETOUR Nearly extinct 100 years ago, elephant seals have made a remarkable comeback along California's coast. From mid-December through March, behemoth bulls return to the beach, followed by females, who soon give birth to pups. The easiest spot to observe the seals is at a vista point 4.8 miles north of Hearst Castle, a 45-minute drive north of Morro Bay. At Hearst State Beach, visit the **Coastal Discovery Center** (☎805-927-6575), on Hwy 1 opposite the entrance to Hearst Castle, to get acquainted with local wildlife.

Further south along the coast, **8** **Montaña de Oro State Park** (simply called "MdO" by locals) is a prize in California's state-park system. It was named "Mountain of Gold" by Spanish explorers, not because any gold was ever found here, but for the golden wildflowers that bloom here in spring, including native poppies. Along the winding entrance road to the state park, the sculpted bluffs of the Pacific at last come into view. "The wind often blows more strongly here than anywhere else on the SLO County coast," Connolly remarks. He occasionally conducts free public astronomy programs here, especially during the Perseid meteor shower in mid-August.

Pull off at Spooner's Cove. Here the grinding of the Pacific and North American plates has uplifted and tilted sedimentary layers of submarine rock, now visible from shore. "Archaeological evidence, such as midden piles containing abalone shells and projectile points, as well as *morteros* (bedrock mortars), are evidence that this spot was once a populous Native American settlement," Connolly tells us. If you go tidepooling, be careful to only touch marine creatures like sea stars, limpets and crabs with the back of one hand, to avoid disturbing them.

Take time out for a short jaunt along the beach and the bluffs, or drive further uphill to the signed trailhead for the 7-mile loop trail tackling Valencia and Oats Peaks. Connolly recommends the latter as a great wilderness escape. "You feel like you're really getting into primitive nature." You'll probably feel some sore muscles, too, ones you'd forgotten you even had, by the time the trail chews you up and spits you out back near the **9 Montaña de Oro State Park Campground**. "Tucked into a small canyon, this is an ideal place to camp: not so close to the shore as to be windy and cold, but close enough to the beach to stay pleasantly cool," Connolly advises. With fewer campsites than many other places along California's central coast, it's typically less crowded here.

South of San Luis Obispo, Hwy 101 passes the turnoff for **10 Avila Beach**. Take your tired self, worn out by all that kayaking and walking against the stiff coastal winds, to **11 Sycamore Mineral Springs**. "These natural springs are surprising, because they're not the first thing you think of as being part of California's central coast," says Connolly. He calls the private hot tubs with wooden decks perched on a hillside "nothing less than dreamy." His favorite time for a long, hot soak in the springs is after dark, when the star-filled skies are visible – that is, unless the coastal fog has already rolled in.

THAR SHE BLOWS!

Almost every port town along California's central coast offers whale-watching boat tours, from Monterey south to Santa Barbara. Gray whales, which migrate from their summer feeding grounds in the arctic Bering Sea to their breeding grounds in Baja, can be spotted off the coast from December through April. Expect to pay $30 to $45 per adult for a two- or three-hour whale-watching trip leaving from Port San Luis or Morro Bay.

Fronting the beach, **12 Avila Grocery & Deli** is a local institution. Connolly says, "It's not simply a market. It's a place to get real flavor as you hang with a local crowd." The entire town of Avila Beach had to be rebuilt from scratch after the environmental catastrophe of the 1992 Unocal underground oil spill, which contaminated the beach and decimated sea otter populations. The Avila Grocery building is still the original, though, having been towed back to Front St after all the other buildings were razed and the beach dug up. If it's a sunny day, take your meal outside onto the new beachfront promenade.

Further along at the north end of the coastal road is **13 Port San Luis**, which harbors a historic California lighthouse. "Its creaky, weather-worn pier is used by one of the biggest fishing operations on the central coast," Connolly tells us. Although most visitors would expect to hear a foghorn sounding in the harbor, it's the bark of harbor seals or the pip of a baby sea otter that you're more likely to hear coming from underneath the pier. Stroll past fresh seafood markets and shacks to the end of the pier, where you can gaze out over the choppy waters.

Make a final wildlife-watching stop further south in ⑭ **Pismo Beach** at the ⑮ **Monarch Butterfly Grove**. To find the grove, look for a gravel parking pullout on the west side of Hwy 1, south of Pismo State Beach's North Beach Campground. Black-and-orange migratory monarch butterflies typically cluster in this shady grove of eucalyptus trees from late October through February. "A single butterfly always catches your eye, but imagine thousands of them fluttering almost in sync in this small grove," says Connolly. In fact, it's the most populous viewing site for monarch butterflies in the western United States. During the winter migration season, volunteers can tell you more about these insects' astonishing journey, which outlasts any single generation of butterflies.

In Pismo Beach, a classic California beach town with a retro vibe, Connolly has stayed at the ⑯ **Sandcastle Inn**, where many of the rooms are mere steps away from the sand and the Pacific. His advice? "The best suite in the house is perfect for a marriage proposal. Just crack open a bottle of wine at sunset on the ocean-view patio. Take it from me, it works like a charm!" You won't need reservations at the nearby ⑰ **Cracked Crab** restaurant, where the famous dish is a bucket of seafood. "When it gets dumped at your table, with flying bits of fish, Cajun sausage, red potatoes and corn cobs," Connolly advises, "make sure you're wearing one of the plastic bibs with a happy red crab printed on it." Unleash your inner Dali with crayons on the white butcher paper–covered tables, while your fresh seafood is being prepped and perfectly cooked.

Sara Benson

TRIP INFORMATION

GETTING THERE
San Luis Obispo is on Hwy 101, about halfway between San Francisco and Los Angeles.

DO

El Moro Elfin Forest
Free guided nature walks given on the third Saturday morning of the month. ☎ 805-528-0392; www.slostateparks.com; off Santa Ysabel Ave, Los Osos; admission free; ☼ 24hr; ♿ ☻

Monarch Butterfly Grove
A shady roadside haven for migratory monarchs. ☎ 800-443-7778; www.monarch butterfly.org; north of Grand Ave, Pismo Beach; admission free; ☼ sunrise-sunset; ♿

Montaña de Oro State Park
Come prepared for wet, windy weather, even if the sun is shining inland. ☎ 805-528-0513; www.parks.ca.gov; Pecho Rd, Los Osos; admission free; ☼ sunrise-sunset; ♿

Morro Bay State Park
Picnic on the waterfront, play golf or go hiking up the *cerros* (hills). ☎ 805-772-2694; www.parks.ca.gov; Morro Bay State Park Rd, Morro Bay; admission free, museum donation $2; ☼ sunrise-sunset, museum 10am-5pm; ♿

Sub-Sea Tours
Make reservations in advance, especially during summer. ☎ 805-772-9463; www.subseatours .com; 699 Embarcadero, Morro Bay; tours from adult/child $14/7, 2hr kayak rental per person $12; ☼ 10am-5pm, tours 11am-4pm; ♿

Sycamore Mineral Springs
Rent your own private hillside hot tub or pick from spa services; reservations advised. ☎ 805-595-7302, 800-234-5831; www.syca moresprings.com; 1215 Avila Beach Dr, Avila Beach; hot-tub per person per hr $13-15; ☼ 7am-midnight Mon-Thu, 7am-2am Fri-Sun

EAT

Avila Grocery & Deli
Old-fashioned service marries modern flavor at this popular beachfront spot. ☎ 805-627-1575; www.avilagrocery.com; 354 Front St, Avila Beach; mains $6-8; ☼ 7am-7pm; ♿

Cracked Crab
Fresh seafood is the staple at this super-casual, family-owned grill. ☎ 805-773-2722; www.crackedcrab.com; 751 Price St, Pismo Beach; mains $9-48; ☼ 11am-9pm Sun-Thu, 11am-10pm Fri & Sat; ♿

Taco Temple
Be enlightened by Cal-Mex fusion fare. ☎ 805-772-4965; 2680 Main St, Morro Bay; mains $5-11; ☼ 11am-9pm Mon & Wed-Sat, 11am-8:30pm Sun

SLEEP

Inn at Morro Bay
Rooms run the gamut of views and amenities, but most are airy. ☎ 805-772-5651; www.innatmorrobay.com; 60 State Park Rd, Morro Bay; r $60-220; ♿

Montaña de Oro State Park Campground
Hike-in environmental sites and horse camps available. ☎ 800-444-7275; www.reserve america.com; Pecho Rd, Los Osos; sites $11-15; ♿ ☻

Sandcastle Inn
Eastern seaboard-style furnishings complement rooms and suites, some with sundecks. ☎ 805-773-2422; www.sandcastleinn.com; 100 Stimson Ave, Pismo Beach; r $110-310; ☻

USEFUL WEBSITES
www.visitslo.com
www.classiccalifornia.com

LINK YOUR TRIP

www.lonelyplanet.com/trip-planner

SOUTHERN CALIFORNIA TRIPS

LA may be a freeway (and a traffic-clogged one at that) but Southern California is much more. Everybody has an image, mood or fantasy linked to the place, thanks largely to Hollywood, the company town for a massive proportion of the world's entertainment. Countless TV shows and movies are shot here, where a mundane coastal park can become Korea, and a rocky outcrop an alien planet. But it doesn't always require a screen for SoCal to transport you. It's the melting pot of the nation: food, culture and even celebrities arrive from elsewhere and are transformed into something new. Even those who have been here for ages are ready for a new age; spas and places centered on "me" are common. If, however, your vision of the region is only the sybaritic coast, from Santa Barbara to the beach towns of the OC to the perfect climes of San Diego, then be ready for a surprise. Head east to the empty, mysterious and forbidding deserts. Death Valley is a stark reminder that all good things come to an end.

PLAYLIST ♫

Half the state's population and the music industry call Southern California home; no wonder a playlist could be in the hundreds, if not thousands. Here's a mix of new and old, legendary and merely familiar, to serenade you on the freeway.

- "LA Woman," The Doors
- "I Love LA," Randy Newman
- "Bad Luck," Social Distortion
- "Californication," Red Hot Chili Peppers
- "Welcome to the Jungle," Guns n' Roses
- "Come On, Let's Go," Ritchie Valens
- "San Diego Serenade," Tom Waits
- "California Soul," The Fifth Dimension

★ BEST TRIP

SOUTHERN CALIFORNIA'S BEST TRIPS

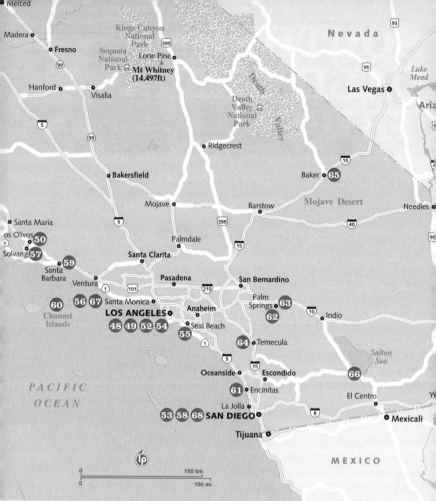

SOUTHERN CALIFORNIA TRIPS

48 Hours in Los Angeles

WHY GO If LA's celebrities "Are just like us!" is LA just like Boise? Well, yes, if Boise bordered 75 miles of sun-dappled coast, basked in the glow of a $275-million concert hall, hosted the Oscars, lured gourmands to savory world-class restaurants. But let's just admit it, shall we? Sometimes leaving home is good.

TIME
2 days

BEST TIME TO GO
Year-round

START
Walt Disney Concert Hall

END
Santa Monica State Beach

According to LA lore, a wannabe starlet once asked Bette Davis for advice on the best way to get into Hollywood. "Take Fountain," was Davis' reply, referencing a lesser-known avenue that runs parallel to Sunset Blvd. Bitchy, perhaps. Practical, yes. But just the attitude needed for navigating this glorious mash-up of a city. In 48 hours you can stroll Hollywood Blvd, nab a studio tour, dine at world-class restaurants, savor a travertine-framed sunset, shop in celebrity style and spend a morning at the beach. Flexibility is key, and if you hear or see the word "Sig-alert," get off the freeway fast.

Downtown, long known for a bustling Financial District that emptied at night, is in the midst of a massive Renaissance that's attracting party animals as well as full-time residents. The symbol of the revitalization is the ❶ **Walt Disney Concert Hall**, the landmark that launched a thousand metaphors. Billowing ship? Blooming rose? Silver bow? No matter which comparison you prefer, it's agreed that this iconic structure – designed by Frank Gehry and completed in 2003 – kick-started Downtown's rebirth. Cascading escalators whisk visitors from the parking garage directly into the airy lobby, where tours highlight Gehry's exquisite attention to detail – air-conditioning units are hidden inside smooth Douglas fir columns – throughout the building and gardens.

Just across Grand Ave, hard hats construct the Grand Ave Cultural Corridor, a high-end cluster of shops, hotels and restaurants set for a

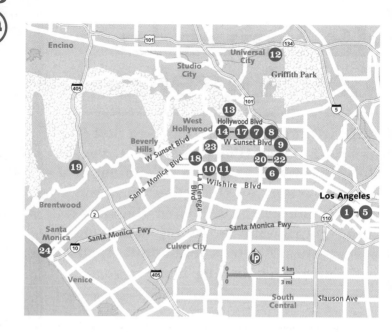

2011 completion. Stroll south to the postmodern charms of the ❷ **Museum of Contemporary Art**, a minimalist masterpiece housing a rotating collection of avante-garde exhibits in its underground galleries. Grand Ave then takes a watch-your-balance plunge before crossing 5th St. Peek inside the 1926 ❸ **Richard Riordan Central Library** on your right to ogle the 64ft-high rotunda with a 42ft span. Here, a 1-ton chandelier laughs in the face of fault lines, hanging with optimistic audacity above a stark marble floor.

Another two blocks – plus an escalator and elevator ride – will take you to the ❹ **Rooftop Bar at the Standard Hotel** and 360-degree views of twinkling city lights, flickering freeways and white-capped mountains. Plot your arrival for weeknights or early evening on the weekend. You'll enjoy the view and the highlights – comfy space pods, fireside lounges – without the long line, $20 cover and maddening crush of scenesters (no offense to scenesters, it's just the numbers that annoy). For downtown lodging without the scene, consider the ❺ **Figueroa Hotel**. Here, a festive Spanish-style lobby, Moroccan-themed rooms and a welcoming poolside bar infuse the hotel with a refreshing join-the-caravan conviviality.

For dinner, the evening can go one of two ways – *burratas* or burgers. For the former, you'll need to be organized (reservations accepted one month ahead) or a little bit lucky because Nancy Silverton and Mario Batali's bustling ❻ **Osteria Mozza** has been the hottest table in town since opening in mid-2007. The highlight at this stylish Melrose and Highland mecca is the central, first-come-first-served mozzarella bar where Silverton whips up *burratas, bufalas* and other Italian cheese-based delicacies. The more casual – but almost equally crowded – Pizzeria Mozza is next door.

So…no one's moved from the mozzarella bar? Consider a deal with bright red **7 Lucky Devils** on Hollywood Blvd, just a short drive north via Highland Ave. The Kobe Diablo, a thick Kobe beef patty slathered with avocado, double-smoked bacon and Vermont cheddar, is so gob-smackingly tasty you'll be tempted to curse aloud. Or you can take another bite, sip one of 15 draft beers, and settle in for some Hollywood people-watching. Cool fact? The owner's Lucky Vanous, the hunky model from the 1990's Diet Coke ads. Just sayin'.

Clubs and condos – not to mention cranes – are transforming the once gritty **8 Hollywood & Vine** intersection into LA's next "it" neighborhood. One popular store that made its mark in the area before things got trendy is **9 Amoeba Music**. For vinyl and liner notes, follow Cahuenga Blvd south from Hollywood Blvd to Amoeba's neon-lit, warehousey digs. Here, the click, click, click of customers flipping through hundreds of thousand of CDs, DVDs and vinyl is soothing in a party-like-it's-1989 sort of way. Slip into nearby Velvet Margarita for tequila sipping and Day of the Dead decor, embrace the historic, divey charms of the Frolic Room, or simply chill out with an acoustic show at Hotel Café.

HAPPY BIRTHDAY, PHILLIPPE

Celebrating your 100th birthday is a big deal in LA, especially since nobody here is a day over 29. It's even more remarkable when the centennial belongs to a restaurant, in this case downtown's **Philippe the Original** (www.philippes.com), which opened in 1908. The restaurant is still hauling in hungry hordes craving juicy French dip sandwiches, created here decades ago by the original Philippe. With 9¢ coffees, sawdust-covered floors and communal tables, Philippes remains a thriving cultural crossroads. North of Union Station, it's worth a trip.

For Mid-City shut-eye, consider the retro charms of the **10 Beverly Laurel Motor Hotel**, the nondescript blue-gray building hiding in plain sight on Beverly Blvd south of Hollywood. Look for the Coffee Shop sign over Swingers, the late-night diner across from the lobby. Inside the hotel, framed photographs and diamond-patterned bedspreads add a hint of style to basic rooms which include an in-room fridge, microwave and sink.

Even the breakfast joints have valet service in LA. Just watch the perpetual flow of cars unloading by the beige umbrellas outside **11 Toast**. Here, parents with strollers, tattooed hipsters, gossiping quartets and an occasional recognizable face come for gourmet breakfasts, easygoing ambiance, and maybe, just maybe, the scene. Add your name to the list and decide on breakfast based on the heaping plates swooping past (scramblettes are always a winner).

If Hollywood is the glamorous face of the entertainment business, then Burbank, with its massive studio production lots, is the hard-working stylist hustling to prep that mug. The two major studios anchoring Burbank are Universal Studios Hollywood and ⑫ **Warner Bros**. For an engaging behind-the-scenes tour, hop the Warner Bros tram for the 2¼-hour VIP tour. It winds past sound stages, sitcom sets and historic sites on the studio's 110-acre lot. Although no two tours are exactly the same, stops can include the Central Perk set, recognizable from the sitcom *Friends,* as well as the Transportation Garage where you'll find the Batmobile from *Batman Begins* and the Mystery Machine from *Scooby Doo.* Tell your guide at the start what you'd most like to see. The tour also includes a stop at the Warner Bros museum, a treasure trove of memorabilia with a well-stocked Harry Potter exhibit on the 2nd floor.

For a great-view detour, grab Mulholland Dr off Cahuenga Blvd, winding an eighth of a mile to the top of the hill. Turn left to enter the small ⑬ **Hollywood Bowl Overlook**. Even on hazy days, the sight of the Hollywood Bowl, Griffith Park, and the city unfurling below is memorable, highlighting the rarely considered juxtaposition of raw nature and urban sprawl. Continue west a third of a mile and make a quick left at the bend onto Outpost Dr, a twisting ride past homes tucked behind hedges, trees and canyon nooks, which will take you back to Hollywood Blvd. If you're in the mood for driving, pass Outpost Dr and continue west on Mulholland Dr. As this famous roadway winds along the summit of the Santa Monica Mountains, you'll have views of the San Fernando Valley to the north and Hollywood to the south. Turn left on woodsy Laurel Canyon Dr to return to Hollywood Blvd.

So Elvis, Batman and Charlie Chaplin walk into a bar...hey, it could happen, at least at the ⑭ **Hollywood & Highland** complex where celebrity impersonators cluster for photo-ops and tips. And while this block is over-the-top touristy, there's a certain undeniable energy that makes the freak-dodging, hustle-and-bustle confusion kind of fun. Be sure to wander the cement handprints and footprints left by big-screen stars from Clark Gable to Judy Garland to Johnny Depp outside ⑮ **Grauman's Chinese Theater**, a 1927 grand movie palace inspired by Chinese imperial architecture.

Crossing Hollywood Blvd here, it can be hard to envision Hollywood's A-listers walking the red carpet in front of the Kodak Theater. In contrast, inside the **16 Hollywood Roosevelt Hotel**, with its dark lobby lounge, antique couches and let-you-be vibe, it's easier to imagine the Hollywood heavyweights who've strolled through, from Marilyn Monroe to Montgomery Clift. The hotel hosted the first Academy Awards ceremony in 1929. Though recently revamped, rooms can feel small, and the elevator is unnerving if you've taken the plunge inside DCA's Tower of Terror. Overall, however, the hotel's history and Hollywood proximity make it an interesting, center-of-the-action choice.

Outside, more than 2000 pink marble stars line the sidewalks between La Brea Ave and Vine St – and a bit beyond – as part of Hollywood's Walk of Fame. Follow the stars east to **17 Skooby's** red-and-white placard reading "gourmet hotdogs." Why this splash of hotdog pretension? Who knows. The chili-slathered masterpieces at this tiny walk-up don't need a fancy adjective. Maybe it's because the fries have dipping sauce.

"…there's a certain undeniable energy that makes the freak-dodging, hustle-and-bustle confusion kind of fun."

To witness pretension on a grand scale, don't miss an Ivy drive-by. Tucked behind a white picket fence on uber-trendy **18 N Robertson Blvd**, the Ivy still holds court as Queen Bee for see-and-be-seen weekday lunches. Scan the patio for A-listers if camera-toting paparazzi crowd the sidewalk. Neighboring boutiques Kitson, Curve and Lisa Kline sell tiny clothes from hot designers to the young, beautiful and moneyed. For designer-style duds at way cheaper prices, follow Robertson north to grittier Melrose Ave, wandering east to the trendy boutiques, denim shops and thrift stores.

If you prefer natural and cultural splendor to commercial, spend your afternoon exploring the **19 Getty Center**, glowing in travertine splendor from its hill-top throne in the Santa Monica Mountains. The natural flow of walkways, skylights, fountains and courtyards on its 110-acre Richard Meier–designed "campus" encourages effortless wandering between Van Gogh's *Irises,* the bright Central Garden, and inspiring citywide vistas framed by Italian-cut stone. Sunsets are simply superb.

For dinner, we recommend two LA restaurants that should never be mentioned in the same breath: **20 AOC** and **21 El Coyote**. But sometimes it's nice to have choices. To maintain the ambiance set by the Getty, make a reservation at Chef Suzanne Goin's ever-popular AOC, a smooth-as-silk wine bar that glows like the wine cellar of a very close, very rich friend. With more than 50 wines by the glass, it's easy to complement the small-plates menu that purrs with such savory morsels as halibut with bacon, and grilled skirt steak with Roquefort butter.

For those who'd prefer to slurp potent margaritas, scarf messy Mexican combos and talk as loud as they want, suit up for a fun-lovin' dinner inside slightly divey El Coyote, the place with red-frocked waitresses and cars spilling out of the parking lot. Trust us, everyone in town's been here at some point. We've seen Nicole Richie chilling on the patio, and they say Sharon Tate ate her last dinner here. Down the street is ㉒ **New Beverly Cinema**, a 30-year-old indie movie house known for nightly double features and themed retrospectives organized by celeb hosts including Quentin Tarantino and Cody Diablo.

To fuel up on your last day, head to Sunset Strip's ㉓ **Griddle Cafe**, a grubby but happenin' spot in the shadows of the Directors Guild. For the best view of the tousled film students and hungry screenwriters that congregate here, sit at the U-shaped bar facing the narrow interior. The pancakes are huge, and the coffee French press. Get there early.

> **DETOUR**
>
> For a short hike to one of LA's best sweeping views, try the 1.4-mile **Charlie Walker Trail**, behind Griffith Park Observatory. This switch-backing path climbs up scorched, scrubby slopes to reach the summit of Mt Hollywood (not the location of the sign). Here, a summit view captures the San Gabriel mountains, the sprawling San Fernando Valley, downtown skyscrapers, and the city grid rolling west to the Pacific Ocean. Round-trip, the hike should take about an hour.

Best way to the beach? To paraphrase Bette Davis: Take Sunset. You'll pass the castlelike visage of Chateau Marmont (look up as you cross Crescent Heights) soon followed by rock icons Whiskey a Go Go, Viper Room and the Roxy. Oh-so-pink Beverly Hills Hotel lurks behind Hollywood hedges, followed by Star Maps, UCLA and posh Bel Air. Sunset then swoops over I-405, cruising west through Brentwood and Pacific Palisades before dropping at the Pacific Coast Hwy. Follow PCH south to ㉔ **Santa Monica State Beach**.

Once there, ride the pier's solar-powered Ferris wheel, pedal the bike path, or simply plop onto your towel on the wide beach and smile at the sun. For historic perspective, glance at the bluffs behind you. A palm-dappled greenway, Palisades Park, runs along the top, passing a marker denoting the western terminus of Route 66. Ponder for a second the appropriateness of America's famed romantic byway ending at this most gorgeous of spots. Then slather on another dollop of lotion and flip for those last few rays.

Amy C Balfour

TRIP INFORMATION

GETTING THERE

Los Angeles is located in Southern California, 381 miles south of San Francisco and 124 miles north of San Diego.

DO

Amoeba Music

Live performances, listening stations and a map are a few of the extras at this vinyl and CD emporium. ☎ 323-245-6400; www.amoeba.com; 6400 W Sunset Blvd; 🕑 10:30am-10:30pm Mon-Sat, 11am-9pm Sun

Getty Center

A driverless tram whisks visitors to art, architecture, gardens and stellar views. ☎ 310-440-7300; www.getty.edu; 1200 Getty Center Dr; admission free, parking $10; 🕑 10am-5:30pm Sun-Fri, 10am-9pm Sat; 🕭

Grauman's Chinese Theater

Stand in the footprints of Gable, Clooney and Schwarzenegger just west of Hollywood & Highland while 200 people jostle you. ☎ 323-463-9576; www.manntheatres.com; 6925 Hollywood Blvd; admission free; 🕭

Hollywood & Highland

Shops, restaurants and movie screens are just part of the spectacle at this towering Hollywood complex. ☎ 323-467-6412; www.hollywoodandhighland.com; 6801 Hollywood Blvd; admission free; 🕑 10am-10pm Mon-Sat, to 7pm Sun; 🕭

Museum of Contemporary Art (MOCA)

Collection spans 1940s to present. ☎ 213-626-6222; www.moca.org; 250 S Grand Ave; adult/under 12yr/student & senior $10/free/5; 🕑 11am-5pm Mon & Fri, to 8pm Thu, to 6pm Sat & Sun

New Beverly Cinema

Indie cinema screens double features and eclectically themed retrospectives. ☎ 323-938-4038; www.newbevcinema.com; 7165 W Beverly Blvd; general/senior & child/student $7/4/6

Richard Riordan Central Library

This 1926 building boasts a grand rotunda, stunning murals, whimsical cascading elevators and 2.1 million books. ☎ 213-228-7000; www.lapl.org; 630 W 5th St; admission free; 🕑 10am-8pm Mon-Thu, 10am-6pm Fri & Sat, 1-5pm Sun; 🕭

Walt Disney Concert Hall

Tours highlight architect Frank Gehry's attention to detail, but concert tickets are needed to see the acoustically precise auditorium. ☎ 323-850-2000 concert tickets, 213-972-4399 tours; www.laphil.com; 111 S Grand Ave; tours free; 🕑 10am-2pm most days

Warner Bros

Hop a tram for a two-hour tour in which the secrets of Hollywood are revealed – forced perspective, fancy facades and fake bricks. ☎ 818-972-8687; www.wbstudiotour.com; 3400 Riverside Dr, Burbank; tours $45, min age 8; 🕑 7:30am-7pm Mon-Fri, tours 8:20am-4pm

EAT & DRINK

AOC

From goat cheese to blue cheese, fancy fromages fill one full page on the menu and add to the epicurean fun. ☎ 323-653-6359; www.aocwinebar.com; 8022 W 3rd St; mains $9-21; 🕑 dinner

El Coyote

Combos are messy and margaritas are strong at this lively Mexican cantina that's been pulling in locals for years. ☎ 323-939-2255; www.elcoyotecafe.com; 7312 Beverly Blvd; mains under $15; 🕑 11am-10pm Sun-Thu; 🕭

Rooftop Bar at the Standard Hotel

Citywide views from the roof are worth hipper-than-thou hassles to get there. ☎ 213-892-8080; 550 S Flower St; cover after 7pm Fri & Sat $20; 🕑 noon-1:30am

Griddle Cafe

Items named Banana Nana Pancakes and Peanut Bubba Crunchy French Toast make reading the menu fun. ☎ 323-874-0377;

7916 W Sunset Blvd; mains $8-12; ☾ 7am-4pm Mon-Fri, 8am-4pm Sat & Sun

Lucky Devils

From Kobe burgers and veggie burgers to fries and shakes, it's all good. ☎ 323-465-8259; 6613 Hollywood Blvd; mains $8-23; ☾ lunch & dinner; ♿

Osteria Mozza

Watch chef Nancy Silverton craft mouthwatering morsels from Italian cheese. ☎ 323-297-0100; www.mozza-la.com; 6602 Melrose Ave; mains $11-30; ☾ dinner

Skooby's

Be sure to order fries with that chili-smothered dog. ☎ 323-468-3647; www.skoobys.com; 6654 Hollywood Blvd; mains $2-8; ☾ 11am-midnight; ♿

Toast

Frothy lattes, hearty scrambles and valet parking at the corner of 3rd St and N Harper Ave. ☎ 323-655-5018; www.toastbakerycafe.net; 8221 W 3rd St; mains $8-17; ☾ 7:30am-11pm; ♿

SLEEP

Beverly Laurel Motor Hotel

Let the retro times roll at this spare but stylin' budget option close to Mid-City and Hollywood. ☎ 323-651-2441; 8018 Beverly Blvd; r $110, pet fee $25; ❋

Figueroa Hotel

Spanish touches and Moroccan-style rooms liven up this property, conveniently located next to the Staples Center. ☎ 213-627-8971; www.figueroahotel.com; 939 S Figueroa St; r $150-185, ste $225-265

Hollywood Roosevelt

Who said historic can't be hip? Open since 1927; reborn in 2005. ☎ 323-466-7000; www.hollywoodroosevelt.com; 7000 Hollywood Blvd; r $350, ste $350-520

USEFUL WEBSITES

www.at-la.com
http://theguide.latimes.com

LINK YOUR TRIP

www.lonelyplanet.com/trip-planner

As Seen on TV

WHY GO John Wayne sparing the life of Natalie Wood, Orson Welles plumbing the depths of dissolution with Marlene Dietrich, Captain Kirk battling a giant lizard: all these happened in and around LA. In two days, you can visit them all, and many more iconic film locations.

TIME
2 days

DISTANCE
210 miles

BEST TIME TO GO
Mar – Nov

START
Los Angeles

END
Venice

Start your tour at LA's most famous erection, ❶ City Hall. You can't help but hear Jack Webb's dull monotone: "This is the city, Los Angeles, California…" There's no need to go inside; rather, recall its role as symbol of law and order in *LA Confidential, DOA* and other noir classics like *Chinatown*.

About 5 miles northwest in the Hollywood Hills (look for that rather famous sign…) is LA's urban back yard, Griffith Park. There are film sites galore within its 4000 acres. But narrow your focus to arid ❷ Bronson Canyon, just five minutes north of the bustle of Hollywood. Many science-fiction films have used these rugged hillsides, including the 1956 version of the classic *Invasion of the Body Snatchers,* wherein Kevin McCarthy and Dana Wynter flee the possessed townfolk. The caves here served as the entrance to the Bat Cave in the camp 1960s TV series *Batman* and they provided the perfect frame as John Wayne decides not to off Natalie Wood in the climax of John Ford's *The Searchers*. (For this location, take Canyon Dr into Griffith Park. From the last parking lot, take a trail through a gate just south – not the continuation of the road to the north – and walk about a quarter of a mile.)

Just outside the park, celebrity-filled mansions line the serpentine roads. Catch views of LA's famous smog (and sometimes the skyline). One notable spread is the ❸ Ennis House, a 1924 concrete-block fantasy designed by Frank Lloyd Wright. Its movie résumé is long, including a role as Harrison Ford's home in *Blade Runner*.

HISTORY & CULTURE

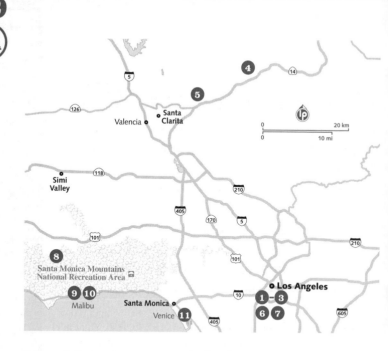

Science fiction and westerns remain the theme as you head to the outer reaches of the Studio Zone. Take Hwy 101 north to I-5, continue to Hwy 14

THE STUDIO ZONE

You can journey through decades of Hollywood history without traveling far thanks to the "Studio Zone," a region that stretches for 30 miles in all directions from the corner of Beverly and La Cienega Blvds in LA near Beverly Hills. Films shot in this zone don't have to pay extra travel fees to the crew and actors – a vital concern to penny-pinching producers and a bonus for day-tripping film buffs.

and head 15 miles east to LA County's **4** **Vasquez Rocks Park**. Huge ancient rocks angle sharply out of the desert here, providing an eye-catching backdrop for hundreds of westerns.

More recently they featured in *Blazing Saddles* and were the town of Bedrock in the live-action *Flintstones*. Four episodes of the original *Star Trek* TV series were shot here, including a memorable one in which William Shatner both chews the scenery and battles a huge homicidal lizard called a Gorn.

Backtrack west on Hwy 14 to Newhall and take Placerita Canyon Rd past some genteel horse ranches until you see the backside of an old west town on your left. **5** **Melody Ranch** has been used as the location for westerns going back to the 1930s. More recently, Al Swearengen, Calamity Jane, Seth Bullock and more spewed prodigious streams of profanity in the remarkable HBO series *Deadwood,* which was entirely shot here.

Finish your day back in LA at a classic Hollywood joint, the ⑥ **Dresden Restaurant**. It's so old-fashioned that it's fashionable again *and* it's the home six nights a week to Marty and Elayne, a pair of lounge singers of the old school (both appeared in the insider Hollywood comedy *Swingers*). Many movies have been shot here, including *Bugsy*. Finally, lay your head upon a down pillow at the ⑦ **Chateau Marmont**, where stars like Garbo, De Niro and Monroe have checked in and Belushi permanently checked out.

"You can almost hear the whup-whup-whup of helicopters and the strains of 'Suicide is Painless'…"

For day two, head to the hills northwest on Hwy 101 at ⑧ **Malibu Creek State Park**, which lies between the valley and the coast off Malibu Canyon Rd. Park in the last lot and follow a trail 4 miles west. You can almost hear the whup-whup-whup of helicopters and the strains of "Suicide is Painless" as you reach the location for the 4077th compound set used for both the movie and TV versions of *M*A*S*H*. Back at the campground, the administration building was built for Cary Grant and company in *Mr Blandings Builds His Dream House*.

Down the hill from the park is ⑨ **Malibu**, which may have the densest collection of celebrities anywhere (you decide whether that refers to IQ, number per square mile or both). Keep your eye peeled for eruptions of paparazzi, especially at ⑩ **Malibu Mutt's Grill**, the deceptively downscale burger joint in the deceptively simple Malibu Country Mart, where the local bold-type crowd like to slum with a hot dog.

Head south down the spectacular Southern California coast to ⑪ **Venice**. This ragtag beach town famous for its schlocky T-shirts, tattoo parlors and amazing sand has been the location for countless movies (and the opening of *Three's Company*). On the stretch of tatty Windward Ave, look for surviving arcaded Spanish-style buildings. These blocks were used for much of *Touch of Evil*, the cult classic set in a Mexican border town. The building at No 25 was the Ritz Hotel, where Charlton Heston foolishly leaves his wife, Janet Leigh, while Orson Welles and Marlene Dietrich take stock of their wasted lives. The landmark opening sequence was shot here as well.

Ryan Ver Berkmoes

ASK A LOCAL

"No SoCal visitor should miss exotic **Leo Carrillo Beach**, northwest of Malibu. The hidden coves (and cave) provided a romantic backdrop for *Pirates'* Johnny Depp & Keira Knightley, *The Karate Kid's* Elisabeth Shue & Ralph Macchio, *50 First Dates'* Adam Sandler & Drew Barrymore, and *Crossroads'* Britney Spears and…herself. Beware of the rough surf here; John Travolta & Olivia Newton-John almost got swept out to sea by a fierce sleeper wave (which you can see on DVD if you play the *Grease* opening in slo-mo)."
Harry Medved, Hollywood, author of Hollywood Escapes *and many more film books*

HISTORY &
CULTURE

TRIP INFORMATION

GETTING THERE
LA is a hub (and a freeway). From San Francisco, it is 350 miles on iconic Hwy 101.

DO
Bronson Canyon
Holy hole in the hill Batman! ☎ 323-913-4688; Canyon Dr, Griffith Park, Los Angeles; admission free; ⊙ dawn-dusk; ♿ 🐾

City Hall
For LA's civic symbol, it's what's on the outside that counts (although inside is also a popular film location). It's right downtown. **200 N Spring St at Temple St, Los Angeles**

Ennis House
The Day of the Locust, Blade Runner, Black Rain and *Rush Hour* are just a few of the movies shot at this landmark mansion, which is not open inside. ☎ 323-660-0607; www.ennishouse.org; 2655 Glendower Ave, Los Angeles

Malibu Creek State Park
Only Hollywood can take you from Korea to New England in a few minutes. ☎ 818-880-0367; www.parks.ca.gov; Malibu Canyon Rd, Calabasas; adult/child $8/4; ⊙ dawn to dusk; ♿ 🐾

Melody Ranch
The setting for *Deadwood* and many more westerns. ☎ 661-259-9669; www.melody

ranchstudio.com; 24715 Oak Creek Ave, Newhall; admission $40; ⊙ by appointment only

Vasquez Rocks Park
Travel back to the old west or another galaxy at these iconic rock formations. ☎ 661-268-0840; http://parks.co.la.ca.us/vasquez_narea.html; 10700 W Escondido Canyon Rd, Agua Dulce; admission free; ⊙ 8am-6pm; ♿ 🐾

EAT
Dresden Restaurant
So old it's new again. ☎ 323-665-4294; www.thedresden.com; 1760 N Vermont Ave, Hollywood; mains $25; ⊙ lunch Mon-Sat, dinner daily

Malibu Mutt's Grill
The place to munch a weinie with the famous. ☎ 310-456-1211; 3835 Cross Creek Rd, Malibu; mains $7; ⊙ 10am-8pm; ♿

SLEEP
Chateau Marmont
The funkiest celebrity hotel in town. ☎ 323-656-1010, 800-242-8328; www.chateaumarmont.com; 8221 W Sunset Blvd, Hollywood; r $350-785

USEFUL WEBSITES
www.moviesites.org
www.seeing-stars.com

LINK YOUR TRIP
www.lonelyplanet.com/trip-planner

TRIP

Scenic Byways & Highways

WHY GO From the Spanish padres to the film moguls of Hollywood, the cowboys to the Road Runner, SoCal's mountains and desert landscapes are the stuff of legend. Even some urban scenes are worth the drive. In the terrain that spawned a million car commercials, this time you get to be the driver.

Starting in the flatlands gives you something to aspire to, and there are plenty of peaks surrounding the lovely, wood-built hamlet of **1** Los Olivos, in the Santa Ynez Valley wine country. Stock up on supplies at small shops, take some *vino* for a picnic (and don't forget drinking water!), and begin your journey by heading southeast on CA 154, the San Marcos Pass Rd. It's pretty much a straight line for the 10 miles before your ascent, through fields the color of brown chalk or, if you're lucky, vineyards ripe with grapes, as you approach the mountains.

Enter the San Marcos Pass and rise through the Santa Ynez Mountains in the **2** Los Padres National Forest. In a bowl to your left is **3** Cachuma Lake, strikingly blue and a surprising find so high up. Around Paradise Rd are some popular hiking trails. Stop for lunch or drinks at **4** Cold Spring Tavern, an 1886 stop for stagecoaches, where game and beer are the specialty and the crowd runs from farmers to bikers, winemakers to vets and lovers young and old(er). Nearby, the tiny **5** Chumash Painted Cave State Historic Park showcases native Chumash petroglyphs, said to date back over four centuries. You'll need a small vehicle to reach it (sorry, no RVs).

As you descend through the pass, Santa Barbara and the Pacific shimmer before you. Turn left a few miles before the city at CA 192 (Foothill Rd) and take in the mansions of tony **6** Montecito. CA 192 changes names a couple of times, but follow the numbered route to

TIME
2 days

DISTANCE
420 miles

BEST TIMES TO GO
Mar – May &
Sep – Nov

START
Los Olivos,
Santa Barbara
County

END
Anza-Borrego
Desert State
Park

ALSO GOOD FOR

OUTDOORS

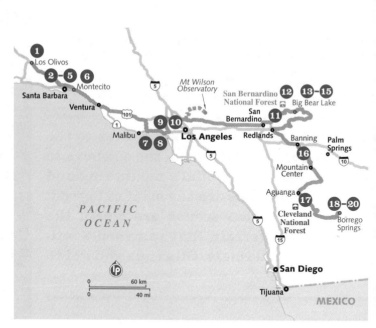

Olive Mill Rd, which links up to Hwy 101. From here, you'll have miles to contemplate California's stunning coast.

As you traverse Ventura County into LA County on Hwy 101, farmland gives way to the all-American suburbs of Thousand Oaks and Westlake Village. Exit at Las Virgenes Rd, which becomes **7 Malibu Canyon Rd**, and travel about 9 miles to the Pacific Coast Hwy (PCH). Of all the crossings between the valley and the ocean, Malibu Canyon's graceful curves and lack of habitation make it the favorite. After viewing all this natural beauty, stop for lunch at **8 Malibu Country Mart**; you never know which specimen of human beauty (aka celebrity) you might spy. Continue on PCH to Sunset Blvd, turn left and roll down the windows to catch the last whiff of the sea breeze as you head past the state parks and golf courses of **9 Pacific Palisades**.

After a few miles, I-405 north takes you to **10 Mulholland Drive**. You may feel like a celebrity yourself as you drive along the roof of LA. To your left, the grid of the San Fernando Valley seems interrupted only by the distant Angeles National Forest, while to your right are glimpses of the LA Basin, over chichi Bel Air, Westwood and Century City. Descend into the Valley via Laurel Canyon Blvd, to hook up again with Hwy 101. Bear to the left where it splits to become CA 134, speeding above the city of Glendale. CA 134 becomes CA 210 through the San Gabriel Valley – it's not the loveliest part of the route, but it is quick (it's a new freeway).

Amuse yourselves playing "license plates" or singing country-and-western tunes. Before you'll know it you'll be at CA 330, which diverts just before Redlands to become CA 18, ⑪ **Rim of the World Scenic Byway**, through the ⑫ **San Bernardino National Forest**. Its curves wend and wind through pine forests, the oranges and yellows of autumn leaves, and pure white above the snow line, up to ⑬ **Big Bear Lake**. It's a favorite getaway among Angelenos for hiking, cycling, boating, skiing in winter and spending the night at 6743ft.

The 1920s cabins of ⑭ **Grey Squirrel Resort** are a homey throwback, and the spicy chicken soup at the Nepalese, Indian and Tibetan specialist ⑮ **Himalayan Restaurant** is an authentic, welcome find.

DETOUR

Just past Glendale on CA 134, take CA 2 north, **Angeles Crest Hwy**, through the **Angeles National Forest**. The drive, via hair-raising curves above thousand-foot cliffs, is one of California's most stunning. Bonus: playing junior astronomer at **Mt Wilson Observatory** (www.mtwilson.edu), where discoveries led to the Big Bang Theory. Take a guided tour on weekends, or wander the grounds yourself (at 5710ft, there's quite the view). Allow two hours round trip, plus sightseeing time.

If you liked yesterday's drive, you'll love this morning's. The Rim of the World (here called CA 38) loops east from Big Bear back to Redlands, about one hour of mostly downhill driving. The gradual descent and relatively few curves mean that even the driver can enjoy the view. From Redlands, head east on I-10 to Banning, and turn off at CA 243, ⑯ **Palms to Pines Scenic Byway**. It's 29 miles to Mountain Center as the Sonora desert gives way to ponderosa forests, with cities and towns spread at your feet. The highway continues on CA 74 east toward Lake Hemet (stop for fishing if you like) and Kern Camp Summit (4917ft), and another 13 miles to CA 371 (Cahuilla Rd). From here travel 21 miles to Aguanga and turn left on CA 79, skirting part of the 460,000-acre ⑰ **Cleveland National Forest**, on your right for about the next 20 miles. California's southernmost national forest, it was the historic home of Luiseño, Cahuilla and Kumeyaay tribes, and later crisscrossed by conquistadors and miners – many of their ancient trails are still in use.

A few miles past Warner Springs, turn left onto San Diego County Rte S2 (San Felipe Rd) and left again after San Diego County Rte S22 (Montezuma Valley Rd) for the last leg of the journey. ⑱ **Borrego Springs** is the only settlement to speak of in ⑲ **Anza-Borrego Desert State Park**, the largest US state park outside Alaska. The descent into town via the Montezuma Grade is just as inspiring as the uphill that began our journey. Pick up information on trails for hiking and how to reach them at the excellent visitor center.

In Borrego Springs, check into the ⑳ **Palms Hotel**, a '50s-mod shell with pool, spa and very decent restaurant. Soak. You've earned it.

Andrew Bender

TRIP
50

TRIP INFORMATION

GETTING THERE
Via Hwy 101, Los Olivos is about 45 miles north of Santa Barbara or 55 miles south of San Luis Obispo.

DO

Anza-Borrego Desert State Park
Pick up maps and access info for hiking trails at the visitor center. ☎ 760-767-4205; www.parks.ca.gov; 200 Palm Canyon Dr, Borrego Springs; 9am-5pm daily Oct-May, 9am-5pm Sat & Sun Jun-Sep;

Big Bear Lake
Get maps, information and room reservations about Big Bear, from the national forest to shopping, from the Big Bear Lake Resort Association. ☎ 909-866-7000, 800-424-4232; www.bigbear.com; 630 Bartlett Rd; 8am-5pm, call center 8am-6pm Mon-Fri, 9am-5pm Sat & Sun

Cachuma Lake
A favorite for boating and fishing, with outdoor accommodations. ☎ 805-686-5050, 805-686-5054 recorded info; www.cachuma.com; admission vehicle $8, tent/RV sites $20/30, yurts $60-70;

Chumash Painted Cave State Historic Park
Four-century-old cave paintings by the native Chumash people off Hwy 154. ☎ 805-733-3713; www.parks.ca.gov; dawn-dusk;

Los Padres National Forest
Info and National Forest Visitor Passes from the visitor center. ☎ 805-968-6640; www.r5.fs.fed.us/lospadres; 6755 Hollister Ave, Suite 150, Goleta; 8am-4:30pm Mon-Fri

EAT

Cold Spring Tavern
Historic Americana roadhouse with wooden plank floors. Good for food; great for local color. ☎ 805-967-0066; www.coldspringtavern.com; 5595 Stagecoach Rd, Santa Barbara; mains lunch $9-13, dinner $17.50-28.50; 11am-3pm & from 5pm daily, 8am-11am Sat & Sun;

Himalayan Restaurant
Surprisingly snappy Indian, Nepalese and Tibetan cooking. ☎ 909-878-3068; www.himalayanbigbear.com; 672 Pine Knot Ave, Big Bear Lake; mains $9-15; 10:30am-9pm Mon-Thu, 10:30am-10pm Fri & Sat;

Malibu Country Mart
Enjoy outdoor dining and spot celebrities coming and going from Nobu, Tra di Noi and Taverna Tony. 3835 Cross Creek Rd, Malibu; various;

SLEEP

Grey Squirrel Resort
Charming 1920s cottages sleep two to 14, a mile from central Big Bear Lake. ☎ 909-866-4335, 800-381-5569; www.greysquirrel.com; 39372 Big Bear Blvd, Big Bear Lake; cottages $94-508;

Palms Hotel
Midcentury midluxury near Anza-Borrego trailheads. It has a decent restaurant too. ☎ 760-767-7788, 800-519-2624; www.thepalmsatindianhead.com; 2220 Hoberg Rd, Borrego Springs; r incl breakfast $159-229

USEFUL WEBSITES
www.fs.fed.us/r5/sanbernardino
www.parks.ca.gov

LINK YOUR TRIP
www.lonelyplanet.com/trip-planner

Kicking Down Route 66

WHY GO Search for the American Dream along Route 66, America's "Mother Road," which brought Dust Bowl refugees, Hollywood starlets and even hippies to California. Pull up alongside retro roadside relics, sleep at vintage motor lodges and stuff yourself at mom-and-pop diners. Spring, when desert wildflowers bloom, is best.

During the 1930s, '40s and '50s, California was the promised land for road-trippers on Route 66. Today you can still follow in their footsteps – or rather, their tire tracks. After running a gauntlet of Mojave Desert ghost towns, motor through railroad stops, such as Barstow and Victorville, then cross the Cajon Summit and wind down into the LA Basin, where crashing ocean waves await at the end of Santa Monica Pier.

At the Arizona border south of I-40, the ❶ Old Trails Arch Bridge carried the Depression-era Joad family across the Colorado River in the movie version of John Steinbeck's novel *Grapes of Wrath*. Drive west past ❷ Needles, a dusty throwback railroad town with a historic depot down by the river. Now under renovation, this depot is one of only a few frontier-era Harvey Houses left standing in the American West. West of Needles, follow to US Hwy 95 north of I-40 for 6 miles, then turn left onto Goffs Rd. Shaded by cottonwood trees, the 1914 Mission-style ❸ Goffs Schoolhouse stands as part of the best-preserved pioneer settlement in the Mojave Desert. Keep going on Goffs Rd through Fenner, crossing under I-40.

Turn right onto the National Old Trails Hwy. Potholed and crumbling in a romantic way, the USA's original transnational highway was established in 1912, more than a decade before Route 66 first ran

TIME
2 days

DISTANCE
325 miles

BEST TIME TO GO
Feb – Apr

START
Needles

END
Santa Monica

ALSO GOOD FOR

HISTORY & CULTURE

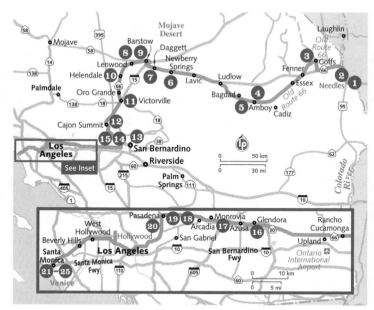

through here. The rutted highway races through tiny towns, sparsely scattered across the Mojave. Only a few landmarks interrupt the horizon, including vintage ❹ **Roy's Motel & Cafe**, a landmark water hole for decades of Route 66 travelers. It's east of ❺ **Amboy Crater**, an almost perfectly symmetrical volcanic cinder cone.

At Ludlow, turn right onto Crucero Rd and pass under I-40, then take the north frontage road west and turn left at Lavic Rd. Back on the south side of I-40, keep heading west on the National Old Trails Hwy. In Newberry Springs, look up the grizzled ❻ **Bagdad Cafe**, made famous by an indie movie in 1987. The highway passes under I-40 again on its way through Daggett, site of the harsh California inspection station faced by Dust Bowl refugees in *Grapes of Wrath*. Two old geezers smoking American Spirits by the railroad tracks is about all the action Daggett sees nowadays, though. Pay your respects to early desert adventurers like Death Valley Scotty at the old ❼ **Stone Hotel**. Drive west to Nebo Rd, turning left to rejoin I-40.

"Loved by Harley bikers, this rural byway is like a scavenger hunt for Mother Road ruins..."

Exit the interstate onto Main St, which runs through Barstow, a railroad settlement and historic crossroads, where murals adorn empty buildings downtown. Follow 1st St north across the Mojave River over a trestle bridge to the 1911 Harvey House, nicknamed "Casa del Desierto," designed by Western architect Mary Colter. Next to a small railroad museum is the **8** **Route 66 "Mother Road" Museum**, displaying black-and-white historical photographs and odds and ends of everyday life in the early 20th century. Drive north on 1st St to Old Hwy 58, turn left and look for a Western pioneer wagon outside **9** **Idle Spurs Steakhouse**. With a tree growing inside the dining room, this cowboy classic has been dishing up prime rib and fruit cobbler since 1950.

Leaving Barstow via Main St, rejoin the National Old Trails Hwy west. It curves alongside the Mojave River through Lenwood, Helendale and Oro Grande. Loved by Harley bikers, this rural byway is like a scavenger hunt for Mother Road ruins, including antique filling stations and tumble-down motor courts. Colorful as a box of crayons, **10** **Elmer's Place** is a roadside folk-art collection of "bottle trees," made from recycled soda-pop and beer containers, telephone poles and railroad signs.

Cross over the Mojave River on a 1930s steel-truss bridge, then roll into downtown Victorville. Opposite the railroad tracks, poke around a mishmash of historical exhibits and contemporary art inside the small **11** **California Route 66 Museum**. The museum building itself was once the Red Rooster Cafe, a famous Route 66 roadhouse. Turn right onto 7th St, then get back on I-15 south over daunting Cajon Summit, a tough haul for Route 66–era autos. Truckers aren't the only ones who know to take the Oak Hill Rd exit for the **12** **Summit Inn**. Surrounded by transportation memorabilia, this old-fashioned truck stop serves ostrich and buffalo burgers and sweet date shakes.

> **ASK A LOCAL**
>
> "The **Aztec Hotel** (☎626-358-3231; 311 W Foothill Blvd, Monrovia) is just about as original as it can be. It's on the old alignment of Route 66. I never get tired of dropping by, and I always see something new here. The hotel is supposedly haunted by a lady who died here during her honeymoon. Historically, Hollywood celebrities would stop by the speakeasy before going to the races at Santa Anita Park."
>
> *Kevin Hansel, California Historic Route 66 Association*

As you descend into San Bernardino, move over onto I-215, then exit at Devore and follow Cajon Blvd down onto Mt Vernon Ave. Detour east on Base Line St, turning left onto "E" St, and look for the Golden Arches outside the **13** **First McDonald's Museum**. Half of the museum is devoted to Route 66, with particularly interesting old photographs and maps. Turn west on 5th St, leaving San Bernardino via Foothill Blvd, which continues straight as an arrow into the urban sprawl of greater Los Angeles.

It's a long haul west to Pasadena, with stop-and-go traffic most of the way. Thankfully, there are more than a handful of gems to uncover along the route. In Rialto, the concrete tepees of the **14** **Wigwam Motel** have been Route 66 icons since 1949. The infamous "Do It in a Tee-Pee" sign out front is gone, as this is now a family-run place. Cruising through Fontana, birthplace of the Hells Angels biker club, you might ask yourself "What the…?!" when you catch sight of the ⑮ **Giant Orange**, a 1920s juice stand of the kind that was once a fixture alongside SoCal's citrus groves. You'll be in desperate need of refreshment by the time you hit Glendora and the ⑯ **Hat** drive-in, which has been piling up hot pastrami sandwiches since 1951. Stay on Route 66 as it detours briefly onto Alosta Ave, then rejoins Foothill Blvd in Azusa. Continue onto Huntington Dr in ⑰ **Duarte**, where a boisterous Route 66 parade happens in mid-September, complete with marching bands, old-fashioned carnival games and a classic car show.

Arriving in Arcadia, 1930s ⑱ **Santa Anita Park** is where the Marx Brothers' *A Day at the Races* was filmed, and where legendary thoroughbred Seabiscuit once ran. Stepping through the soaring art-deco entrance into the grandstands, you'll feel like a million bucks – and that's even if you don't win any wagers. Continue along Colorado Blvd into wealthy Pasadena. Its motto "timeless appeal with modern luxuries," the vintage ⑲ **Saga Motor Hotel** still hands out quaint metal room keys to its guests. Downtown in Old Pasadena, turn left onto Fair Oaks Ave and drive south to the neighborhood ⑳ **Fair Oaks Pharmacy**, an old-fashioned drugstore, soda fountain and candy shop operating on the same corner since 1915.

Join the jet-set modern world on the Pasadena Fwy (CA 110), which streams south into LA. Although many Route 66 relics have been lost in LA, you can glimpse a few remnants of the past by following Sunset Blvd west onto Santa Monica Blvd, which crawls through West Hollywood, Beverly Hills and West LA. Route 66 reaches its finish line, over 2200 miles from its starting point in Chicago, on an ocean bluff in ㉑ **Palisades Park**, where a Will Rogers Hwy memorial plaque marks the official end of the Mother Road. Celebrate on ㉒ **Santa Monica Pier**, where you can ride a 1920s carousel featured in *The Sting*, gently touch starfish and tide-pool critters at the ㉓ **Santa Monica Pier Aquarium**, and soak up a sunset atop the solar-

HOLLYWOOD REDUX

Like a resurrected diva of the silver screen, **Hollywood** is making a comeback. Although it hasn't recaptured its Golden Age glamour, this historic neighborhood is still worth visiting for its restored movie palaces, unique museums and of course, the pink stars on the Walk of Fame. Start exploring at the Hollywood & Highland complex, north of Santa Monica Blvd; the **Hollywood Visitor Information Center** (www.discoverlosangeles.com) is upstairs.

powered Ferris wheel at ㉔ **Pacific Park**. Say "So long!" to your retro Route 66 road trip at the time-warped ㉕ **Sea Shore Motel**. Although the noisy, no-frills rooms have seen better days, they're so close to the beach that you can inhale the sea-salted breezes.

Sara Benson

TRIP INFORMATION

GETTING THERE
From Los Angeles, take I-10 east, then I-15 north and I-40 east to Needles and the Arizona state line.

DO
Amboy Crater
It's a 1-mile scramble up the volcano's west side from the parking lot. Skip it in strong winds or summer heat. ☎ 760-326-7000; www.blm.gov/ca; admission free; 1 mile west of Amboy; ☼ sunrise-sunset

California Route 66 Museum
Past the volunteer-run gift shop is a gallery of rotating art and historical exhibits. ☎ 760-951-0436; www.califrt66museum.org; 16825 "D" St, Victorville; donations welcome; ☼ 10am-4pm Thu-Mon, sometimes 11am-3pm Sun

Elmer's Place
American folk-art style garden of "bottle trees" brightens a lonely stretch of the Mother Road. 24266 National Old Trails Hwy, Helendale; ☼ 24hr

First McDonald's Museum
In 1940 the McDonald brothers moved their first fast-food restaurant to San Bernardino, where carhops once served burgers and fries. ☎ 909-885-6324; 1398 N "E" St, San Bernardino; donations welcome; ☼ 10am-5pm

Giant Orange
Look for the boarded-up OJ stand next to Bono's Restaurant & Italian Deli, just west of Sultana Ave. 15395 Foothill Blvd, Fontana; ☼ no public entry

Goffs Schoolhouse
Public open-house tours are offered on select weekends by the Mojave Desert Heritage & Cultural Association. ☎ 760-733-4482; www.mdhca.org; 37198 Lanfair Rd, Goffs; donations welcome; ☼ usually 9am-4pm Sat & Sun

Old Trails Arch Bridge
Although vehicular traffic is prohibited, this river crossing is worth a souvenir photo from afar. Off I-40 exit 1, east of the California-Arizona border; ☼ no public access

Pacific Park
Year-round carnival rides include the West Coast's only oceanfront steel roller coaster. ☎ 310-260-8744; www.pacpark.com; unlimited rides over/under 42" tall $20/11; 380 Santa Monica Pier, Santa Monica; ☼ call for hr; ♿

Route 66 "Mother Road" Museum
Venture across the railroad tracks from downtown to this volunteer-staffed museum of Mother Road lore. ☎ 760-255-1890; http://route66museum.org; 681 N First Ave, Barstow; donations welcome; ☼ 10am-4pm Fri-Sun Apr-Oct, 11am-4pm Fri-Sun Nov-Mar

Roy's Motel & Cafe
Although the motel has been abandoned, the gas station, mini mart and café are occasionally open. National Old Trails Hwy, Amboy; admission free; ☼ vary

Santa Anita Park
During race season, tram tours go behind the scenes into the jockeys' room and training areas; reservations required. ☎ 626-574-7223, tour info ☎ 626-574-6677; www.santa anita.com; 285 W Huntington Dr, Arcadia; tours free, race tickets $5-10; ☼ live racing Thu-Mon Dec 26-Apr 20

Santa Monica Pier
The free summer Twilight Dance Series hosts rock, jazz, reggae, salsa and swing concerts. ☎ 310-458-8900; www.santamonicapier .org; west of Ocean Ave, Santa Monica; admission free; ☼ 24hr; ♿ ☺

Santa Monica Pier Aquarium
Stop by for family-oriented natural science on the beach, below the pier's carousel. ☎ 310-393-6149; www.healthebay.org; 1600 Ocean Front Walk, Santa Monica; adult/child $5/free; ☼ 2-6pm Tue-Fri, 12:30-6pm Sat & Sun; ♿

Stone Hotel
This late-19th-century hotel once housed miners, desert explorers and wanderers, including Sierra Nevada naturalist John Muir. **National Old Trails Hwy, Daggett;** no public entry

EAT
Bagdad Cafe
The original café in Bagdad is gone, but this roadhouse diner survives. Browse through tourists' scribblings from around the world in piled-up notebooks. ☎ 760-257-3101; 46548 **National Old Trails Hwy, Newberry Springs; mains $5-10;** vary

Fair Oaks Pharmacy
Road weary? Stop by this early-20th-century soda fountain for egg creams, hand-dipped malts and gooey-good chili cheeseburgers. ☎ 626-799-1414; www.fairoakspharmacy .net; 1526 Mission St, Pasadena; mains $4-8; 9am-9pm Mon-Fri, 9am-10pm Sat, 10am-7pm Sun;

Hat
The pastrami burger on French bread topped with Thousand Island dressing will keep you going strong. ☎ 626-857-0017; 611 W Route 66, Glendora; mains $3-8; 10am-1am;

Idle Spurs Steakhouse
Yeehaw! It's an Old West steakhouse and fully stocked saloon (it's even got microbrews) to slake your desert cottonmouth. ☎ 760-256-8888; www.idlespurssteakhouse.com; 690 Hwy 58, Barstow; mains $13-27; 11am-9pm Mon-Fri, 4-9pm Sat & Sun

Summit Inn
Authentic 1950s truck stop with a retro jukebox and exotic specialties on its time-tested menu. ☎ 760-949-8688; 5960 Mariposa Rd, Oak Hills; mains $5-10; 6am-8pm Mon-Thu, to 9pm Fri & Sat

SLEEP
Saga Motor Hotel
Take a dip in the heated outdoor swimming pool, which is surrounded by Astroturf, and pretend it's the 1950s. ☎ 626-795-0431, 800-793-7242; www.thesagamotorhotel .com; 1633 E Colorado Blvd, Pasadena; r $92-108;

Sea Shore Motel
Well-worn motor lodge is a budget-saving bargain near the beach. Bring earplugs (thin walls, traffic noise). ☎ 310-392-2787; www .seashoremotel.com; 2637 Main St, Santa Monica; r $105-175;

Wigwam Motel
Rescued from its formerly run-down state, this vintage motor court lets Route 66 travelers sleep inside concrete tepees. It's not in the safest neighborhood, so exercise caution in the immediate vicinity. ☎ 909-875-3005; www.wigwammotel.com; 2728 W Foothill Blvd, Rialto; r $65-80;

USEFUL WEBSITES
www.cart66pf.org
www.route66ca.org

LINK YOUR TRIP
TRIP
www.lonelyplanet.com/trip-planner

Loony LA

WHY GO It's not called La La Land for nothing. For more than a century, dreamers and nonconformists have flocked to the city, trotting out their quirks, obsessions and passions for all to see. Like an indulgent parent, LA has encouraged such behavior with a shrug and one simple word: whatever.

TIME
2 – 3 days

DISTANCE
58 miles

BEST TIME TO GO
Year-round

START
Echo Park

END
East LA

ALSO GOOD FOR

CITY

It's Fight Club. It's Preakness. It's that scary girl from study hall who used to give you rope burn – only now she's on wheels whooshing round a track like her skates are on fire. ❶ **LA Derby Dolls**, just west of Downtown, is the hottest thing going since Pinkberry. Even Drew Barrymore's scouting the roller derby scene. Follow the signs to the Doll Factory on Temple St and join the roaring, tattooed mob watching the "half-clad, all bad" dolls – with names like Demolicious and Thora Zeen – who've shoved, blocked and hauled ass on a banked track since 2003.

Ratchet down the adrenaline with another kitschy gal, this one adorning the ❷ **Farmer's Daughter**, a midcity hotel where the decor is flirty, fun and steeped in blue gingham and roosters. Located across the street from CBS Studios, The Grove and the Farmers Market, the Daughter's faux country charms are popular with *Price is Right* contestants and hard-core shoppers.

Brain still rattled from roller derby? Then beware Jonathan Borofsky's ❸ **Ballerina Clown** at the corner of Rose Ave and Main St. It too can mess with your equilibrium: "Why is a sad-faced man clown – in a tutu – dancing above the entrance to Longs Drugs?" Because you're in ❹ **Venice**, baby, so drink the tea, jump down the rabbit hole, and look south at something curiouser: three-story ❺ **binoculars** (designed by Claes Olenburg and Coosje van Bruggen) flanking the Frank Gehry–designed former offices of Chiat/Day.

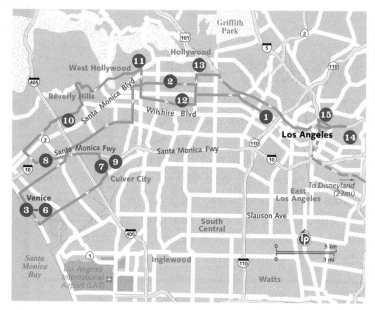

Go with the offbeat flow on Venice's Ocean Front Walk, a cacophonous mix of rollerblading exhibitionists, sweaty bodybuilders, and white men who can't jump – all sharing the mile-long beach boardwalk between Rose Ave and Venice Pier. "People are strange..." sang The Doors, so it's appropriate that a **⑥ mural of Jim Morrison**, former Venice resident, now poses in eternal, black-leathered badness over the 18th and Speedway intersection. Museums can be strange too, as you'll discover 6 miles east in Culver City. Pause outside the deceptively nondescript **⑦ Museum of Jurassic Technology** and re-adjust everything you know about permanent collections. Then ring the doorbell. Inside, a maze of dark, off-kilter exhibit rooms highlight old wives' tales, trailer park relics and Russian space dogs. Is it real? Is it fake? Created by MacArthur Fellow David Wilson, whatever it is, you'll be pondering it for days.

For gastronomic looniness, backtrack to the Santa Monica airport for the Pan-Asian menu at **⑧ Typhoon**, where stir-fried Tawainese crickets and fried chambai ants join kung pao chicken and moo shu pork. For a visual dessert, the viewing deck offers close-up views of private planes lifting off. You might also ponder the long line spilling out of nearby **⑨ Tender Greens**. It's not a nightclub, just a salad-centric eatery famous for its fresh, mostly organic produce.

Those who prefer views of celebrity graves will appreciate the efficiency of pocket-sized **⑩ Pierce Brothers Westwood Memorial Park** where the grounds can be walked in 10 minutes. Here, 4.5 miles northeast of Typhoon, you'll find the red-lipped kiss prints of Marilyn Monroe fans adorning her marble crypt. The tombstones of Rodney "…there goes the neighborhood" Dangerfield and new neighbor Merv Griffin (we won't spoil the fun, check it out) are laugh-out-loud appropriate. Other lawn-covered luminaries include Natalie Wood, Truman Capote and Jack Lemmon.

Even the park ranger at ⓫ **Greystone Mansion & Park** admits that the place is spooky. This English Gothic mansion may be perched above palm-dappled Beverly Hills, but the mood is melancholy. But then, the stone-walled fortress was the site of the mysterious murder-suicide of oil heir Ned Doheny by his male assistant in 1929. The home is closed – and apparently vacant – but the grounds and gardens are open.

> **ASK A LOCAL**
>
> "The big event at **Hollywood Forever Cemetery** (www.hollywoodforever.com) is for Rudolf Valentino on August 23. They have a death celebration with a whole ceremony in a mausoleum with someone playing the piano, and a lady in black comes in and puts a flower on [his grave]."
>
> *Chris Palmeri, Los Angeles*

The next morning, kick-start your day with an LA classic: the smell of hot tar and the sight of a dying mammoth at the ⓬ **La Brea Tar Pits & Page Museum** on Wilshire Blvd. Wander the percolating pits, stopping by Pit 91 in summer to watch scientists pull fossils from the muck. Inside the museum, skeletons of ancient carnivores continue to fascinate the kiddies. A quick drive north to Hollywood takes you to ⓭ **Hannibal Lector's prison cell**. After *Silence of the Lambs* wrapped shooting at Universal Studios, Lector's entire cellblock was dismantled piece by piece and delivered to the basement of the Hollywood Museum on Highland Ave. The dark prison corridor is available for private parties; Police Chief William J Bratton's dined there twice. For your own over-the-top meal, head back toward downtown to ⓮ **El Tepeyac**, a scrappy East Side stalwart serving the gargantuan Manuel's Special Burrito. Named after the owner, this gastronomic marvel – variously described as football-sized, head-sized, or weighing four pounds – is crammed with pork, rice, beans and chili. Order at the window, and dig in at a picnic table.

> **DETOUR**
>
> Why is Cinderella talking to that Marilyn Manson look-a-like? Because it's **Bats Day in the Fun Park**, an annual gathering of Goths and their kind in Disneyland, making it the Gothiest Place on Earth one day a year. Picture 5000 Goths moping together at the event's 10th anniversary in 2008. See www.batsday.net for more info.

Nearby is delightfully macabre ⓯ **Skeletons in the Closet**, the LA morgue's tiny, tongue-in-cheek souvenir shop. Friendly staff members swap tales about ghost towns and eerie dreams as visitors peruse plastic skeletons, "Body Bag" garment bags, and $25 beach towels emblazoned with the outline of a crime scene corpse – the most popular item. The morgue itself is just two stories below.

Amy C Balfour

TRIP 52

TRIP INFORMATION

GETTING THERE
From LAX take I-105 east to I-110, then head north to downtown. Exit at W Temple St, follow it west.

DO

Greystone Mansion & Park
This Gothic mansion, seen in *Ghostbusters*, was the site of an infamous 1929 murder-suicide. ☎ 310-550-4796; www.greystone mansion.org; 905 Loma Vista Dr, Beverly Hills; admission free; ⏱ 10am-5pm Nov-Mar, to 6pm Apr-Oct; ♿

Hannibal Lector's Prison Cell
The entire creepy set from *Silence of the Lambs* is in the Hollywood Museum basement. ☎ 323-464-7776; www.thehollywood museum.com; 1660 N Highland Ave, Hollywood; adult/student & senior $15/12; ⏱ 10am-5pm Wed-Sun

La Brea Tar Pits & Page Museum
Cool bones pulled from nearby goo. ☎ 323-934-7243; www.tarpits.org; 5801 Wilshire Blvd, Mid-City; adult/child/student, senior & youth $7/2/4.50; ⏱ 9:30am-5pm Mon-Fri, 10am-5pm Sat & Sun; ♿

LA Derby Dolls
Two teams of skate-wearing dolls tear around a banked track, trying to hold back the point-scoring jammer. Park on Temple St or at City of Angels Medical Center for $8. ☎ 310-285-3766; www.derbydolls .com/la; 1910 W Temple St, Echo Park; admission $20

Museum of Jurassic Technology
Off-kilter collection of "relics and curiosities" from the Lower Jurassic. ☎ 310-836-6131; www.mjt.org; 9341 Venice Blvd, Culver City; suggested donations adult/12-21yr US$5/3; ⏱ 2-8pm Thu, noon-6pm Fri-Sun

Pierce Brothers Westwood Memorial Park
This tiny cemetery, tucked behind an office building, is packed tight with famous post-lifers including Marilyn Monroe and Truman Capote. ☎ 310-474-1570; 1218 Glendon Ave, Westwood; admission free; ⏱ 8am-dusk

Skeletons in the Closet
It's coroner couture and collectibles at this tiny shop above the LA morgue. ☎ 323-343-0760; www.lacoroner.com; 1104 N Mission Rd, East LA; ⏱ 8:30am-4:30pm Mon-Fri

EAT & SLEEP

El Tepeyac
Scruffy but popular Mexican joint in East LA serves gargantuan burritos. ☎ 323-268-1960; 812 N Evergreen Ave, Boyle Heights; mains $9-17; ⏱ 6am-9:45pm Sun-Thu, 6am-11pm Fri & Sat

Farmer's Daughter
Flirty, faux-country motel rooms across from CBS studios, the Farmers Market and The Grove. ☎ 323-937-3930; www.farmers daughterhotel.com; 115 S Fairfax Ave, Mid-City; r $165-189, suites $199-265

Tender Greens
Salads headline the menu at this health-minded eatery, where servers mix your order in a bowl as you move down the line. ☎ 310-842-8300; www.tendergreensfood.com; 9523 Culver Blvd, Culver City; ⏱ 11:30am-9pm Sun-Thu, 11:30am-10pm Fri & Sat

Typhoon
Nosh on stir-fried crickets while planes take off at Santa Monica Airport. ☎ 310-390-6565; www.typhoon.biz; 3221 Donald Douglas Loop S, Santa Monica; mains lunch $7-20, dinner $8-21; ⏱ lunch Sun-Fri, dinner daily

USEFUL WEBSITES
www.gridskipper.com/travel/los-angeles
www.lamag.com

LINK YOUR TRIP

www.lonelyplanet.com/trip-planner

A Wild Ride in the Parks

WHY GO The world's first theme park opened in 1940 when Walter Knott threw open the gates to an Old West attraction beside his fried chicken restaurant in Buena Park. Nearly 70 years later, parks circle the globe, but for sheer density, variety and scream-your-head-off craziness, SoCal remains King of the Thrill.

TIME
5 – 6 days

DISTANCE
160 miles

BEST TIME TO GO
Apr – Sep

START
San Diego

END
Valencia

When it comes to 8000lb killer whales, Shamu at San Diego's ❶ SeaWorld is pretty darn cute. In fact, if you're not yelling "Shamu, Shamu!" with the rest of the crowd during the 25-minute show *Believe,* your heart is assuredly made of plankton. For ooohs and ahhhs beyond the Shamu zone, wander habitats housing frolicking polar bears, menacing reef sharks and honking seals (you can feed 'em sardines for $5). The handful of rides are low-key, but coaster junkies can get a tiny fix on the plummeting coaster-flume *Journey to Atlantis.* Avoid the front seat if you're wearing white.

For nearby shut-eye, unpack your bags inside an oceanfront cottage at ❷ Beach Cottages in Pacific Beach. Shuffleboard and Ping-Pong – not to mention the beach – keep the under-12 set occupied. For breakfast, dodge joggers and dog walkers on an oceanside stroll north to scruffy ❸ Kono's across from Crystal Pier. The line moves fast and, for a hearty breakfast burrito under $5, what's a short wait?

If you're traveling with kids under 13, take a coastal drive north on Hwy 101 to Carlsbad's ❹ Legoland. The rides aren't constructed of Lego, but almost everything else is, just ask that nice-looking family in the parking lot…oh, wait, they're made out of plastic blocks. Inside the park, people can't stop staring at the tiny Lego newlyweds gliding blissfully from the quickie wedding chapel in Miniland Las Vegas. Will they be getting a quickie Lego divorce or is life somehow better

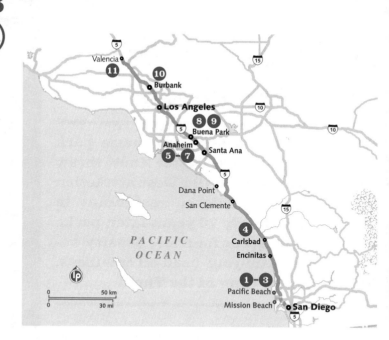

when you're made of connectible blocks? Young sharpshooters will enjoy 2008's Lost Kingdom Adventure with its point-and-blast laser guns (the 16ft Pharaoh is made from 300,000-plus blocks). For small-sized shrieks, climb aboard the twisting Project X Technic minicoaster.

For sheer attention to detail, no park does it better than Anaheim's **⑤ Disneyland**, 60 miles north, which welcomed 14.9 million guests in 2007. From the bright floral Mickey at the entrance to the buffeting Star Speeder in Star Tours to the screeching monkeys inside Indiana Jones Adventure, there's a magical detail ready to tease one of your senses. The latest high-dollar attraction is 2007's $100-million Finding Nemo Submarine Voyage. Look for Nemo from inside a sub and rumble though an underwater volcanic eruption. Coasterwise, use the Fastpass system and you'll be hurtling through Space Mountain – still the park's best adrenaline pumper – in no time.

Elevator issues? Avoid the Tower of Terror at **⑥ Disney's California Adventure** (DCA), across from Disneyland. The heart-stopping plunge down a 183ft

DETOUR

Pompadoured waiters, "Splish Splash" on the stereo, cherry-topped milkshakes. What is this? *Happy Days?* Nope, it's the next best thing: **Corvette Diner** in Hillcrest, San Diego, 8.3 miles south of Pacific Beach. At this doo-wop diner the singing waitstaff has happily forgotten it's a new millennium, but nobody seems to mind. We dare you not to finish the banana, peanut butter and marshmallow Elvis Shake that's all shook up.

elevator shaft is an experience you won't forget. Themed areas in DCA high-light the best of California, including numerous adventures that don't involve losing your lunch. Except Rockin' California Screamin' at Paradise Pier. This whip-fast coaster looks like an old school carnival ride, but from the moment it blasts forward with a cannon-shot whoosh, this 10-acre monster never lets go. DCA began a $1.1-billion makeover in 2008, with a Little Mermaid "dark ride," a state-of-the-art water show, and a new Car Land theme area scheduled.

Of the three Disney lodgings at the resort, the one most enjoying its theme is 489-room ❼ **Paradise Pier Hotel.** Hallways are aqua blue, mini-surfboards display your room number, and interiors celebrate coastal living with a bright, surfy joie de vivre reflected in multicolored bedspreads, lighthouse lamps, and sunburst mirrors.

> *"Inside the park, people can't stop staring at the tiny Lego newlyweds..."*

For 11th-century joie de vivre, get your gas-guzzling steed to rowdy ❽ **Medieval Times,** 7 miles northwest of Disneyland. Here, crown-wearing guests gnaw on roast chicken with their bare hands while knights joust, fence and display their horsemanship in a central arena. The next morning, slow down at the corner of Beach and La Palma Aves. Hear the screams? Got your teens? Hello, ❾ **Knott's Berry Farm,** America's first theme park, where eight high-scream coasters lure middle-schoolers and fast-track fanatics. Look up as you enter. The suspended coaster careening past is the Silver Bullet, popular for its corkscrew, double spiral and outside loop. Barefoot riders removed their flip-flops for a reason. The *Peanuts* gang keeps moppets happy in Camp Snoopy.

Thirty miles north, it's bye-bye to the future, hello to *The Simpsons* at ❿ **Universal Studios Hollywood,** where a $40-million simulator ride featuring Homer and the gang has replaced the lurching *Back to the Future.* An 80ft screen is the backdrop for a whirlwind journey through Krustyland. The short-but-screamworthy *Revenge of the Mummy* hurtles through Imhotep's Tomb (ride as a solo to avoid long lines) and *Jurassic Park* ends with a splashy plunge. Hop a tram for the Studio Tour, the park's best "ride." The guided tram winds past the Bates Motel from *Psycho,* a lunging Jaws, and Wisteria Lane from *Desperate Housewives* (when the show's not shooting). After a devastating 2008 fire, the studio has plans for a replacement for the destroyed *King Kong* attraction.

Ready to ratchet and roll? Look north to the steel-framed harbingers of doom rising from the grounds of Valencia's ⓫ **Six Flags Magic Mountain** off the I-5 northwest of Burbank. With 15 daredevilicious coasters ranging from Scream (which rips through seven loops) to revamped X2 (with a hurtling car spinning 360 degrees), Magic Mountain caters to its base. Bumper cars, kiddie plunges and Thomas the Tank Engine are tyke-friendly alternatives.

Amy C Balfour

TRIP INFORMATION

GETTING THERE
SeaWorld is 5 miles northwest of San Diego International Airport via I-5 and SeaWorld Dr.

DO

Disneyland & Disney's California Adventure
Happiest Place on Earth still lures 'em in by the tram load. ☎ 714-781-4565; www.disney land.com; 1313 S Harbor Blvd, Anaheim; 1-day Disneyland or DCA adult/3-9yr $66/56; ♿

Knott's Berry Farm
A shriek fest of horrorific mazes and spine-tingling shows complement the coasters during Halloween season. ☎ 714-220-5200; www.knotts.com; 8039 Beach Blvd, Buena Park, adult/3-11yr & senior $52/23; ♿

Legoland
A Lego-made family greets DNA-made families in the parking lot at this mazelike ode to plastic connectable blocks. ☎ 760-918-5346; www.legoland.com; 1 Legoland Dr, Carlsbad; adult/3-12yr $60/50; ⊙ 10am-6pm, with seasonal variation; ♿

SeaWorld
Creatures of the deep are the reason to come. ☎ 619-226-3901; www.seaworld.com; 500 SeaWorld Dr, San Diego; adult/3-9yr $61/51; ⊙ 9am-11pm Jul–mid-Aug, shorter hours rest of year; ♿

Six Flags Magic Mountain
Scream. Ninja. Viper. Goliath…15 roller coasters. Fifteen ways to lose it. ☎ 661-255-4111; www.sixflags.com/parks/magicmoun tain; 26101 Magic Mountain Pkwy, Valencia; adult/child under 4ft $60/30; ⊙ vary by season; ♿

Universal Studios Hollywood
Rides are tied to movies at this Burbank theme park, and the highlight is the Studio Tour. ☎ 818-622-3801; www.universal studioshollywood.com; 100 Universal City Plaza; admission over/under 48in $67/57 (see online specials); ⊙ vary by season; ♿

EAT

Kono's
Join the quick-moving line for plates piled high with eggs, bacon, pancakes and hearty burritos. ☎ 858-483-1669; 704 Garnet Ave, Pacific Beach; dishes from $5; ⊙ breakfast & lunch; ♿

Medieval Times
Feast on roast chicken while knights on horseback joust before you. ☎ 714-523-1100; www.medievaltimes.com; 7662 Beach Blvd, Buena Park; adult/12yr & under $53/35; ⊙ daily, show times vary; ♿

SLEEP

Beach Cottages
Celebrating its 60th birthday in 2008, this mom-and-pop motel with oceanfront cottages is south of Crystal Pier. ☎ 858-483-7440; www.beachcottages.com; 4255 Ocean Blvd, Pacific Beach; r $140-160, apt $285-345, cottage $295-335; ♿

Paradise Pier Hotel
Ask for a room overlooking DCA at this beach-inspired retreat, the newest and brightest of the three Disney hotels. ☎ 714-999-0990; www.disneyland.com; 1717 S Disneyland Dr, Anaheim; r $270-300; ♿

USEFUL WEBSITES
www.latimes.com/funland
www.westcoaster.net

LINK YOUR TRIP
www.lonelyplanet.com/trip-planner

Seeing Stars

WHY GO Los Angeles is Mt Olympus for today's gods and goddesses, a centralized playground where leading men chase puppies up canyon trails, A-list movie mommas push strollers through outdoor markets and dime-a-dozen reality stars nibble muffins at organic cafés. Jennifer Godwin, an E! Online editor who tracks their shenanigans, reveals the best hotspots.

Strolling past the arrival gates at ❶ **Los Angeles International Airport** (LAX), don't be surprised if people look vaguely familiar. The arrival gates are prime celeb-spotting territory, says Godwin, and that grungy guy with the tattered man-bag could be a big-screen superhero. And really, we're not advocating stalking, but if you were in a chocolate factory, you'd certainly admire the bon bons, no?

If it's early, head toward Hollywood and an order of chocolate French toast at ever-so-sharp ❷ **Joan's on Third**, a gourmet deli and café where you'll find crumbly cheese stacks, bright gelato tubs, swirled frosty cupcakes and, on occasion, a not-so-crumbly Jake Gyllenhaal. But no matter what time you arrive, the patio will inevitably be full and the crowd undeniably chic. Next up – and a short drive west – is the swanky ❸ **Four Seasons at Beverly Hills**, a favored locale for movie premiere press junkets, says Godwin, and a prime spot for catching A-listers dashing in and out between interviews. Most junkets start at 9am, so drop by early for a glimpse of the good life and a chance to see what's doing.

If celeb-watching in Beverly Hills induces shoe envy, ladies, covet no more. Get thee to the nearby shrine of pedicured couture – the shoe department at ❹ **Barneys New York.** "Katie Holmes and Chloe Sevigny love their Barneys," says Godwin. And why shouldn't they? Standing

TIME
2 days

DISTANCE
50 miles

BEST TIME TO GO
Aug – May

START
LAX

END
Cross Creek
Plaza, Malibu

ALSO GOOD FOR

CITY

BEST TRIP

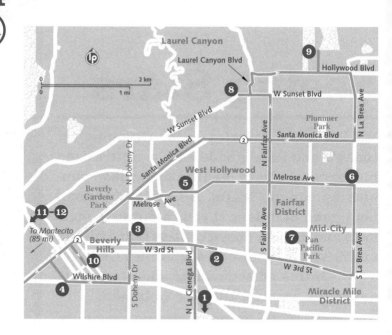

above the traffic-clogged fray of Wilshire Blvd like a centurion of style, four-story Barneys is a reliable, if occasionally snooty, purveyor of trendy duds.

And for lunch? "Pretend you're vegan," says Godwin, because there's no better celeb-bait than a vegan-conscious lunch joint. For primo stargazing try the high-octane patio at West Hollywood's best-known coffee house, **5** **Urth Caffé**. Dressed-down starlets sip organic lattes, but truth is you're more likely to see a reality star looking for that 16th minute. Better for stargazing is tiny **6** **M Café de Chaya** (M Chaya Café for short), where Angela Bassett, Giovanni Ribisi and Jason Schwartzmann nosh on macrobiotic specialties – natural whole foods eaten in season – at the tightly packed tables. Order at

IMPROVE YOUR ODDS

Zoo curators will tell you that certain times are better for catching exotic animals in action. There's a similar theory for celebs. Many TV stars flee the city during summer hiatus, which generally runs from May to July. In general, weeknights are often better than weekends because stars – like everyone else – run errands, catch movies and blow off steam after work. And with fewer tourists around, they're easier to spot.

the counter – try the bi bim bop (marinated pan-fried tofu, Korean-style vegetables, spicy miso and kim chee), grilled tuna burger or organic fries.

From here, follow La Brea Ave south to 3rd St, turn right, and head west until you reach the palazzo-style outdoor mall **7** **The Grove** next to the Farmers Market at Fairfax Ave. Word of warning: exuberant fountains, a clanging trolley, and roving masses of humanity will distract you from your mission. Acclimate, then grab a fountain-side spot between Pacific Theaters and the Apple store and see who struts past. Godwin spotted Nathan Lane and Natalie Portman within minutes of each other at the theater, while we've spied America Ferrera and Scott Speedman near the Apple store.

Drive northwest to Sunset Strip for a nap at the infamous **8 Chateau Marmont**, where dark hallways lead to Gothic-style (but modern) rooms, decadent indulgences and, well, we just can't spill the beans on all the naughtiness here. Postnap, stroll the cacophony of sound, light and excess otherwise known as The Strip, keeping in mind the party doesn't start before 11pm. For late-night star-peeping, a shabby-chic couch in the Chateau's lobby lounge is the place to be. The hotel is a top choice for those hitting movie- and award-show circuits, and the dark, well-trodden lounge never misses a whisper.

Next morning, don your best $200 hoodie for a hike up dog-friendly **9 Runyon Canyon**. "There's a jogging path that all the celebs use to walk their dogs," says Godwin. And if you don't spot a starlet, no worries. The citywide view from the summit is worth the half-hour climb. Insider tip? Park on N Vista St and walk north to enter. The larger entrance on N Fuller St has tight parking, not to mention a smell that is markedly ripe. As the children's book says, everybody poops, and that includes celebrity dogs.

Posthike, grab a picnic at the Beverly Hills **10 Whole Foods Market**. Famous folks grocery shop too, and Whole Foods, with its colorful fruit displays, natural and organic products, and choice-laden take-out section, is hard to resist. For A-list movie mommas looking to feed their broods with California-grown fare, try the Sunday **11 Brentwood Farmers Market**, where Reese Witherspoon and Jennifer Garner wander the stalls.

DETOUR ➤ Celeb-heavy **Montecito** is a leafy community tucked between the Santa Ynez mountains and the Pacific east of Santa Barbara, 78 miles northwest of Malibu. Heavy hitters like Oprah Winfrey, Ellen Degeneres, Steven Spielberg and Dick Wolf have homes here. Though many houses hide behind manicured hedges, the big names occasionally venture out to the boutique-and-patio-lined main drag, Coast Village Rd.

With picnic packed, drive north on the Pacific Coast Hwy (PCH) to canyon-cloaked Malibu, stomping grounds for one-name powerhouses like Barbra, Mel and, until recently, a Starbucks-slurping, underwear-avoiding popstar who will not be named. But a Malibu hotspot will be: **12 Cross Creek Plaza**, an everyday strip mall (theater, coffee shop and bookstore) that happens to sit across the street from star-studded Malibu Colony and is frequented by Leonardo DiCaprio. Done scoping? Park on PCH and wander over to gawk at Malibu's two most enduring celebrities: Surf and Sand.

Amy C Balfour

TRIP 54

TRIP INFORMATION

GETTING THERE
Los Angeles is 381 miles south of San Francisco and 124 miles north of San Diego.

DO

Barneys New York
Four-story ode to fashion where Young Hollywood converges for designer duds and swoon-inducing shoes. ☎ 310-276-4400; 9570 Wilshire Blvd; ☷ 10am-7pm Mon-Wed, Fri & Sat, until 8pm Thu, noon-6pm Sun

Brentwood Farmers Market
On Sundays, locals converge for fresh, California-grown produce, flowers and crafts. ☎ 818-591-8161; S Gretna Green Way & San Vicente Blvd; ☷ 9am-2:30pm Sun

Cross Creek Plaza
This isn't just any strip mall, this is a Malibu strip mall where the stars are almost as ubiquitous as the photographers. Cross Creek Rd near Pacific Coast Hwy, Malibu

Grove
Mega-stars mix with the masses to shop, watch movies or browse the Apple store. ☎ 323-900-8080; www.thegrovela.com; 189 The Grove Dr; ☷ 10am-9pm Mon-Thu, until 10pm Fri & Sat, 11am-8pm Sun; ☷

Los Angeles International Airport (LAX)
When stars swoop into town, the LAX arrival areas are eventually where they land. ☎ 310-646-5252; www.lawa.org/lax

Whole Foods Market
Even celebrities need milk, or its closest natural substitute, and this organic and natural foods market is a fave. ☎ 310-274-3360; www.wholefoodsmarket.com; 239 N Crescent Dr; ☷ 7am-10pm

EAT & DRINK

Joan's on Third
Gourmet market where rich cupcakes, crisp baguettes, spicy olives and trendy stars jostle for attention. ☎ 323-655-2285; www.joansonthird.com; 8350 W 3rd St; mains $4-16; ☷ 8am-8pm Mon-Sat, to 6pm Sun

M Café de Chaya
Vegan celebs love the macrobiotic cuisine at this compact restaurant. ☎ 323-525-0588; www.mcafedechaya.com; 7119 Melrose Ave; mains breakfast $5-11, lunch $9-16; ☷ 9am-10pm Mon-Sat, 9am-9pm Sun

Urth Caffé
For a dash of scenester pretension with your organic coffee, settle in on the patio at this jumpin' café. Oops, caffé. ☎ 310-659-0628; www.urthcaffe.com; 8565 Melrose Ave

SLEEP

Chateau Marmont
A castlelike hideaway where the mood is portentous, the lighting dim, and the clientele discreetly indulged. ☎ 323-656-1010; www.chateaumarmont.com; 8221 W Sunset Blvd; r from $370

Four Seasons at Beverly Hills
A posh doyenne on Doheny and Burton known for impeccable service and daylong movie junkets. ☎ 310-273-2222, www.fourseasons.com/losangeles; 300 S Doheny Dr; r from $455

USEFUL WEBSITES
www.defamer.com
www.eonline.com

LINK YOUR TRIP
www.lonelyplanet.com/trip-planner

Beach Towns of the OC

WHY GO You can drive the entire Orange County coast in a few hours, but really, why would you? With six distinctly different communities lining its shores, Orange County has a beach town catering to every type of traveler. Artist? Shopper? Surfer? Here's a peek at the communities behind the coastline.

TIME
3 days

DISTANCE
68 miles

BEST TIME TO GO
Year-round

START
Seal Beach

END
Dana Point

ALSO GOOD FOR

OUTDOORS

Train journeys start with "All aboard!" Space expeditions start with "10-9-8." And this 68-mile road trip starts with "I'd like a breakfast burrito, please." But not just any breakfast burrito. We'll be having a scrambled-eggs-bacon-chorizo-potatoes-and-cheese-stuffed tortilla from ❶ **Nick's Deli** in ❷ **Seal Beach**. Why? Because the surfers, hard hats and beach bunnies parading into this scrappy mainstay never order anything else. Between bites, watch shopkeepers unlocking their stores, silver-haired seniors gossiping over coffee, and board-toting surfers trotting toward the beach. It's small-town life with an oceanfront spin. It's also the place to sneak in lessons before heading south. Students at ❸ **M&M Surfing School** take advantage of gentle waves here while first-time kiteboarders at ❹ **Kitesurfari** benefit from wind conditions that'll have them catching air – up to 40ft – in no time.

A short bridge to the south drops you onto a 1-mile spit of land known as ❺ **Sunset Beach**. Like a gruff old salt who just wants to be left alone, this ornery community has resisted the trendy, prefab blandness gobbling up coastal towns to the south. One bar holding tight to its divey charms is tiny ❻ **Mother's Tavern**, where the Harleys line up like horses. If kayaking's more your style, stop by ❼ **OEX Sunset Beach** for a rental then drop in at yacht-filled Huntington Harbor. At dinnertime, follow the twinkling white lights to ❽ **Roman Cucina**, where the hearty Italian fare is just as hot as the waiters.

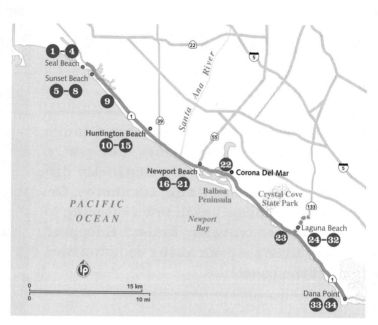

The OC coast is popular with another sort of vagabond: migrating birds that refuel at the handful of wetlands hanging tough beside overdeveloped Pacific Coast Hwy (PCH). At 1700-acre **9 Bolsa Chica State Ecological Reserve**, a wooden walkway meanders over reedy marshes where plovers, egrets and other feathered fly-bys swoop in for breakfast. Note the pumping oil derricks to the east – a common sight in this oil-rich community – as you cruise into **10 Huntington Beach** for your own fresh breakfast at **11 Sugar Shack**. Long popular with early-rising surfers for its good food, sunny patio and supercheap prices, it maintains an upbeat individuality on recently revamped, slightly bland Main St.

Though the city's moniker is the Jan & Dean–inspired *Surf City,* there's more to this town than hanging ten. Drive northeast on Goldenwest St to enjoy the leafy trails at 354-acre **12 Huntington Central Park**. Toss a disc at the park's 18-hole frisbee golf course, horseback ride on shady bridle paths, or let the kids loose on the muddy Adventure Playground. Back at the beach, dust off your Rollerblades for a glide down the 8.5-mile Ocean Strand or let Fido romp on **13 Dog Beach** 2 miles north of the pier.

For a glimpse of Surf City style, browse the sunglasses, flip-flops and board shorts preening on the racks at **14 Huntington Surf & Sport** and **15 Jack's Surfboards**, the twin sentries of surf culture towering over PCH and Main St. And speaking of surf culture, is that crackling evening glow a beach bonfire?

Sure is, and you can build one too at one of the nearly 600 fire rings nestled in the sand south of Huntington Beach Pier.

Further south, two-story ⑯ **Newport Channel Inn** welcomes cyclists, families and groups with down-to-earth hospitality, big rooms and affordable prices. Enjoy the mom-and-pop sincerity while you can. Next up are the superficial charms of glitzy ⑰ **Newport Beach**, a very good place to be rich. Yacht dealerships line the coastal highway here, a fitting prelude to retail shrine ⑱ **Fashion Island**, a chic Mediterranean-style outdoor mall with koi ponds and fountains scattered among its nearly 200 stores.

Cyclists hug the shoulder on Back Bay Dr, a one-way lane winding along the eastern coast of bird-and-wildlife haven ⑲ **Newport Bay Ecological Preserve**, another coastal marsh teeming with wildlife. Extreme sports more your speed? Just past West Jetty Park on Balboa Peninsula, adrenaline junkies cluster near the ⑳ **Wedge** to watch perfectly hollow waves – that can reach up to 30ft – fling bodysurfers against the sand like rag dolls. Since these shore breakers crest on the sand not the sea, smashing your noggin is a distinct possibility.

> **ASK A LOCAL**
>
> Maggie Susich of Newport Beach has two pieces of advice for visitors. One, think carefully before pedaling a "surrey" on the bike path between Newport Pier and Balboa Pier. Seems locals aren't big fans and may just bombard you with water balloons. Two, if it's Tuesday, hit up Great Mex for $1 tacos and $1 beers. It's on Balboa Blvd across from the Fun Zone – you'll see the surfers spilling out the door.

Slip into your Fashion Island finest for cocktails at ㉑ **3-Thirty-3 Waterfront**. Perfect for a low-key happy hour (try the gourmet sliders and fries), this harborside lounge morphs into the stereotypical Newport scene as the night rolls on. Think Botoxed former beauties (we won't say cougars on sheer principle) and overtanned yachtsmen on a midnight prowl. The next morning, shake off late night mistakes and head to the best thing going in these parts – the coastal views. One of the best vistas is at breezy ㉒ **Lookout Point** on Ocean Blvd in chichi Corona del Mar, where expansive views of Newport Harbor and Balboa Peninsula unfurl below the rocky cliffs.

"In this melding of art and reality, human models re-create famous paintings with eerie accuracy."

While slurping a thick date milkshake at ㉓ **Ruby's Crystal Cove Shake Shack** on the road to ㉔ **Laguna Beach**, it's easy to push aside thoughts of MTV's *Laguna Beach* and its spin-offs. Lauren Conrad and the show's other slack-jawed beauties may be scoring magazine covers, but it's the galleries, art festivals and sculpture-lined parks that will lure crowds to Laguna for years to come. Most locals here, though wealthy, are also live-and-let-live, and there's a palpable, artistic joie de vivre in the air that increases the sense of fun. Immerse yourself in the Laguna mindset at **25 Casa Laguna Inn**. With its bougainvillea-draped walls, terracing courtyards and plush bungalows (once housing artists), Casa Laguna is a work of art posing as a 22-room inn.

Also posing as a work of art are the performers in the **26 Pageant of the Masters**, which celebrated its 75th anniversary in 2008. In this melding of art and reality, human models re-create famous paintings with eerie accuracy. Held in July and August, the pageant is part of the coinciding **27 Festival of the Arts**. Catch a free shuttle from town to the festival, where you can wander jury-selected art by more than 140 exhibiting artists. Another Laguna classic is the sticker-covered Mexican food shack **28 Taco Loco**, where the tempting list of fillings – fish, shrimp, lobster, chicken, beef and tofu – makes it hard to commit.

29 Heisler Park is one of the most gorgeous coastal landscapes in SoCal. Sitting atop a bluff north of Laguna's Main Beach, its primary path winds past public art, palm trees, picnic tables and grand views of rocky shores and tide pools before sloping south to **30 Main Beach**. Wander past the volleyball players, sunbathers, and beachcombers here before heading into downtown, where it's easy to wile away an afternoon in the galleries, boutiques and one-of-kind gift shops.

DETOUR   If you've got a soft spot for pinnipeds, drive 3.5 miles northeast on Laguna Canyon Rd from downtown Laguna to the **Pacific Marine Mammal Center** (www.pacificmmc.org). Outdoor holding pens house ailing seals and sea lions that are being nursed back to health for eventual return to the sea. Displays detail the history of the organization as well as the diseases plaguing these coastal creatures. Visitors welcome, just follow the posted rules.

For an aesthetically pleasing dinner – that also tastes fantastic – try compact **31 242 Café Fusion Sushi**, where one of Orange County's few female sushi chefs slices and preps the best sushi rolls in town. After dinner, it's time to thank the mojito gods: a rooftop bar has opened in Laguna. Just one look at the overflowing crowds at stylish **32 k'ya Rooftop Lounge**, perched atop La Casa del Camino hotel, suggests its arrival is long overdue. For the best odds of entry, arrive early. Its upscale cocktails, friendly service and prime coastal views are topping many locals' to-do lists.

Last up is marina-flanked **33 Dana Point**, namesake of 19th-century adventurer Richard Dana, who famously called the area "the only romantic spot on the coast." Put his words to the test by pitching camp on the sand-duned shores of **34 Doheny State Beach**. With the surf pounding just a few yards away, you'll see firsthand why Doheny's annually voted the county's "Best Camping Site" by readers of the *OC Register*.

Amy C Balfour

TRIP INFORMATION

GETTING THERE
From LAX, follow I-405 28 miles south to Seal Beach.

DO

Bolsa Chica State Ecological Reserve
This restored salt marsh is an environmental success story now teeming with birdlife. It's across from Bolsa Chica State Beach. ☎ 714-846-1114; Pacific Coast Hwy, Huntington Beach; ⏱ 6am-8pm; ♿

Fashion Island
Rising from the center of a massive traffic loop, this open-air island of retail has nearly 200 stores. ☎ 949-721-2000; www.shopfashionisland.com; 401 Newport Center Dr, Newport Beach; ⏱ 10am-9pm Mon-Fri, 10am-7pm Sat, 11am-6pm Sun

Festival of the Arts
Two-month celebration of art with 140-plus jury-selected artists displaying their handiwork in all its forms. ☎ 949-494-1145 info, 949-497-6582 tickets; 650 Laguna Canyon Rd, Laguna Beach; www.foapom.com; adult/student & senior $7/4; ⏱ 10am-11:30pm Jul & Aug

Huntington Surf & Sport
High-energy surf shop has coffee stand beside cement handprints of surfing greats. ☎ 714-841-4000; www.hsssurf.com; 300 Pacific Coast Hwy, Huntington Beach; ⏱ 8am-10pm Mon-Fri, to 11pm Fri & Sat, earlier in winter

Jack's Surfboards
Just like surf shops everywhere – surf videos, sunglasses, flips-flops, bored clerks – but bigger. ☎ 714-536-4516; www.jackssurfboards.com; 10 Main St, Huntington Beach; ⏱ 8am-10pm

Kitesurfari
Learn the ups and downs of kiteboarding in a two-day course in Seal Beach. ⏱ 562-596-6451; www.kitesurfari.com; 452 Pacific Coast Hwy, Seal Beach; 2-day lessons $440; ⏱ 11am-6pm Thu-Mon, to 4pm Sat & Sun

M&M Surfing School
For surf lessons, look for its van in the parking lot north of Seal Beach pier. ☎ 714-846-7873; www.surfingschool.com; Seal Beach; 1-day lesson $65-80, 5-day lesson $250

OEX Sunset Beach
Rent kayaks just off PCH. ☎ 562-592-0800; www.oexsunsetbeach.com; 16910 Pacific Coast Hwy, Sunset Beach; single/double kayak for 2hr $15/25; ⏱ 9am-6pm

Pageant of the Masters
Human models blend into life-size re-creations of famous paintings in this thrilling experience that coincides with the Festival of the Arts. ☎ 949-494-1145 info, 949-497-6582 tickets; www.pageanttickets.com; 650 Laguna Canyon Rd, Laguna Beach; admission $15-100

EAT

242 Café Fusion Sushi
Order the yellowtail with spicy miso sauce, and your night will be on course. ☎ 949-494-2444; 242 N Coast Hwy, Laguna Beach; mains $6-19; ⏱ dinner Tue-Sun

Nick's Deli
This Seal Beach stalwart, three blocks from the beach, sells about one breakfast burrito per minute. ☎ 562-598-5072; 223 Main St, Seal Beach; mains $5-7; ⏱ breakfast & lunch

Roman Cucina
Twinkling lights mark the spot at this popular Italian restaurant known for heaping plates of pasta and $5 Martini Mondays. ☎ 562-592-5552; 16595 Pacific Coast Hwy, cnr 20th St, Sunset Beach; mains $12-18; ⏱ dinner

Sugar Shack
Put your name on the clipboard at this long-popular breakfast joint. ☎ 714-536-0355; 213 Main St, Huntington Beach; mains under $8; ⏱ 6am-4pm Mon, Tue & Thu, 6am-8pm Wed, 6am-5pm Fri-Sun

Taco Loco
Order tacos and Coronas at the counter then sit among surfers at this Mexican sidewalk

café. ☎ 949-497-1635; 640 S Coast Hwy,
Laguna Beach; mains under $8; ☾ 11am-
midnight Sun-Thu, to 2am Fri & Sat

DRINK

3-Thirty-3 Waterfront
Dial up your style and dust off your pick-up
lines for a late-night prowl at this quintes-
sentially Newport lounge. ☎ 949-673-8464;
333 Bayside Dr, Newport Beach

k'ya Rooftop Lounge
Ride the elevator to the roof at Hotel La
Casa del Camino for open-air cocktails with
the stunning Laguna coast as the backdrop.
☎ 949-376-9718; www.kyarestaurant.com;
1287 S Coast Hwy, Laguna Beach

Mother's Tavern
This rowdy dive in the tiny red building by
the barber shop somehow squeezes a band
inside most Sunday afternoons. ☎ 562-
592-2111; 16701 Pacific Coast Hwy, Sunset
Beach

Ruby's Crystal Cove Shake Shack
This easy-to-miss wooden shack has been
selling shakes for more than 60 years. It's on
low bluffs just east of the Crystal Cove/Los
Trancos entrance to Crystal Cove State

Park. ☎ 949-464-0100; 7703 E Coast Hwy;
☾ 10am-sunset

SLEEP

Casa Laguna Inn
Couples swoon for the cozy courtyards,
cushy beds and chef-prepared breakfasts at
romantic, 22-room Casa Laguna Inn. ☎ 949-
494-2996; www.casalaguna.com; 2510 S
Coast Hwy, Laguna Beach; r $280-400, suites
$400-550

Doheny State Beach
Pitch your tent on the sand at the only Orange County park that allows camping on the
beach. ☎ 949-496-6172; www.dohenystate
beach.org; 25300 Dana Point Harbor Dr,
Dana Point; campsites $25-35

Newport Channel Inn
Big rooms, the beach bike path and friendly
service lure 'em in year after year at this family-owned motel west of town. ☎ 949-642-
3030; www.newportchannelinn.com; 6030
W Coast Hwy, Newport Beach; r $119-200

USEFUL WEBSITES
www.lagunabeachinfo.org
www.surfcityusa.com

LINK YOUR TRIP
www.lonelyplanet.com/trip-planner

TRIP
1 Up the Pacific Coast Highway p37
3 Best of the Beaches p53
8 Surfing USA p81

Spa Time

WHY GO Sometimes you need a getaway from your getaway. How better to escape than to contemplate the grace of nature, or to go inward and have your cares rubbed, scrubbed or rub-a-dubbed away? Southern California bubbles with hot springs and day spas ethnic, hip and froufrou, and grand hikes and explorations that are just as rejuvenating.

TIME
5 days

DISTANCE
200 miles

BEST TIME TO GO
Year-round

START
Culver City

END
Indian Wells

Third gear...second gear...stop. Transit out of the world of cars and freeways with a realignment at ❶ **Massage Garage** in the LA suburb of Culver City. "We Fix Bodies" is the slogan at this hipster haven, and the basic 60-minute massage is called the "tune up". The industrial decor – lighting, car seats, tanker desk – may feel a little gimmicky, but there's plenty to love among the staff of 30 therapists and reasonable prices for shiatsu, pregnancy massages, reflexology, facials and more.

While plenty of LA hotels pamper with service, the ❷ **Hotel Palomar**, in the Westwood neighborhood, does it with an urban aesthetic, in-room spa services and central location at rates that won't fray your nerves. Even the TV is good for you, with health and fitness programs and the Yoga Channel.

The next morning, earn your next spa treatment by driving west to the coast for a moderately vigorous hike in ❸ **Topanga Canyon State Park**. Amid the woods, 800ft elevations and rocky outcroppings of the 6.5-mile Eagle Rock Loop, you'll scarcely believe that you're in the middle of America's second-biggest metropolis. The Pacific shines blue in the distance.

Then head to West Hollywood, where the Russian day spa ❹ **Voda** helps you recover from your rushin'. Lunch at Voda's café is heartier-

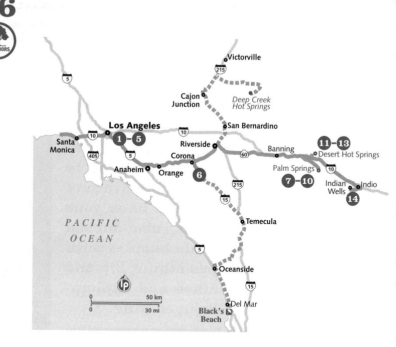

than-your-average-spa cuisine (eg wraps) but still good for you, and the signature treatments are Russian-inspired *banyas,* hot-stone saunas accompanied by a cold plunge pool – jump in and out of both to your heart's content.

> "...masseuses pull, stretch and pulverize every limb and, yes, walk on your back."

Platza involves vigorous massage and whacking with a *venik,* a water-soaked bundle of birch, oak and eucalyptus. Call before setting out, as some days are single-sex, and swimsuits are required on the rest.

On your way to Downtown LA, **5 Pho Siam** day spa literally walks all over you. This family-owned place, friendly and superclean, specializes in "no pain, no gain" Thai massage – imagine a sports massage on (herbal) steroids. You lie on a mat on the floor while masseuses pull, stretch and pulverize every limb and, yes, walk on your back. You sort of wonder where they get the strength. There are dozens of treatment booths (leave your shoes outside them) and silk sheers above the hallways.

The next day, head east into the desert, where the red-clay pool nicknamed "Club Mud" is the most famous among the 18 pools and spas filled with naturally heated mineral water at **6 Glen Ivy Hot Springs**. It's in Corona, near the border of Orange and Riverside Counties. On 11 acres bursting with bougainvillea, eucalyptus and palms, you can wallow in the water, lounge in the moisturizing confines of the "grotto" cave, take an aqua aerobics class, treat yourself to a massage in a private outdoor cabana, swim laps or feel ocean-fresh in the saline pool. Swimsuits are required – bring an old one if you want to hit the mud.

Seventy-five miles further east, there's a reason it's called **7 Palm Springs**. Its home, the Coachella Valley, sits atop a giant aquifer, which the native Agua Caliente band of Cahuilla Indians long used for curative purposes. A hike through the Cahuilla-owned **8 Tahquitz Canyon** outside the city center explains some of the legend, beauty and history of the area, and rangers lead informative excursions. In downtown Palm Springs, the Cahuilla run the **9 Spa Resort Casino**, where the bargain-priced "Taking of the Waters" package lets you course through multiple baths, steam rooms and saunas.

> **DETOUR** **Black's Beach**, in the Torrey Pines neighborhood north of central San Diego and about 90 miles south of Corona, is SoCal's favorite nude beach. It stretches most of a mile and gets its share of families and volleyballers; gay men congregate around the northern end.

At the other end of the scale is the **10 Palm Springs Yacht Club**, 16,500 sq ft worth of spa, pool and gym at the splashy Parker Palm Springs hotel. Jonathan Adler's tongue-in-cheek nautical decor (yacht club in the desert? – think about it) lets you contemplate knot patterns in the carpet as the Wringer deep-tissue massage takes the knots out of your body. The Voodoo We Do massage incorporates Thai stretches.

> **DETOUR** To frolic in nature while wearing nature's own, hippy-dippy **Deep Creek Hot Springs**, in the desert near Apple Valley in the San Bernardino National Forest, is a secluded SoCal classic. It's a 2-mile Joshua Tree– and cactus-lined hike from the parking lot to Deep Creek's smattering of clothing-optional pools. Take plenty of drinking water and an open mind.

Northwest of Palm Springs, the city of **11 Desert Hot Springs** lives up to its name, with waters bubbling from deep below the desert floor. The 56 acres of the **12 Two Bunch Palms** spa sit atop an actual oasis, with pools and sunbathing areas (including clothing-optional), a very decent restaurant and a code of silence. Imitate Tim Robbins in Robert Altman's *The Player* and have a mud bath here, or get wrapped, massaged and more. Nearby, chic, minimalist hotels make for a smart stay; **13 Hope Springs** is an eternal favorite for midcentury design and vistas across the valley.

And down valley, amid the golf courses of Indian Wells, advanced spa-goers hit **14 The Well** spa at Miramonte Resort. Enjoy a wine bath or lemon-extract exfoliation, or a painting party for you and your honey. Decompress in a Vichy shower, settle back in your own private cabana to contemplate the mountains towering nearby and become one with the world.

Andrew Bender

TRIP INFORMATION

GETTING THERE
Culver City is surrounded by the city of Los Angeles, near the intersection of the I-10 and I-405 freeways.

DO

Glen Ivy Hot Springs
The original "Club Mud". ☎ 888-453-6489; www.glenivy.com; 25000 Glen Ivy Rd, Corona; admission Mon-Thu $35, Fri-Sun & holidays $48; 🕘 9:30am-6pm early-Mar–Oct, 9:30am-5pm Nov-early Mar

Massage Garage
Hipster day spa in up-and-coming Culver City. ☎ 310-202-0082; www.themassagegarage.com; 3812 Main St, Culver City, Los Angeles; massages per 30/60/90min $30/45/70, facials from $45; 🕘 10am-9pm

Palm Springs Yacht Club
Slick and playful spa at the Parker. ☎ 760-321-4606; www.parkerpalmsprings.com; 4200 E Palm Canyon Dr, Palm Springs; treatments $80-295; 🕘 vary by season, phone in advance

Pho Siam
Thai massage, plus reasonably priced facials and waxing. ☎ 310-652-2250; www.phosiam.com; 1525 Pizarro St, Los Angeles; massage from $25; 🕘 9am-10:30pm Mon-Fri, 8am-5pm Sat, 9am-5pm Sun

Spa Resort Casino
Owned by native Cahuilla peoples. ☎ 760-778-1772; www.sparesortcasino.com; 100 N Indian Canyon Dr, Palm Springs; treatments from $40; 🕘 8am-7pm

Tahquitz Canyon
Hike through waterways and legends. ☎ 760-416-7044; www.tahquitzcanyon.com; 500 W Mesquite Ave, Palm Springs; adult/child $12.50/6; 🕘 7:30am-5pm daily Oct-Jun, Fri-Sun Jul-Sep

Topanga Canyon State Park
Urban hiking that may make you forget you're in the city. ☎ 310-455-2465; www.parks.ca.gov; off Entrada Rd, Los Angeles; parking $6; 🕘 8am-dusk

Two Bunch Palms
Spa in an oasis, with a code of silence. Adults only. ☎ 760-329-8791, 800-472-4334; www.twobunchpalms.com; 67425 Two Bunch Palms Trail, Desert Hot Springs; admission $25, treatments from $115

The Well
Italian-inspired surroundings and innovative services. ☎ 760-341-2200, 866-843-9355; www.miramonteresort.com; 45-000 Indian Wells Lane, Indian Wells; baths/treatments from $45/80; 🕘 9am-6pm Mon-Thu, 9am-8pm Fri, 9am-8pm Sat, 8am-6pm Sun

EAT

Voda
Mod, Russian day spa, also serving meals of more-than-spa cuisine. ☎ 323-654-4411; www.vodaspa.com; 7700 Santa Monica Blvd, West Hollywood; mains lunch $8.50-10, dinner $11-26; platza massage from $25, other treatments from $125; 🕘 9am-midnight Mon-Fri, 7am-midnight Sat & Sun

SLEEP

Hope Springs
Midcentury-minimalist, modernist mecca, with period furniture and three natural mineral pools. ☎ 760-329-4003; www.hopespringsresort.com; 68075 Club Circle Dr, Desert Hot Springs; r from $125

Hotel Palomar
Cool, contemporary and central with a good-for-you vibe. ☎ 310-475-8511, 800-472-8556; www.hotelpalomar-lawestwood.com; 10740 Wilshire Blvd, Los Angeles; r from $249

LINK YOUR TRIP

www.lonelyplanet.com/trip-planner

It's a Small World: Ethnic Food Tour

WHY GO Southern California is perhaps the world's greatest melting pot, and pots always remind us of food. Whether your passion is burrowing into burritos or scarfing pad Thai to Elvis music, SoCal's all that and a bag of chips – here's just a sampler platter. Loosen that seat belt.

TIME
4 days

DISTANCE
350 miles

BEST TIME TO GO
Year-round

START
**Solvang,
Santa Barbara
County**

END
**Tijuana,
Mexico**

ALSO GOOD FOR

HISTORY &
CULTURE

SoCal is known for foods from Latin America and Asia, but we begin our journey with old-world comfort food in Solvang, which bills itself as the Danish capital of America. No trip to this quaint red-painted timber-built town is complete without *æbelskiver* (apple fritters) at ❶ **Solvang Restaurant**; they're so popular that there's a special takeout window. ❷ **Bit o' Denmark** serves a classic smorgasbord (Danish buffet) of over two dozen items in Solvang's oldest building (1911); don't miss the *frikadeller* (Danish meatballs).

Hwy 101 takes you into Santa Barbara. It's one of the West Coast's ritziest cities, but ❸ **La Super-Rica** looks downright humble, tucked away in the closest thing Santa Barbara gets to a barrio. This taco shack has become a sort of pilgrimage site as the favorite Mexican restaurant of the late great Julia Child, Santa Barbarian and America's first celebrity chef. Your tacos might come filled with oddball but delicious ingredients like zucchini and potato, flank steak or *adobado* (marinated pork). Roasted *pasilla* chiles stuffed with pork are another specialty of the house.

From here continue south on Hwy 101, and give thanks to the Ventura County farmland that may well have birthed those veggies you've been savoring. It's about 1½ hours into LA and America's first Thai Town. Browse the market at ❹ **Thailand Plaza** shopping center, or go upstairs, where the food court is a California take on Bangkok street stalls: look for "silver and gold bags" (ground pork and shrimp in wonton

wrappers), "crying tiger" (grilled, marinated beef) or some 100 curries and rice and noodle dishes. Down the street, **5** **Palms Thai** offers classics on both plate and stage. Pad Thai, curries, beef jerky and barbecue are second to none (there's also a special menu of venison, frog and more). *Then,* Palms throws in a Thai Elvis impersonator at night. "Can't help falling in love" indeed.

DETOUR

Bakersfield is not on many tourist maps...except for foodies'. That's thanks to its **Basque community**, one of the largest outside of the Pyrenees, who originally settled here as sheepherders. **Wool Growers** restaurant is much loved for its hearty portions of roast lamb, steaks and garlic chicken. They're all served with the "set-up," a half-dozen family-style side dishes. After dinner, two-step the night away at a country-western honky-tonk; Bakersfield's often called the "Nashville of the West."

Head south on Western Ave to Koreatown, 900-some restaurants spreading for miles. **6** **Chosun Galbee** offers a busy but chic setting for *galbi* (marinated beef ribs), *dak bulgogi* (chicken) and more cooked on a grill set into your table. **7** **Manna Korean BBQ**, a block away, is its open-air equivalent, with cheaper all-you-can-eat deals. Walk off your meal (and pick up takeout) at the gigantic supermarket amid the boutiques for toys, chic car accessories and traditional bedding at **8** **Koreatown Galleria** shopping center.

A few miles west, the Fairfax District is the historic hub of LA's Jewish community. **9** **Canter's Deli** is an institution, having sold over 2 million pounds of lox and 24 million bowls of chicken soup since 1931. Twenty-four hour service means that you can be harassed by Canter's sassy waiters whenever you want.

A couple of miles south on Fairfax Ave is Little Ethiopia. While the main pedestrian strip through the neighborhood is like Main St, Anywhere, USA, the cooking is brazen and fiery. Use your hands to tear apart large spongy millet crepes called *injera,* the better to scoop up curry stews and roasted meats at ⑩ **Rosalind's.**

> *"Pad Thai, curries, beef jerky and barbecue (and) a Thai Elvis impersonator..."*

I-10 and CA 110 take you to Little Tokyo in Downtown LA. In the shadow of City Hall, it looks more Californian than Japanese, but the cooking's authentic and the browsing fun. ⑪ **Daikokuya** specializes in steaming bowls of ramen noodles or *domburi* (rice topped with chicken, pork or egg). A short drive away, ⑫ **R-23** is a forward-thinking sushi bar/art gallery known for Dungeness crab salad and lobster tempura, exposed brick walls, Frank Gehry chairs and the occasional celebrity customer.

Lots of places have *a* Chinatown, but LA County has about a half-dozen. ⑬ **Empress Pavilion** rules Downtown LA's historic Chinatown for brunch of dim sum, a cacophony of servers wheeling carts of steamed, fried and baked dumplings. Barbecue at ⑭ **Sam Woo** is sweet and tangy – duck, chicken, pork and more.

Amid LA's hoards of taco and burrito stands, the gourmet ⑮ **La Serenata de Garibaldi** is a beacon in East LA's Mexican neighborhood, fancy and fine, with a large menu of fish and seafood. If you like your evenings as eclectic as your cuisine, the 1925 ⑯ **Figueroa Hotel** in Downtown LA makes a good break. A Spanish-style lobby leads to a bougainvillea- and cactus-laden poolside garden and Moroccan-themed rooms. It's close to Staples Center and LA Live for evening entertainment.

Other Chinatowns line the cities of the San Gabriel Valley east of LA: Monterey Park, San Gabriel, Rosemead, Alhambra and Arcadia. The rambling, Spanish-colonial confines of ⑰ **Mission 261** are so stately that you order dim sum off a menu. If you're a fan of Taiwanese soup dumplings (little steamed packets filled with meat and broth), you'll be in dumpling heaven at ⑱ **Din Tai Fung.** It's the Arcadia branch of Taipei's most venerated dumpling house.

It'd be easy to spend another week browsing LA's ethnic restaurants and shops – with 140 nationalities here, we've barely scratched the surface – but this morning the great south beckons. Head out of town on I-5 to Little India, on Pioneer Blvd in the Orange County city of Artesia. ⑲ **Tirupathi Bhimas** serves famous vegetarian cuisine; look for *koota*, a lentil stew with chili and coconut. ⑳ **Surati Farsan Mart** is a large and new Indian market with an extensive dine-in menu and all the vittles – savory, sweet and in packages – that you could want for the road.

Eat quickly, though, because it's not a long drive to Little Saigon, the world's largest community of overseas Vietnamese, straddling the OC communities of Garden Grove and Westminster. Try Vietnam's national dish, *pho* (noodle soup), at ㉑ **Pho 79**; there's a great version using chicken. It's inside Asian Garden Mall, a hulking Vietnamese shopping center that makes for excellent browsing and local color before or after your meal. ㉒ **Brodard** serves famous Nem Nuong Cuon – rice paper wrapped tightly around pork paste – way more addictive than it sounds!

EVEN SMALLER SMALL WORLDS

Food courts inside LA landmarks serve world specialties, blessedly minus the chain stores.

At Downtown LA's beaux arts **Grand Central Market**, **Maria's Fresh Seafood** dishes up fish tacos and seviche tostadas, **China Café** serves shrimp noodle soup, and other choices run from Middle Eastern to Hawaiian. The original **Farmers Market** (Third St and Fairfax Ave) offers fab multi-culti fare: tacos in shocking combos from ¡**Loteria!**; Brazilian-style *churrascuria* (grilled meats) at **Pampas Grill**; French bistro classics at **Monsieur Marcel**; and dishes perfumed with peanut, mango and tamarind at **Singapore Banana Leaf**.

I-5 continues south, where Old Town San Diego is one of the state's oldest settlements. Mexican restaurants here range from margarita-pouring dives to white-tableclothed boîtes. It may look for the tourists, but some of the restaurants are tops. ㉓ **Old Town Mexican Café** makes tortillas right there in the window; enjoy yours with *machacas* (shredded pork with onions and peppers). Meanwhile, the refined ㉔ **El Agave** pours from some 1500 tequilas to accompany its renowned dishes of *mole* (spicy sauce of chili and chocolate).

A short ride away, just north of downtown San Diego, is California's biggest Little Italy south of San Francisco. The brass-railed confines of ㉕ **Zucchero** are a homey, almost Brooklyn setting to enjoy a short phone-book's worth of pizzas, seafood dishes and gelati. ㉖ **Filippi's** is both an Italian deli and a red-and-white checked pizza grotto.

And with your passport, Tijuana is just across the border in Mexico. In the center of the tourist fray, ㉗ **Hotel Caesar** gave its name to the salad, and ㉘ **La Especial** serves standard-setting versions of familiar faves like *carne asada* (thinly sliced grilled beef). Across town, in Tijuana's Zona Gastronomica, the mystical menu at ㉙ **La Diferencia** is like something out of *Like Water for Chocolate* – and isn't that magic the reason you're here?
Andrew Bender

TRIP INFORMATION

GETTING THERE
Santa Barbara is on Hwy 101. Head south to LA and pick up I-5 into Orange and San Diego counties.

DO

Koreatown Galleria
Three-story mall with a supermarket to make you go "hmm?" ☎ 323-733-6000; www.koreatowngalleria.com; cnr Olympic Blvd & Western Ave, LA; ⏲ 7am-midnight; ⚞

Surati Farsan Mart
Known far and wide for sweets and spices, samosas to lassi. ☎ 562-860-2310; www.suratifarsan.com; 11814 Pioneer Blvd, Artesia; ⏲ 11am-8:30pm

Thailand Plaza
Thai shopping mall with supermarket and large food court. ☎ 323-993-9000; www.thailandplazala.com; 5321 Hollywood Blvd, LA; ⏲ 11am-1am Mon-Thu, 11am-2am Fri-Sun

EAT

Bit o' Denmark
Famous smorgasbord from the people who invented it. ☎ 805-688-5426; 473 Alisal Rd, Solvang; mains $13-22; ⏲ 11am-9pm Mon-Fri, 9am-9pm Sat & Sun

Brodard
Out-of-the-way fave for rice paper rolls. ☎ 714-530-1744; 9892 Westminster Ave, Garden Grove; mains $6-12; ⏲ 8am-9pm Wed-Mon

Canter's Deli
LA's Jewish deli of record, *and* late-night party place. ☎ 323-651-2030; www.cantersdeli.com; 419 N Fairfax Ave, LA; mains $7-18; ⏲ 24hr, closed Rosh Hashanah & Yom Kippur; ⚞

Chosun Galbee
Contempo-chic Korean barbecue. Great for first-timers. ☎ 323-734-3330; www.chosungalbee.com; 3300 Olympic Blvd, LA; dishes $11-23; ⏲ 11am-11pm

Daikokuya
Ramen and *donburi* specialist in Little Tokyo. ☎ 213-626-1680; 327 E 1st St, LA; ⏲ 11am-2.30pm & 5pm-midnight Mon-Sat

Din Tai Fung
LA outpost of Taiwan's most venerable house of dumplings, served in steamers. ☎ 626-588-1666; www.dintaifungusa.com; 1108 S Baldwin Ave, Arcadia; dumpling plates $5-9; ⏲ lunch & dinner

El Agave
Old world bungalow that's *muy romántico*. ☎ 619-220-0692; www.elagave.com; 2304 San Diego Ave, San Diego; mains lunch $10-18, dinner $18-27; ⏲ lunch & dinner

Empress Pavilion
Chinatown dim sum palace; seats 500. ☎ 213-617-9898; www.empresspavilion.com; Bamboo Plaza, 988 N Hill St, LA; dim sum plate $2-5, dinner $20-25; ⏲ 10am-3pm & 5:30-9pm Mon-Fri, 9am-3pm & 5:30-10pm Sat & Sun; ⚞

Filippi's
Old-school American-Italian in Little Italy. ☎ 619-232-5094; www.realcheesepizza.com; 1747 India St, San Diego; dishes $5-20; ⏲ 11am-10pm Sun & Mon, 11am-10:30pm Tue-Thu, 11am-11pm Fri & Sat; ⚞

Hotel Caesar
Not much atmosphere, but you can get the namesake salad where it was invented. ☎ 011-52-664-685-1606; Av Revolución 827, Tijuana, Mexico; Caesar salad $6; ⏲ 9am-midnight

La Diferencia
Dress up for fancy Mexican away from Tijuana's tourist fray. ☎ 052-664-634-3346; Blvd Sánchez Taboada 1061, Tijuana, Mexico; mains around $15; ⏲ noon-10:30pm Mon-Sat, noon-8pm Sun

La Especial
Mexican classics done right, in a basement of carved hardwood. ☎ 052-664-685-6654; Av Revolucíon 718, Tijuana, Mexico; mains breakfast $5-12, lunch & dinner $6-12; ⏲ 9am-10pm Sun-Thu, 9am-11:30pm Fri & Sat

La Serenata de Garibaldi

This East LA hacienda will convince you that "gourmet Mexican" isn't an oxymoron. ☎ 323-265-2887; www.laserenataonline.com; 1842 E 1st St, Los Angeles; mains $10-25; ⏱ 11:30am-10:30pm Mon-Fri, 9am-10:30pm Sat & Sun

La Super-Rica

Low-slung taco shack with happy hordes spilling out the door. ☎ 805-963-4940; 622 N Milpas St, Santa Barbara; dishes under $7; ⏱ 11am-9:30pm Thu-Tue; ♿

Manna Korean BBQ

Indoor-outdoor grill-fest, with bargain-priced all-you-can eat plan. ☎ 323-733-8516; www.mannakoreanbbq.com; 3377 Olympic Blvd, Los Angeles; mains $17-19; ⏱ 11am-11pm Sun-Thu, to midnight Sat & Sun

Mission 261

Elegant dim sum in a century-old adobe. ☎ 626-588-1666; www.mission261.com; 261 S Mission Dr, San Gabriel; dim sum each $2-7; ⏱ 10:30am-3pm & 5:30-9:30pm Mon-Fri, 9am-3pm & 5:30-10pm Sat & Sun

Old Town Mexican Café

Fresh made tortillas – even for breakfast! – and famous margaritas. ☎ 619-297-4330; www.oldtownmexcafe.com; 2489 San Diego Ave, San Diego; dishes $3-14; ⏱ 7am-midnight

Palms Thai

Thai classics, adventuresome meats and a Thai King (of rock 'n' roll, that is). ☎ 323-462-5073; www.palmsthai.com; 5900 Hollywood Blvd, Los Angeles; mains $7-16; ⏱ noon-11pm

Pho 79

Famous Vietnamese noodle soup in a Vietnamese mall with some 400 other shops. ☎ 714-893-1883; Asian Garden Mall, 9200 Bolsa Ave, Westminster; mains under $7; ⏱ 8am-7:30pm Thu-Tue, to 5pm Wed

R-23

East of Little Tokyo, is it Japanese cuisine or art gallery? We say both! ☎ 213-687-7178; www.r23.com; 923 E 2nd St, Los Angeles; ⏱ 11:30am-2pm Mon-Fri, 5:30-10pm Mon-Sat

Rosalind's

In the heart of Little Ethiopia. ☎ 323-936-2486; www.rosalindsrestaurant.com; 1044 S Fairfax Ave, Los Angeles; mains $11-17; ⏱ 11am-2am

Sam Woo

With Chinese-style barbecue this good, who cares if there's no atmosphere? ☎ 213-687-7238; 803 Broadway, Los Angeles; dishes $6-12; ⏱ 9am-midnight Sun-Thu, to 1am Fri & Sat

Solvang Restaurant

Come for æbelskiver dumplings, and you may also recognize the woodwork from the film *Sideways*. ☎ 805-688-4645; 1672 Copenhagen Dr, Solvang; mains $6-10; ⏱ 6am-3pm Mon-Fri, 6am-4pm summer, 6am-5pm Sat & Sun

Tirupathi Bhimas

Vegetarian cooking in the heart of Little India. ☎ 562-809-3806; www.tirupathibhimas.com; Little India Village, 18792 Pioneer Blvd, Artesia; mains $5-10; ⏱ 11:30am-2:30pm Tue-Fri, 6-9:30pm Tue-Thu, 6-10pm Fri

Zucchero

Brass-rail and marble-tiled backdrop for pizzas, pastries and gelati. ☎ 619-531-1731; www.cafezucchero.com; 1731 India St, San Diego; mains lunch $8-17, dinner $13-20; ⏱ 7am-10pm

SLEEP

Figueroa Hotel

Historic and eclectic in Downtown LA. ☎ 213-627-8971, 800-421-9092; www.figueroahotel.com; 939 S Figueroa St, Los Angeles; r $148-184, suites $225-265

www.lonelyplanet.com/trip-planner

LINK YOUR TRIP

Astronauts, Hotrods & Cowpokes

WHY GO When it comes to museums, So-Cal is like a school for the gifted. There's so much talent vying for attention in one place, it's easy to overlook the quirky kid. On this tour, we'll take time for the quirky, visiting those unique collections that deserve a closer look.

At first glance, the banged-up silver pod inside the ❶ **San Diego Air & Space Museum** looks like a space-age junker left up on blocks. But step closer. That's *Gumdrop*, the Apollo 9 command module used during a 1969 space mission to test the lunar module. Exhibits like *Gumdrop* are what's cool about this warehouselike museum in Balboa Park where historic treasures from the aviation age (plus a few reproductions) are plunked just inches from exhibit-floor walkways. From the Air & Space Museum, a short walk through the park leads to the Spanish Colonial charms of ❷ **Prado**, a bustling lunch spot in the heart of Balboa Park's museum district. Best bet is the terracing patio, where button-downed but friendly waitstaff offer knowledgeable recommendations about heirloom tomato salads and lobster & asparagus quiches. A short drive west leads to pedestrian-friendly Little Italy, where the four-story ❸ **La Pensione Hotel** offers European-style digs and a frescoed courtyard.

An easy 88-mile drive north on I-5 to Orange County's ❹ **Discovery Science Center** continues the technology and science theme. See the 10-story cube seemingly balanced on its point? Stop there. This hands-on museum has more than 100 exhibits explaining the science of everything from tornado formation to T-Rex digestion. Inside the Discovery Earth telephone booth, winds of 78 mph whip your hair – not to mention your vanity – in every direction. Small children run from the Shake Shack where a 6.9 earthquake rattles its occupants. Finally, stick your face into a board of plastic pins – we're not sure of the science – for a disconcerting imprint of your mug.

TIME
3 – 4 days

DISTANCE
260 miles

BEST TIME TO GO
Year-round

START
San Diego

END
Santa Barbara

ALSO GOOD FOR

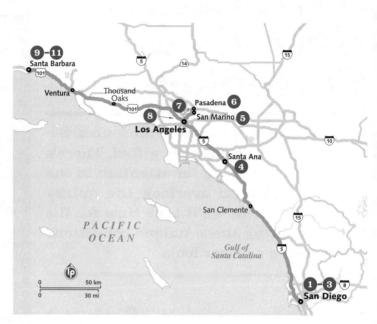

For cultural charms, point your car north toward the San Gabriel foothills, where wealthy mid-Westerners were lured in the 1880s by warm weather and healthier climes. Railroad tycoon Henry Huntington established his collection of manuscripts and art here in 1919. Today, the **5 Huntington Library, Art Collections, and Botanical Gardens** are open to the public at his magnificently landscaped former estate. Angelenos may rave about the finger sandwiches served in the dainty tea room or their lazy afternoon in the delightful gardens, but it's the paper-based library exhibits garnering the most wows, at least among the bookworm set. On display are a vellum Gutenberg Bible (c 1455) – with margin smudges from centuries of admiration – as well as an Ellesmere edition of Chaucer's *Canterbury Tales* (c 1400–05), and numerous early editions, letters and scribblings from literary and political heavyweights.

A leafy drive northwest leads to Pasadena's **6 Pacific Asia Museum**, where the Chinese porcelain bowls, beautiful in their delicate simplicity, are worth the admission price. The museum contains more than 14,000 works of art from Japan, the Himalayas, Southeast Asia and Tibet. Engaging exhibit summaries – contained in nine galleries around a courtyard – make the art accessible to newcomers. Pasadena, with its small town friendliness and walkable downtown, is a nice spot to spend the night before the drive into LA and beyond.

With its dangerous curves and narrow tunnels, the Arroyo Parkway from Pasadena to LA has a Wild West vibe, perhaps appropriate for the **7 Museum** of the American West. A few exhibits feel hokey – like the Shootout at the OK Corral diorama – but then you'll find a historic relic, like Doc Holliday's gun or Wyatt Earp's handwritten notes that explain what really went down. It's these real-life links to America's mythologized past that make this Griffith Park museum so darn fun. Equally engaging exhibits examine daily realities for pioneer families, immigrants, gold miners and Native Americans.

If the Wild West is the most romantic of American icons, the automobile and open road are a close second. Ask most guys to recommend their favorite LA museums, and the ⑧ **Petersen Automotive Museum** inevitably makes the top three. America's love affair with the automobile is front and center at this 300,000-sq-ft showplace, established in 1994 by the creator of *Hot Rod* magazine, Robert E Petersen. The permanent exhibit traces the history of the automobile while three separate galleries – Hotrods, Hollywood and Motorcycles – showcase a rotating lineup that has included a 2006 Bugatti and a Batmobile.

SOCAL: HOME OF SHRUNKEN HEADS

A quirky museum tour doesn't live up to its name unless it includes one or two oh-gross! exhibits. Based on our research, there's nothing creepier in SoCal than a tennis ball–sized shrunken head. Kids flock to the tiny noggins displayed near the mummies in San Diego's **Museum of Man** (www.museumofman.org), in Balboa Park. Further north, the squinch-faced head just past the jungle corridor in Buena Park's **Ripley's Believe It or Not!** (www.ripleysbp.com) is another doozy. You've been warned.

A 95-mile drive northwest leads to the low-key ⑨ **Karpeles Manuscript Library Museum**, another museum built on the passion of one avid collector. This under-the-radar trove of written artifacts, pulled from the collection of real-estate developer David Karpeles, has numerous intriguing finds – from the original draft of the Bill of Rights to Einstein's description of the theory of relativity. For another written masterpiece, the menu at ⑩ **Tupelo Junction Cafe** around the corner bubbles with Southern-minded specialties – think deep dish cheddar and Gouda mac-n-cheese with smoked bacon collard greens. Sleep it off a few blocks south at breezily sophisticated ⑪ **Hotel Santa Barbara**. The sunny Mediterranean colors should provide a bit of morning inspiration before a day exploring the museums and historic sites that fill Santa Barbara's pedestrian-friendly downtown.

DETOUR ▶ Its centennial celebrated in 2008, Pasadena's **Gamble House** (www.gamblehouse.org) is a masterpiece of Craftsman architecture built by Charles and Henry Green for Proctor & Gamble heir David Gamble. The entire home is a work of art; its foundation, furniture and fixtures all united by a common design and theme inspired by its southern California environs. The Gamble house is 1.5 miles northwest of the Pacific Asia Museum. Take E Walnut St west to N Orange Grove Ave and drive north.

Amy C Balfour

HISTORY & CULTURE

TRIP INFORMATION

GETTING THERE
The San Diego Air & Space Museum is located in Balboa Park, 3.5 miles southeast of San Diego International Airport.

DO
Discovery Science Center
Parents, resist the temptation to push your kids aside to get to the hands-on exhibits. ☎ 714-542-2823; www.discoverycube.org; 2500 N Main St, Santa Ana; adult/child $13/10; ☎ 10am-5pm; ♿

Huntington Library, Art Collections, and Botanical Gardens
A Gutenberg bible, Gainsborough's *Blue Boy* and the Japanese Garden are highlights. ☎ 626-405-2100; www.huntington.org; 1151 Oxford Rd, San Marino; adult $15-20, 5-11yr $6, student $10, senior $12-15; ☀ vary seasonally

Karpeles Manuscript Library Museum
Historic written artifacts are the draw at this free museum in downtown Santa Barbara. ☎ 805-962-5322; www.rain.org/~karpeles; 21 W Anapamu St, Santa Barbara; admission free; ☀ 10am-4pm

Museum of the American West
Engaging museum endowed by Gene Autry that highlights the romance and reality of life in the Wild West. ☎ 323-667-2000; www.autrynationalcenter.org; 4700 Western Heritage Way, Los Angeles; adult/student & senior/3-12yr $9/3/5; ☀ 10am-5pm Tue-Sun; ♿

Pacific Asia Museum
Nine galleries highlight Chinese, Japanese, Himalayan, Tibetan and Southeast Asian artwork. ☎ 626-449-2742; www.pacificasiamuseum.com; 46 N Robles Ave, Pasadena; adult/student & senior $7/5; ☀ 10am-6pm Wed-Sun

Petersen Automotive Museum
Celebrate car culture with a California spin. ☎ 323-930-2277; www.petersen.org; 6060 Wilshire Blvd, Los Angeles; adult/child/student & senior; $10/3/5; ☀ 10am-6pm Tue-Sun; ♿

San Diego Air & Space Museum
Hellcats, Wildcats and Spitfires fight for attention at this ode to aviation. ☎ 619-234-8291; www.aerospacemuseum; 2001 Pan American Plaza, San Diego; adult/6-11yr/senior $15/6/12; ☀ 10am-4:30pm

EAT
Prado
Join museum-hoppers, business people, military officers and ladies-who-lunch for an upscale museum-district meal. ☎ 619-557-9441; 1549 El Prado, San Diego; mains lunch $9-20, dinner $9-43; ☀ lunch daily, dinner Tue-Sun

Tupelo Junction Cafe
Enjoy hearty Southern gourmet meals and desserts such as malt ice-cream pie with Oreo & Whopper crust. ☎ 805-899-3100; www.tupelojunction.com; 1218 State St, Santa Barbara; mains $7-23; ☀ breakfast, lunch & dinner

SLEEP
Hotel Santa Barbara
Centrally located downtown hotel open since 1925. ☎ 805-957-9300; www.hotelsantabarbara.com; 533 State St, Santa Barbara; r $219-289

La Pensione Hotel
Great budget find in Little Italy that's close to downtown and the Embarcadero. ☎ 619-236-8000; www.lapensionehotel.com; 606 W Date St, San Diego; r $90

USEFUL WEBSITES
www.balboapark.org
www.pasadenacal.com

www.lonelyplanet.com/trip-planner

LINK YOUR TRIP

Sideways in Santa Barbara

FOOD & DRINK

WHY GO The 2004 Oscar winner Sideways may have gotten the party started, but passionate vintners, eco-minded entrepreneurs and gorgeous wine trails are keeping Santa Barbara and its wineries in the juice. Bryan Hope, sustainable-winery guru, recommends a few cinematic and sustainable highlights for your wine-tasting weekend.

TIME
2 – 3 days

DISTANCE
134 miles

BEST TIME TO GO
Year-round

START
Downtown Santa Barbara

END
El Capitan Canyon

ALSO GOOD FOR

OUTDOORS

Bryan Hope shows that green travel can be easy. On half-day trips with his company, Sustainable Vine Wine Tours (www.sustainable vine.com), he explains organic and sustainable growing practices in a way that's so accessible and engaging you're left wondering why other wineries are lagging behind.

Though most of his tours are in rural Santa Barbara County, Hope lives in the city and swaps the latest econews with the city's other earth-friendly entrepreneurs. One tasting room Hope recommends in ❶ Santa Barbara proper is ❷ Jaffurs Wine Cellars, which sits inside garage-style digs where the walls are adorned with surfboards. Known for Rhone varietals sourced from local growers, Jaffurs – located nine blocks east of State St – is a tiny but welcoming operation that produces about 4000 cases per year.

For stunning views of the city's mountain-flanked coastline, tread down the splintered wooden pier at Stearns Wharf at the southern end of State St. Turn left at the first cluster of shops, walk past the pirate mugs and painted starfish then climb one story to the tasting room at ❸ Stearns Wharf Vintners. Here, local wines are poured within view of chichi yachts and sun-dappled seas. "Most locals avoid the pier," says Hope, but Stearns Wharf Vintners is his recommended exception.

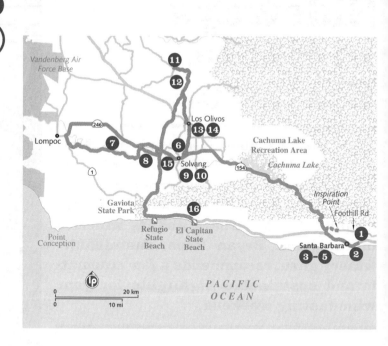

Unpack your bags, and maybe grab a catnap, behind the cream picket fence at the Victorian ❹ **Cheshire Cat Inn**, one of Santa Barbara's more eco-conscious accommodations. The inn, whose owner hails from Cheshire County, England, has 17 rooms inspired by *Alice in Wonderland,* all decorated with fun – but never overdone – English flair. The mood is communal, with guests sharing a large breakfast table in the morning. Eccentric Mad Hatters and grumpy Queen of Hearts can ease into the day at one of the shaded spots perfect for solo nibbling in the crisply manicured back yard. Those who suffer from cat allergies need not stay away – the grinning cats here are purely literary.

LOOK MOM, NO CAR!

If you're serious about traveling in an eco-conscious manner and visiting green-minded destinations, then Santa Barbara's your city. Public transportation is convenient, energy conscious and easy to use. One simple tip is to ride Amtrak's *Pacific Surfliner* from LA's Union Station to the Santa Barbara station, which is just steps from the beach, downtown and several hotels. Electric shuttles travel along State St as well as the coast. For trip planning details, check out www.santabarbarcarfree.org.

Before dinner, walk one block east to downtown's main drag, State St. Work up an appetite strolling past the upscale boutiques, bustling café patios and stately historic buildings – all sporting the same faux-Mediterranean style required by city codes. Look up to see the red clay tile roofs that tie them all together.

Hungry? Amble three blocks east from State St on Victoria St for dinner at
⑤ Spiritland Bistro. "It's small, quaint, and not open every day," says Hope.
Inside this classy but welcoming dining nook, perched on the corner of Victoria and Garden Sts, a vegetarian- and vegan-centric menu offers "organic global cuisine." The seasonal dinner menu recently included Greek moussaka, Italian vegetable risotto and Hawaiian nut-crusted mahimahi. Look for a special wine and food pairing menu on the last Wednesday night of the month.

In the morning, rise and shine for a drive north on Hwy 154 to the rolling hills and dusty roads of Santa Barbara's wine country, about 30 miles north of the city. Given a public relations boost by the wine-centric buddy movie *Sideways,* the area now boasts six wine trails and more than 100 wineries. Before that first sip of wine, however, pick your designated driver then load up on organic picnic fixings at the busy back counter inside **⑥ New Frontiers Natural Marketplace,** at the intersection of Hwy 246 and Old Mission Rd. Here, the produce is organic, the meat hormone-free and the sandwiches always above average. Loaded up, continue west on Hwy 246 past the windmills of Solvang and the ostriches of Buellton.

DETOUR The southern foothills of the Santa Ynez mountains are crisscrossed by shaded hiking trails that cut through rugged chaparral and steep canyons. Hope recommends the short but scenic hike along the Tunnel Trail to **Inspiration Point** for the latter's sweeping views of Santa Barbara and the Pacific Ocean. The trailhead is 2 miles from downtown. Park at the end of Tunnel Rd, off Mission Canyon Rd, keeping all four wheels completely within the painted lines.

Tractors, road bikes and Harleys will inevitably join your loop in the rolling **⑦ Santa Rita Hills.** Sporting the area's newest wine appellation (Sta Rita Hills) on their labels, the wineries on this trail are known for their top-notch pinots. To bypass the longer scenic loop, follow Hwy 246 west across Hwy 101 and turn left almost immediately onto Santa Rosa Rd. For the leisurely drive, stay on Hwy 246, continuing about 30 miles west, passing several wineries and the La Purisima State Historic Park. Turn left onto Hwy 1, following it south to Santa Rosa Rd, turning left to continue the loop. This route is popular with cyclists, and it's a scenic leg of the Solvang Century bike race every March.

At the eastern end of Santa Rosa Rd, follow the cacti and cobblestones to the **⑧ Alma Rosa Winery & Vineyards** tasting room. Look familiar? The room and its gregarious tasting manager, Chris Burroughs, enjoyed screen time in *Sideways.* Local wine pioneers Peter and Thekla Sanford, former owners of powerhouse Sanford Wineries, opened Alma Rosa in 2005 to focus on sustainable growing practices. "They're very ecominded," says Hope and "they've been farming organically for years." Consider purchasing a bottle and enjoying your picnic here. Tables are available in the shade or under the sun.

Finish the Santa Rita Hills loop by taking Santa Rosa Rd back to Hwy 246 and following it east to return to the kitschy, Danish charms of tiny ❾ Solvang. The town's windmills, *abelskivers* (gooey Danish pastries) and knickknack stores make for an entertaining – if sticky sweet – afternoon stroll. When it gets to be too much, step into the ❿ Presidio Vineyard & Winery tasting room at the corner of Hwy 246 and Atterdag Rd. Known for its pinots and chardonnays, Presidio is the only area vineyard that's certified both organic and biodynamic.

TASTING ROOM TIPS

To make the most of your wine tour, Chris Burroughs, the tasting room manager at Alma Rosa Winery & Vineyards, recommends small groups, open-minded attitudes and an itinerary focused on just a handful of wineries. Picnicking on site is always welcome, and you'll be considered especially cool if you complement your lunch with wine purchased on site. Not so cool? Heavy perfume and smoking. Otherwise, enjoy yourself and don't be afraid to ask questions – winemakers love beginners.

Next up is the wine trail through ⓫ Foxen Canyon, where there's nary a windmill to be seen. What you will find are oak-dotted hillsides, tidy rows of grapevines and some of the prettiest wineries in the county. From Solvang, take Hwy 246 east to Hwy 154, following it northwest to Foxen Canyon Rd. Turn right. If time allows, follow this meandering country lane about 18 miles, passing several wineries – Fess Parker, Zaca Mesa, Foxen Vineyard – before reaching tiny San Ramon Chapel for a turnaround.

Just north of bus-filled Fess Parker Winery & Vineyard is ⓬ Demetria Estate. With its curving arches and thick wooden doors, Demetria looks like the grand country home of a beloved Greek uncle. It's also the winery most enjoyed by Sustainable Vine patrons and is one of Hope's favorites as well. Why? "The location, the people, and the wines," says Hope. Tastings are by appointment only, but it's worth the extra effort to sample Demetria's biodynamically farmed pinots and Rhone varietals.

For shopping, head south to the upscale boutiques, fine galleries. and country-chic furniture stores clustering around the five short blocks comprising downtown ⓭ Los Olivos. This charming gourmet town enjoys a prime location between the Foxen Canyon Wine Trail to the northwest and the Santa Ynez Wine Trail to the south. To make it all the more perfect, it even has a few inviting tasting rooms of its own.

While in town, stop by ⓮ Los Olivos Café. Savor Caprese salads, smoked salmon pizzas, butternut squash ravioli and other outstanding Cal-Mediterranean specialties with just the right glass of wine on the restaurant's wisteria-draped patio. Another memorable scene from *Sideways* – Miles, Jack, Maya and Stephanie's evening double date – was filmed inside. The café also offers a 3pm to 5pm "grazing" menu – think baked brie, beef skewers and marinated olives – that's just right for a leisurely afternoon respite.

For a more substantial meal, follow Grand Ave south – it becomes Alamo Pintado Rd – to Hwy 246, backtracking through Solvang to Buellton. On the south side of the road is the bustling parking lot at **15** **Hitching Post II**. This sturdy roadside chophouse – which makes its own pinot noir – is the restaurant where Maya waitressed in the movie. It's also one of numerous sites where Miles overimbibed. Too bad he didn't focus on the food as well as the wine. Old-school mains like oak-grilled steak, baby-back ribs and California quail come with a veggie tray, shrimp cocktail or soup, salad, and a starch. It's the perfect place for toasting, laughing and swapping stories about the day.

"Another memorable scene from Sideways – *Miles, Jack, Maya and Stephanie's evening double date – was filmed inside."*

Before hitting the sack, unwind beside your fire pit at **16** **El Capitan Canyon**, 20 miles west of Santa Barbara. This upscale, woodsy retreat is a current darling of glossy travel mags, scoring a recent cover of *Sunset* magazine. It's also a hit with couples looking for a more pampered outdoor experience, and families with rambunctious kids looking for semiwild distractions. In other words, if you want to sleep close to nature without pitching your own tent, El Capitan Canyon is the place to do it. In addition to toasting marshmallows, watching for Bambi and wishing on shooting stars, guests can indulge themselves with on-site massages, a gourmet café and a yoga yurt. The best part? The top-quality snooze between the fancy mattress and high-thread-count sheets.

Amy C Balfour

TRIP INFORMATION

GETTING THERE

From Los Angeles, drive 95 miles northwest via Hwy 101 to downtown Santa Barbara. Ecominded? Hop the Pacific Surfliner.

EAT

Hitching Post II

Old-school steakhouse on main drag – by the ostrich farm – makes its own pinot noir. ☎ 805-688-0676; 406 E Hwy 246, Buellton; mains $23-49; ☺ 5-9:30pm, from 4pm Sat & Sun

Los Olivos Café

Savor Cal-Mediterranean specialties at this breezy bistro known for its wine selection, outstanding food and *Sideways* cameo. ☎ 805-688-7265; www.losolivoscafe.com; 2879 Grand Ave, Los Olivos; mains $11-25; ☺ lunch, "3pm-5pm" menu, dinner

New Frontiers Natural Marketplace

Pick up healthy sandwiches – Avocado Delight, Turkey Galore – on the way to the wine country. ☎ 805-693-1746; 1984 Old Mission Dr (off Alamo Pintado Rd at Hwy 246); mains $7-8; ☺ 8am-8pm Mon-Sat, to 7pm Sun

Spiritland Bistro

White linens, raw walnut taco salads, communal wine nights, and vegetarian- and vegan-centric menu. ☎ 805-966-7759; www.gjspiritland.com; 230 E Victoria St, Santa Barbara; mains lunch $15-25, dinner $35-45; ☺ lunch daily, dinner Wed-Sun

DRINK

Alma Rosa Winery & Vineyards

Welcoming winery in the Santa Rosa Hills offers fantastic organically grown wines. ☎ 805-688-9090; www.almarosawinery.com; 7250 Santa Rosa Rd, Buellton; tasting fee $10; ☺ 11am-4:30pm

Demetria Estate

Greek-style hospitality enchants visitors at this Foxen Canyon tasting room where grapes are farmed sustainably and biodynamically. ☎ 805-686-2345; www.demetriaestate.com; 6701 Foxen Canyon Rd, Los Olivos; tasting fee $10; ☺ by appointment

Jaffurs Wine Cellars

Small batch Rhone varietals are served up in a surfboard-adorned tasting room. ☎ 805-962-7003; www.jaffurswine.com; 819 E Montecito St, Santa Barbara; tasting fee $8; ☺ 11am-5pm Fri-Sun

Presidio Vineyard & Winery

Try organically farmed pinots and chardonnays in the heart of downtown Solvang. ☎ 805-693-8585; www.presidiowinery.com; 1603 Copenhagen Dr #1, Solvang; tasting fee $7.50, to keep the glass $10; ☺ 11am-6pm

Stearns Wharf Vintners

Yacht-dotted coastal views from 2nd-floor tasting room halfway down the pier. ☎ 805-966-6624; www.stearnswharf.org/Pages/page19.html; 217g Stearns Wharf, Santa Barbara; tasting fee $15; ☺ 11am-6pm

SLEEP

Cheshire Cat Inn

Victorian inn, inspired by the grinning cat from Lewis Carroll's classic, is eco-minded and close to downtown. ☎ 805-569-1610; www.cheshirecat.com; 36 W Valerio St, Santa Barbara; r $199-299, cottages $279-399

El Capitan Canyon

High style meets the big woods at this upscale campground where fire pits accompany rustic-chic cabins and tents. ☎ 805-685-3887; www.elcapitancanyon.com; 11560 Calle Real, Goleta; tents $145, cabins $225-350; ⚓

USEFUL WEBSITES

www.greensantabarbara.com
www.sbcountywines.com
www.lonelyplanet.com/trip-planner

LINK YOUR TRIP

OUTDOORS

Santa Barbara Islands & Hikes

WHY GO Santa Barbara is catnip for outdoor adventurers. Cove-dotted coastlines, rocky swimming holes, shady mountain trails, and a national park where there's nary a car to be seen – all within 50 miles of downtown. Meow. Kerry Kellogg, trails manager in Los Padres National Forest's Santa Barbara Ranger District, shares some favorites.

The warning on the website reads: "There is no transportation available on the islands. All areas must be accessed on foot or by private boat or kayak." If that message lures you instead of scares you, then ❶ **Channel Islands National Park** is the SoCal destination for you. Best of all, a short boat ride from Ventura with ❷ **Island Packers** – one of the park's concessionaires – can have you on the islands in under hour. Try ❸ **Channel Islands Kayak Center**, next door to Island Packers, for rentals and tours.

Of the park's four largest islands, ❹ **Anacapa,** with its haunting rocky spires and proximity to the mainland, works best for camera-toting day-trippers. Just west, multifaceted ❺ **Santa Cruz** is the top choice for hikers and kayakers looking for easy camping and light adventure. ❻ **Santa Rosa** kicks it up a notch, drawing backcountry campers who don't mind lugging water and gear to less convenient campsites. Which leaves rugged ❼ **San Miguel** – with its wet landings and harsh terrain – for the hardy few. Prepare for serious isolation and potentially torrid weather.

Which one wins Best All Around? Kellogg, who grew up in Santa Barbara, picks 22-mile-long Santa Cruz. Though campers haul their own equipment, it's only about a half mile from the Scorpion's Bay dock to the eucalyptus-shaded campsites. Kayakers can paddle

TIME
5 days

DISTANCE
150 miles

BEST TIME TO GO
Apr – Oct

START
Channel Islands

END
Santa Barbara

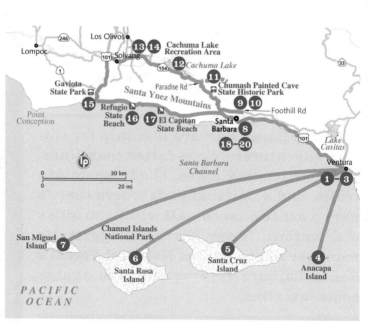

newbie-accessible coves and sea caves while hikers scramble scrub-and-brush-lined trails to bluffs "where you can look back at Santa Barbara and Ventura," says Kellogg. "It's spectacular."

To look back at the Channel Islands from the mainland, follow the coast 30 miles northwest from Ventura to the Santa Ynez mountains. Here, front-country trails crisscross the foothills above downtown Santa Barbara. Pre-hike, load up with gourmet cheeses and meats – and maybe a bottle of pinot – at sunny **8** **Metropulos**, a well-stocked deli-and-wine shop in the eclectic Funk Zone neighborhood off Hwy 101.

For summit hounds, Kellogg recommends hiking the **9** **Tunnel Trail** which starts at the end of Tunnel Rd off Mission Canyon Rd. About 4 miles one way, the trail "will take you up to La Cumbre peak, the highest point on the range." If peak bagging isn't a priority, try **10** **Rattlesnake Canyon Trail** east of Skofield Park off Las Canoas Rd. It's a more moderate hike that winds past waterfalls and the old mission dam.

If the weather's bad, don't write off the day, says Kellogg. A 20-minute drive north from Santa Barbara on Hwy 154 through the San Marcos pass can take you from coastal cold and fog to inland sun and 100°F heat. From Hwy 154, follow Paradise Rd east to the Lower Santa Ynez Recreation Area (grab a $5 Adventure Pass at the kiosk). The **11** **Red Rock Trail** starts here and passes large rocks and cool-water swimming holes. "If getting tanned and sunburned is your goal," says Kellogg, "this is the place."

Just north is ⑫ **Cachuma Lake Recreation Area**, a county park resembling a small village with its general store, gas station, laundry and 350 campsites. Here you can trout fish, boat, even sleep in a yurt. What you can't do is dip a toe in all that gorgeous blue. The lake is a source for drinking water so bodily contact is a no-no.

> **DETOUR**
> For an unexpectedly harrowing drive (that's arguably more exciting than the destination) turn right onto Painted Cave Rd 8 miles north of Santa Barbara off Hwy 154. The road narrows as it twists up into a canyon, shrinking to nearly one lane by the time it reaches **Chumash Painted Cave State Historic Park**. Look for the small sign on your left. The bright pictographs, protected by a metal screen, were painted more than 400 years ago.

Due to its proximity to several wine trails, nearby Santa Ynez is a farm town teetering on the precipice of chichi wine village. Wine meets West at ⑬ **Trattoria Grappolo**, a tony Italian joint sitting behind a kitschy Wild West facade. The chef, hailing from Tuscany, lures a loyal, convivial crowd with rigatoni, ravioli and a list of fancy pizzas. Chase your cappuccino with a shot of whiskey – after sticking a dollar bill on the wall – next door at ⑭ **Maverick Saloon**, a country-and-western bar where the two-steppin' is never ironic.

The next morning, follow Hwy 101 south past the Santa Rita Hills. As the coast approaches, the highway swings east, passing three rugged coastal state parks – ⑮ **Gaviota State Park**, ⑯ **Refugio State Beach** and ⑰ **El Capitan State Beach** – in quick succession. All have camping, but Kellogg recommends the slightly more commercial charms of Refugio, where pitching a tent is no hassle and there's a concessionaire on site. "As a local person, I like going there. It's easy living." It's also hard to score a reservation. Call exactly seven months before your desired date. With its sheltered put-ins, Refugio is also good for launching kayaks because you rarely fight the surf. For a scenic two-hour paddle, Kellogg recommends two cars, dropping one at El Capitan then returning to Refugio (both have day parking). "It's pretty primitive beach lined with coves and cliffs," says Kellogg. "The clarity of the water, especially in summertime, is like having a glass-bottom boat. You can look down and see starfish." A paved bike path links the two parks – 2.5 miles apart – so a kayak-biking combo is another way to explore. ⑱ **Paddle Sports of Santa Barbara** can help with rentals and logistics.

Refuel with a bowl of chunky seafood stew on the deck at harborside ⑲ **Brophy Brothers**. For the best sunset Kellogg recommends ⑳ **Arroyo Burro Beach**, called Hendry's Beach by locals, a few miles west. As Kellogg explains: "Right as the sun dips into the ocean, 100 people get quiet and sometimes cheer."

Amy C Balfour

TRIP INFORMATION

GETTING THERE

From LAX, follow Hwy 101 northwest 70 miles to Ventura.

DO

Channel Islands Kayak Center

Beside Island Packers, this outfitter rents kayaks, with maps, and offers guided tours. Call for appointment. ☎ 805-644-9699; www.cikayak.com; 1691 Spinnaker Dr, Ventura; day rentals single/double $35/55

Channel Islands National Park

Stop by the Visitor Center in Ventura for brochures and weekend lectures at the in-house tide pool. ☎ 805-658-5730; www.nps.gov/chis; 1901 Spinnaker Dr, Ventura; admission free, campsite $15; ⏲ Visitor Center 8:30am-5pm; ♿

Island Packers

Boats depart daily for Anacapa and Santa Cruz. ☎ 805-642-1393; www.islandpackers.com; 1691 Spinnaker Dr, Suite 105b, Ventura; trips adult $45-75, child $28-58, senior $42-70; ⏲ 8:30am-5pm

Paddle Sports of Santa Barbara

Rents kayaks and guides multisport tours. ☎ 805-899-4925; www.kayaksb.com; 117b Harbor Way, Santa Barbara; half-day rentals single/double $30/40; ⏲ 10am-6pm

EAT & DRINK

Brophy Brothers

For the perfect melding of surf and stew, slurp cioppino on the upstairs deck. ☎ 805-966-4418; www.brophybros.com; 119 Harbor Way, Santa Barbara; mains $10-24; ⏲ lunch & dinner

Maverick Saloon

Pick yer pardner and do-si-do – or just stick to drinkin' – at this fun-loving saloon.

☎ 805-686-4785; www.mavericksaloon.org; 3687 Sagunto St, Santa Ynez; ⏲ noon-2am Mon-Fri, 10am-2am Sat & Sun

Metropulos

Grab gourmet sandwiches, cheese and wine from this upbeat corner deli. ☎ 805-899-2300; www.metrofinefoods.com; 216 E Yanonali St, Santa Barbara; mains $8-10; ⏲ 8:30am-6pm Mon-Fri, 10am-4pm Sat

Trattoria Grappolo

Yep, that's fine Tuscan Italian they're serving behind that rootin' tootin' facade. ☎ 805-688-6899; www.trattoriagrappolo.com; 3687 Sagunto St, Santa Ynez; mains $7-30; ⏲ lunch Tue-Sun, dinner daily

SLEEP

Cachuma Lake Recreation Area

Find tents, cabins and yurts at this fisher-friendly campground, 20 miles northwest of Santa Barbara. ☎ 805-686-5055; www.cachuma.com; 59, Hwy 154, Santa Ynez Valley; day use vehicles $8, campsites $20-30, yurts $60-70, cabins $135-210; ♿

El Capitan State Beach

Tide pools, fishing, and surfing 17 miles northwest of Santa Barbara. ☎ 805-968-1033; www.parks.ca.gov; 10 Refugio Beach Rd, Goleta; day use vehicles $8, campsites peak/nonpeak $25/20; ⏲ 8am-sunset; ♿ 🐾

Gaviota State Park

Swimming, boating and 39 campsites 33 miles northwest of Santa Barbara. ☎ 805-968-1033; www.parks.ca.gov; 10 Refugio Beach Rd, Goleta; day use vehicles $8, campsites peak/nonpeak $25/20; ⏲ 7am-sunset; ♿ 🐾

Refugio State Beach

Between Gaviota and El Capitan; has sheltered put-ins perfect for launching kayaks. ☎ 805-968-1033; www.parks.ca.gov; 10 Refugio Beach Rd, Goleta; day use vehicles $8, campsites peak/nonpeak $25/20; ⏲ 8am-

LINK YOUR TRIP

www.lonelyplanet.com/trip-planner

Lift Your Spirits

WHY GO The journey of self-discovery isn't a competition but honestly, is there anywhere prettier than the SoCal coast to contemplate the meaning of it all? Crashing surf, cradling bluffs, multicolored sunsets. Sometimes the universe says it's OK to be pretty on the outside too.

It's not every day you see golden lotus domes breaking up a palm-dotted coastal horizon. Unless you're at the southern border of Encinitas, of course, where the ❶ **Self-Realization Fellowship Retreat & Hermitage** sets a charmingly offbeat mood for a road trip. Founded by Yogi Paramahansa Yogananda in 1937, the retreat lures spiritual pilgrims seeking to balance their body, mind and soul. Though the main grounds are closed to casual visitors, solace seekers are welcome to wander the tranquil koi ponds and burbling waterfalls nestled in the retreat's public meditation garden on K St.

This lush oasis sits on a bluff overlooking ❷ **Swami's Beach**, where territorial locals surf a powerful reef break. For a more laid-back vibe, try ❸ **Swami's Café**, just across South Coast Hwy 101. This come-as-you-are beach joint serves smoothies, omelets, burritos and abundant veggie options to an appreciative, flip-flop wearin' crowd. Order at the counter, settle in on the umbrella-shaded patio.

Ready to dig deeper? A short coastal drive north leads to Carlsbad's ❹ **Chopra Center**. Inside this den of serenity, complimentary healing tea makes spiritual self-analysis a downright pleasant experience. It's easy to lose track of time browsing guides on mind-body healing – most by alternative medicine pioneer Deepak Chopra and other ayurveda practitioners – and the center offers intriguingly named courses like Primordial Sound Meditation and Soul of Healing. Even if you only have time to flip through the pamphlets, you'll better understand your dosha or, in

TIME
3 days

DISTANCE
202 miles

BEST TIME TO GO
Year-round

START
Encinitas

END
Ojai

ALSO GOOD FOR

OUTDOORS

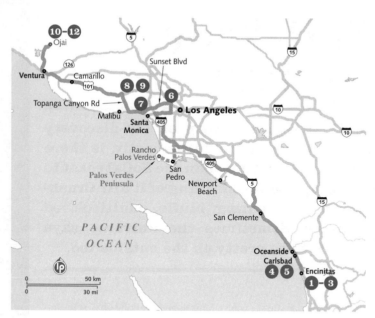

lay terms, get an inkling why you're always cranky and stressed out. If you leave unbalanced, the pampered grounds of the luxurious ❺ **La Costa Resort & Spa**, which the Chopra Center calls home, will lighten your mood. Floral bursts of orange, purple and yellow thrive in the breezy shadows of swaying palms and tiled fountains. Two PGA golf courses, a spa with 42 treatment rooms, 17 tennis courts and an array of children's programs round out the appeal.

As you step inside ❻ **Bodhi Tree Bookstore** from bustling Melrose Ave in LA, the patchouli scent and the clinking of wind chimes mark the transition from urban chaos to no-stress zone. The loudest sounds inside this cottage-style bookstore are the wooden floorboards creaking as readers peruse the tightly packed stacks, wandering from Astrology to Christianity to UFOs to Western Mysticism and beyond. Psychics offer daily readings in the store's annex, and used books are sold in a separate building near a thriving 35ft Bodhi tree. A small poster offers a definition of New Agers: "People taking conscious responsibility for their own lives, not blaming others for their problems." An admirable philosophy, but one that's hard to appreciate while dodging maniacs on the Pacific Coast Hwy. Destination? Paramahansa Yogananda's 10-acre ❼ **Self-Realization Fellowship Lake Shrine**. The fellowship's headquarters were established here in 1925; the Lake Shrine opened to the public in 1950.

One of the most striking features here is the Gandhi World Peace Memorial, which sits beside the path circling the shrine's spring-fed lake. A portion of

Gandhi's ashes rests in a brass coffer inside the memorial's stone sarcophagus. Elsewhere, solitude seekers enjoy the numerous benches dotting the flower-dappled foliage. Stop by the small museum adjacent to the gift store for exhibits highlighting the yogi's meetings with international leaders in the 1920s and '30s as well as his accurate pre-death pronouncement.

For lunch, continue up the coast to Malibu, following serpentine Topanga Canyon Rd into the hills. After about 5 miles, turn left at Old Topanga Rd, then park just past the ivy-draped sign for **❽ Inn of the Seventh Ray**. With its burbling fountains, shaded nooks and chirping birds, one would hardly be surprised if the staff started speaking Elvish. The seasonal menu has Zen-like appeal as well, with fresh ginger lemonade complementing veggie quiches, raw salads and fresh fish sandwiches. Tolkien-esque visions continue inside the hobbit-sized **❾ Spiral Staircase** bookstore next door. Jam-packed with candles, inspirational stickers and spiritual-minded books and CDs, it too exudes Zen-like tranquility. Just beware the world's loudest – and most persistent – set of wind chimes hanging in the sideroom corner. There's no hiding for the clumsy; we can attest.

> **DETOUR** The stunning **Wayfarers Chapel** (www.wayfarers chapel.org) in Rancho Palos Verdes, south of Los Angeles, isn't exactly New Age but it certainly inspires reflection. Perched on a bluff above the Pacific Ocean, 20 miles southwest of the Long Beach Airport, this small glass church is cradled by towering redwoods. Built by Lloyd Wright (Frank's son) in 1951, it's a beautiful spot for meditation, and the Swedenborgian congregation here welcomes wayfarers of all denominations.

You know a town deserves its New Age rep when stacks of holistic health magazines vie for attention in towering racks outside the public library. But that's **❿ Ojai**, the "New Agey-ist" of SoCal's small towns. Tucked in a tiny valley 14 miles north of Ventura, this mystical Shangri-la is dotted with spiritual retreats and learning centers as well as several top-notch spas. At sunset, look to the Topa Topa mountains for "The Pink Moment," an occasional weather-based phenomenon causing the summits to turn a rosy shade of pink.

For Mission-style lodging with amphibian flair, check into Ojai's **⓫ Blue Iguana Inn**. Rustic wooden furniture, patterned throw rugs and blue-tiled displays – not to mention decorative iguanas – keep the mood convivial. Continue the happiness with a soul-nourishing dinner on the patio at **⓬ Boccali's**. The gooey pizza, warm bread and fresh salads – don't miss the tomatoes – are so good that most meals end with the same thing: a completely clean plate. In sum, maybe that's what it all comes down to, a hot slice of pizza and a mountain-flanked view.

Amy C Balfour

TRIP INFORMATION

GETTING THERE
Encinitas is 25 miles north of San Diego International Airport and 102 miles south of Los Angeles International Airport.

DO

Bodhi Tree Bookstore
Cozy cottage of enlightenment carries a wide array of spiritual and philosophical books. ☎ 310-659-1733; www.bodhitree.com; 8585 Melrose Ave, West Hollywood; ◷ new 10am-11pm, used until 7pm

Chopra Center
Healing tea, engaging books and welcoming staff assist visitors seeking mind-body balance. ☎ 760-494-1600; www.chopra.com; 2013 Costa del Mar Rd, Carlsbad; ◷ 6:30am-8pm Mon-Fri, 7:30am-6pm Sat & Sun

Self-Realization Fellowship Lake Shrine
Still your thoughts on a stroll around a swan-dotted, spring-fed lake. ☎ 310-454-4114; www.lakeshrine.org; 17080 Sunset Blvd, Los Angeles; ◷ 9am-4:30pm Tue-Sat, 12:30pm-4:30pm Sun

Self-Realization Fellowship Retreat & Hermitage
Meditate, read or watch Swami's Beach surfers from a lush garden that was originally landscaped by Yogi Paramahansa Yogananda. www.yogananda-srf.org; 215 K St, Encinitas; ◷ 9am-5pm Tue-Sat, 11am-5pm Sun

Spiral Staircase
A tiny New Age bookery jammed beside Inn of the Seventh Ray. ☎ 310-455-3370; 128 Old Topanga Canyon Rd, Topanga; ◷ noon-11pm

EAT

Boccali's
Savor home-style Italian at this convivial east-of-town spot. ☎ 805-646-6116; www.boccalis.com; 3277 Ojai-Santa Paula Rd, Ojai; mains lunch $7-10, dinner $7-18; no credit cards; ◷ lunch & dinner; ♿

Inn of the Seventh Ray
Leafy patio beside stream provides Zen-dy backdrop for organic-minded dining. ☎ 310-455-1311; www.innoftheseventhray.com; 128 Old Topanga Rd, Topanga; mains lunch $10-16, dinner $24-35; ◷ lunch & dinner

Swami's Café
It's all good at this omelet and burrito joint across the street from the golden lotus domes. ☎ 760-944-0612; 1163 S Coast Hwy 101, Encinitas; mains under $10; ◷ 7am-4pm

SLEEP

Blue Iguana Inn
Kick back at this breezy Mission-style motel where fun-loving iguanas set the mood. ☎ 805-646-5277; www.blueiguanainn.com; 11794 N Ventura Ave, Ojai; r $119-159, suites $159-269

La Costa Resort & Spa
Flower-dotted retreat offers golf, tennis the Chopra Center, and numerous ways to relax. ☎ 760-438-9111; www.lacosta.com; 2100 Costa del Mar Rd, Carlsbad; r from $299

USEFUL WEBSITES
www.ojaichamber.org
www.wholepersoncalendar.com

LINK YOUR TRIP
www.lonelyplanet.com/trip-planner

Palm Springs & Joshua Tree Oases

OUTDOORS

WHY GO Southern California's deserts can be brutally hot, barren-looking places. But that's not always the case in the Coachella Valley and around Joshua Tree National Park, where shady fan-palm oases hide in geologically wonderful canyons and fertile date gardens. Spring is best, when desert wildflowers bloom.

SoCal deserts at first look hostile to human life, but Native Americans have thrived here for millennia. Especially around Palm Springs, streams flowing from the San Jacinto Mountains sustain a rich variety of plant life in the desert canyons. Walk in the footsteps of the ancestors of the Agua Caliente band of Cahuilla Indians into ❶ **Indian Canyons**, where sculpted cliffs overshadow oases of native California fan palms. Hike out with a knowledgeable tribal ranger or independently explore Murray Canyon, where bighorn sheep and birds come seeking water.

In 1774 Spanish explorer Juan Bautista de Anza was the first European to encounter the Cahuilla tribe, after which the name Agua Caliente came to refer to both the people and the natural hot springs, which still flow restoratively today through the town of ❷ **Desert Hot Springs**. There are dozens of old-fashioned motels and resorts with day spas to choose from. The midcentury modern hideaway of ❸ **Hope Springs** attracts cool hipsters from LA and beyond.

Hwy 62 (aka Twentynine Palms Hwy) curves north past ❹ **Big Morongo Canyon Preserve**, yet another hidden oasis in the high desert. Tucked into the Little San Bernardino Mountains, it's a bird-watching hot spot, thanks to a native riparian habitat with a collection of cottonwood and willow trees. Starting from the parking lot by the educational kiosk, you can tramp along wooden boardwalks through

TIME
2 – 3 days

DISTANCE
175 miles

BEST TIME TO GO
Feb – Apr

START
Palm Springs

END
Palm Springs

marshy woodlands as hummingbirds flutter atop flowers and woodpeckers hammer away.

In the forgotten northwest corner of Joshua Tree National Park, **⑤Black Rock Campground** is a beautiful spot to set up base camp for a long weekend, with easy access to hiking trails into Black Rock Canyon. Young kids will get a kick out of the **⑥ Black Rock Nature Center**, too. Hwy 62 keeps rolling east into the soulful, artistic town of **⑦ Joshua Tree**, just outside the national park's west entrance. Tap into the indie vibes and chat with the alternative-minded, occasionally eccentric locals at the **⑧ Crossroads Cafe**, a rustic coffeehouse with art displays. Just as much of a pleasure is an overnight stay at **⑨ Spin & Margie's Desert Hide-a-Way**, where unusual design motifs include corrugated tin, old license plates and cartoon art. Or you can motor on down the highway to the military base town of Twentynine Palms. With country-kitsch tables and a weather vane, the cheerful **⑩ Wonder Garden** café mixes up smoothies, wraps and bagel sandwiches, but it's the ice-cream freezer that gets the most business when temperatures soar in the desert. Trickier to find is the idiosyncratic **⑪ 29 Palms Inn**, a mellow collection of very rustic adobe-and-wood cabins built around the Oasis of Mara.

Once you've gotten your bags unpacked and refueled both your stomach and the car, it's time to jump into the heart of **⑫ Joshua Tree National Park**, a wonderland of jumbo rocks interspersed with sandy forests of Joshua trees. The trees got their name from Mormon settlers, who thought the twisted, spiky arms resembled the arms of a prophet stretching up toward God.

Start exploring at the **13** **Oasis Visitor Center**, with its must-see exhibits about California's desert fan palms *(Washingtonia filifera)*. These palms are often found growing up to 75ft tall along fault lines, where cracks in the earth's crust allow subterranean water to surface. Each tree can live for up to 80 or 90 years and may weigh as much as 3 tons. Outside the visitor center a gentle nature trail leads you around the Oasis of Mara, named by the indigenous Serrano tribespeople for the natural springs and green grasses. When gold miners arrived in the late 19th century, the original 29 palm trees found growing here later gave the town its name. Although this gorgeous grove is easily accessible today, desert fan–palm oases are a rare gift, with just over 150 mapped across North America.

> **DETOUR**
>
> From the town of Yucca Valley, head 5 miles north along hilly Pioneertown Rd, and you'll drive straight into the past. **Pioneertown** (www.pioneertown.com) was built as a Hollywood movie backdrop for Western movies in 1946, and has hardly changed since. Witness a "real" Old West–style gunfight, hit the 1940s-era bowling alley built for Roy Rogers, then scarf down plates of barbecue as live bands play at honky-tonk **Pappy & Harriet's Pioneertown Palace** (www.pappyandharriets.com).

With your curiosity whetted by the Oasis of Mara, backtrack along Hwy 62 and head south past **14** **Indian Cove Campground** to the hard-baked trailhead for the 3-mile round-trip to **15** **49 Palms Oasis**, which takes you over a ridge, then drops you into a rocky gorge, doggedly heading down past barrel cacti toward that distant speck of green. You might fear that it's a mirage, but instead it reveals itself to be a lush grove of desert fan palms. Sit under their shade and beside small pools of water that attract birds, bugs and bighorn sheep. Like anywhere else in the national park, stay on the trail to avoid crushing fragile cryptobiotic soil, upon which a healthy desert depends.

"...desert fan–palm oases are a rare gift, with just over 150 mapped across North America. "

Not all of the park's oases are natural. Anyone who enjoys history and Western lore should take the 90-minute walking tour of **16** **Keys Ranch**, where pioneer homesteaders once tried their hand at cattle ranching, mining and farming, thanks to a man-made mill and irrigation works. Nearby is another artificial oasis at **17** **Barker Dam**, where a nature trail loops for about a mile past a pretty little lake and a rock engraved with Native American petroglyphs. If you find it so refreshing here that you just can't seem to leave, pitch a tent at **18** **Hidden Valley Campground**.

Get an early start the next morning and take the winding road south through the park. You'll pass the abundant ⑲ **Cholla Cactus Garden**, where handily labeled specimens burst into bloom in early spring, as well as a roadside patch of ocotillo plants, which look like green octopus tentacles adorned with flaming scarlet flowers later in the spring. Next, you'll arrive at the humble ⑳ **Cottonwood Visitor Center**, named for the nearby Cottonwood Springs oasis. Once used by the Cahuilla people, who left behind archaeological evidence such as mortars and clay pots, the springs became a hotbed of gold mining and milling activity in the late 19th century. Far more hidden is ㉑ **Lost Palms Oasis**, reached only by a strenuous hiking trail. After 3.6 miles, the trail delivers you an eerily remote canyon filled with boulders, where beautiful stands of desert fan palms wave. The precipice views of the multicolor desert look limitless.

There's a more interesting way to get back to Palm Springs than backtracking through the park. Drive south from Cottonwood Springs and over I-10 to pick up scenic Box Canyon Rd, which burrows a hole through the desert, twisting its way toward Mecca to join Hwy 111. Heading north, the Coachella Valley is the ideal place to find the date of your dreams – the kind that grows on trees, that is. The valley's most famous variety, the medjool, arrived in the 1920s from Morocco. Today, date orchards let you sample different varieties for free, but the signature taste of the valley is the date shake. Try one at the tasty

GOING VERTICAL

From boulders to cracks to multi-pitch faces, there are more rock-climbing routes in 'J-Tree' than anywhere else in SoCal. The longest climbs are not much more than 100ft, but there are many challenging technical routes. Pick up climbing guidebooks and gear in town at **Nomad Ventures** (www.joshuatreevillage .com/515/nv.htm). For a day of instruction or a guided climb, talk to **Uprising Adventure Guides** (www.uprising.com).

㉒ **Oasis Date Gardens**, or at ㉓ **Shields Date Gardens**, where you can watch the free movie *Romance & Sex Life of the Date*.

Nearer to Palm Springs, you've got one last chance to uncover a desert oasis at the ㉔ **Coachella Valley Preserve**, where a nature trail winds through the Thousand Palms Oasis, also the habitat of the endangered fringe-toed lizard. Heading back into Palm Springs, stop off for a bite at two modern-day culinary oases: ㉕**Manhattan in the Desert**, where Jewish deli sandwiches and layer-cake slices are as big as dinner plates, or at the organic, healthy-minded ㉖ **Native Foods**, a casual wood-furnished eatery with candlelit outdoor tables at night.

Sara Benson

TRIP INFORMATION

GETTING THERE
From Los Angeles, take I-10 east, then follow Hwy 111 south into downtown Palm Springs.

DO
Big Morongo Canyon Preserve
This haven for 240 species of birds attracts rare bighorn sheep to its watering holes. ☎ 760-363-7190; www.bigmorongo.org; 11055 East Dr, off Hwy 62, Yucca Valley; admission free; ⏱ 7:30am-sunset; ♿

Black Rock Nature Center
Family friendly exhibits explain the park's varied desert ecology. ☎ 760-367-3001; www.nps.gov/jotr; 9800 Black Rock Canyon Rd, off Joshua Lane, Joshua Tree; admission free with national park entry; ⏱ 8am-4pm Sat-Thu & noon-8pm Fri Oct-May; ♿

Coachella Valley Preserve
Walk atop the San Andreas fault, wandering past dozens of native flora and fauna species. ☎ 760-343-2733; http://coachellavalleyp reserve.org; Thousand Palms Canyon Rd, off I-10 exit Ramon Rd, Thousand Palms; admission free; ⏱ sunrise-sunset Sep-Jun, 5am-10am Jul & Aug

Cottonwood Visitor Center
Basic visitor services near the national park's southern entrance. ☎ 760-367-5500; www .nps.gov/jotr; off Cottonwood Springs Rd, 8mi north of I-10; admission free with national park entry; ⏱ 9am-3pm

Indian Canyons
Call ahead for schedules of 90-minute tribal ranger-led hikes. ☎ 760-323-6018; www .indian-canyons.com; off South Palm Canyon Dr, Palm Springs; adult/child $8/4, incl guided hike $11/6; ⏱ 8am-5pm daily Oct-May, 8am-5pm Fri-Sun Jun-Sep; ♿

Joshua Tree National Park
There are no facilities besides rest rooms, so gas up and bring food and plenty of water. ☎ 760-367-5500; www.nps.gov/jotr; 7-day entry pass per car/bicycle $15/5; ⏱ 24hr daily; ♿

Keys Ranch
Call between 8am and 4:30pm daily to book your guided tour in advance. ☎ 760-367-5500; www.nps.gov/jotr; Park Blvd, Joshua Tree National Park; adult/child 6-12yr $5/2.50; ⏱ 10am & 1pm Sat & Sun, weekday tour schedules vary

Oasis Date Gardens
Taste the Coachella Valley's famous dates, not too far from the Salton Sea. ☎ 800-827-8017; www.oasisdategardens.com; 59-111 Hwy 111, Thermal; admission free; ⏱ 9am-4pm

Oasis Visitor Center
Stop by for free information, to buy field guides and maps, and to watch videos on demand (from 11am to 3pm). ☎ 760-367-5500; www.nps.gov/jotr; National Park Blvd at Utah Trail, 3 miles south of Hwy 62; admission free with national park entry; ⏱ 8am-5pm; ♿ ⚲

Shields Date Gardens
It's the classic choice, if only to view the laughable 1950s-style educational film. ☎ 760-347-7768; www.shieldsdates.com; 80-225 Hwy 111, Indio; admission free; ⏱ 9am-5pm

EAT
29 Palms Inn
The inn's poolside restaurant bakes its own bread, grills steaks and seafood, and pours bottled microbrews, too. ☎ 760-367-3505; www.29palmsinn.com; 73950 Inn Ave, Twentynine Palms; mains $6-23; ⏱ 11am-2pm daily, 5-9pm Sun-Thu & 5-9:30pm Fri & Sat

Crossroads Cafe
Homemade breakfast hash, fruit smoothies, fresh sandwiches and dragged-through-the-garden salads make both omnivores and vegan tree-huggers happy. ☎ 760-366-5414; www.crossroadscafeandtavern.com; 61715 Twentynine Palms Hwy, Joshua Tree; mains $5-11; ⏱ 6:30am-3pm Sun-Tue, 6:30am-8pm Thu-Sat

Manhattan in the Desert
It's always busy, but worth any wait for heaping plates of West Coast–style Jewish deli fare. ☎ 760-322-3354; 2665 E Palm Canyon Dr, Palm Springs; most mains $6-18; ⏱ 7am-9pm Sun-Thu, 7am-10pm Fri & Sat; ♿

Native Foods
This LA import dishes up a half-dozen types of vegan burgers, Southwestern salads and sizzling veggie rice bowls with seitan and tofu. ☎ 760-416-0070; www.nativefoods .com; Smoke Tree Village, 1775 E Palm Canyon Dr, Palm Springs; mains $7-11; ⏱ 11am-9:30pm Mon-Sat; 🐾

Wonder Garden
This veggie-friendly café is a local institution, opposite the Rio Ranch Market. ☎ 760-367-2429; 73511 Twentynine Palms Hwy, Twentynine Palms; mains $4-8; ⏱ 7:45am-3pm Mon-Sat

SLEEP

29 Palms Inn
Some of the rustic cabins have decks and fireplaces, perfect on cool desert evenings; small TVs and no telephones keep the atmosphere serene. ☎ 760-367-3505; www.29palmsinn .com; 73950 Inn Ave, Twentynine Palms; r $90-325; 🐾

Black Rock Campground
Family-oriented national-park campground with equestrian sites available. ☎ 760-367-3001, reservations 877-444-6777; www .recreation.gov; 9800 Black Rock Canyon Rd, off Joshua Ln, Joshua Tree; campsites $15; ♿ 🐾

Hidden Valley Campground
First-come, first-served campsites are available year-round, in the middle of the park. ☎ 760-357-5500; www.nps.gov/jotr; Park Rd, Joshua Tree National Park; campsites $10; ♿ 🐾

Hope Springs
A modernist motel mecca, with artful public spaces and 10 rooms boasting authentic period furniture. A two-night minimum stay is required; rates rise on weekends. ☎ 760-329-4003; www.hopespringsresort.com; 68075 Club Circle Dr, Desert Hot Springs; r from $195

Indian Cove Campground
This quieter, less crowded campground also has group sites available. ☎ reservations 877-444-6777; www.recreation.gov; off Indian Cove Rd, 3mi south of Hwy 62, Twentynine Palms; sites $15-40; ♿ 🐾

Spin & Margie's Desert Hideaway
Four boldly colorful, snappy-looking suites each have their own kitchen at this homey, hacienda-style inn; the studio cabin is more private. ☎ 760-366-9124; www.deserthide away.com; 6920-6923 Sunkist Rd, Joshua Tree; r $125-160

USEFUL WEBSITES
www.desertusa.com
www.visit29.org

LINK YOUR TRIP

www.lonelyplanet.com/trip-planner

Retro-Modern Palm Springs

WHY GO For this fab midcentury modern architectural tour of Palm Springs, where you can drive by masterpieces from the Rat Pack era, tour Elvis' honeymoon hideaway and stay overnight inside Frank Sinatra's vacation home, we've teamed up with local expert Tony Merchell, a well-known architectural historian.

TIME
2 days

DISTANCE
16 miles

BEST TIME TO GO
Oct – Mar

START
Palm Springs

END
Palm Springs

After WWII, Hollywood celebrities flocked to Palm Springs, where their newfound wealth built desert palaces, many in the midcentury modern architectural style. Today, this retro-flavored resort town shows off some of the best-preserved modern buildings in Southern California.

Your first stop is at the ❶ **Palm Springs Visitor Center**. "This building, with its hyperbolic paraboloid roof structure," Merchell points out, "is an icon of Palm Springs. It's an adaptive reuse of the Tramway Gas Station designed by Albert Frey and Robson C Chambers in 1965." The distinctive space-age structure, with its stark metal roof cutting diagonally across an organic background of toothily peaked San Jacinto Mountains, is a standout example of modern design, rescued from demolition by the city in 2002. You can pick up a copy of the Palm Springs Modern Committee's full-color tour map here; the self-driving tour takes you past many of the important architectural buildings still standing in Palm Springs.

Everyone interested in modern architecture visits the ❷ **Kaufmann Desert House** designed by Richard Neutra, an Austrian-born architect who worked with Frank Lloyd Wright and later Rudoph Schindler. We admit it's partly concealed by mature landscape, but don't worry: parts of this masterpiece are still visible from the road. Its exterior is

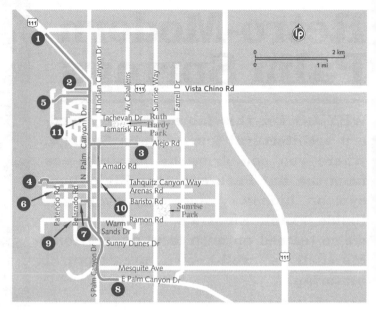

dominated by square lines and flat-topped metal roofs. But some building materials, including sandstone and sliding glass walls, soften the look, making the house fit more harmoniously with the desert landscape.

Next up is the ③ **Frank Sinatra House**, designed by modern architect E Stewart Williams. Ol' Blue Eyes wanted a Georgian-style mansion, but Williams, a contemporary of Frey and Neutra, proposed a low-lying modern design. You can only get a good view of the Sinatra House if either the front or rear gate is open – but it's also available to rent. Famous for its grand piano-shaped pool, the house is stylishly outfitted with authentic period pieces.

"…sheer glass walls and corrugated roofs built dramatically into a rocky canyon."

Very few modern houses are open to the public in any regular manner. However, as Merchell points out, "Architect Albert Frey's own house, ④**Frey House II**, now owned by the Palm Springs Art Museum, is open on rare occasions." It's an incredible piece of art, with sheer glass walls and corrugated roofs built dramatically into a rocky canyon. The Swiss-born architect apprenticed with Le Corbusier, master of the International Style, before moving to Palm Springs in 1939. Other modernist designs by the prolific Frey include the 1950s-era City Hall.

One house that is regularly open to the public is the ⑤ **Alexander Estate**, also known as "The House of Tomorrow" and the "Elvis Honeymoon Hideaway."

This spectacular midcentury modern party house was built for Robert Alexander, who, along with his father George, was the largest builder of modern homes in Palm Springs. Elvis leased it for a year and, after marrying Priscilla Beaulieu at the Aladdin casino hotel in Las Vegas, he escaped to Palm Springs, as many celebs did both then and now, to get away from Hollywood paparazzi.

"There are many hotels to choose from in Palm Springs," Merchell points out, "but if you want something of the retro Rat Pack experience, you've got a few good choices." Just off the main drag in downtown Palm Springs, Merchell highlights the ❻ **Orbit In**. "It was the first modern hotel to be refurbished in Palm Springs. It's all first-class, with serious furniture and a great outdoor bar by the pool." Throwback touches include LP record players (juxtaposed with plasma-screen TVs), a fire pit by the Jacuzzi and 1950s-style beach cruiser bikes for guests to borrow.

Also conveniently downtown, the ❼ **Del Marcos Hotel** dates from 1947. This was the first building in the desert designed by architect William F Cody, who worked on many other private homes, hotels and country clubs around Palm Springs. "It has a great pool with a wonderful view of the mountains. Two of the upper-level rooms have private balconies that offer a view of Frey House II," Merchell comments. Groovy tunes in the lobby usher you to a saltwater pool and ineffably chic rooms named for local architectural luminaries. On the south side of Palm Springs, you'll find the ❽ **Horizon Hotel**, which was also designed by Bill Cody and has been meticulously restored to its former glory. Notice there are no 90-degree angles visible anywhere on the property.

STAR HOMES

Another way to get the "Rat Pack" experience is to rent a Palm Springs vacation home. "There are hundreds of vacation rentals available in the desert, many of which are perfectly furnished in the modern style," says our expert Tony Merchell. Many can be found through **Vacation Rentals by Owner** (www.vrbo.com). Listings include the immaculately furnished "Alexander," which was restored "with the assistance of the original architect William Krisel, who also designed the new front landscape," says Merchell.

"There aren't that many Rat Pack–era restaurants left in Palm Springs," Merchell remarks. "One of the best is ❾ **Melvyn's** at the Ingleside Inn. The restaurant is good, but the bar is fantastic: a small dance floor, and old-timers partying down to the wee hours." Come for the Sunday afternoon jazz jams. Casual ❿ **Sherman's Deli & Bakery** is "where old Palm Springs and tourists hang out," Merchell reveals. "Sandwiches are enormous!" Grab a sidewalk table and watch PS society pass by, often dressed in outrageously colorful California-chic resort wear by ⓫ **Trina Turk**, whose original storefront boutique looks right at home inside a 1960s Albert Frey design.

Sara Benson

HISTORY & CULTURE

TRIP INFORMATION

GETTING THERE
From Los Angeles, take I-10 east, then follow Hwy 111 south into downtown Palm Springs.

DO
Alexander Estate
Tour the midcentury modern home that's nicknamed the "Elvis Honeymoon Hideaway." ☎ 760-322-1192; www.elvishoneymoon .com; 1350 Ladera Circle, Palm Springs; admission $25-35; ◷ tours 1pm Mon-Fri, by reservation only Sat & Sun

Frey House II
Owned by the Palm Springs Museum, which has an impressive collection of Julius Shulman's midcentury modern architectural photographs. ☎ 760-322-4800; www.psmuseum.org; 686 Palisades Dr, Palm Springs; admission varies; ◷ by reservation

Kaufmann Desert House
Painstakingly restored, this home's pavilions are the final evolution of Neutra's domestic style. 470 W Vista Chino Rd, Palm Springs; ◷ no public entry

Palm Springs Visitor Center
Look for the converted gas-station at the start of the Tramway Rd. ☎ 760-778-8418; www. palm-springs.org; 2901 N Palm Canyon Dr, Palm Springs; admission free; ◷ 9am-5pm

Trina Turk
Find shagadelic drag-worthy fashions at PS' signature clothing boutique. ☎ 760-416-2856; www.trinaturk.com; 891 N Palm Canyon Dr, Palm Springs; ◷ 10am-5pm Mon-Fri, 10am-6pm Sat, noon-5pm Sun

EAT
Melvyn's
Frank Sinatra numbered among the early customers at this swanky resto lounge. ☎ 760-325-2323; www.inglesideinn.com; Ingleside Inn, 200 W Ramon Rd, Palm Springs; mains $10-50; ◷ restaurant 11:30am-3pm Mon-Fri, 9am-3pm Sat & Sun, 6-11pm daily, lounge 10am-2am daily

Sherman's Deli & Bakery
This deli serves early-bird dinners and is festooned with headshots of aficionados like Don Rickles. ☎ 760-325-1199; www .shermansdeli.com; 401 E Tahquitz Canyon Way, Palm Springs; mains $5-15; ◷ 7am-9pm; ♿ ⚘

SLEEP
Del Marcos Hotel
After suffering years of bad remodels, this 16-room oasis shines at last. ☎ 760-325-6902, 800-676-1214; www.delmarcoshotel.com; 225 W Baristo Rd, Palm Springs; r $99-300

Frank Sinatra House
A three-night minimum rental is required at Blue Eyes' "Twin Palms" estate. ☎ 877-318-2090; www.timeandplace.com/loca tions/palmsprings/twinpalms; 1148 E Alejo Rd, Palm Springs; house rental per night $1500-2600

Horizon Hotel
Marilyn Monroe and Betty Grable once lounged by the poolside bar at this modern gem. ☎ 760-323-1858, 800-377-7855; www.thehorizonhotel.com; 1050 E Palm Canyon Dr, Palm Springs; r $99-440

Orbit In
Swing back into the 1950s during the complimentary "Orbitini" happy hour. ☎ 760-323-3585, 877-996-7248; www.orbitin.com; 562 W Arenas Rd, Palm Springs; r $129-450

USEFUL WEBSITES
www.psmodcom.com
www.pspf.net

LINK YOUR TRIP

www.lonelyplanet.com/trip-planner

Southern Fruit Loop

WHY GO Make a quick getaway into the San Diego backcountry for some old-fashioned fun in Temecula, famous for its grapes and wineries; Julian, a one-horse town surrounded by rolling hills of apple orchards and horse ranches; and the remote desert settlement of Borrego Springs, which bursts with citrus groves.

TIME
2 days

DISTANCE
250 miles

BEST TIME TO GO
Sep – Apr

START
San Diego

END
San Diego

ALSO GOOD FOR

HISTORY &
CULTURE

For San Diegans, Temecula has become a popular short-break destination for its Old West–Americana main street, nearly two dozen wineries and California's largest casino, Pechanga. Temecula means "Place of the Sun" in the language of the indigenous Luiseño tribespeople. In the 1820s, this sun-drenched region became a ranching outpost for nearby Mission San Luis Rey. Although you may imagine nothing but desert down here, Temecula is only 20 miles inland from the Pacific Ocean. Every night, coastal fog and strong breezes cool off the valley's 5000-acre citrus and vineyard zone. That's why wine grapes flourish here, especially sun-seeking Mediterranean red varietals.

Five-block Front St is the heart of ❶ **Old Town Temecula**. Stroll past turn-of-the-last-century storefronts, many of which now house antique dealers, and sample Temecula's agricultural products at places like the ❷ **Temecula Olive Oil Company**. See if you can taste the difference between their olives harvested early in autumn, which have a more robust flavor, and those picked during the new year, which tend to be richer, more golden and mellow tasting. Some of the oils are pressed from the same type of olives that Spanish padres cultivated at early California missions in the late 18th and early 19th centuries. Nearby in Old Town, laid-back ❸ **Sweet Lumpy's BBQ** was voted best barbecue in the Inland Empire. It doesn't have tattoo-flashing biker chicks like its competitor across the street, but it does make

darn good hickory-smoked 'cue, hand-pulled pork and beef sandwiches, and homemade fruit pies.

Never mind that many of Temecula's wineries aspire to be like lavish Napa estates. You can still find some down-to-earth, diamond bottles in the rough here, especially if it's Italian-style *vino* you crave. Rancho California Rd is the main route into wine country. **4 Loma Vista B&B** is a welcoming B&B with vineyard-view balconies and a hot tub for relaxing after an afternoon of wine tasting. On another hilltop further east, **5 Mount Palomar Winery** is one of Temecula's oldest wineries, growing diverse varietals since 1969. In the Spanish Mission–style tasting room, Italian wines like Sangiovese are what most folks love, along with a distinctive dry Riesling and a nutty cream sherry aged in California's only outdoor solera, a Spanish system of barrel aging and blending different vintages together. At Ponte Family Estate Winery, known for its Italian blends, **6 Smokehouse Restaurant** is a locals' fave lunch and weekend brunch spot, with an airy garden-ensconced patio.

PICK YOUR OWN

Along Hwy 78 outside Julian, many family-owned orchards let you pick your own apples and pears during September and October. The 1930s **Calico Ranch** (www.spencervalley.com) is just east of town, or visit **Peacefield Orchard** (www.peacefieldorchard.com), which has a 105-year-old Gravenstein apple tree. Backtracking to Temecula, the **Temecula Berry Company** (www.temeculaberryco.com) is open typically from May until the July 4 holiday.

Thin-crust pizzas baked in a grapevine-fired oven taste best when married to a glass of spicy Nebbiolo. Youthful **7 Wilson Creek Winery** makes an odd, but undeniably creative almond champagne (infused with almond oil during fermentation) and a chocolate port. For the big finish, go out of your way to find **8 Leonesse Cellars**, pouring award-winning viognier and mélange des rêves, for its panoramic mountain and vineyard views gained from a Tudor-esque tower.

Winding through the pine-covered mountains and tree-shade valleys of the San Diego backcountry, it's less than an hour's drive to **9 Julian**, a late-19th-century gold-rush town. Settled by ex-Confederate soldiers after the Civil War, flecks of gold were found in the creek here in 1869, sparking a short-lived burst of speculation. Not much mineral ore was ever extracted here, but more lasting riches were found in the fertile soil. Today apple orchards and equestrian ranches fill the countryside. To experience the past for yourself first, take the kids with you to **10 Eagle and High Peak Mine**, where tour guides will lead you through the underground tunnels of an authentic 19th-century hard-rock mine.

TOURING TEMECULA

To leave the designated driving to someone else, **Grapeline Temecula** (www.gogrape.com) offers day-long minivan tours that can include four winery tastings and lunch. To get a different perspective on the vineyards, **California Dreamin'** (www.californiadreamin.com) operates sunrise balloon rides out of Temecula.

Julian's apple harvest takes place in early autumn, but crowds descend year-round on its pint-sized main street, merrily jammed by motorcyclists out for a Sunday-afternoon ride. False-fronted shops along the wooden sidewalks all claim to make the very best apple pie, cider, jams and jellies. The classic pick is the family-owned **11 Julian Pie Company**, which churns out apple cider and cinnamon-dusted cider donuts alongside its apple-filled pastry goodies. To savor the flavor of the Old West, stay at the **12 Julian Gold Rush Hotel**, a historical landmark. If it's fully booked, the surrounding countryside is full of enticing rural B&B retreats.

"…guides will lead you through the underground tunnels of an authentic 19th-century hard-rock mine."

Keep driving over the mountains, deeper into the desert, to lonely, wind-buffeted **13 Borrego Springs**. Apart from losing yourself in the palm-canyon oases and salt beds of Anza-Borrego Desert State Park, another good reason to make the trek out here is for the grapefruit harvest in early spring, when roadside fruit stands on Christmas Tree Circle open their shutters. To get back to San Diego, backtrack to Julian, then follow Hwy 79 and/or the Sunrise Hwy (County Rd S1) south, both scenic routes that connect with I-8 westbound.

Sara Benson

TRIP INFORMATION

GETTING THERE
From San Diego, take I-15 north for about an hour to Temecula.

DO

Eagle and High Peak Mine
Be regaled with tales of the hardscrabble life of the town's early pioneers during an hour-long underground tour; call ahead to confirm hours. ☎ 760-765-0036; end of C St, Julian; adult/child $10/5; 🕙 10am-2pm Mon-Fri, 10am-3pm Sat & Sun; 🚻

Leonesse Cellars
A renowned winery on the unhurried, eastern side of Temecula Valley. ☎ 951-302-7601; www.leonessecellars.com; 38311 De Portola Rd, Temecula; tasting fee $10; 🕙 10am-5pm

Mount Palomar Winery
Elevate your senses at this well-established winery and deli, perfect for picnic lunches. ☎ 951-676-5047; www.mountpalomar .com; 33820 Rancho California Rd, Temecula; tasting fee $10; 🕙 10am-6pm Mon-Thu, 10am-7pm Fri-Sun

Old Town Temecula
Print out free coupons and a digital visitors-guide from the website. ☎ 951-506-0056; www.temeculacvb.com; visitor center 42031 Main St, Temecula; admission free; 🕙 visitor center 10am-5pm; 🚻

Temecula Olive Oil Company
Roasted garlic, herb and citrus-infused oils are made by a master from olives grown in pesticide-free groves. ☎ 951-693-0607; www.temeculaoliveoil.com; 28653 Old Town Front St, Temecula; 🕙 10am-5pm

Wilson Creek Winery
Take a pass on the sparkling wines to taste the rich, estate-bottled zinfandels and syrahs instead. ☎ 951-699-9463; www.wilsoncreek winery.com; 35960 Rancho California Rd, Temecula; tasting fee $10; 🕙 10am-5pm

EAT

Julian Pie Company
Hot apple pie à la mode will make you smile. ☎ 760-765-2449; www.julianpie .com; 2225 Main St, Julian; mains $3-15; 🕙 9am-5pm; 🚻

Smokehouse Restaurant
California wine-country cuisine is delicately touched by Italian influences at this busy winery. ☎ 951-694-8855; www.pontewin ery.com; Ponte Winery, 35053 Rancho California Rd, Temecula; mains $13-23; 🕙 11am-5pm Mon-Thu, 11am-9pm Fri & Sat, 10am-7pm Sun Apr-Oct, winter hours vary; 🚻

Sweet Lumpy's BBQ
Sweet and spicy sauces accompany fall-off-the-bone tender meats, with all the fixin's on the side. ☎ 951-506-3747; www.sweet lumpysbbq.com; 28464 Front St, Temecula; mains $8-25; 🕙 11am-8:30pm Mon-Fri, 11am-4pm Sat; 🚻

SLEEP

Julian Gold Rush Hotel
A turn-of-the-20th-century B&B with antique ambience and a quaint honeymoon cottage. ☎ 760-765-0201, 800-734-5854; www.julian hotel.com; 2032 Main St, Julian; r $130-210

Loma Vista B&B
Known for delicious breakfasts, this hacienda's 10 rooms have rustic country-and-western, Euro-Victorian and art-deco accents. ☎ 951-676-7047, 877-676-7047; www .lomavistabb.com; 33350 La Serena Way, Temecula; r $130-220

USEFUL WEBSITES
www.julianca.com
www.temeculawines.org

http://www.lonelyplanet.com/trip-planner

LINK YOUR TRIP
TRIP
50 Scenic Byways & Highways p307
68 48 Hours in San Diego p391

Life in Death Valley

WHY GO Dive deep into the Mojave Desert on our grand tour of Death Valley National Park, a forbidding-sounding place where the incredible forces of natural and human history collide. Time your trip for early spring to catch blossoming wildflowers and blessedly lower temperatures.

Death Valley is a land of extremes – you'll find the lowest elevation in the US here, not far from Mt Whitney, the highest peak in the lower 48 states. Death Valley is also the hottest place in the nation. If you don't believe us, just take a look at the ❶ **World's Largest Thermometer**, off I-15 in Baker. It stands 134ft tall to commemorate the record-breaking temperature of 134° F measured in nearby Death Valley on July 10, 1913. Try to visit the desert in the cooler spring months, when wildflowers are in full bloom. That is, if enough rain has fallen over the winter.

Even when the desert is bone-dry, you can still find an oasis at ❷ **Tecopa Hot Springs Resort**. Soak in the natural mineral springs used by Native Americans for centuries, then try the fresh, organic cooking at ❸ **Pastels**, a humble little desert bistro. On new moon nights, when the desert sky twinkles with celestial diamonds, you can roll out your sleeping bag for star-viewing parties. Further north in Shoshone, look for ❹ **Cafe C'est Si Bon**, a solar-powered internet café decorated with vibrant local art and UFOs ("Unusual and Found Objects").

Harley riders speed along Hwy 178 on the winding, southern approach to ❺ **Death Valley National Park**. Cresting Jubilee Pass, the highway at last dips down into the valley itself, enfolded by steep, rugged mountains. The peaks are the ages-old product of geological uplift and erosion along thrust faults. Despite its name, this harsh-looking valley

TIME
2 – 3 days

DISTANCE
350 miles

BEST TIME TO GO
Feb – Apr

START
Baker

END
Death Valley National Park

ALSO GOOD FOR

OUTDOORS

BEST TRIP

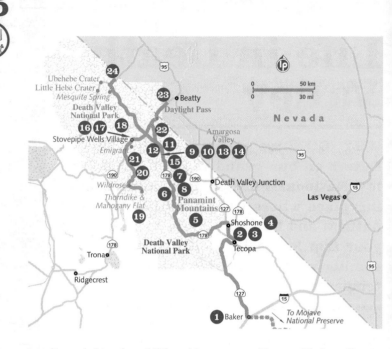

is a diverse habitat for wildlife and has supported human life for millennia, starting with the Timbisha Shoshone people, followed much later by Old West pioneers, gold seekers and borax miners. It's the silence and solemnity of the vast expanse that inspires travelers today.

That cracked, parched-looking salt pan extending across the valley floor is **6 Badwater**. At 282ft below sea level, Badwater is the lowest point in North America. Here a boardwalk hovers over the constantly evaporating bed of salty, mineralized water, otherworldly in its beauty. Prehistoric Lake Manly, which covered the entire valley during the ice age, reappeared here in 2005 for the first time in recorded human history. Although the lake evaporated again within weeks, its surprising reemergence just goes to show the tenacity of life in this barren-looking valley. And that means human endurance, too: in July, the Badwater Ultramarathon race travels 135 miles from Badwater to Mt Whitney Portal (elevation 8360ft) in 120°F-plus heat.

Many of Death Valley's most outstanding natural features also reflect the human history of the place. Take **7 Zabriskie Point**, for example. Rising over 5000ft above the valley floor, this panoramic vision of an inferno of badlands gets its name from an early 20th-century manager of the Pacific Borax Company. **8 Twenty Mule Team Canyon** is where the mule skinners once guided the famous 20-mule wagon trains hauling borax out of Death Valley to a railway stop nearby in the Mojave Desert. As your car rattles along an unpaved road through the canyon, pause to ponder the arduous 165-mile, 10-day trip those mule teams made in the late 19th century.

The 20-mule teams' journey actually began far below at ❾ **Furnace Creek**. Find out exactly why borax, a mineral mostly used to make everyday household detergents, was so valuable, at the ❿ **Borax Museum**. Out back is a pioneer-era collection of old wagons and stagecoaches. A short drive north, passing the interesting ⓫ **Furnace Creek Visitor Center**, you can walk in the footsteps of the Chinese laborers who dug borax out of the earth and examine the adobe ruins of the ⓬ **Harmony Borax Works**, which operated for just five years during the 1880s.

When sunset seems to set the desert rocks aflame, check into the rustic, family-style motel rooms or Western cabins at ⓭ **Furnace Creek Ranch**, which can arrange horseback rides. Beside the general store, chow down at the ⓮ **Forty-Nine Cafe & Wrangler Steak House**. Over at the elegant oasis of the ⓯ **Furnace Creek Inn**, guests soak up elevated views across the desert salt pans as they swim laps in a warm, natural spring–fed pool. On the site of the valley's original tourist camp, ⓰ **Stovepipe Wells Village** is a quieter, more down-to-earth place to rest your head, with renovated motel rooms. At its cowboy-style ⓱ **Toll Road Restaurant**, the flapjacks and biscuits-and-gravy breakfasts go like gangbusters.

"As they left, one woman reputedly looked back and uttered the words 'Good-bye, death valley.'"

The next day, take up another strand of history in Death Valley: the story of the lost '49ers. When the California gold rush began in 1849, a small group of pioneers took what they hoped would be a shortcut to the California goldfields, leaving behind the Old Spanish Trail. Exhausted, dangerously running out of food and water, and struggling with broken wagons and worn-out pack animals, the woeful group arrived near Furnace Creek on Christmas Eve. (Today, an Old West festival featuring a historical reenactment of the ill-fated '49ers takes place here every November.)

Failing to get their wagons across the Panamint Mountains, the survivors slaughtered their oxen and burned their wagons near ⓲ **Mesquite Flat sand dunes**, outside of what was later named Stovepipe Wells Village. The pioneers proceeded to walk out of the torturous valley over Emigrant Pass. As they left, one woman reputedly looked back and uttered the words "Good-bye, death valley." Follow the '49ers' escape route by driving up Emigrant Canyon Rd, which winds through Wildrose Canyon up to the ⓳ **Charcoal Kilns**. Built in the 1876, these beehive-shaped kilns produced the fuel needed to process silver and lead ore. Historically, it wasn't just borax that miners unearthed in Death Valley.

During the 19th and 20th centuries, gold was discovered around Death Valley, including at **20** **Eureka Mine**, a short detour off the main road out toward vertigo-inducing Aguereberry Point, and at the ghost town site of **21** **Skidoo**, a boomtown that went bust in the early 20th century, and where the influential silent movie *Greed* was filmed in 1923. The **22** **Keane Wonder Mine** also sparked a mini gold rush in Death Valley. Get out of your car here for a stiff uphill hike to the mine, which feels like an Old West movie set. You're free to carefully explore around the ruins, but don't venture inside any mine shafts, which can collapse without warning. Finally, just over the Nevada state line is **23** **Rhyolite**, the queen of Death Valley's mines during its heyday (1905–11). Today it's the best-preserved ghost town around, featuring the photogenic ruins of a three-story bank and a miner's house built with 50,000 glass beer, whiskey and medicine bottles.

DETOUR For even more Wild West history, visit the **Mojave National Preserve** (www.nps.gov/moja), south of Baker. Tour the gloriously restored Kelso Depot, with its fascinating historical museum. At Hole-in-the-Wall, scale the cliffs Native Americans used to escape Western ranchers, then drive through Wild Horse Canyon or follow the old Mojave Rd blazed by Spanish missionaries, fur trappers and traders, and oddly enough, camels on an 1867 military expedition. Finally, detour to **Nipton** (www.nipton.com), a turn-of-the-20th-century mining and whistle-stop railway town.

No historical tour of Death Valley would be complete without a tour of **24** **Scotty's Castle**, where guides in authentic period dress lead you around a grandiose Spanish villa built by a wealthy Chicago businessman, Albert Johnson, and his wife in the 1920s. The castle's most famous resident was a bogus prospector named "Death Valley Scotty." This ex-Buffalo Bill sideshow performer, hustler and raconteur claimed that this ranch in Grapevine Canyon actually was his, and that he had built it from gold he mined in Death Valley. That was a big, fat lie, but Albert Johnson played along, even after he had lost a ton of money investing in Scotty's legendary mine. Scotty himself lived at the ranch off and on until his death in 1954; his passing signaled the end of the Old West era in Death Valley.

Sara Benson

TRIP INFORMATION

GETTING THERE
From Los Angeles, take I-10 east toward San Bernardino, then I-15 north past Barstow to Baker.

DO
Borax Museum
Poke around historical exhibits covering mining and the famous 20-mule teams that hauled mineral ore out of Death Valley. ☎ 760-786-2345; Hwy 190, Furnace Creek; admission free; ⊙ 10am-5pm

Death Valley National Park
Pay your entrance fee at the Furnace Creek visitor center. If you didn't fill up outside the park, there are gas stations with 24-hour credit-card pumps at Furnace Creek and Stovepipe Wells. ☎ 760-786-3200; www.nps .gov/deva; PO Box 579, Death Valley; 7-day entry pass $20; ⊙ 24hr; ♿

Furnace Creek Visitor Center
Staff hand out free information and brochures, including schedules of ranger-guided hikes, kid-friendly educational programs and after-dark slide shows in the auditorium. ☎ 760-786-3200; www.nps.gov/deva; Hwy 190, Furnace Creek; ⊙ 9am-5pm; ♿

Rhyolite
A worthy detour east of Death Valley, this mining ghost town is made for just wandering around. Get advice from the resident caretaker at the 1906 bottle house. ☎ 775-553-2967; www.rhyolitesite.com; Hwy 374, 4 miles west of Beatty, NV; admission free; ⊙ 24hr; ♿ 🚻

Scotty's Castle
Show up early, because living-history tour tickets are sold on a first-come, first-served basis. "Underground Mystery Tours" of the castle's technologically innovative inner workings and Lower Vine Ranch tours of Death Valley Scotty's cabin are available seasonally. ☎ 760-786-2392; www.nps.gov /deva; Hwy 267, Death Valley National Park;

tour $11; ⊙ 9am-4:30pm summer, 8:30am-5pm winter

Tecopa Hot Springs Resort
Sex-segregated bathhouses shelter therapeutic mineral springs, where tribal elders, snowbird RVers and curious passersby all soak together. ☎ 760-852-4420; www.tecopa hotsprings.org; 860 Tecopa Hot Springs Rd, Tecopa; admission $8; ⊙ 6am-10pm daily Oct-May

EAT
Cafe C'est Si Bon
Savor the fresh-cooked, chef-made crepes and quiche, while world music plays in the background, interrupted only by the happy oinks of Pizza, the pet pig. ☎ 760-852-4307; www.tecopaca.com; Hwy 127, Shoshone; mains $6-8; ⊙ 8am-4pm Fri-Wed

Forty-Niner Cafe & Wrangler Steak House
Be prepared for very long waits and only average American food at this Old West family-style restaurant and steakhouse. Avoid the buffet. ☎ 760-786-2345; www.furnace creekresort.com; Hwy 190, Furnace Creek; mains $8-25; ⊙ café 7am-9pm daily mid-Oct–mid-May, 11:30am-9pm mid-May–mid-Oct, steakhouse 5-9pm mid-Oct–mid-May, 6-9:30pm mid-May–mid-Oct; ♿

Furnace Creek Inn Dining Room
Reserve a table in the formal dining room (where a dress code applies), or stay casual at the sociable bar, where you can order the same menu of Southwestern fare. Afternoon tea ($18) is served from 3:30pm to 5pm daily, except in summer when the inn is closed. ☎ 760-786-2345; www.furnace creekresort.com; Hwy 190, Furnace Creek; mains $12-37; ⊙ 11am-2:30pm & 5-9pm mid-Oct–mid-May

Pastels
Chef John Muccio, an expat from Las Vegas, runs the friendly "flexitarian" kitchen here, where the California fusion menu is always changing and bread is baked fresh daily.

☎ 760-852-4307; www.pastelsbistro.com; Tecopa Hot Springs Resort, Tecopa Hot Springs Rd, Tecopa; mains $5-15; ☺ usu 7am-7pm

Toll Road Restaurant

Above-par cowboy cooking is dished up inside a ranch house with a toasty fireplace, Native American blankets on the walls, and wooden chairs and tables that really feel like the Old West. ☎ 760-786-2387; www.stove pipewells.com; Stovepipe Wells Village, Hwy 190, Stovepipe Wells; mains $5-25; ☺ 7am-10am, 11:30am-2pm & 5:30-9pm; ♿

SLEEP

Death Valley National Park Campgrounds

Furnace Creek Campground accepts reservations from mid-October through mid-May. All other campgrounds are first-come, first-served; some have potable water. Emigrant is tents-only; more remote Wildrose, Thorndike and Mahogany Flat are also free. Mesquite Springs has spacious sites that are much less congested than at Furnace Creek. ☎ reservations 877-444-6777; www.recreation.gov; campsites free-$18; ☺ some campgrounds year-round; ♿ ☼

Furnace Creek Inn

At this hilltop adobe hotel, elegant Mission-style buildings dating from 1927 lie among palm-shaded garden terraces. Stripped-down rooms with cable TV are overpriced, yet the Zen-like atmosphere is priceless. Perks include a swimming pool and tennis courts. ☎ 760-786-2345, reservations 303-297-2757, 800-236-7916; www.furnace creekresort.com; Hwy 190, Furnace Creek; r $305-425; ☺ mid-Oct–mid-May

Furnace Creek Ranch

Popular with families, this dusty ranch is just south of the Furnace Creek Visitor Center. It has very ordinary cabins and motel rooms, but also a swimming pool, horseback-riding stables and a desert golf course. ☎ 760-786-2345, reservations 303-297-2757, 800-236-7916; www.furnace creekresort.com; Hwy 190, Furnace Creek; r $119-191; ♿

Stovepipe Wells Village

Basically, it's just a roadside motel with a small swimming pool, but it's the best bargain in the valley itself. Rooms are renovated, but have no phone or TV. ☎ 760-786-2387; www.stovepipewells.com; Hwy 190, Stovepipe Wells; r $75-115; ☼

USEFUL WEBSITES

www.deathvalleychamber.org
www.nps.gov

LINK YOUR TRIP

www.lonelyplanet.com/trip-planner

TRIP
51 Kicking Down Route 66 p311
62 Palm Springs & Joshua Tree Oases p363
66 Hidden Deserts opposite

Hidden Deserts

WHY GO Southern California's deserts are definitely weird places. Forget about Nevada's Burning Man festival, because more remote Mojave Desert outposts have it beat when it comes to artistic, way-out happenings. Uncover the most offbeat, eccentric and just plain strange spots in Southern California on our psychedelic road trip.

TIME
3 – 4 days

DISTANCE
575 miles

BEST TIME TO GO
Oct – Apr

START
Palm Springs

END
Beatty, NV

ALSO GOOD FOR

OUTDOORS

With the quixotic windmills of the San Gregorio Pass in your rearview mirror, it's time to leave civilization behind. Snaking along Hwy 111 out of the Coachella Valley, what looks like a mirage sparkles on the horizon. Wait, no. It couldn't be, right? But yes, it is! In the middle of the Colorado Desert is an artificial lake, the ❶ **Salton Sea**. Created by a disastrous accident in 1905, when flooding on the Colorado River caused Imperial Valley irrigation canals to overflow, it's now California's largest lake. After burying a railroad town and Native American lands, and enduring a host of ecological problems, the Salton Sea has become a vacation destination – of sorts. On the empty beaches of ❷ **Salton Sea State Recreation Area**, pitch a tent or go swimming (though salt may sting your eyes). A more popular activity is birding, with over 400 migratory and native species spotted at the national wildlife refuge on the lake's south side.

Niland, with its boarded-up businesses and dusty thoroughfares, is a typically hardscrabble lakeshore community. It takes a special kind of freak to live way out here, and we say that with love. Heading east on Main St, drive out to ❸ **Salvation Mountain**, where the motto is "God Never Fails." Made of concrete and adobe covered in a rainbow patchwork of acrylic paint, it's the vision of folk artist Leonard Mc-Knight, who smilingly waves visitors over from the roadside. Further east along Beal Rd is the welcome sign for ❹ **Slab City**. An abandoned

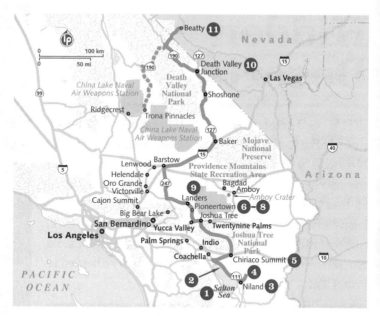

WWII-era Marine barracks, here you'll find thousands of snowbird RVers camped over the winter, and a few hard-core residents even in summer. This is the true Wild West, where hippies, vets, conspiracy theorists and social outsiders congregate to swap stories and books, to make music and love, and often to escape the long arm of the law. Alexander Supertramp stayed here during his epic journey, which was depicted in the movie *Into the Wild*.

Drive narrow Box Canyon Rd to I-10 east. At Chiriaco Summit, pull off at the **5 General Patton Memorial Museum**, standing at the entrance to the WWII-era Desert Training Center. Here more than one million troops trained for battle in harsh conditions overseas, especially for desert warfare in North Africa. Besides exhibits of army tanks and about the ruthless, soldier-slapping general himself, the gigantic 3D relief map of Southern California showing the Colorado River aqueduct system and Patton's training camps is literally the big attraction here.

"Alexander Supertramp stayed here during his epic journey, which was depicted in Into the Wild."

Take the scenic route north through Joshua Tree National Park, rising from the Colorado (Sonoran) Desert into the Mojave. Exit the park near the artsy, beatnik town of Joshua Tree, then follow Hwy 62 west to Yucca Valley, turning right on Pioneertown Rd. Built in 1946 by Hollywood Western movie and TV producers, **6 Pioneertown** is a time-warped place. Mane St is lined with wooden boardwalks and faux frontier-style buildings. Hokey Old West gunfights are still acted out on Sunday afternoons from April through October. Pioneer Bowl, an old-fashioned bowling alley built for Roy Rogers in 1947, is usually open on weekends, too. Drop by **7** **Pappy and Harriet's Pioneertown Palace**, a real-live honky-tonk, dishing up saucy roadhouse barbecue plates and live bands most nights. After the show, it's a short tipsy stumble back to the **8** **Pioneertown Motel**, with rustic cabins where Western movie stars such as Gene Autry once slept.

Built by George Van Tassel (who worked with eccentric billionaire Howard Hughes), supposedly using telepathic help from extraterrestrial beings, the **9** **Integratron** supposedly sits on a "powerful geomagnetic vortex" near the town of Landers, just east of Hwy 247. Thousands of people, from rock stars to UFO fans to meditative yogis, have visited this white dome-shaped building for a healing "sonic bath" courtesy of singing crystal bowls. Van Tassel believed the Integratron's resonant inner chamber was a rejuvenating, antigravity time machine. Judge for yourself by taking a private tour.

DETOUR Head west out of Death Valley to the **Trona Pinnacles** (www.blm.gov/ca/ridgecrest/trona.html), an awesome national landmark, where tufa spires rise out of an ancient lakebed in an alien fashion. Déjà vu? You may recognize this place from the 1960s TV show *Lost in Space* or the movie *Star Trek V: The Final Frontier*. Look for the signposted turnoff from Hwy 178, then drive about 5 miles along a dirt road, usually accessible to 2WD vehicles.

At Death Valley Junction, a 200-plus-mile drive north via Barstow and I-15, the **10** **Amargosa Opera House and Hotel** is a stranger pit stop. A ghost town built in the 1920s by the Pacific Borax Company, this Mexican colonial-style courtyard building was revived by New York dancer Marta Becket after her car broke down nearby in 1967. She has painted a trompe l'oeil audience for herself on the walls of the opera house, where she continues to give heartbreakingly bizarre dance and mime performances, even though she's over 80 years old.

Of course, Death Valley National Park is full of natural oddities with intriguing names like Devils Golf Course, Hells Gate and also the Racetrack, where rocks mysteriously move across the desert playa. But nothing around the valley is as disturbing as the larger-than-life statues – a ghostly biblical last supper, a mining prospector with a penguin – of the **11** **Goldwell Open Air Museum**, created in 1984 by Belgian artist Albert Szukalski. The sculpture garden is just outside the ghost town of Rhyolite, with its three-story boomtown bank ruins and folk-art bottle house. Both are on the Nevada side of the border, a short drive east of the national park.

Sara Benson

TRIP INFORMATION

GETTING THERE

From Los Angeles, drive I-10 east about 125 miles to Indio, then cruise Hwy 111 south.

DO

Amargosa Opera House

Octogenarian Marta Becket performs original stage shows for curious tourists from around the world. ☎ 775-852-4441; www .amargosaoperahouse.com; Hwys 127 & 190, Death Valley Junction; adult/child $15/12; ☽ shows usually 8:15pm Sat Nov–mid-May

General Patton Memorial Museum

WWII aficionados won't want to miss this Desert Training Center storehouse. ☎ 760-227-3483; www.generalpattonmuseum.com; I-10 at Chiriaco Summit; adult/child $4/free; ☽ 9:30am-4:30pm

Goldwell Open Air Museum

Innovative installation art or simply a blight on the landscape? You decide. ☎ 702-870-9946; www.goldwellmuseum.org; off Hwy 374, Rhyolite, NV; admission free; ☽ 24hr daily, visitor center open some weekends Sep–May;

Integratron

Make advance reservations for a private tour or sound-bath experience. ☎ 760-364-3126; www.integratron.com; 2477 Belfield Blvd, Landers; sound baths per person $10-55, private tours from $60; ☽ hours vary

Salton Sea State Recreation Area

Stop at the visitor center to find out more about this accidental desert oasis. ☎ 760-393-3052; www.parks.ca.gov; 100-225 State Park Rd, Mecca; day-use fee $6; ☽ 24hr, visitor center Fri-Sun summer;

Salvation Mountain

Chat with the artist, then snap some photos of his Bible-themed desert monument. www.salvationmountain.us; Beal Rd, Niland; donations welcome; ☽ hours vary;

Slab City

Tread lightly when you visit this free-for-all, truly alternative desert community. www .slabcity.org; Beal Rd, Niland; admission free; ☽ 24hr;

EAT & SLEEP

Amargosa Opera House Hotel

Rooms lack TV or telephone but come with colorful murals, air-con and heating. ☎ 760-852-4441; www.amargosaopera house.com; Hwys 127 &190, Death Valley Junction; r $68-84

Pappy and Harriet's Pioneertown Palace

Kick up your cowboy boots' heels, then chow down on BBQ ribs while indie bands play. ☎ 760-365-5956; www.pappyandharriets .com; 53688 Pioneertown Rd, Pioneertown; mains $5-25; ☽ 11am-1am Thu-Sun, 5pm-midnight Mon

Pioneertown Motel

Bikers, horseback riders and fun-minded families stay in memorabilia-filled rooms equipped with kitchenette, satellite TV and wi-fi internet. There are no phones though. ☎ 760-365-4879; www.pioneertownmotel .com; 5040 Curtis Rd, Pioneertown; r $75-95;

Salton Sea State Recreation Area

Pitch a tent by the beach – there's almost always room here. ☎ reservations 800-444-7275; www.reserveamerica.com; 100-225 State Park Rd, Mecca; campsites $12-23; ☽ 24hr;

USEFUL WEBSITES

www.desertusa.com

www.roadsideamerica.com

www.lonelyplanet.com/trip-planner

LINK YOUR TRIP

Cocktails on the Coast

WHY GO Here's lookin' at you, kid. In fact, everyone's lookin' at you. And you're lookin' at them. And you're all lookin' at the scene. Even the designated driver will have fun at swanky bars from Santa Monica to San Diego. We've even included bars in hotels in case, you know...

Not too long ago, the margarita was SoCal's unofficial cocktail. Then new-wave martinis muscled in, in a fit of Rat Pack bravado. Now a new breed of bartenders is mixing it all up again, with unheard-of ingredients from cucumber to ginger. The results: a party up and down the coast.

Dig the scene at the ❶ **Penthouse** at Santa Monica's Huntley Hotel. Designer Thomas Schoos' mod silver bar, retracting roof and sheer curtains for (semi) privacy accent the view 19 stories up. It's awe-inspiring as the sun sets over the ocean, and merely fab thereafter. The Huntley cocktail is vodka, white grape juice and dry riesling. The Cucumber Squeeze sounds like salad in a glass: cucumber, basil and lemon juice. Oh, plus sake and vodka. The Penthouse's food menu features seasonal selections from Santa Monica's famed farmers market, and influences from France and Spain. Head east on Wilshire Blvd into Beverly Hills, where ❷ **Blue on Blue**, the poolside restaurant at the Avalon Hotel, is chic and sleek with a mid-century-meets-Zen vibe. Cozy into your private cabana while club beats play, and dip into the Elixir cocktail. Its ingredients read like the recipe for a tonic: cucumber-dill infused vodka, sweetened lime juice and white cranberry juice. The Dark & Stormy is rum with ginger beer and ground nutmeg, or try seasonal cocktails like the Winter Wonderland (raspberry vodka, white chocolate liqueur, peach schnapps, whipped cream and raspberry puree).

A few minutes' drive away in West Hollywood's Boys' Town, the ❸ **Abbey** is a must-stop for gay men, or anyone who's ever met a

TIME
2 – 3 days

DISTANCE
160 miles

BEST TIME TO GO
Year-round

START
Santa Monica

END
Coronado

ALSO GOOD FOR

CITY

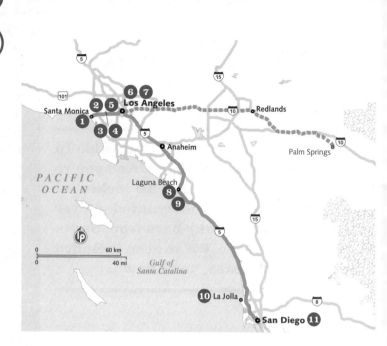

gay man. Its model-licious indoor-outdoor space (your own private divan, anyone?) has come a long way from its humble coffee-shop origins to a menu of two-dozen varieties of flavored martinis. They are not cheap, but it's hard to complain when the bartenders are so disarmingly hunk-o. David Myers, the Michelin-starred chef behind nearby **4 Comme Ça**, the French bistro that's taken LA by storm, is obsessed with old-school bartending – think crystal-clear chunks of ice and diminutive glassware. Alongside Comme Ça's cheese bar and plates of precision-prepared French-bistro cuisine, the Penicillin cocktail will cure what ails you with scotch, ginger, lemon and honey. The Rumble is rum, lemon, blackberries and crushed ice.

If you can get in to **5 Katsuya Hollywood**, go! (But be cool about it.) At the legendary corner of Hollywood and Vine, this high-flying, geisha-inspired, Philippe Starck–designed Japanese restaurant is home to the Dragon Lounge, where oversized curtains are printed with interiors of French chateaux and the mismatched chairs are works of art. Cocktails from the "Liquid Kitchen" include the Burning Mandarin (orange vodka with serrano chili, orange and lemon) and the Sugarsnap (sugarsnap pea–infused vodka with citrus). Head Downtown, way Downtown, where the industrial-chic boîte **6 Edison** hearkens back to the hidden lounges of Prohibition. Sip Edisons (lavender-honey infused liquor, with pear liqueur and pear nectar) surrounded by turbines and other machinery from when this was a boiler room. It's dressed up with cocoa leather couches and three cavernous bars. You should dress up too.

Topiaries. Egg-shaped cabanas. Hippo waste baskets. The rooftop bar at the **7** **Standard Downtown** hotel takes camp seriously, and it's seriously fun to party amidst gleaming skyscrapers – look for nighttime films playing on the walls of neighboring buildings. The bar specializes in bottle service, so go with friends. Rooms are just as playful, with beds that seem to float on platforms in the center of the floor, and clear glass walks between the bedroom and bathroom.

After spending the night Downtown, head south on I-5 into Orange County. Splashes, at the **8** **Surf & Sand Resort**, is about the only watering hole on the water in artsy Laguna Beach. Enjoy dead-on ocean views while quaffing a Peach on the Beach (peach schnapps, vodka, Grand Marnier, OJ and CJ) or Splashes Lemonade, less innocent than it sounds. Every guest room upstairs also looks on the ocean –

DETOUR ▶ Palm Springs, about 1½ hours from Downtown LA, has been all about cocktails since the Rat Pack days. Steve McQueen and Ali McGraw were among the first customers at the burnished bar at **Melvyn's** at the Ingleside Inn, and today the **Parker Palm Springs** hotel is the place to scene and be scene. Or just honor local history with a pitcher of martinis poolside at your condo.

fall asleep to the sound of waves. A few miles away at the high-toned **9** **Montage Resort**, the Lobby Lounge is the place to go if you've got someone to woo, stat. Amid California Arts and Crafts furnishings and crystal glassware, the drink menu alone is 16 pages. The Timeless Love – Hennessy "Timeless" Cognac and Dom Perignon – costs $350 (see under "someone to woo").

The love continues in La Jolla – **10** **La Sala** bar at the 1926 La Valencia Hotel is an old-world classic, perched above the Pacific and La Jolla Cove.

Old Hollywood from Greta Garbo to Gregory Peck used to hang out here, so while there are newfangled martinis, a place like this calls for a classic: gin or vodka with vermouth, an olive or twist. Speaking of old school, San Diego's **11** **Hotel del Coronado** has been a landmark for over a century; this whitewashed grande dame conjures images of panama hats and linen suits. Even if the Del has evolved – rooms in the original building ooze the charm of a bygone era; the newer building less so – the Babcock & Story Bar remains a tribute to those

THE MARILYN MANHATTAN

In *Some Like it Hot,* filmed at the **Hotel del Coronado,** Marilyn Monroe whipped up a Manhattan using "bourbon whiskey," shaken in a hot-water bottle. Here's how the Del's Babcock & Story Bar makes them today:

   2oz Woodford Reserve bourbon
   ½oz each of sweet and dry vermouth (suggest Cinzano and Noilly Prat respectively)
   dash of Angostura bitters and maraschino cherry juice
Stir with ice and strain into a chilled glass; garnish with a maraschino cherry.

days. The 46ft-long bar came from Philadelphia via Cape Horn. Order a Manhattan, ease back, and consider how far *you've* come.

Andrew Bender

TRIP INFORMATION

GETTING THERE
The Huntley Hotel is just north of the Third Street Promenade in Santa Monica.

EAT
Blue on Blue
Fifties mod meets Zen in this minimalist poolside restaurant. Lucille Ball once lived upstairs. ☎ 310-277-5221; www.avalon beverlyhills.com; Avalon Beverly Hills, 9400 W Olympic Blvd, Beverly Hills; mains $14-38; ⊘ 7am-11pm

Comme Ça
French bistro cooking and precision-prepared cocktails from a Michelin-starred chef. ☎ 323-782-1178; www.commecarestaurant .com; 8479 Melrose Ave, Los Angeles; mains $19-28; ⊘ 8am-midnight

Katsuya Hollywood
Chic space with dishes including crispy rice with spicy tuna, and baked white fish with truffle. ☎ 323-871-8777; www.sbe.com /katsuya; 6300 Hollywood Blvd, Los Angeles; mains $20-35; ⊘ 11am-3pm & 5pm-midnight Mon-Fri, 11am-1am Sat & Sun

Penthouse
Sparkling top-story design fest with views of Santa Monica Bay. ☎ 310-393-8080; www.thehuntleyhotel.com; Huntley Hotel, 1111 2nd St, Santa Monica; mains $25-35; ⊘ 6:30am-12:30am Mon-Thu, 6:30am-1:30am Fri & Sat

DRINK
Abbey
Standard-setting gay bar that's becoming straight-friendly, like it or not. ☎ 310-289-8410; www.abbeyfoodandbar.com; 692 N Robertson Blvd, West Hollywood; ⊘ 8am-1:45am

Edison
Sets the standard for cool in hip Downtown LA. No baggy jeans or flip-flops allowed. ☎ 213-613-0000; www.edisondown town.com; 108 W 2nd St, off Harlem Alley, Los Angeles; ⊘ 5pm-2am Wed-Fri, 6pm-2am Sat

La Sala
Quaff like a star of yesteryear in this classic 1926 bar in La Jolla, north of San Diego. ☎ 858-454-0771; www.lavalencia.com; La Valencia Hotel, 1132 Prospect St, La Jolla; ⊘ 4pm-2am

Montage Resort
Dress up and watch the sunset at the lobby lounge of this OC Craftsman hotel. ☎ 949-715-6000, 866-271-6953; www.montage lagunabeach.com; 30801 South Coast Hwy, Laguna Beach; ⊘ 10:30am-1am

SLEEP
Hotel del Coronado
San Diego's iconic hotel is pricey, but what history! Quaff in the Babcock & Story Bar. ☎ 619-435-6611, 800-468-3533; www.hotel del.com; 1500 Orange Ave, Coronado; r $300-500; ⓐ

Standard Downtown
Mod, minimalist and shag-happy. ☎ 213-892-8080; www.standardhotel.com; 550 S Flower St, Los Angeles; r from $245; ⊘ rooftop bar noon-1:30am

Surf & Sand Resort
Every one of its large, well-appointed rooms has an ocean view, as does Splashes Bar. ☎ 949-497-4477, 800-524-8621; www.surf andsandresort.com; 1555 S Coast Hwy, Laguna Beach; r $335-565

USEFUL WEBSITES
www.eaterla.com

http://www.lonelyplanet.com/trip-planner

LINK YOUR TRIP
TRIP

48 Hours in San Diego

WHY GO Most Americans work all year for a two-week vacation. San Diegans will tell you they work all week for a two-day vacation. And it's easy to see why. With top-notch beaches, parks, museums and nightlife immediately accessible, packing a holiday into 48 hours is a breeze.

If you're cruising into town on I-5, exit at Washington St for a pit stop at ❶ **Bronx Pizza**. Yeah, Tony Soprano is on the wall, Donald Trump, a few boxers…but you're here for the pie not the pictures, and they know it. Order up at the counter, grab your slice at the window and be on your way; no fuss, great slice, fuggitaboutit. San Diego may be easy to navigate, but there's a lot we gotta see.

First up is the Embarcadero, where a lineup of historic ships ends at the massive ❷ **USS Midway Museum**. Though *Top Gun's* Goose and Maverick may spring to mind at the sight of this floating city, they're no match for the aircraft carrier's docents – the real thing – who love dishing about life on board. This tour is living history at its best, with engaging first-person accounts on the audio tour through the engine room, brig and tiny compartments. Hoist yourself up the Island Super-structure towering over the 4-acre flight deck and imagine the captain and flight control choreographing a high-stakes ballet of fighter jets, helicopters and 1000 crew – on a 69,000 ton ship heaving atop the sea.

Sightlines into Petco Park are so good from ❸ **Altitude Skybar** at the Gaslamp Marriott that you'd hardly blink if a well-spun homer dropped into your beer. Fire pits, sleek couches and burly bouncers exude LA cool, though an easy-going crowd keeps pretension at bay. But times they are a changing in the 16-block ❹ **Gaslamp Quarter**, with rapid-fire openings of boutique hotels and velvet-rope clubs marking a second, youthful wave of gentrification, which is amping the weekend intensity

TIME
2 days

BEST TIME TO GO
Year-round

START
Hillcrest

END
Mission Hills

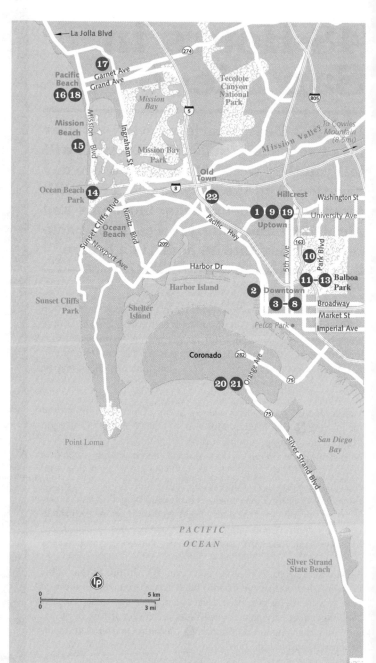

in this former red-light district. Voted 2008's Best Seafood Restaurant by *San Diego Magazine* in three polls, swanky **5** **Oceanaire Seafood Room** is a cherished Gaslamp gathering spot cruising in luxury-liner style. Lawyers and bankers from downtown towers chatter elbow-to-elbow at the oyster bar, or move to red booths while nibbling on "ultra fresh" halibut, snapper and mahimahi prepared with seasonal flair. White leather banquettes set an equally chic tone at **6** **Confidential** (Andrew Firestone is an investor), open since 2006 and leading this second, high-octane wave of revitalization.

If you'd like a room with a stripper pole at new-but-naughty **7** **Ivy Hotel**, just ask. This adult playground spins a loud, Vegas-party vibe, especially on weekends, and it's already hosted A-listers from Brad Pitt to Eric Clapton. Of Ivy's three nightclubs, firepit-and-cabana dotted **8** **Eden** – San Diego's

ASK A LOCAL

"The lobster BLT at **C-Level Lounge** (880 Harbor Island Dr) is so good you'd step on your mother's face to get to it. It's a BLT made with lobster, bacon and avocados, and comes with a little cup of lobster bisque to dunk it in. It's just amazing. Get it with Deborah's mai tai. C-Level is on Harbor Island and it has panoramic views of downtown."

Brian Murphy, San Diego

largest rooftop bar – draws the most ogles from nearby condo dwellers enjoying *Rear Window*-esque views of the action. Don't ask for a mint after breakfast at **9** **Hash House a Go Go**, back in Hillcrest. With its heaping skillets of hash, massive flapjacks and hearty gourmet scrambles, a wafer-thin mint could push you over the edge. Walk it off on bamboo-lined pathways at the new, 3-acre Monkey Trails & Forest Tales inside Balboa Park's sprawling **10** **San Diego Zoo**. Conservation-minded signs dot multilevel walkways, where face-to-face encounters – beware the gremlinlike mug of the Wolf's guenon – aren't uncommon. "Oohs" and "ahhhs" mark the always-popular Polar Bear Plunge, Panda Discovery Center and Koala Exhibit and the 35-minute tour on the double-decker Express Shuttle provides an efficient orientation for first timers.

Spanish-Colonial pavilions add a dash of romantic flair to an afternoon of museum hopping in **11** **Balboa Park**, a 1200-acre urban retreat home to gardens, theaters, 15 museums, the zoo and a very large outdoor organ. For sheer density of Old Masters, drop by the **12** **Timken Museum of Art**, where the impressive Putnam collection includes works by Rembrandt, Rubens and Cézanne. There's always something intriguing at the white-walled **13** **Museum of Photographic Arts**: from 1850s daguerreotypes to MRI images, exhibits embrace photography in all its forms.

Give that tan a workout with a short drive west from Balboa Park on I-8 toward the city's main beaches, an introduction to which best starts with the fish taco, the city's most famous contribution to America's culinary lexicon. While the foundation never varies – a soft tortilla topped with fish, salsa, cabbage and special sauce – every beach bum has a favorite based on taste, location and sometimes affordability. With one exception. The fish tacos at fun-lovin' **14 South Beach Bar & Grill**, in scruffy Ocean Beach, transcend local snobberies. Whether it's the white sauce, the lightly fried mahimahi, the salsa or their combined triple magic, these tacos rock. Insider tip? The rule here is to order your food from the waiter and your beer from the bar. Grab a post-lunch nap on the 3 miles of beach between South Mission Jetty and Pacific Beach Point. Cyclists, bladers and dog walkers keep the peace on bustling **15 Ocean Front Walk**. For the ultimate Pacific Beach experience, kick back inside a white Cape Cod–style cottage adorned with flower boxes, blue shutters and loads of charm at **16 Crystal Pier Hotel & Cottages**, atop Crystal Pier.

> **ASK A LOCAL**
>
> "One of my…favorite spots [for hiking] is **Cowles Mountain** (www.mtrp.org). It's right near San Diego State. That's a great hike because it doesn't take that long: 45 minutes up and 45 minutes back. It's really popular and you'll see people running up and down [or with] dogs and two year olds. Once you get to the top, it's so scenic. On a clear day you can see from Coronado to La Jolla."
>
> *Katie Wallace, San Diego*

If it's Tuesday and you're under 25, praise your maker, slip on your cleanest dirty flip-flops and hustle to **17 Garnet Ave** for Taco Tuesday – cheap eats, drink specials and loads of glowing sun worshippers clustered in one place. If your pub-crawling days are past, swap tacos and brews for martinis and views amidst sleek, contemporary lines at **18 JRDN Restaurant and Tower Bar** in Tower 23 Hotel. Breakfast on the go can hit a speed bump at neighborhood bakery **19 Bread & Cie**, back in Hillcrest, where the sensory overload of aromatic fresh bread, chattering diners and racks of pastries can make it hard to focus. But try, because it's time to swoop over the Coronado Bay Bridge to San Diego's grand dame, the historic **20 Hotel del Coronado**. Built in 1888, the all-timber, white-washed Hotel Del was the world's largest resort at the time, and its conical red towers, balconies and polished wood interiors exuded a snappy, look-at-me exuberance, which is still palpable to this day. Guests have included US presidents and royalty, and the hotel enjoyed a non-speaking role in Billy Wilder's 1959 classic, *Some Like it Hot*. Book a room in the original Victorian building for the most historic experience. Guest or not, a languorous hour sipping margaritas on the ocean-view patio at **21 Babcock & Story Bar**, named after the hotel's founders, is a relaxing way to soak in the scene.

Our trip started with pizza but in San Diego it can end with no less than *taquitos,* tacos and other addictive Mexican fare. For an almost-full-circle trip, exit off I-5 at Washington St and turn right on India St. One block up on the left is come-as-you-are **22 El Indio**. *Taquitos* were created here, and crowds have been coming to this family-owned joint for 60 years. Best part? The homemade tortilla chips and fresh chunky salsa are available to go for a post–San Diego fix.

Amy C Balfour

TRIP INFORMATION

GETTING THERE
San Diego is 120 miles south of Los Angeles, via I-5 south, and 500 miles south of San Francisco.

DO

Balboa Park
Planning to visit more than a handful of museums in Balboa Park? The Passport to Balboa Park provides admission to 13 museums within a one-week period. www.balboapark .org; adult/child $39/2, incl zoo $65/36

Museum of Photographic Arts
Deceptively small, the museum's genre-pushing special exhibits will engage you longer than you'd planned. ☎ 619-238-7559; www .mopa.org; 1649 El Prado, Balboa Park; adult/ student & senior $6/4; ☽ 10am-5pm Tue-Sun

San Diego Zoo
See the pandas early. They're more active and the lines are shorter. ☎ 619-231-1515; www.sandiegozoo.org; 2920 Zoo Dr, Balboa Park; adult/child $25/17; ☽ 9am-5pm, later in summer; ♿

Timken Museum of Art
With free admission and a healthy selection of grand masters, this Balboa Park museum is a top pick. ☎ 619-239-5548; www.timken museum.org; 1500 El Prado; admission free; ☽ 10am-4:30pm Tue-Sat, 1:30-4.30pm Sun, closed Sep

USS Midway Museum
This famous aircraft carrier saw action in Vietnam and the Gulf War before being decommissioned in 1992. ☎ 619-544-9600; www .midway.org; 910 N Harbor Dr, Embarcadero; adult/child/senior & student $17/9/13; ☽ 10am-5pm; ♿

EAT

Bread & Cie
This neighborhood bakery bustles with an upbeat mix of children, seniors and solos on any given morning. ☎ 619-683-9322; 350 University Ave; mains $2-10; ☽ 7am-7pm Mon-Fri, 7am-6pm Sat, 8am-6pm Sun; ♿

Bronx Pizza
No credit cards, no delivery, no pineapple, no beer – gotta problem? ☎ 619-291-3341; www.bronxpizza.com; 111 Washington St, Hillcrest; mains $13-19; ☽ 11am-10pm Sun-Thu, 11am-11pm Fri & Sat; ♿

El Indio
Visible from I-5, this 60-year stalwart just off the Washington St exit still packs 'em in. ☎ 619-299-0333; www.el-indio.com; 3695 India St, Mission Hills; mains $1-9; ☽ 8am-9pm; ♿

Hash House a Go Go
Hashes are breakfast potatoes tossed with meat (or veggies) and topped with two eggs. ☎ 619-298-4646; www.hashhouseagogo .com; 3628 Fifth Ave; breakfast & lunch mains $8-15, dinner $14-36; ☽ breakfast & lunch daily, dinner Tue-Sun

Oceanaire Seafood Room
Attentive staff, luxury liner digs and simple but elegant fresh seafood are the bait at this swanky Gaslamp fave. ☎ 619-858-2277; www.theoceanaire.com; 400 J St, Gaslamp; mains $20-39; ☽ dinner

South Beach Bar & Grill
For loaded fish tacos, follow the noise to the nondescript building at the end of Newport Ave. ☎ 619-226-4577; www.southbeachob .com; 5059 Newport Ave; mains $3-11; ☽ lunch & dinner

DRINK

Altitude Skybar
It's altitude, not attitude, that's bringing 'em to this popular rooftop lounge where the vibe's more "Hey man" than "Who do you know?" ☎ 619-696-0234; www.altitudesky bar.com; 660 K St, Gaslamp

Babcock & Story Bar
Indoors flows into outdoors at this breezy bar, where margaritas and tropical drinks mix well with the ocean view. ☎ 619-435-6611,

ext 7919; www.hoteldel.com/dining
/babcock.cfm; 1500 Orange Ave, Coronado;
🕐 11am-1am

Confidential

An infusion of LA style in the heart of the
Gaslamp Quarter. ☎ 619-696-8888; www
.confidentialsd.com; 901 4th Ave at E St,
Gaslamp; 5pm-2am Tue-Sat

Eden

Candlelight and cushions make the Ivy's
rooftop lounge the sexiest temptation in
town. ☎ 619-814-1000; www.ivyhotel
.com/eden.aspx; 600 F St, Gaslamp;
🕐 10am-midnight Sun-Wed, 10am-2am
Thu-Sat

JRDN Restaurant and Tower Bar

A blue-violet glow sets an upscale mood –
and keeps the crowd lookin' hot. ☎ 858-
270-5736; www.jrdn.com; 4551 Ocean Blvd,
Pacific Beach

SLEEP

Crystal Pier Hotel & Cottages

Park your car on the pier – right in front of
your cottage – if you're overnighting here.
☎ 858-483-6983; www.crystalpier.com;
4500 Ocean Blvd, Pacific Beach; cottages
$300-500; ♿

Hotel del Coronado

For the history of this iconic hotel, check out the
photo exhibit below the lobby. ☎ 619-435-
6611; www.hoteldel.com; 1500 Orange Ave,
Coronado; r $380-750, suites $1060-1880; ♿

Ivy Hotel

A sultry newcomer to the Gaslamp District,
where Eden is only an elevator ride away.
☎ 619-814-1000; www.ivyhotel.com; 600 F
St, Gaslamp; r $279-379, suites from $479; ♿

USEFUL WEBSITES

www.sandiego.org
www.gaslamp.org

LINK YOUR TRIP

http://www.lonelyplanet.com/trip-planner

TRIP

1 Up the Pacific Coast Highway p37
3 Best of the Beaches p53
53 A Wild Ride in the Parks p321

Day Trips from LA & San Diego

Mountain trails, shaggy bison, poppy fields and mud spas are all within 60 to 120 miles of Los Angeles. Further south, apple pie, black rhinos, mariachi bands and a monument honoring a liar are within a two-hour drive of San Diego.

PASADENA

For an easy, car-free day of shopping and museum-hopping, take the Metro Rail Gold Line from Downtown LA northeast to Pasadena, which sits above the sprawl in the safety of the San Gabriel foothills. After a 20-minute ride from LA's Union Station, you'll step from the train into Old Town Pasadena, a bustling 20-block shopping and entertainment district set among restored historic buildings along Colorado Blvd. Though there are plenty of chain stores here, there's a refreshing selection of indie-minded bookstores – check out Distant Lands for travel books – as well as mom-and-pop eateries and small museums. Of the latter, walk past Rodin's *The Thinker* into the impressive and accessible Norton Simon Museum, which teems with choice works from Rembrandt, Renoir, Raphael and Van Gogh. If you're here on New Year's Day, snap open your foldout chair and nab a sidewalk spot for viewing the Rose Bowl Parade's flower-festooned floats. **From the Pershing Sq metro station downtown (500 S Hill St), take the Red Line to Union Station, then catch the Gold Line to the Del Mar station in Pasadena (www.metro.net).**

See also **TRIP 51**

SANTA MONICA MOUNTAINS

Hiking may not be the first thing on your to-do list when visiting LA but trust us, exploring the city's wild side will be one of the things you remember most about your visit (except that glimpse of Johnny Depp on Sunset Blvd of course). Chumash Native Americans once roamed the hilly, tree-and-chaparral-covered coastal range that is now protected as the Santa Monica Mountains National Recreation Area. It stretches from Griffith Park in Hollywood to Point Magu across the Ventura County line, and the 65-mile Backbone Trail tags along the ridgeline for the whole ride. Numerous trails crisscross these foothills. For a nice mix of waterfalls, shady canyons and sweeping coastal views, tackle the 3-mile Temescal Canyon trail north of Sunset Blvd at the intersection of Temescal Canyon Rd – just before Sunset Blvd reaches the Pacific Coast Hwy. **For trail maps, biking information, and details about public buses that stop near park areas and trailheads within the Santa Monica Mountains, visit www.nps.gov/samo.**

See also **TRIP 60**

CATALINA

There's no need to drive to Yellowstone to see a herd of bison. Just hop a one-hour ferry (www.catalinaexpress.com) to Catalina Island, where more than 150 of the shaggy beasts – left over from a 1924 film shoot, natch – graze away their days in the island backcountry. Mediterranean-flavored Catalina Island is a popular getaway for harried Angelenos, but can sink under the weight of day-trippers in summer. Stay overnight though and feel the ambience go from frantic to romantic. After an hour or two exploring the shops of Avalon, spend the rest of the day hiking, taking to the water or checking out those buffalo on an island tour. For bluff-top views with a bit more isolation, take the ferry to Two Harbors, the only other settlement on the island. Here you'll find one lodge, a general store, a restaurant…and not much else. **For ferries to Avalon and Two Harbors, follow I-405 south from LAX to I-110, then head south following signs to N Harbor Blvd and Berth 95.**

See also **TRIP 55**

COSTA MESA

Best piece of advice for visiting South Coast Plaza, the sprawling shopping complex just east of Newport Beach? Grab a map at one of the four concierge booths. With more than 300 luxury and department stores, this destination mall, located on 128 acres and containing 2.8 million sq ft of retail and dining space, can be tricky to navigate. And that's without mentioning the 12,750 parking spaces surrounding the megalith. For shoppers not into the mega-mall scene, just south are two smaller shopping areas, The Lab and The Camp. The first caters to indie-minded shoppers preferring vintage and unique styles, while the latter targets vegans, tree-huggers and rock climbers. But Costa Mesa isn't all about shopping; its downtown serves as Orange County's cultural center. The Orange County Performing Arts Center, with its acoustically stunning 3000-seat Segerstrom Hall, is here, as is the South Coast Repertory, which is known for its social-minded, groundbreaking plays. **To get to South Coast Plaza from LA, drive 40 miles southeast on I-405.**

See also **TRIPS 53 & 55**

GLEN IVY HOT SPRINGS

Grab your BFF for an indulgent spa day with a twist – red clay mud pools where you can soak yourself in the wet muck, spread it all over your skin and then let it dry in the sun. Skin benefits? We can't say for sure but it sure looks fun. Nicknamed Club Mud, this lovely 11-acre day spa (www.glenivy.com), 75 miles from Los Angeles, has 18 pools and spas (not all of them muddy) filled with naturally heated mineral water – all surrounded by landscaped grounds lush with bougainvillea, eucalyptus and palm trees. You can relax on a lounge chair in the saunas and steam rooms, take an aqua aerobics class, swim laps in one of the larger pools or, for a small extra fee, treat yourself to a massage. Heaping salads are the big draw at the on-site restaurant, Café Sole. **From LA, follow I-15 south to Temescal Canyon Rd and turn right. Drive 1 mile to Glen Ivy Rd, turn right again and continue straight to the end. Minimum age is 16.**

See also **TRIP 56**

BIG BEAR

So you want to surf in the morning and ski in the afternoon? Try the low-key resort at Big Bear Lake (6750ft), 110 miles northeast of Los Angeles in the San Bernardino Mountains. Snowy winters lure scores of ski bunnies and snowboarders to its two mountains (with 55 runs and 26 ski lifts), while summers bring hikers, mountain-bikers and water-sports enthusiasts looking to escape LA's stifling heat. Steel your nerves for Hwy 18's Rim of the World Drive. As it quickly ascends from the basin to 5000ft, its hair-raising twists and turns beside plummeting drop-offs will have you clutching the wheel. Remember, breathing is good. **From LA, drive east on I-10 to I-215 north then exit east on Hwy 30. Follow signs to Hwy 18 and Lake Arrowhead, continuing on Hwy 18 to Big Bear.**

See also **TRIP 50**

SAN DIEGO'S NORTH COAST

The oceanside towns of San Diego's North Coast are a well-kept secret of rugged coastlines, indie-minded communities and low-key friendliness. In ritzy Del Mar, 10 miles north of La Jolla, you'll find pricey restaurants, unique galleries and the Del Mar Racetrack and Fairgrounds. The more interesting community of Solana Beach, just north, is known for its beaches, the Cedros Design District (with unique home furnishing stores) and the concerts at Belly Up Tavern. In Cardiff-by-the-Sea there's a 1000-acre ecological preserve, a campground overlooking the surf and great happy hour deals at The Beach House, where you sip cocktails almost over the waves. Continuing north, the gold lotus domes of the Self Realization Fellowship Retreat & Hermitage have been luring spiritual seekers and infusing the town of Encinitas with a New Age sensibility since 1937. A powerful, locally guarded reef break known as Swami's is next door. About 8 miles further north is Carlsbad, home to Legoland and Carlsbad Ranch, a 50-acre field of carmine, saffron and the snow-white blossoms of ranunculuses that come ablaze from early March to mid-May. **From downtown San Diego via I-5 north and Hwy 101 north, it's 20 miles to Del Mar, 23 miles to Solana Beach, 25 miles to Cardiff, 28 miles to Encinitas and 37 miles to Carlsbad.**

See also **TRIP 61**

SAN DIEGO ZOO'S WILD ANIMAL PARK

How close can you get to the animals at San Diego Zoo's Wild Animal Park? Consider this sign: "In gorilla society prolonged eye contact is not only impolite, but is considered a threat. Please respect the social signals of our gorillas and do not stare at them directly." Seems we're so close we need to be reminded of our manners. The sign is indicative of the experience at this 1800-acre open-range zoo, where protecting wild animals and their habitats – while educating visitors in a soft-handed manner – is the primary goal. On the Journey to Africa tram you'll pass black rhinos, giraffes, ostriches and other herbivores chilling out on a rolling plain (for slightly better views, sit on the left-hand side of the tram). By law, predators and prey must be separated so you won't see any battles to the death during the 25-minute tour. Guides do, however, weave an engaging mix of animal facts and ecominded considerations. For up-close views of big cats, follow the signs to the Lion Camp and the Safari Walk Backcountry – and pray there's not a park-disrupting earthquake. **From San Diego, follow I-15 north to the Via Rancho Parkway exit, turn right and continue to San Pasqual Rd. Turn right and follow signs to the park.**

See also **TRIP 53**

JULIAN

Autumn is prime time in Julian, the mountain hamlet with a three-block main street and a heart made of apple pie. In fall, city folk flock here to buy fresh local apples, wander the 1870s streetscape and attend the Grape Stomp and Apple Days Festival, held in early September and early October respectively. Although Julian (elevation 4450ft) is near the geographical center of San Diego County, by the time you reach it from the city it really feels like you've been on a journey. Historically, prospectors arrived here after the Civil War (1861–65). The discovery of gold in 1869 led to a growth spurt (to a whopping 600), and mining continued for over 60 years. Later, much of the land was given over to farming, and Julian-grown apples won prizes at world fairs. In addition to poking around downtown – don't miss the mishmash of local history and artifacts at the Pioneer Museum – you can tour a now-defunct gold mine or take a short scenic drive to the Menghini Winery. But whatever you do, make sure it includes a bite of apple pie à la mode. **From San Diego, take I-8 east to SR67, toward Ramona, where it turns into SR78. Continue to Julian. Loop back on SR79 south to I-8 for new scenery.**

See also **TRIP 64**

ANZA-BORREGO DESERT STATE PARK

If you've got the late-February blahs, call the Wildflower Hotline (☎760-767-4684) and see what's blooming. Winter and spring are the high seasons and the spring wildflowers can be absolutely stunning. The little-developed park comprises almost a fifth of San Diego County and extends almost all the way to Mexico. At 640,000 acres it's the largest US state park outside Alaska.

Northeast of Borrego Springs is the Peg Leg Smith Monument, a pile of rocks honoring legendary mountain man – and local liar – Peg Leg Smith. According to lore, his stories about finding pure gold rocks in the area inspired others to come here. At Elephant Trees Discovery Trail at Onctillo Wells, you'll find a fragrant herd of the elusive elephant tree, related to myrrh and named for the tree's resemblance to a pachyderm's leg. East of Borrego, a 4-mile dirt road, sometimes passable without 4WD, leads to Font's Point and its spectacular panorama of Borrego Valley and the Borrego Badlands. **From San Diego, take I-8 east to Hwy 79 north, following it to Hwy 78 east. From Hwy 78, take County Hwy S3 north, following it to County Hwy S22 west and the visitors center (☎ 760-767-4205; www.parks .ca.gov).**

See also **TRIPS 62 & 66**

TEMECULA

What's it take to become a popular weekend destination these days? Old West storefronts, nearly two dozen wineries and a really big casino did the trick for Temecula, in the southeast corner of Riverside County. Temecula means "Place of the Sun" in the language of the native Luiseno people, who were present when the first Spanish missionary visited in 1797. In the 1800s the area was a ranching outpost for the Mission San Luis Rey and, later, a stop on the Butterfield stagecoach line and the California southern railroad. What's most amazing is Temecula's astonishing growth, rocketing from 2700 people in 1970 to 101,000 residents in 2008. Hiding behind the Old West facades lining Old Town's Front St are antique stores, wine shops and the Temecula Olive Oil Company, which offers free samples of flavorful oils. A 10-minute drive east leads to the wineries and their patio views of vine-dotted hillsides. A few have breezy restaurants. If you don't like crowds, start your wine tasting fairly early on the weekends because the tasting rooms and terraces can get crowded late in the day. **Temecula is 60 miles north of downtown San Diego. Take Hwy 163 north to I-15 north.**

See also **TRIPS 59 & 64**

TIJUANA

Times are tough for Tijuana. A recent spate of violent kidnappings and fatal shoot-outs – mostly due to gang-related turf wars – has turned once-bustling tourist areas into near ghost towns. Still, locals want tourists to return, and if you refrain from doing anything illegal, getting stumbling drunk or flashing your money around, you shouldn't have any problems. During Prohibition in the 1920s, Tijuana (pronounced "tee-hwah-na," or TJ for short) was the darling of the Hollywood crowd. Until recently, easy-flowing tequila and beer pulled in college students, sailors and other revelers, who flocked to the rollicking bars and nightclubs on La Revo (Av Revolution). Curio stores still overflow with kitschy souvenirs, and touts bark at passersby from liquor stores and low-priced pharmacies, but things have definitely calmed down.

Instead of boozing it up, check out the excellent history of Baja California in the Museo de las California at the Centro Cultural Center (which has English signage), or visit some of the city's best restaurants in Zona Centro and Zona Rio. **Take the San Diego Trolley blue line south to San Ysidro station (about an hour). Driving your own car is not recommended; if you do, pre-buy Mexican car insurance. Drive 45 minutes south on I-5. Short-term US visitors don't need a passport; all other visitors must bring their passport and US visa for re-entry.**

Amy C Balfour

See also **TRIP 57**

Behind the Scenes

THIS BOOK

This guidebook was commissioned in Lonely Planet's Oakland office and produced by the following:

Product Development Manager Heather Dickson
Commissioning Editor Suki Gear
Coordinating Editor Kirsten Rawlings
Coordinating Cartographer Hunor Csutoros
Coordinating Layout Designer Jim Hsu
Managing Editor Sasha Baskett
Managing Cartographer Alison Lyall
Managing Layout Designers Celia Wood
Assisting Editors Charlotte Orr, Victoria Harrison, Laura Stansfeld, Diana Saad, Simone Egger
Assisting Cartographers Mick Garrett, Andy Rojas
Assisting Layout Designers Paul Iacono, Wibowo Rusli
Series Designer James Hardy
Cover Designers Gerilyn Attebery, Jennifer Mullins
Project Manager Eoin Dunlevy

Thanks to Owen Eszeki, Mark Germanchis, Chris Girdler, Michelle Glynn, Brice Gosnell, Liz Heynes, Lauren Hunt, Laura Jane, John Mazzocchi, Darren O'Connell, Paul Piaia, Julie Sheridan, Glenn van der Knjiff

THANKS

Ryan Ver Berkmoes Huge thanks to the kindness of Harry Medved, author of many books on Hollywood, including the iconic *50 Worst Films of All Time,* which I once read on a plane and got to laughing so disruptively that the flight attendant cut off my drinks (thank God I wasn't 86d). Also thanks to Suki Gear, who never cut anything off me, but cuts an amazing figure as a Commissioning Editor; and to Kirsten Rawlings and the editors who added literacy to my writing. Finally: Nate Cavalieri is a music god!

Alexis Averbuck Deep thanks to Patti Averbuck, David Averbuck, Douglas Fir, Susan Butler, Aggie Brenneman, Roger Edwards, Jennifer Hale, Rachel Averbuck, Lemont Hale, Oren Averbuck, Reuben Weinzveg, Padi Selwyn, Kris Brown, Tom Brown, Kent Rosenblum, George Baker, Frank Cardozo, Kristin 'Kale' Bowling, Jacob Averbuck, Jennifer Averbuck, Ned Averbuck, Maxine Averbuck, Suki Gear and Heather Dickson.

Amy C Balfour Big thanks to John & Cindy Klinedinst for their Gaslamp hospitality and to the gang at Klinedinst for up-to-the-minute recs. Thank you Katie, Tyler, Paul and Brian for San Diego guidance, Cheryl for Laguna, Allison and Chris for LA. Kudos to experts Bryan, Kerry and Jen. Thanks Suki for answering all my questions with patience, and Ryan for tying it all together with skill. I'd also like to thank Kirsten Rawlings and Charlotte Orr for their spot-on editorial assistance.

Andrew Bender Thanks to Karen & Wayne Olmsted, Carol Martinez and staff at LA Inc, friends, advisors and suggesters from Santa Barbara to Indian Wells to Tijuana, and the Center for High Angular Resolution Astronomy at Georgia State University (seriously). In-house acknowledgments go to Suki Gear, Ryan Ver Berkmoes and Kirsten Rawlings.

Sara Benson Big thanks to Suki Gear for this fun gig. Heaps of gratitude are due to all of the folks that I interviewed for this book: Tony Merchell, Sondra Brown, Richard Stenger, Kevin Hansel, Rich Levin, Pamela Connolly, Evan Baxter, Amy Starbin and, most of all, Mike Connolly, Jr.

Alison Bing Thanks California gurus Suki Gear and Ryan Ver Berkmoes at Lonely Planet, plus road-trippers extraordinaire Marco Flavio Marinucci and Anais LaRocca for car-stereo DJing to rock out in the redwoods and seeking out beaches with maximum bumming potential.

Nate Cavalieri Thanks to Florence Chien, Joe Hayes, Jessica Belcher, and Jerry and Helenan Cavalieri, who joined me to make these so fun, and to Suki Gear, whose warmth and support are deeply appreciated. Also thanks to Alice Waters, for directing me towards a life-affirming chicken.

Dominique Channell I'd like to thank Brad and Zack at Calistoga Bike Shop, as well as all the local Napa and Sonoma folks-in-the-know who helped with my research. Thanks to Suki Gear and Alison Lyall at Lonely Planet for asking me to help with this very fun, exciting new title, and to my dear family and friends for their continued support and feedback.

Beth Kohn A big thanks to Suki Gear for signing me up, and Heather Dickson and Ryan Ver Berkmoes for making it happen. For their insight and suggestions, applause to Sam Benson, Jane Coughran, Amanda Holder and Richard Schave. Hugs go to the very patient Jenny G and Claude Moller.

ACKNOWLEDGMENTS

Many thanks to the following for the use of their content:

Internal photographs by Lonely Planet Images, and by Judy Bellah p19 (bottom); Richard Cummins p13, p21 (bottom), p23; Lee Foster p15 (top), p16 (top), p16 (bottom), p17, p24 (top); Hanan Isachar p21 (top); David Peevers p14, p22 (top); Anthony Pidgeon p18, p24 (bottom); Carol Polich p19 (top); Witold Skrypczak p22 (bottom); Brent Winebrenner p15 (bottom); Corey Wise p20.

All images are the copyright of the photographers unless otherwise indicated. Many of the images in this guide are available for licensing from Lonely Planet Images: www.lonelyplanetimages.com.

SEND US YOUR FEEDBACK

Got feedback? We'd love to hear your corrections, suggestions, compliments or complaints, so feel free to use our feedback form: **lonelyplanet.com/contact**.

Note: We may edit, reproduce and incorporate your feedback comments in Lonely Planet products such as guidebooks, websites and digital products. If you send it in, then that counts as permission for us to use it. If you don't want your name acknowledged, please let us know.

To read our privacy policy, visit **lonelyplanet.com/privacy**.

Index

000 map pages
000 photograph pages

GreenDex

It seems like everyone's going "green" in California these days, but how can you know which businesses are actually ecofriendly and which are simply jumping on the bandwagon?

The following have been selected by our authors because they demonstrate an active sustainable-tourism policy. Some are involved in conservation or environmental education, others engage with biodynamic agriculture and many are locally owned and operated, thereby maintaining and preserving local identity, arts and culture.

For more information about sustainable tourism and Lonely Planet, see www.lonelyplanet.com/responsibletravel.

Southern California

LONELY PLANET OFFICES

USA
150 Linden St, Oakland, CA 94607
☎ 510 250 6400, toll free 800 275 8555
fax 510 893 8572
info@lonelyplanet.com

Australia
Head Office
Locked Bag 1, Footscray, Victoria 3011
☎ 03 8379 8000, fax 03 8379 8111
talk2us@lonelyplanet.com.au

UK
2nd fl, 186 City Rd,
London EC1V 2NT
☎ 020 7106 2100, fax 020 7106 2101
go@lonelyplanet.co.uk

Published by Lonely Planet Publications Pty Ltd
ABN 36 005 607 983